5th Workshop on Research in Computational Typology and Multilingual NLP (SIGTYP 2023)

Dubrovnik, Croatia
6 May 2023

ISBN: 978-1-7138-7387-7

Printed from e-media with permission by:

Curran Associates, Inc.
57 Morehouse Lane
Red Hook, NY 12571

Some format issues inherent in the e-media version may also appear in this print version.

Association for Computational Linguistics
209 N. Eighth Street
Stroudsburg, Pennsylvania 18360

Phone: 1-570-476-8006
Fax: 1-570-476-0860

acl@aclweb.org

Additional copies of this publication are available from:

Curran Associates, Inc.
57 Morehouse Lane
Red Hook, NY 12571 USA
Phone: 845-758-0400
Fax: 845-758-2633
Email: curran@proceedings.com
Web: www.proceedings.com

SIGTYP 2023

The 5th Workshop on Research in Computational Linguistic Typology and Multilingual NLP

Proceedings of the Workshop

May 6, 2023

The SIGTYP organizers gratefully acknowledge the support from the following sponsors.

Supported By

Google

Introduction

SIGTYP 2023 is the fifth edition of the workshop for typology-related research and its integration into multilingual Natural Language Processing (NLP). The workshop is co-located with the 17th Conference of the European Chapter of the Association for Computational Linguistics (EACL 2023), which takes place in Dubrovnik, Croatia. This year our workshop features a shared task on cognate and derivative detection for low-resourced languages.

Encouraged by the 2019 – 2022 workshops, the aim of the fifth edition of SIGTYP workshop is to act as a platform and a forum for the exchange of information between typology-related research, multilingual NLP, and other research areas that can lead to the development of truly multilingual NLP methods. The workshop is specifically aimed at raising awareness of linguistic typology and its potential in supporting and widening the global reach of multilingual NLP, as well as at introducing computational approaches to linguistic typology. It fosters research and discussion on open problems, not only within the active community working on cross- and multilingual NLP but also inviting input from leading researchers in linguistic typology.

The workshop provides focused discussions on a range of topics, including the following:

1. Integration of typological features in language transfer and joint multilingual learning. In addition to established techniques such as "selective sharing", are there alternative ways to encode heterogeneous external knowledge in machine learning algorithms?

2. Development of unified taxonomy and resources.Building universal databases and models to facilitate understanding and processing of diverse languages.

3. Automatic inference of typological features. The pros and cons of existing techniques (e.g. heuristics derived from morphosyntactic annotation, propagation from features of other languages, supervised Bayesian and neural models) and discussion on emerging ones.

4. Typology and interpretability. The use of typological knowledge for interpretation of hidden representations of multilingual neural models, multilingual data generation and selection, and typological annotation of texts.

5. Improvement and completion of typological databases. Combining linguistic knowledge and automatic data-driven methods towards the joint goal of improving the knowledge on cross-linguistic variation and universals.

6. Linguistic diversity and universals. Challenges of cross-lingual annotation. Which linguistic phenomena or categories should be considered (near-)universal? How should they be annotated?

7. Bringing technology to document and revitalize endangered languages. Improving model performance and documentation of under-resourced and endangered languages using typological databases, multilingual models and data from high-resource languages.

The final program of SIGTYP contains 2 keynote talks, 3 shared task papers, 12 archival papers, and 5 extended abstracts. This workshop would not have been possible without the contribution of its program committee, to whom we would like to express our gratitude. We should also thank Ella Rabinovich and Natalia Levshina for kindly accepting our invitation as invited speakers. The workshop is sponsored by Google. Please find more details on the SIGTYP 2023 website: https://sigtyp.github.io/ws2023-sigtyp.html

Organizing Committee

Workshop Organizers

Lisa Beinborn, Vrije Universiteit Amsterdam
Koustava Goswami, Adobe Research
Saliha Muradoğlu, Australian National University
Alexey Sorokin, Moscow State University
Ritesh Kumar, Dr. Bhimrao Ambedkar University
Andreas Shcherbakov, The University of Melbourne
Edoardo M. Ponti, The University of Edinburgh
Ryan Cotterell, ETH Zürich
Ekaterina Vylomova, The University of Melbourne

Program Committee

Program Chairs

Emily Ahn, University of Washington
Miriam Butt, University of Konstanz
Daan van Esch, Google AI
Elisabetta Ježek, University of Pavia
Paola Merlo, University of Geneva
Joakim Nivre, Uppsala University
Robert Östling, Stockholm University
Ivan Vulić, The University of Cambridge
Richard Sproat, Google Japan
Željko Agić, Corti
Edoardo Ponti, The University of Edinburgh
Alexey Sorokin, Moscow State University
Andrey Shcherbakov, The University of Melbourne
Tanja Samardžić, University of Zurich
Aryaman Arora, Georgetown University
Samopriya Basu, The University of North Carolina at Chapel Hill
Badr M. Abdullah, Saarland University
Guglielmo Inglese, KU Leuven
Olga Zamaraeva, University of Washington
Borja Herce, University of Zurich
Michael Hahn, Stanford University
Giuseppe Celano, Leipzig University
Richard Futrell, University of California, Irvine
Gerhard Jäger, Universität Tübingen
Eitan Grossman, Hebrew University of Jerusalem
Johann-Mattis List, University of Passau
Miryam de Lhoneux, KU Leuven
Giulia Venturi, Istituto di Linguistica Computazionale Antonio Zampolli
Kristen Howell, University of Washington
Barend Beekhuizen, University of Toronto
Claire Bowern, Yale University
Thomas Proisl, University of Erlangen-Nuremberg
Michael Regan, University of Washington

Table of Contents

Program

Saturday, May 6, 2023

08:50 - 09:00 *Opening Remarks*

09:00 - 09:50 *Keynote by Ella Rabinovich*

09:50 - 10:20 *Cross-lingual Transfer*

Identifying the Correlation Between Language Distance and Cross-Lingual Transfer in a Multilingual Representation Space
Fred Philippy, Siwen Guo and Shohreh Haddadan

Gradual Language Model Adaptation Using Fine-Grained Typology
Marcell Richard Fekete and Johannes Bjerva

Cross-lingual Transfer Learning with Persian
Sepideh Mollanorozy, Marc Tanti and Malvina Nissim

10:20 - 10:35 *Cross-Lingual Transfer of Cognitive Complexity (Findings)*

10:35 - 11:15 *Break*

11:15 - 11:30 *Does Transliteration Help Multilingual Language Modeling Long (Findings)*

11:30 - 12:30 *Multilinguality*

Multilingual BERT has an Accent: Evaluating English Influences on Fluency in Multilingual Models
Isabel Papadimitriou, Kezia Lopez and Dan Jurafsky

The Denglisch Corpus of German-English Code-Switching
Doreen Osmelak and Shuly Wintner

Trimming Phonetic Alignments Improves the Inference of Sound Correspondence Patterns from Multilingual Wordlists
Frederic Blum and Johann-Mattis List

Saturday, May 6, 2023 (continued)

	On the Nature of Discrete Speech Representations in Multilingual Self-supervised Models Badr M. Abdullah, Mohammed Maqsood Shaik and Dietrich Klakow
	You Can Have Your Data and Balance It Too: Towards Balanced and Efficient Multilingual Models Tomasz Limisiewicz, Dan Malkin and Gabriel Stanovsky
12:30 - 12:45	*Evaluating the Diversity, Equity and Inclusion of NLP Technology: A Case Study for Indian Languages (Findings)*
12:45 - 13:00	*A Large-Scale Multilingual Study of Visual Constraints on Linguistic Selection of Descriptions (Findings)*
13:00 - 14:15	*Lunch (with Linguistic Trivia at 13:45–14:15)*
14:15 - 15:05	*Keynote by Natalia Levshina*
15:05 - 15:50	*Linguistic Complexity*
	Information-Theoretic Characterization of Vowel Harmony: A Cross-Linguistic Study on Word Lists Julius Steuer, Johann-Mattis List, Badr M. Abdullah and Dietrich Klakow
	A Crosslinguistic Database for Combinatorial and Semantic Properties of Attitude Predicates Deniz Özyıldız, Ciyang Qing, Floris Roelofsen, Maribel Romero and Wataru Uegaki
	Revisiting Dependency Length and Intervener Complexity Minimisation on a Parallel Corpus in 35 Languages Andrew Thomas Dyer
15:50 - 16:10	*Break*
16:10 - 16:40	*Shared task on Cognate and Derivative Detection For Low-Resourced Languages*
	Findings of the SIGTYP 2023 Shared task on Cognate and Derivative Detection For Low-Resourced Languages Priya Rani, Koustava Goswami, Adrian Doyle, Theodorus Fransen, Bernardo Stearns and John P. McCrae

Saturday, May 6, 2023 (continued)

	ÚFAL Submission for SIGTYP Supervised Cognate Detection Task Tomasz Limisiewicz
	CoToHiLi at SIGTYP 2023: Ensemble Models for Cognate and Derivative Words Detection Liviu P. Dinu, Ioan-Bogdan Iordache and Ana Sabina Uban
16:40 - 16:45	*Break*
16:45 - 18:05	*Syntax and Morphology*
	Grambank's Typological Advances Support Computational Research on Diverse Languages Hannah J. Haynie, Damián Blasi, Hedvig Skirgård, Simon J. Greenhill, Quentin D. Atkinson and Russell D. Gray
	Language-Agnostic Measures Discriminate Inflection and Derivation Coleman Haley, Edoardo M. Ponti and Sharon Goldwater
	Does Topological Ordering of Morphological Segments Reduce Morphological Modeling Complexity? A Preliminary Study on 13 Languages Andreas Shcherbakov and Ekaterina Vylomova
	Multilingual End-to-end Dependency Parsing with Linguistic Typology knowledge Chinmay Choudhary and Colm O'riordan
	Using Modern Languages to Parse Ancient Ones: a Test on Old English Luca Brigada Villa and Martina Giarda
	Corpus-based Syntactic Typological Methods for Dependency Parsing Improvement Diego Alves, Božo Bekavac, Daniel Zeman and Marko Tadić
18:05 - 18:10	*Best Paper Awards, Closing*

You Can Have Your Data and Balance It Too: Towards Balanced and Efficient Multilingual Models

Tomasz Limisiewicz[♠*†] **Dan Malkin**[♢*] **Gabriel Stanovsky**[♢]
[♢] School of Computer Science, The Hebrew University of Jerusalem
[♠] Faculty of Mathematics and Physics, Charles University in Prague
{dan.malkinhueb,gabriel.stanovsky}@mail.huji.ac.il
limisiewicz@ufal.mff.cuni.cz

Abstract

Multilingual models have been widely used for cross-lingual transfer to low-resource languages. However, the performance on these languages is hindered by their under-representation in the pretraining data. To alleviate this problem, we propose a novel multilingual training technique based on teacher-student knowledge distillation. In this setting, we utilize monolingual teacher models optimized for their language. We use those teachers along with balanced (sub-sampled) data to distill the teachers' knowledge into a single multilingual student. Our method outperforms standard training methods in low-resource languages and retains performance on high-resource languages. [1]

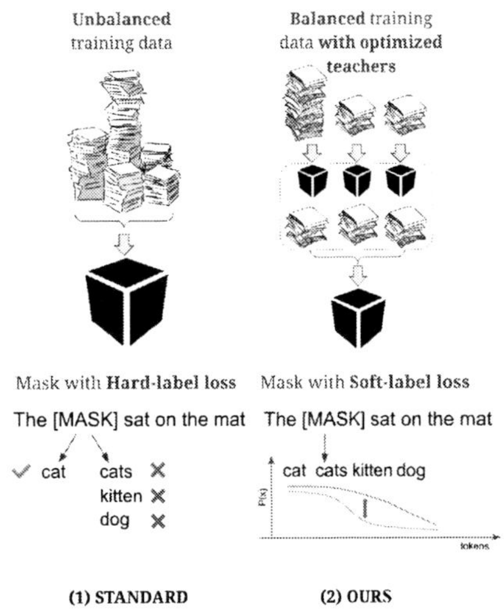

Figure 1: We train a student for multilingual language modeling using a collection of teachers optimized for each of the target languages and multilingual data sub-sampled to the data size of the lowest resource language. Our approach achieves a better trade-off in performance between high- and low-resource languages.

1 Introduction

While multilingual language models have been gaining popularity, largely thanks to their cross-lingual transfer ability, their performance has been shown to be skewed toward languages with abundant data (Joshi et al., 2020; Wu and Dredze, 2020). Introducing language models that better incorporate diverse and low-resource languages can increase accessibility to NLP technologies in these languages and help improve cross-lingual transfer (Malkin et al., 2022).

In this work, we address two research questions. First, we ask if we can we improve performance on low-resource languages without hurting it on high-resource ones? Second, does a better trade-off between high- and low-resource languages improve cross-lingual transfer?

To answer these two questions, we distill multiple monolingual teacher models optimized for various languages into a single multilingual student model, using a small balanced multilingual dataset (Figure 1). Our experiments show that this allows taking advantage of data in high-resource languages while avoiding under-fitting low-resource languages.

2 Background: Soft Vs. Hard Labels

We compare two alternatives for the masked LM loss functions: the original loss used for masked language modeling, i.e., *hard labeling* and *soft labeling* as defined in Sanh et al. (2019):
(1) *hard labeling*, which takes into account a single gold masked token in a sentence, y_{gold}, and evaluates the model's prediction for this word, i.e., standard cross-entropy loss:

$$\mathcal{L}_{HARD} = -\log(P(y_{gold})) \qquad (1)$$

[*] Equal contribution. The order was decided by a coin toss.

[†] Work done while visiting the Hebrew University.

[1] We will make all of our code and resources publicly available.

Proceedings of the 5th Workshop on Research in Computational Linguistic Typology and Multilingual NLP (SIGTYP 2023), pages 1–11
May 6, 2023

(2) *soft labeling*, which allows for multiple valid candidates using the output distribution of an oracle (or a strong LM) $\hat{M}_l$ as a soft label:

$$\mathcal{L}_{SOFT} = -\sum_{y \in V} P_{\hat{M}_l}(y) \log \frac{P(y)}{P_{\hat{M}_l}(y)} \quad (2)$$

Where y denotes tokens in the model's vocabulary V. Please note that $\mathcal{L}_{SOFT}$ is also equivalent to a KL-divergence between oracle and predicted distributions.

In the following sections, we will explain how soft labeling allows us to distill multiple teachers into a single multilingual student while accounting for balanced performance in high- and low-resource languages.

3 Teacher-Student Distillation for Multilingual Language Models

We train a multilingual student using the masked-language modeling objective and a collection of monolingual teachers optimized for each student's language. All models share one multilingual vocabulary. Sharing vocabulary was necessary to apply our *soft labeling* loss, which requires that the student's and teacher's probability space (in the case of language models: vocabularies) are the same.[2]

To avoid under-fitting low-resource languages, we naively balance the students' training data by truncating data in all target languages to the data size of the lowest resource language. To make the most out of high-resource languages, we rely on soft labeling. For a mask in a given language, we use the *high-resource* language-specific teacher's distribution over the mask and use it as the oracle $\hat{M}_l$ in Equation 2 as a soft label. Our intuition is that this allows the student to gain the broader teachers' knowledge in its language and thus compensate for the sub-sampled data size. Figure 1 provides a visual scheme for this approach.

Formally, given a set of languages $L = \{l_1, l_2, ..., l_K\}$, their corresponding teachers $T_{l_1}, T_{l_2}, ..., T_{l_K}$, and their data $D = \{D_1, D_2, ..., D_K\}$ we teach the student model using the K teachers (which are trained for each of the languages). For student training, we truncate the data size of all languages in D to the smallest dataset size ($min(|D_1|, |D_2|, ..., |D_K|)$).

[2]Please refer to Section 8, "Teacher model availability" for discussion about vocabulary sharing across monolingual models.

Size [characters]	Shared Script	Diverse Script
100M	English	Russian
100M	German	German
50M	Spanish	Korean
30M	Hungarian	Greek
20M	Vietnamese	Hindi
10M	Turkish	Telugu
10M	Basque	Urdu

Table 1: Pre-training datasets for each language (in millions of characters) sampled from Wikipedia for high-resource (top) and low-resource (bottom) languages. Some of the selected low-resource languages are actually widely spoken. They were chosen because of relatively smaller Wikipedia sizes (as shown in Appendix B).

Data selection and processing. We collect pre-training data from Wikipedia,[3] aiming to capture a diverse set of high and low-resource languages, as summarized in Table 1. We subsample the corpora by randomly choosing sentences from each language's full corpus. We designate high-resource languages as ones with 50 or 100 million characters in their corpus after sampling, while low-resource languages' corpora consist of 10, 20, and 30 million characters.

Throughout our experiments, we compare 7 languages that share the Latin script versus 7 languages with varying scripts, as the script was found to be an essential factor for multilingual performance (K et al., 2020; Muller et al., 2021; Malkin et al., 2022). We include German in both sets (as one of 7 languages), to compare its performance in both settings.

Models' Architecture and Hyper-parameters. Each of our models comprises of 6 hidden layers and 4 attention heads, an MLM task head. The embedding dimension is 512 and sentences were truncated to 128 tokens. In total, our models consist of 51193168 parameters. We train a single uncased wordpiece tokenizer (Wu et al., 2016) on the 100mb splits of 15 languages.[4] Before tokenization, we strip accents for all languages except Korean.

We train all models for 10 epochs, with a batch size of 8. We used linear decay of the learning rate

[3]Obtained and cleaned using wikiextractor (Attardi, 2015). We chose Wikipedia as it consists of roughly similar encyclopedic domains across languages and is widely used for training PLMs (Devlin et al., 2019).

[4]13 languages presented in Table 1 with Hebrew and Lithuanian that were added for future experiments.

with the initial value of 5e-5. Exact configurations and parameters are available in our code.

4 Experiments

We validate our method using two experiments. First, we ascertain that our method indeed improves performance for low-resource languages while maintaining performance for high-resource languages. This is done by comparing the performance of our approach in masked language modeling with two multilingual baselines. Second, we show that our method is competitive for downstream tasks and cross-lingual transfer by probing the pre-trained models for POS and NER tagging.

Multilingual modeling. We evaluate masked language modeling performance on monolingual test sets by measuring *mean reciprocal rank* (MRR). Since the performance of multilingual models is often compared to the performances of monolingual baselines, we report the *average performance difference* between a multilingual model and the monolingual models trained on the same set of respective languages.

Downstream probing. We use the models trained in the previous experiment and train a probe,[5] keeping the base model parameters frozen, to predict part-of-speech tagging (POS) and name entity recognition (NER), as provided respectively by universal dependencies (Nivre et al., 2020) and the XTREME benchmark (Hu et al., 2020).[6] We chose those two tasks because they commonly appear in NLP pipelines (Manning et al., 2014; Honnibal and Montani, 2017). We measure the models' performance in two cases: when the training and test datasets are in the same language (denoted IN-LANG) and when a probe trained for a language l_1 is tested on another one l_2 (denoted ZERO-SHOT). As noted by Hu et al. (2020), zero-shot evaluation is a good measure of a model's cross-lingual transfer. We use probing because it offers a good insight into the representation learned by the model (Belinkov, 2022).

Baselines. We compare the students' performance to multilingual models trained with *hard labels*, on the same data and languages as the student and its teachers. One such model was trained on all the available data in each language to examine the extent of under-fitting low-resource languages, denoted ***HL***. Additionally, to measure how much our student gains from its teacher's knowledge, we train another model on the corpora constrained to the size of the least resourceful language using the standard *hard labels*, denoted ***HL balanced***.

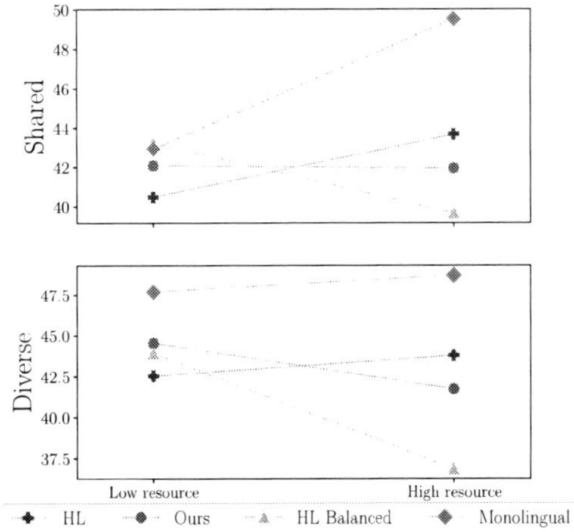

Figure 2: Our balanced teacher-student approach using soft labels presents the overall best combination for low and high-resource languages among multilingual models. This figure presents average MRR results in masked language modeling for both low- and high-resource languages. Results are reported for a Latin-script language set (Shared) and a set with diverse scripts (Diverse).

Experimental Setup Each teacher is a monolingual model trained with *hard labels*. The teachers are trained on the entire training corpus available in their language. In a student model, we distill the knowledge of multiple monolingual teachers into a multilingual student using *soft labels*, as described above. The distillation into the student is performed on groups of shared and diverse script languages. The data is constrained to 10 million characters for each language. All our models are trained using default BERT hyper-parameters detailed in Section 3.

5 Results

We report the experimental results on our test sets, in three language sets grouped by the amount of data available in pre-training, i.e., low-resource, high-resource, and all data. We address our research questions in light of the results:

5

6 See Section D.2 in the Appendix for more information.

Script	Lang. Set	HL	HL Balanced	Ours
Shared	Low-Res.	-2.5	**0.3**	-0.1
	High-Res.	**-5.8**	-10	-7.6
	All	-3.9	-4.0	**-3.7**
Diverse	Low-Res.	-5.1	-3.8	**-3.1**
	High-Res.	**-5.0**	-12	-7.0
	All	-5.0	-7.2	**-4.7**

Table 2: Average difference from monolingual baselines (higher is better) calculated on MRR scores. Our teacher-student model achieves better results overall in both shared and diverse scripts. It is otherwise between the baselines, except for shared script, where it is better for low-resource.

	Lang. set	HL I-L	HL Z-S	HL balanced I-L	HL balanced Z-S	Ours I-L	Ours Z-S
Shared	Low-Res	35.2	33.4	35.5	34.3	**36.6**	**34.5**
	High-Res	83.3	33.7	81.2	32.4	**84.3**	**33.8**
	{de}	**87.1**	32.3	84.1	32.2	86.8	**33.0**
	All	55.8	33.5	55.1	33.5	**57.0**	**34.2**
Diverse	Low-Res	53.1	35.8	54.6	34.9	**55.7**	**35.9**
	High-Res	76.8	36.2	73.4	34.7	**77.3**	**36.8**
	{de}	**87.7**	36.8	83.3	35.3	87.4	**38.1**
	All	63.3	36.0	62.7	34.8	**64.9**	**36.3**

(a) Accuracy of POS probing.

	Lang. set	HL I-L	HL Z-S	HL balanced I-L	HL balanced Z-S	Ours I-L	Ours Z-S
Shared	Low-Res	26.5	23.7	27.9	**24.3**	**29.8**	23.9
	High-Res	34.2	24.9	34.7	24.7	**37.6**	**26.0**
	{de}	31.4	**27.4**	**32.1**	25.7	32.0	23.9
	All	29.8	24.2	30.8	24.5	**33.1**	**24.8**
Diverse	Low-Res	25.7	12.8	28.0	**13.8**	**29.9**	12.9
	High-Res	32.8	14.9	29.9	15.1	**37.2**	**17.1**
	{de}	32.5	14.8	31.5	15.7	**35.3**	**17.2**
	All	28.7	13.7	28.8	14.4	**33.0**	**14.7**

(b) Macro F1 of NER probing.

Table 3: For each model and language set, we report average IN-LANG performance (probe trained and tested on the same language) and average ZERO-SHOT performance (probe trained on one language and tested on another). Each ZERO-SHOT number is an average result across all source languages and target languages in the indicated language set. Each entry is a mean of 5 runs with different probe initialization. The Results with significance intervals for each language can be found in Appendix (Tables 6, 7).

Our method offers a good trade-off between performance on high- and low-resource languages. Figure 2 shows the trend of language modeling scores (MRR) when changing from low- to high-resource set. Table 2 summarizes performance differences from monolingual models for our method and the two control baseline models.

In low-resource setting, our model outperforms *HL* and achieves similar results to *HL balanced*. For high-resource languages, our approach closely trails *HL* and is better than *HL balanced*, which was trained on the same data as our student model. It indicates that the student model effectively acquires knowledge from the teachers' distributions. Our model achieves the best results overall when calculated over all languages.

Better trade-off between high- and low-resource languages improves results on downstream. Table 3 shows that IN-LANG and ZERO-SHOT results of probing for POS and NER labels. Our method achieves better or on-par average results in both tasks and language sets. The only exception is *HL balanced* baselines, which scores better in NER for low-resource languages.

Sharing script is not necessary for good multilingual performance. As seen in Figure 2 and Table 2 for low-resource languages, shared script results are consistently closer to monolingual results compared to the diverse script setting. Whereas, for high-resource set, the average difference between the results of monolingual models and our model or *HL* is smaller in the diverse script scenario. For the language included in both sets (German), MRR is higher when coupled with distinct script languages. The performance difference is 0.4 and 0.9 percent in favor of diverse scripts, for *HL* and our model. *HL balanced* scores 2.8% better in shared script scenario. This implies that diverse scripts can benefit multilingual modeling when we reveal enough monolingual data (as in high-resource setting).

In Table 3, we observe that the results for German in the shared-script scenario are better for POS tagging and worse for NER in comparison to diverse-script. Those findings align with previous results suggesting that shared vocabulary is not necessary for cross-lingual transfer and has a varying effect depending on the task (K et al., 2020; Malkin et al., 2022).

6 Related Work

Recent work utilized knowledge distillation in training NLP models. However, to the best of our knowledge, we are the first to do this in low-resource, balanced data settings. Contrary to the approaches of Tsai et al. (2019); Sanh et al. (2019), we do not scale down student models but constraint training datasets.

Sun et al. (2020) use one teacher model and train for machine translation, and Heffernan et al. (2022) use a single multilingual teacher to train a sentence embedding model for low-resource languages. Both rely on parallel corpora for target low-resource languages. Other works on multilingual language modeling addressed how to improve low-resource performance, largely using post-hoc or language-specific solutions. Chau et al. (2020) change the vocabulary to account for low-resource languages, while Muller et al. (2021) transliterate tokens of low-resource languages to the most similar available high-resource language.

Finally, Pfeiffer et al. (2020) introduce cross-lingual adapters, compact components that allow adapting a given model pre-trained for a task in a different desired language.

7 Conclusions

We train multilingual language models aimed at balancing the models' performance for languages with uneven data sizes. We outperform standard models for low-resource languages while maintaining performance on high-resource languages. Noticeably, our method gives better results overall than the naive data sub-sampling. Lastly, our model is a good representation learner for downstream tasks, outperforming baselines for two probing tasks.

Taken together, our results suggest a new direction for multilingual modeling that accounts for a more even performance across low- and high-resource languages and improves cross-lingual transfer.

8 Limitations

Restricted model size and training. Due to limited computational resources, we performed experiments for models significantly smaller than the ones developed by the industry. We based our down-scaling choices on previous ablation studies on cross-lingual models (K et al., 2020). In line with their findings, we prioritized model depth (6 hidden layers) over width (4 attention heads). Also, we examine only BERT based models. This work serves as a proof of concept for a new multilingual language modeling, and future work can extend the study to bigger models with different architectures.

Restricted data. We decided to train our models on sub-sampled Wikipedia to achieve reasonable training times. As shown in appendix B.2 the chosen sample follows the resource-richness trend across languages but does not fully reflect the imbalance between high- and low-resource languages. Nevertheless, we think that this issue does not weaken our point, as even our "unbalanced" baseline model is trained on less skewed data than currently deployed multilingual models. Furthermore, we train our models on 7 languages. Our method needs to be verified on larger data sizes and broader language sets.

Working with limited training data might still be valuable in several aspects. First, there's a growing interest in efficient, and green AI. Smaller and more efficient models will reduce training and inference costs while allowing them to run on less capable hardware and make them accessible to a wider community. Second, from a linguistic perspective, many of the world's languages lack large corpora, and hence will benefit from models that leverage a limited amount of available resources (Joshi et al., 2020).

Naive balancing method. We truncate our training to the size of the smallest low-resource languages, which might be a naive and aggressive approach leading to a sub-optimal performance on our available data. However, our simple approach achieves good results even with naive balancing. Future work can extend it with complex data balancing approaches, such as weighing training data using a learned data scorer (as done in Wang et al. (2020)).

Teacher model availability. Our teacher-student training method assumes the existence of pre-trained monolingual teachers for each considered language, which is considerably less sustainable than training only one multilingual model. Nevertheless, we believe that it is possible to re-use publicly available models as teachers for high-resource languages, while for low-resource languages, competitive results can be obtained with smaller models requiring less computation (Hoffmann et al., 2022). Because our distillation method works on predicted distribution and not latent representations, to combine knowledge of teachers from multiple source languages, we will need to align their vocabularies, which was shown to be feasible by Artetxe et al. (2020); Rust et al. (2021). We leave this engineering task for future work.

Metrics for probing tasks. To evaluate probing for NER we used macro-F1 measured per token and not per entity as in usual NER evaluation. We observed that the probes underperformed in correctly classifying all tokens in a single entity. It led to overall low results in regular F1 that would not allow meaningful comparison between analyzed models. Importantly, macro-F1 equally weights the performance in predicting each class. Thus, it is appropriate to evaluate NER task, where most tokens are annotated as not belonging to any entity.

Acknowledgements

We thank anonymous reviewers for their valuable comments on the previous versions of this article. This work was supported in part by a research gift from the Allen Institute for AI, and a research grant 2336 from the Israeli Ministry of Science and Technology. Tomasz Limisiewicz's visit to the Hebrew University has been supported by grant 338521 of the Charles University Grant Agency and the Mobility Fund of Charles University.

References

Mikel Artetxe, Sebastian Ruder, and Dani Yogatama. 2020. On the cross-lingual transferability of monolingual representations. In *Proceedings of the 58th Annual Meeting of the Association for Computational Linguistics*, pages 4623–4637, Online. Association for Computational Linguistics.

Giusepppe Attardi. 2015. Wikiextractor. `https://github.com/attardi/wikiextractor`.

Yonatan Belinkov. 2022. Probing classifiers: Promises, shortcomings, and advances. *Computational Linguistics*, 48(1):207–219.

Ethan C. Chau, Lucy H. Lin, and Noah A. Smith. 2020. Parsing with multilingual BERT, a small corpus, and a small treebank. In *Findings of the Association for Computational Linguistics: EMNLP 2020*, pages 1324–1334, Online. Association for Computational Linguistics.

Jacob Devlin, Ming-Wei Chang, Kenton Lee, and Kristina Toutanova. 2019. BERT: Pre-training of deep bidirectional transformers for language understanding. In *Proceedings of the 2019 Conference of the North American Chapter of the Association for Computational Linguistics: Human Language Technologies, Volume 1 (Long and Short Papers)*, pages 4171–4186, Minneapolis, Minnesota. Association for Computational Linguistics.

Kevin Heffernan, Onur Çelebi, and Holger Schwenk. 2022. Bitext mining using distilled sentence representations for low-resource languages. *arXiv preprint arXiv:2205.12654*.

Jordan Hoffmann, Sebastian Borgeaud, Arthur Mensch, Elena Buchatskaya, Trevor Cai, Eliza Rutherford, Diego de Las Casas, Lisa Anne Hendricks, Johannes Welbl, Aidan Clark, Tom Hennigan, Eric Noland, Katie Millican, George van den Driessche, Bogdan Damoc, Aurelia Guy, Simon Osindero, Karen Simonyan, Erich Elsen, Jack W. Rae, Oriol Vinyals, and Laurent Sifre. 2022. Training compute-optimal large language models. *CoRR*, abs/2203.15556.

Matthew Honnibal and Ines Montani. 2017. spaCy 2: Natural language understanding with Bloom embeddings, convolutional neural networks and incremental parsing. To appear.

Junjie Hu, Sebastian Ruder, Aditya Siddhant, Graham Neubig, Orhan Firat, and Melvin Johnson. 2020. XTREME: A massively multilingual multitask benchmark for evaluating cross-lingual generalisation. In *Proceedings of the 37th International Conference on Machine Learning, ICML 2020, 13-18 July 2020, Virtual Event*, volume 119 of *Proceedings of Machine Learning Research*, pages 4411–4421. PMLR.

Pratik Joshi, Sebastin Santy, Amar Budhiraja, Kalika Bali, and Monojit Choudhury. 2020. The state and fate of linguistic diversity and inclusion in the NLP world. In *Proceedings of the 58th Annual Meeting of the Association for Computational Linguistics*, pages 6282–6293, Online. Association for Computational Linguistics.

Karthikeyan K, Zihan Wang, Stephen Mayhew, and Dan Roth. 2020. Cross-lingual ability of multilingual BERT: an empirical study. In *8th International Conference on Learning Representations, ICLR 2020, Addis Ababa, Ethiopia, April 26-30, 2020*. OpenReview.net.

Dan Malkin, Tomasz Limisiewicz, and Gabriel Stanovsky. 2022. A balanced data approach for evaluating cross-lingual transfer: Mapping the linguistic blood bank. In *Proceedings of the 2022 Conference of the North American Chapter of the Association for Computational Linguistics: Human Language Technologies*, pages 4903–4915, Seattle, United States. Association for Computational Linguistics.

Christopher Manning, Mihai Surdeanu, John Bauer, Jenny Finkel, Steven Bethard, and David McClosky. 2014. The Stanford CoreNLP natural language processing toolkit. In *Proceedings of 52nd Annual Meeting of the Association for Computational Linguistics: System Demonstrations*, pages 55–60, Baltimore, Maryland. Association for Computational Linguistics.

Benjamin Muller, Antonios Anastasopoulos, Benoît Sagot, and Djamé Seddah. 2021. When being unseen from mBERT is just the beginning: Handling new languages with multilingual language models. In *Proceedings of the 2021 Conference of the North American Chapter of the Association for Computational Linguistics: Human Language Technologies*, pages 448–462, Online. Association for Computational Linguistics.

Joakim Nivre, Marie-Catherine de Marneffe, Filip Ginter, Jan Hajič, Christopher D. Manning, Sampo Pyysalo, Sebastian Schuster, Francis Tyers, and Daniel Zeman. 2020. Universal Dependencies v2: An evergrowing multilingual treebank collection. In *Proceedings of the 12th Language Resources and Evaluation Conference*, pages 4034–4043, Marseille, France. European Language Resources Association.

Jonas Pfeiffer, Ivan Vulić, Iryna Gurevych, and Sebastian Ruder. 2020. MAD-X: An Adapter-Based Framework for Multi-Task Cross-Lingual Transfer. In *Proceedings of the 2020 Conference on Empirical Methods in Natural Language Processing (EMNLP)*, pages 7654–7673, Online. Association for Computational Linguistics.

Phillip Rust, Jonas Pfeiffer, Ivan Vulić, Sebastian Ruder, and Iryna Gurevych. 2021. How good is your tokenizer? on the monolingual performance of multilingual language models. In *Proceedings of the 59th Annual Meeting of the Association for Computational Linguistics and the 11th International Joint Conference on Natural Language Processing (Volume 1: Long Papers)*, pages 3118–3135, Online. Association for Computational Linguistics.

Victor Sanh, Lysandre Debut, Julien Chaumond, and Thomas Wolf. 2019. Distilbert, a distilled version of bert: smaller, faster, cheaper and lighter. In *NeurIPS EMC2 Workshop*.

Haipeng Sun, Rui Wang, Kehai Chen, Masao Utiyama, Eiichiro Sumita, and Tiejun Zhao. 2020. Knowledge distillation for multilingual unsupervised neural machine translation. In *Proceedings of the 58th Annual Meeting of the Association for Computational Linguistics*, pages 3525–3535, Online. Association for Computational Linguistics.

Henry Tsai, Jason Riesa, Melvin Johnson, Naveen Arivazhagan, Xin Li, and Amelia Archer. 2019. Small and practical BERT models for sequence labeling. In *Proceedings of the 2019 Conference on Empirical Methods in Natural Language Processing and the 9th International Joint Conference on Natural Language Processing (EMNLP-IJCNLP)*, pages 3632–3636, Hong Kong, China. Association for Computational Linguistics.

Xinyi Wang, Yulia Tsvetkov, and Graham Neubig. 2020. Balancing training for multilingual neural machine translation. In *Proceedings of the 58th Annual Meeting of the Association for Computational Linguistics*, pages 8526–8537, Online. Association for Computational Linguistics.

Shijie Wu and Mark Dredze. 2020. Are all languages created equal in multilingual BERT? In *Proceedings of the 5th Workshop on Representation Learning for NLP*, pages 120–130, Online. Association for Computational Linguistics.

Yonghui Wu, Mike Schuster, Zhifeng Chen, Quoc V Le, Mohammad Norouzi, Wolfgang Macherey, Maxim Krikun, Yuan Cao, Qin Gao, Klaus Macherey, et al. 2016. Google's neural machine translation system: Bridging the gap between human and machine translation. *ArXiv preprint*, abs/1609.08144.

Lang.	POS		NER	
	train	test	train	test
de	166849	22458	20000	10000
es	28492	3147	20000	10000
en	21253	5440	20000	10000
eu	5396	1799	10000	10000
hu	910	449	20000	10000
tr	3664	4785	20000	10000
vi	1400	800	20000	10000
ru	67435	11336	20000	10000
ko	27410	4276	20000	10000
el	28152	2809	20000	10000
hi	13304	2684	5000	1000
te	1051	146	1000	1000
ur	4043	535	20000	1000

Table 4: Number of training and testing sentences for POS and NER tasks in XTREME data collection. The data were used to train and evaluate probes on top of analysed models.

A Appendix

In the appendix: we provide details on datasets used in this work Section B; show how proposed teacher-student distillation behaves in the monolingual scenario with just one teacher Section C; present detailed results of our two experimental for each language Section D; provide details of our training procedure and hardware usage Section E.

B Datasets Details

B.1 Data Splits

For pre-training (monolingual) teacher and *HL* models, we use Wikipedia splits of sizes indicated in Table 1, for training student and *HL balanced* models, we subsample training corpus to 10 million characters. We use validation and test sets containing 10000 Wikipedia sentences each.

For downstream probing, we use train and test splits from XTREME. The numbers of sentences in these splits per language are shown in table 4.

B.2 Correspondence of the Sizes of Our Corpora and Wikipedias

Figure 3 shows the per language correspondence between our corpora size and the whole Wikipedia. The latter was used to pre-train MBERT (Devlin et al., 2019). We observe a good linear fit between character numbers in our corpora and the logarithm of Wikipedia byte size. It suggests that the multilingual imbalance is even more severe in the original dataset than in our sample.

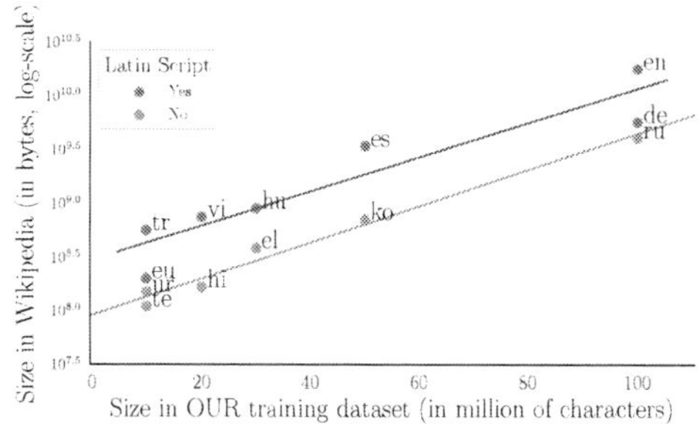

Figure 3: A comparison of subsampled corpora sized and the data available in Wikipedia, which was MBERT's training corpus.

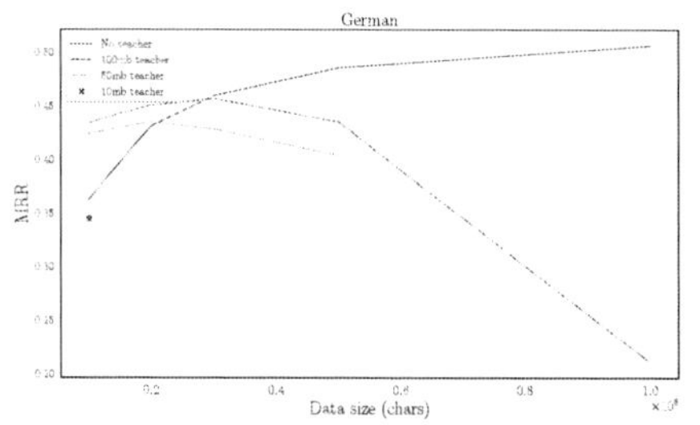

Figure 4: Performance of a language model as the function of training corpora size. The regular HL training is compared with the knowledge distillation to a student on the dataset lower or equal in size than the teacher's training set.

C Teacher-Student Method in the Monolingual World

The purpose of this experiment is to visualize how the model's performance scales with the size of the pre-training dataset. Also, we check the behavior of the teacher-student knowledge distillation with the change of data size used to train a teacher and a student in a monolingual setting.

We train a monolingual model on German Wikipedia data with five sizes (in millions of characters): 10, 20, 30, 50, and 100. Subsequently, we designate 10, 50, and 100 million character models as teachers and distill their knowledge into students on the same size or smaller corpus.[7]

As presented in figure 4, the teacher performance

[7] In monolingual knowledge distillation, we used a learning rate 5 times higher than in the default BERT training script. This choice led to better results.

	Shared script	Diverse script
HL	-2.9	**-2.5**
HL Balanced	**-9.2**	-12
Ours	-6.1	**-5.2**

Table 5: Difference from monolingual baseline, for German. German achieves better results in diverse script, except for *HL Balanced*. This suggest that diverse script might help increase language modeling performance.

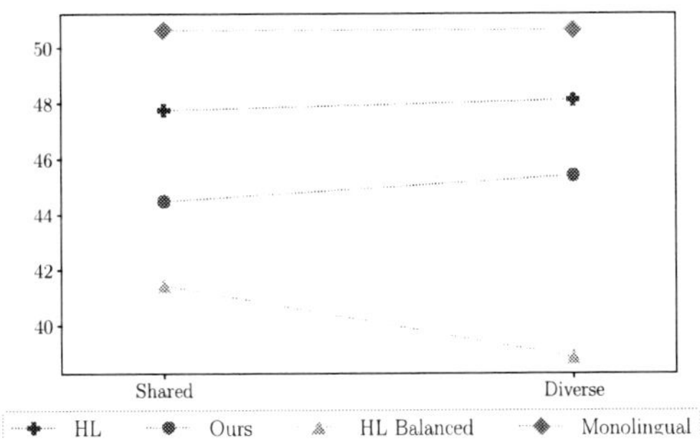

Figure 5: MRR scores for German trained in the set of languages with shared script and diverse script. We observe slight improvement for diverse script over shared script, and significant deterioration for *HL Balanced*.

can be nearly matched by a student trained on a considerably smaller corpus. For the teacher trained on the largest split, the student performance rises steadily with the increase of distillation detest from 10 to 30 million characters and drops after that point. The performance of the student trained on 100 million characters is noticeably low. It is a sign of over-fitting, as in our setting, distillation set is always a subset of the teacher's training set. Also, in the case of teachers trained on smaller corpora, distillation on the dataset of the same size (as the teacher training set) leads to a drop in performance. Therefore, we claim that the distillation is beneficial when the teacher's training set is larger than the student's one.

D Per Language Results

D.1 German: Comparing Shared and Diverse Scripts

Table 5 and Figure 5 present masked language modeling performance for German for three analyzed multilingual model types. German is the language included both in the shared and diverse script language sets. Therefore the results allow comparing which setting is more effective in multilingual language modeling.

D.2 Results for Every Language

We present per language results in masked language modeling performance in Figure 6 and for probing tasks (POS and NER) in Tables 6 and 7.

E GPUs and training procedures

All of our models (monolingual teachers, students, and multilingual models trained using *hard labels*) are trained on a single GPU core.

We used varying GPUs architectures allocated for each model upon availability (nvidia gtx 980, tesla M60, and RTX 2080Ti). Training time varied between 1 to 3 hours for monolingual models (depending on the data size, language, and GPU core). Multilingual models' training took around 18 hours to complete. Early stopping was used for all models based on results on a balanced dev set.

MLM evaluation was run on the same machines as training or on CPU. the run time ranged from 2 to 4 hours. Training a probe on top of a frozen model took from 1 to 20 minutes, depending on the number of training examples available for a language. The evaluation time on a downstream task was less than 2 minutes.

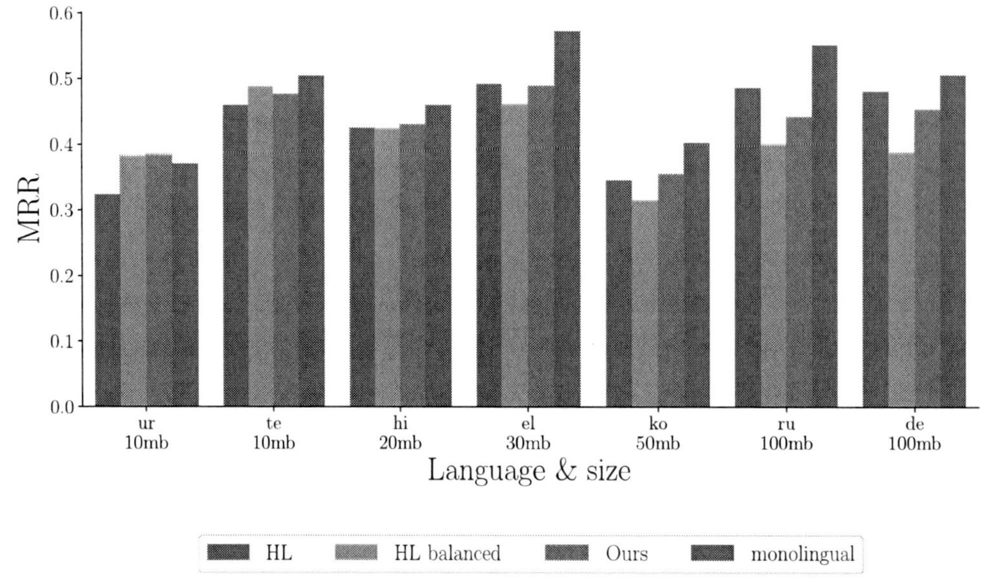

(a) Shared Script (Latin)

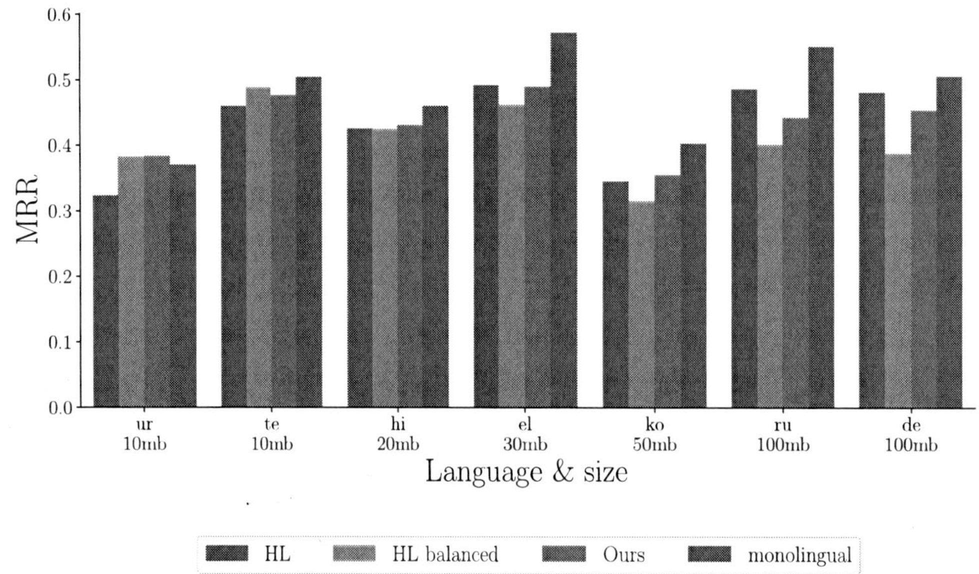

(b) Diverse Script

Figure 6: The figures present MRR results for each language. Our model is compared with baselines: *HL balanced*, *HL* and monolingual models. We observe similar trends as in Figure 2 at higher granularity.

Script	Lang.	HL		HL balanced		Ours	
		In-Lang	Zero-Shot	In-Lang	Zero-Shot	In-Lang	Zero-Shot
Shared	de	87.1 $\pm$0.0	32.3 $\pm$0.9	84.1 $\pm$0.0	32.2 $\pm$1.0	86.8 $\pm$0.0	33.0 $\pm$1.1
	en	79.5 $\pm$0.1	34.2 $\pm$1.4	77.4 $\pm$0.2	32.1 $\pm$2.1	81.1 $\pm$0.2	34.1 $\pm$1.3
	es	83.1 $\pm$0.1	34.6 $\pm$1.7	82.0 $\pm$0.1	32.8 $\pm$1.7	84.8 $\pm$0.1	34.2 $\pm$1.0
	eu	56.3 $\pm$1.2	34.1 $\pm$1.2	58.1 $\pm$1.5	35.0 $\pm$2.7	58.2 $\pm$0.7	33.1 $\pm$2.2
	hu	18.5 $\pm$3.5	37.4 $\pm$1.0	16.6 $\pm$3.4	37.9 $\pm$1.7	18.5 $\pm$5.2	39.5 $\pm$1.2
	tr	40.5 $\pm$2.2	33.3 $\pm$1.5	40.6 $\pm$3.8	34.5 $\pm$2.2	42.1 $\pm$2.6	34.1 $\pm$2.6
	vi	25.5 $\pm$2.2	28.7 $\pm$1.1	26.9 $\pm$3.1	29.9 $\pm$1.3	27.7 $\pm$4.5	31.3 $\pm$1.9
Diverse	de	87.7 $\pm$0.0	36.8 $\pm$0.9	83.3 $\pm$0.0	35.3 $\pm$1.1	87.4 $\pm$0.0	38.1 $\pm$0.3
	ru	79.0 $\pm$0.0	36.9 $\pm$0.9	74.0 $\pm$0.1	36.9 $\pm$1.2	78.6 $\pm$0.1	38.8 $\pm$1.5
	ko	63.7 $\pm$0.2	34.8 $\pm$1.6	62.8 $\pm$0.2	31.9 $\pm$1.8	65.8 $\pm$0.2	33.5 $\pm$1.2
	el	66.6 $\pm$0.2	29.9 $\pm$1.1	66.7 $\pm$0.2	27.0 $\pm$1.0	69.0 $\pm$0.3	30.8 $\pm$1.4
	hi	70.7 $\pm$0.2	34.9 $\pm$0.8	69.6 $\pm$0.1	34.7 $\pm$1.9	70.8 $\pm$0.4	36.0 $\pm$1.6
	te	25.1 $\pm$9.9	42.1 $\pm$1.8	30.0 $\pm$8.4	43.0 $\pm$1.2	28.4 $\pm$6.0	42.6 $\pm$1.3
	ur	50.0 $\pm$1.0	36.3 $\pm$0.6	52.2 $\pm$3.4	34.7 $\pm$0.8	54.4 $\pm$2.0	34.1 $\pm$1.4

Table 6: Accuracy of POS probing for each language. Standard deviations and mean results are computed based on 5 runs with different initialization of the probe.

Script	Lang.	HL		HL balanced		Ours	
		In-Lang	Zero-Shot	In-Lang	Zero-Shot	In-Lang	Zero-Shot
Shared	de	31.4 $\pm$0.6	27.4 $\pm$1.0	32.1 $\pm$0.4	25.7 $\pm$0.4	32.0 $\pm$0.7	26.9 $\pm$1.1
	en	33.0 $\pm$0.5	24.9 $\pm$0.7	33.3 $\pm$0.4	24.8 $\pm$0.2	37.8 $\pm$0.7	25.9 $\pm$0.9
	es	38.2 $\pm$0.6	22.6 $\pm$0.3	38.8 $\pm$1.3	23.7 $\pm$0.7	42.9 $\pm$1.0	25.4 $\pm$1.7
	eu	20.6 $\pm$2.0	27.3 $\pm$0.9	18.5 $\pm$1.3	27.9 $\pm$0.9	20.5 $\pm$0.9	25.9 $\pm$1.0
	hu	26.6 $\pm$0.5	24.3 $\pm$0.9	26.8 $\pm$1.0	25.3 $\pm$0.4	30.2 $\pm$0.6	26.1 $\pm$0.9
	tr	27.3 $\pm$0.5	24.4 $\pm$1.0	30.8 $\pm$0.5	25.4 $\pm$0.4	29.5 $\pm$0.4	24.2 $\pm$0.4
	vi	31.5 $\pm$1.4	18.7 $\pm$0.5	35.5 $\pm$0.5	18.6 $\pm$0.5	39.0 $\pm$1.5	19.2 $\pm$1.3
Diverse	de	32.5 $\pm$0.8	14.8 $\pm$0.6	31.5 $\pm$0.7	15.7 $\pm$0.7	35.3 $\pm$0.4	17.2 $\pm$1.0
	ru	33.7 $\pm$0.8	15.8 $\pm$0.7	29.9 $\pm$0.7	14.6 $\pm$0.7	38.0 $\pm$0.2	16.8 $\pm$0.7
	ko	32.1 $\pm$0.4	14.2 $\pm$0.4	28.2 $\pm$0.5	15.0 $\pm$0.4	38.3 $\pm$0.8	17.3 $\pm$1.1
	el	27.4 $\pm$0.7	16.6 $\pm$0.6	26.5 $\pm$0.9	17.2 $\pm$0.8	31.5 $\pm$0.6	16.6 $\pm$0.6
	hi	16.3 $\pm$0.7	12.8 $\pm$0.4	18.1 $\pm$1.0	14.4 $\pm$1.2	15.7 $\pm$1.1	13.2 $\pm$0.7
	te	13.3 $\pm$1.1	13.8 $\pm$0.5	14.6 $\pm$2.0	13.7 $\pm$0.4	14.2 $\pm$0.6	13.9 $\pm$0.2
	ur	45.6 $\pm$1.1	7.9 $\pm$1.4	52.7 $\pm$1.2	10.0 $\pm$1.2	58.0 $\pm$1.0	8.0 $\pm$0.9

Table 7: Macro-F1 of NER probing for each language. Standard deviations and mean results are computed based on 5 runs with different initialization of the probe.

Multilingual End-to-end Dependency Parsing with Linguistic typology knowledge

Chinmay Choudhary
National University of Ireland
c.choudhary1@nuigalway.ie

Dr. Colm O'riordan
National University of Ireland
colm.oriordan@nuigalway.ie

Abstract

We evaluate a *Multilingual End-to-end BERT based Dependency Parser* which parses an input sentence by directly predicting the relative head-position for each word within it. Our model is a Cross-lingual dependency parser which is trained on a diverse polyglot corpus of high-resource source languages, and is applied on a low-resource target language.
To make model more robust to typological variations between source and target languages, and to facilitate the cross-lingual transferring, we utilized the Linguistic typology knowledge, available in typological databases **WALS** and **URIEL**. We induce such typology knowledge within our model through an auxiliary task within Multi-task Learning framework.

1 Introduction

Linguistic typology is the classification of human languages according to their syntactic, phonological and semantic features. There are numerous available typological databases such as WALS (Haspelmath, 2009), SSWL (Collins and Kayne, 2009), LAPSyd (Maddieson et al., 2013), ValPal (Hartmann and Bradley Taylor, 2013), AUTOTYP (Bickel et al., 2017), APCLS (Michaelis and Magnus Huber, 2013) etc. These databases provide taxonomies of typological features and their possible values, as well as the respective feature values for most of the world's languages.
Linguistic typology existed as an independent research domain since long (Greenberg, 1963; Comrie, 1989; Nichols, 1992) but recently it has been used along with *Cross-lingual/Multi-lingual* NLP (Ponti et al., 2018; Wang and Eisner, 2017; Agić, 2017; Bender, 2016; O'Horan et al., 2016) to address the issue of data-sparsity in low-resource languages.
However all the popular typological databases suffer from a major shortcoming of limited coverage. In fact, values of many important typological features for most languages (specially less documented ones) are missing in these databases. This sparked a line of research on automatic acquisition of such missing typology knowledge. Many researchers (Malaviya et al., 2017; Bjerva and Augenstein, 2018; Bjerva et al., 2019; Bjerva and Augenstein, 2017; Östling and Tiedemann, 2016) indeed successfully used Multi-lingual NLP and ML techniques to predict these missing feature values. Thus Multilingual NLP and Language typology feature prediction are very closely related tasks which would complement each other. Based on this intuition, we propose a model that performs both Multilingual NLP and Linguistic typology feature prediction tasks simultaneously, in a multi-tasking setup.
Multi-task Learning (MTL) (Ruder, 2017) is neural network framework which involves performing of two or more tasks simultaneously leading to knowledge/parameter sharing. These tasks are closely related thus complement each other leading to improved performance on all of them. Even in scenarios where we primarily care about a single task, using a closely related task as an auxiliary task for MTL can be useful (Caruana, 1998; Zhang et al., 2014; Liu et al., 2015; Girshick, 2015; Arik et al., 2017).
In this work, we use *Linguistic Typology* feature prediction task as auxiliary task for *End-to-end Cross-lingual Dependency Parsing*. Hence, we make following contributions.

1. We evaluated the performance an *End-to-end BERT Based Parser* which can parse a sentence by directly predicting relative head-position tag for each word within input sentence. This is inspired by (Li et al., 2018) which is an *End-to-end Seq2seq Dependency Parser*. We evaluated the performance of this BERT based End-to-end parser in both monolingual and cross-lingual/multilingual setups (using mBERT). We will refer to this model

Proceedings of the 5th Workshop on Research in Computational Linguistic Typology and Multilingual NLP (SIGTYP 2023), pages 12–21
May 6, 2023 ©2023 Association for Computational Linguistics

as *Base E2E BERT parser* in this paper.

2. We added the auxiliary task of Linguistic typology prediction to our *Base E2E BERT parser* to observe the change in performence under different settings. We will refer to this model as *Multitasking E2E BERT Parser* in this paper.

2 Related Work

Cross-lingual *Model-transfer* approaches to Dependency Parsing such as (McDonald et al., 2011; Cohen et al., 2011; Duong et al., 2015; Guo et al., 2016; Vilares et al., 2015; Falenska and Çetinoğlu, 2017; Mulcaire et al., 2019; Vania et al., 2019; Shareghi et al., 2019) involve training a model on high-resource languages and subsequently adapting it to low-resource languages.
Participants of CoNLL 2017 shared-task (Daniel et al., 2017) and CoNLL 2018 shared task (Zeman et al., 2018) also provide numerous approaches to dependency parsing of low-resource languages.
Some approaches such as (Naseem et al., 2012; Täckström et al., 2013; Barzilay and Zhang, 2015; Wang and Eisner, 2016a; Rasooli and Collins, 2017; Ammar, 2016; Wang and Eisner, 2016b) used typological information to facilitate cross-lingual transfer. All these approaches directly feed the linguistic typology features into the model whereas we induce the linguistic typology knowledge through Multitask learning.
Inducing typology knowledge through MTL rather than directly feeding it along with word-embeddings have following advantages.

1. The model can also be applied to low-resource languages for which many typology feature values are unknown/missing.

2. The auxiliary task should help to improve the performance on the main dependency parsing task as well, since it would make the model give special emphasis on the syntactic typology (specially word-order typology) of language being parsed while predicting the dependency relations.

3 Base End-to-end BERT Parser

This section elaborates the details of our *End2End BERT based Dependency Parser* which directly predicts the relative head position tag of each word within input sentence.

Given a sentence of length T, its dependency parse-tree can be represented as a sequence of T relative head-position tags as demonstrated in figure 1a. Figure 2a depicts the architecture of our baseline model. The depicted architecture comprises of three components namely *BERT Encoder, Output Network* and *Tree-decoder* described as section 3.1, 3.2 and 3.3.

3.1 BERT Encoder

It is a BERT based network which takes as input, the entire sentence as sequence of tokens. The model outputs $d-1$ dimensional word-embeddings for all words within the input sentence. Thus for a sentence of length T, it would output matrix $E \in R^{T*(d-1)}$.
We use WordPiece tokenizer (Wu et al., 2016) to tokenize input sentence and extract embeddings. For each word within input sentence, we use the BERT output corresponding to the first wordpiece of it as its embedding, ignoring the rest.

3.1.1 POS tag information

We add pos-tag information in our parser by appending index of pos-tag of each word, to the encodings outputted by BERT encoder as evident in figure 2b. Thus matrix $\hat{E}$ is derived from E through equation 1 .

$$\hat{E} = E; [t_1; t_2; ....; t_T] \quad (1)$$

Here t_i is POS-tag index of ith word. $\hat{E} \in R^{T*d}$

3.2 Output Network

Its a simple feed-forward network with *softmax* activation. The network takes-in embedding matrix from the BERT encoder and outputs the probabilities of all possible relative head position tags at each word by applying equation 1.

$$Pr = softmax(\hat{E} * W + b) \quad (2)$$

Here W,b are weights and biases. $Pr \in R^{T*N}$ where N is the number of valid relative head-position tags.
For the sentence of length T, set of all possible relative head position tags S_T is given as

$$S_T = [L_1, L_2, ..., L_T, R_1, R_2, ..., R_{T-1}, \\ < root >, < EOS >]$$

Here $< root >$ and $< EOS >$ are tags to be assigned to $< s >$ and $< /s >$ tokens at the begin

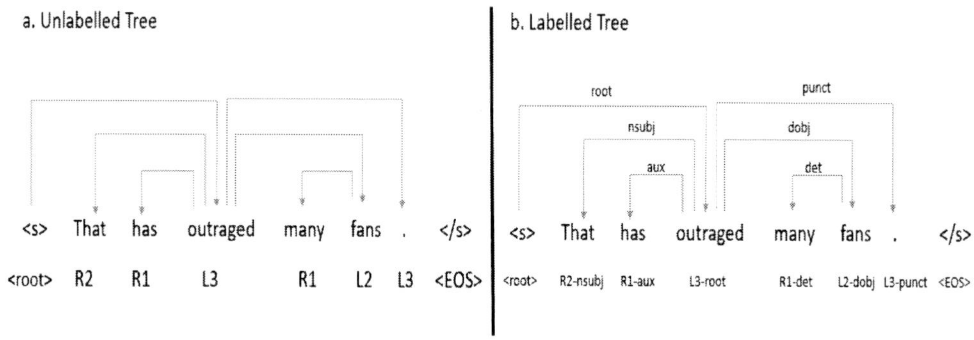

Figure 1: Examples of dependency parse tree being represented as relative head-position tag sequence

and end of the input sentence as shown in figure 1a.

For training and evaluations, we always computed probabilities of all relative head-position tags within the tag-set for a sentence of length *Max* i.e. S_{Max} as the dimensions of model parameters should be fixed. Here *Max* is the length of largest sentence from all copra used during experiments.

In this paper we experimented with only Unlabeled Dependency Parsing however same architecture can be used for Labeled Dependency Parsing as well. In such case the output tags would comprise of relative head positions as well as relationship labels (eg: L2-nsubj). Hence, the set of all possible relative head position tags S would be much larger. Figure 1b depicts a labelled parse-tree being represented as sequence of head-position tags.

3.3 Tree-Decoder

This component decodes the most probable correct label sequence from Probabilities outputted by Output Network. The correct label sequence would satisfy following constraints.

1. Sequence should start with $< root >$ and end with $< EOS >$ tags. These tags should not appear anywhere else.

2. At each index (of word being labelled) the assigned label should be within the range of sentence. For eg: Word 'That' within sentence shown in figure 1a can not have tags L_2, L_3, L_4, L_5, L_6 and word '.' in the sentence can not have any right tags as these are outside the range of sentence.

3. Label sequence should not generate any cycles within dependency tree.

4. One of the words should have the head at $< root >$ token.

We used dynamic programming with beam-search to efficiently extract the most probable label sequence which satisfies the above listed constraints, out of all possible label sequences.

3.4 Multitasking End-to-end BERT Parser

Figure 2b demonstrates the architecture of our proposed model. The model is very similar to the *Base E2E BERT Parser* described in section 3 with one extra component namely *Linguistic typology predictor* which predicts the typology features of language being parsed. Thus model is Multi-tasking model with hard-parameter sharing (Ruder, 2017).

3.4.1 Linguistic typology predictor

It is a simple deep feed forward neural network which takes in the embedding generated by BERT Encoder for token $< /s >$ and outputs probabilities of values of binary syntactic typology features for the language being parsed as 1. Such features are provided by URIEL database (Littell et al., 2017). Let $\hat{N}$ be the number of syntactic typology features provided by URIEL database. The *Linguistic typology predictor* would then predict probability matrix $Pr_{ty} \in R^{\hat{N}}$ by applying equation 2.

$$Pr_{ty} = sigmoid(e_{</s>} * U + c) \tag{3}$$

Here $e_{</s>} \in R^d$ is embedding from BERT Encoder for $< /s >$ token. $U \in R^{d*\hat{N}}$ and $c \in R^{\hat{N}}$ are weights and biases respectively.

3.5 Training

We trained both *BERT Encoder* (fine-tuning of pre-trained BERT model) and *Output Network* components of *Base E2E BERT Parser* model jointly, by

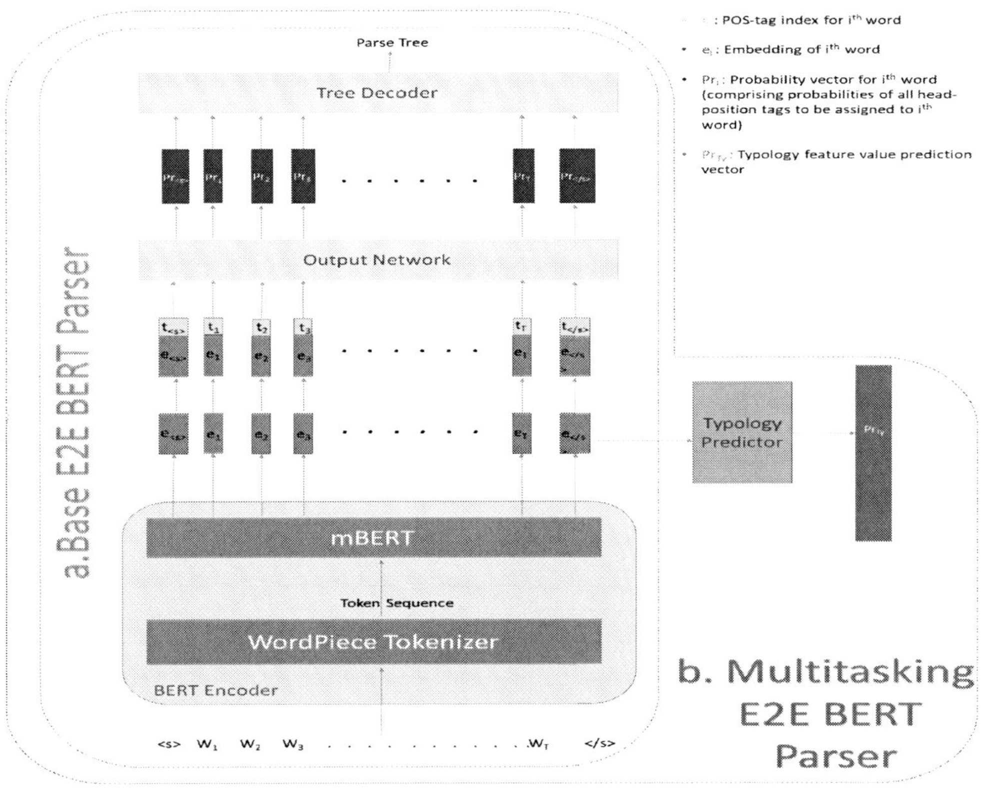

Figure 2: a. Base End-to-end BERT parser architecture. b.Multitasking End-to-end BERT parser architecture. Its an extension of Base End-to-end BERT parser architecture with one extra component namely *Typology Predictor*.

optimizing the cross-entropy loss (Gómez, 2018) between true relative head-position tags and probabilities outputted by the *Output Network*.

On the other hand, *Multitasking E2E BERT parser* is trained to perform tasks of *Prediction of relative heap-position tag sequence* and *Prediction of typology features* simultaneously through MTL, by optimizing the total-loss as the sum of cross-entropy loss over true head-position tag-sequence and the binary cross-entropy loss over true typology values.

Table 4 outlines values of hyper-parameters used during experimentation. These values are obtained by minimizing loss on *Validation* dataset for English language.

4 Experiments

4.1 Experimental setups

We evaluated the monolingual and multilingual variants of our proposed models within two distinct experimental setups namely *Monolingual* and *Cross-lingual* setups. These are described as sections 4.1.1 and 4.1.2 respectively.[1].

4.1.1 Monolingual Setup

In this setup we conducted experiments to evaluate the performance of fully monolingual variants of our proposed *Base E2E BERT Parses* and *Multitasking E2E BERT Parser*. In these settings we experimented in two languages namely *English* and *Chinese*. These monolingual variants use pretrained monolingual English and Chinese BERT models provided by [].

For all experiments within this setup, we used the *Deep Biaffine Parser* (Dozat and Manning, 2016) as baseline. Its is a neural graph-based dependency parser which uses biaffine attention classifiers to predict the arcs and labels of the required parse-tree for an input sentence.

4.1.2 Cross-lingual setups

We conducted numerous experiments to evaluate the performance of Multilingual/Cross-lingual variants of our proposed *Base BERT Parses* and

[1]Source code at https://github.com/XXXXX

Experimental Settings	Source Languages	Target Languages
Monolingual	English, Chinese	English, Chinese
Cross-lingual with single source language	English	German, Croatian, Italian, Hindi, Chinese, Estonian, Vietnamese
Cross-lingual with multiple source languages	English, Urdu, French, Arabic, Japanese, Polish, Latvian, Tamil, Greek, Coptic, Kazakh, Turkish	German, Croatian, Italian, Hindi, Chinese, Estonian, Vietnamese

Table 1: Source and Target Languages used during experiments

Languages	Corpus
English	en_ewt-ud-train
Urdu	ur_udtb-ud-train
French	fr_ftb-ud-train
Arabic	ar_padt-ud-train
Japanese	ja_gsd-ud-train
Polish	pl_pdb-ud-train
Latvian	la_ittb-ud-train
Tamil	ta_ttb-ud-train
Greek	el_gdt-ud-train
Coptic	cop_scriptorium-ud-train
Kazak	kk_ktb-ud-train
Turkish	tr_imst-ud-train

Table 2: Copra for source languages listed in table 1 used during experiments. All copra are part of Universal Dependencies dataset.

Languages	Corpus	Dev Corpus*
German	de_hdt-ud-test	de_hdt-ud-dev
Croatian	hr_set-ud-test	hr_set-ud-dev
Italian	it_isdt-ud-test	it_isdt-ud-dev
Hindi	hi_hdtb-ud-test	hi_hdtb-ud-dev
Chinese	zh_gsd-ud-test	zh_gsd-ud-dev
Estonian	et_edt-ud-test	et_edt-ud-dev
Vietnamese	vi_vtb-ud-test	vi_vtb-ud-dev

Table 3: Copra for target languages listed in table 1 used during experiments. All copra are part of Universal Dependencies dataset. * A small subset of sentences are sampled from these copra to be added to the source copra in *Few-shot* scenarios

Multitasking E2E BERT Parser models in cross-lingual settings. These Multilingual variants use pre-trained Multilingual BERT (mBERT) (Wu and Dredze, 2019) model which is trained on data from Wikipedia in 104 languages.
We evaluated the Multilingual variants of our models under following two Cross-lingual setups.

1. *Cross-lingual with single source language (CL-Single)*: In this setup, all the parsers are trained in single source language English, but tested on a diverse range of target languages

2. *Cross-lingual with multiple source languages (CL-Poly)*: In this setup, all the parsers are trained on diverse polygot corpus and tested on a diverse range of target languages. There is no overlap between source and target language sets.

Furthermore, the experiments within *Cross-lingual with single source language (CL-Single)* and *Cross-lingual with multiple source languages (CL-Poly)* setups are conducted under both *Few-shot* and *Zero-shot* learning scenarios.
Within *Zero-shot* learning scenario the training corpus does not contain any sentence in the target language on which the model is being evaluated. On the other hand, within *Few-shot* learning scenario the training corpus consists of few sentences in the target language on which the model is being evaluated, along with other source language sentences (covering over 80% the corpus). In Cross-lingual setups we used Graph-based mBERT parser by (Wu and Dredze, 2019) as baseline. It is a multilingual parser that uses same architecture as (Dozat and Manning, 2016) except the LSTM encoder which is replaced by mBERT.

4.2 Languages

Table 1 lists various source and target language used in each of the experimental settings. In *CL-Poly* setup, we trained our models on joint polygot corpus of all twelve source languages listed in Table 2. All these twelve languages belong to distinct

Hyper-parameter	Value
d	768
Dropout prob.	0.01
Bach-size	32
Number of steps per epoch	Size of training corpus / 32
Epochs	50
BERT dimensions	cased_L-12_H-768_A-12

Table 4: Hyper-parameters

Model	en	zh
Deep Biaffine Network	93.77	93.77
Base E2E BERT Parser	93.00	93.77
Multitasking E2E BERT parser	93.13	93.77

Table 5: Unlabeled Attachment Scores (UAS) achieved in *Monolingual* experimental settings.

linguistic families thus making the corpus typologicaly diverse.

For all experiments, the training corpus size is always fixed to 30,000 sentences. The joint polygot corpus to train *CL-Poly* is created by randomly sampling 2500 sentences from the training coprus for each of the 12 source languages listed in Table 1, concatenating them as one treebank and randomly shuffling the order.

Our *Cross-lingual* models are tested on seven target languages, belonging to distinct linguistic families. Three of these seven languages namely *Chinese*, *Estonian* and *Ammheric* belong to a linguistic family which is distinct from language families of all the source languages listed in Table 2. Thus performance on these languages indicate true robustness of the evaluated models to typological variations between source and target languages.

4.3 Treebank and Typology datasets

Tables 2 and 3 list the treebank copra for each of the languages listed in Table 1, used during experiments. All these copra are downloaded from Universal Dependencies[2] .

For Linguistic typology feature prediction auxiliary tasks we used Linguistic typology feature values provided by URIEL database (Littell et al., 2017). URIEL database is a collection of binary features extracted from multiple typological, phylogenetic, and geographical databases such as WALS (Haspelmath, 2009), PHOIBLE (Moran and Richard Wright, 2014), Ethnologue (M. Paul Lewis and Fennig, 2015) and Glottolog (Harald Hammarstrom and Bank, 2015). URIEL database can be accessed through Pyton PyPi library called *lang2vec*[3]. Library also allows users to access only a subset of all binary features as well.

For the experiments within this paper, we used only syntactic binary features generated from WALS database (categorised as *Syntax-WALS* within URIEL database).

4.3.1 Missing Typology

As with most typology databases, URIEL also comprises of several missing values of features for many languages. These missing values are indicated as '–' in typology vector provided by URIEL (rather than having values 0 or 1). A typology feature can also have value as '–' for a well-documented language if that feature has no dominant value observed within the respective language

These missing features pose a problem during training of *Multitasking BERT Parser* as there are no true-values for these to optimize loss with. We address this issue through masking technique (Vaswani et al., 2017). We masked the missing typology features and train only on available ones for each source language.

4.3.2 Short tree-bank copra

For each experiment under *Few-shot learning* scenario, we extracted a small set of target language sentences (on which model is being evaluated), to be added to the source training corpus before training.

We extracted this subset by randomly sampling sentences from the *dev* corpus of the respective target-language tree-bank dataset until the token-size becomes approximately equal to 3000. This is inspired by (Ammar et al., 2016) who used same yardstick to evaluate their *Multi-lingual Dependency Parser (MALOPA)*.

5 Results and Inference

Tables 5 outlines Unlabeled Attachment Score (UAS) achieved by the baseline *Deep Biaffine Parser* as well as our *Base E2E BERT Parser* and

[2]https://universaldependencies.org/

[3]https://pypi.org/project/lang2vec/

	CL-Single				CL-Poly			
	mBERT	**Base E2E**	**Multi E2E**	**Aux task***	**mBERT**	**Base E2E**	**Multi E2E**	**Aux task***
zh	43.32	42.98	41.74	0.01	66.81	66.52	65.35	0.28
hr	72.49	72.07	70.91	0.07	75.28	75.01	74.05	0.14
et	71.05	70.69	69.72	0.05	67.2	66.8	65.67	0.26
de	78.07	77.68	76.67	0.04	78.85	78.54	77.33	0.21
hi	44.83	44.42	43.18	0.11	74.68	74.4	73.32	0.22
it	86.63	86.32	85.23	0.04	77.77	77.4	76.3	0.21
vi	40.74	40.34	39.25	0.08	66.89	66.56	65.45	0.24

Table 6: Unlabeled Attachment Scores (UAS) achieved in both Cross-lingual settings under *Zero-shot* scenario. *F1 values achieved on the auxiliary task of linguistic typology prediction (excluding missing values)

	CL-Single				CL-Poly			
	mBERT	**Base E2E**	**Multi E2E**	**Aux task***	**mBERT**	**Base E2E**	**Multi E2E**	**Aux task***
zh	44.04	43.69	44.29	0.57	67.68	67.37	68.19	0.76
hr	73.38	73.0	73.46	0.6	75.93	75.58	76.28	0.68
et	71.89	71.5	71.96	0.56	67.91	67.55	68.45	0.78
de	78.8	78.47	79.08	0.57	79.74	79.45	80.25	0.71
hi	45.63	45.33	45.91	0.61	75.59	75.16	76.13	0.62
it	87.44	87.12	87.63	0.61	78.51	78.14	78.98	0.66
vi	41.44	41.16	41.62	0.61	67.68	67.41	68.37	0.75

Table 7: Unlabeled Attachment Scores (UAS) achieved in both Cross-lingual settings under *Few-shot* scenario. *F1 values achieved on the auxiliary task of linguistic typology prediction (excluding missing values)

Multitasking E2E BERT Parser in monolingual settings, on both English and Chinese.

Tables 6 and 7 outline Unlabeled Attachment Scores (UAS) obtained under the *Few-shot* and the *Zero-shot* learning scenarios respectively. Results indicate that in both *Monolingual* and *Cross-lingual settings*, our *Base E2E BERT parser* performed at par with the baseline *Deep Biaffine Parser* (Dozat and Manning, 2016) and *Graph-based mBERT parser* (Wu and Dredze, 2019) models respectively, despite being much simpler in design as its end-to-end.

5.1 Effect of Polygot Training

It is evident from results that in *CL-Single* setup under both *Few-shot* and *Zero-shot* scenarios, all the evaluated mBERT based cross-lingual models (baseline and proposed models) perform better on target languages which are genealogically or geographically closer to the source language English. Thus high performance is observed for the European languages **de**, **et**, **it** and **hr**, whereas performance drop significantly on Asian languages **zh**, **hi** and **vi** as these are both genealogically and geographically apart from English.

On the other hand, in *CL-Poly* setup, these models show almost uniform performance across all target languages. However even in *Cl-Poly* setup, the models achieved comparatively lower UAS on languages **zh**, **et** and **vi** than on other target languages, as these languages belong to a language family which is distinct from language families of all source languages listed in table 2 (section 4.2). Since **zh**, **et** and **vi** are fully unknown languages in both *CL-Single* and *CL-Poly*, the performance on these languages indicate the cross-lingual transfer ability of the evaluated mBERT based dependency parsing models.

It is evident from results outlined in Tables 6 and 7 that both baseline and our proposed End-to-end parsing models show very strong improvement in performance on languages **zh**, **et** and **vi** when trained on mixed polygot corpus as compared to when trained on single source language copra.

Thus it can be inferred that Cross-lingual transfering ability of an mBERT based multilingual dependency parser, to a distinct and unseen target language increases significantly as a result of polygot training, as polygot training allows the model to generalise better over a diverse set of languages.

5.2 Effect of Auxiliary task

Tables 2, 3 and 4 also outline the F1-scores achieved by our *Multitasking E2E BERT parser* model on the auxiliary task of predicting linguistic-typology features in Monolingual settings as well as both *Cross-lingual with single source language* and *Cross-lingual with multiple source languages* under both *Zero-shot* and *Few-shot* scenarios.

5.2.1 Effect in Monolingual setting

Results in Table 1 show that within Monolingual setup, our *Multitasking E2E BERT parser* showed marginal improvement over *Base E2E BERT parser* for both English and Chinese. In-fact the monolingual variant of our *Multitasking E2E BERT parser* outperformed the baseline *Deep Biaffine Parser* (Dozat and Manning, 2016) for both English and Chinese.

Hence it can be inferred that in Monolingual settings, the auxiliary task of predicting linguistic typology features does lead to improvement in parsing performance indeed, as it enables the model the model to emphasize on syntactic typology of language being parsed (specifically word-order features) while predicting the dependency relations within the sentence.

5.2.2 Effect in Cross-lingual settings

Under the *Zero-shot learning* scenario, our *Multitasking E2E BERT parser* under-performed *Base E2E BERT parser* in both *CL-Single* and *CL-Poly* settings for all target languages.

On the other hand under *Few-shot learning* scenario, our *Multitasking E2E BERT parser* showed improvement in performance for all target languages, in both *CL-Single* and *CL-Poly* settings.

Within *CL-Poly* setting under *Few-shot learning* scenario, our *Multitasking E2E BERT parser* shows an average improvement of 4.6% in UAS across all target languages over *Base E2E BERT parser*. This is much higher than average improvement of 1.93% shown by our*Multitasking E2E BERT parser* over *Base E2E BERT parser* within *CL-Single* settings under *Few-shot learning* scenario.

Based on these trends it can be inferred that the auxiliary task does not help the model to improve the cross-lingual transfer parsing in an unseen language (which are not the part of training corpus). However the task does enable the model to better learn to distinctively parse in each of the languages on which it is trained, even if the training corpus consists of only few sentence in the language.

Further the improvement is higher in *CL-Poly* settings than *CL-Single* settings as the model generalizes better on the auxiliary task due to polygot training.

6 Conclusion and Future Work

In this paper we evaluated the performance of our proposed *End-to-end BERT Based Dependency Parser* which can parse a sentence by directly predicting relative head-position tag for each word within input sentence. Subsequently we added the auxiliary task of Linguistic typology prediction to our *Base E2E BERT parser* to observe the change in performance under different settings.

Our results show that adding such auxiliary task leads to improvement in performance of *Base E2E BERT Parser* within Cross-lingual settings under *Few-shot* learning scenario whereas no improvement is observed within the *Zero-shot* learning scenario.

References

Željko Agić. 2017. Cross-lingual parser selection for low-resource languages. In *Proceedings of the NoDaLiDa 2017 Workshop on Universal Dependencies (UDW 2017)*, pages 1–10.

Waleed Ammar. 2016. *Towards a Universal Analyzer of Natural Languages*. Ph.D. thesis, Ph. D. thesis, Google Research.

Waleed Ammar, George Mulcaire, Miguel Ballesteros, Chris Dyer, and Noah A Smith. 2016. Many languages, one parser. *Transactions of the Association for Computational Linguistics*, 4:431–444.

Sercan O Arik, Mike Chrzanowski, Adam Coates, Gregory Diamos, Andrew Gibiansky, Yongguo Kang, Xian Li, John Miller, Andrew Ng, Jonathan Raiman, et al. 2017. Deep voice: Real-time neural text-to-speech. *arXiv preprint arXiv:1702.07825*.

Regina Barzilay and Yuan Zhang. 2015. Hierarchical low-rank tensors for multilingual transfer parsing. Association for Computational Linguistics.

Emily M Bender. 2016. Linguistic typology in natural language processing. *Linguistic Typology*, 20(3):645–660.

Balthasar Bickel, Johanna Nichols, Taras Zakharko, Alena Witzlack-Makarevich, Fernando Hildebrandt, Kristine, and John B Lowe. 2017. The autotyp typological databases. *Version 0.1. 0. Online:* `https://github.com/autotyp/autotyp-data/tree/0.1.0`.

Johannes Bjerva and Isabelle Augenstein. 2017. Tracking typological traits of uralic languages in distributed language representations. *arXiv preprint arXiv:1711.05468*.

Johannes Bjerva and Isabelle Augenstein. 2018. From phonology to syntax: Unsupervised linguistic typology at different levels with language embeddings. *arXiv preprint arXiv:1802.09375*.

Johannes Bjerva, Robert Östling, Maria Han Veiga, Jörg Tiedemann, and Isabelle Augenstein. 2019. What do language representations really represent? *Computational Linguistics*, 45(2):381–389.

R Caruana. 1998. Multitask learning. autonomous agents and multi-agent systems.

Shay B Cohen, Dipanjan Das, and Noah A Smith. 2011. Unsupervised structure prediction with non-parallel multilingual guidance. In *Proceedings of the 2011 Conference on Empirical Methods in Natural Language Processing*, pages 50–61.

Chris Collins and Richard Kayne. 2009. Syntactic structures of the world's languages. `http://sswl.railsplayground.net/..`

Bernard Comrie. 1989. *Language universals and linguistic typology: Syntax and morphology*. University of Chicago press.

Zeman Daniel, Popel Martin, Straka Milan, Hajic Jan, Nivre Joakim, Ginter Filip, Luotolahti Juhani, Pyysalo Sampo, Petrov Slav, Potthast Martin, et al. 2017. Conll 2017 shared task: Multilingual parsing from raw text to universal dependencies. In *CoNLL 2017 Shared Task: Multilingual Parsing from Raw Text to Universal Dependencies*, volume 1, pages 1–19. Association for Computational Linguistics.

Timothy Dozat and Christopher D Manning. 2016. Deep biaffine attention for neural dependency parsing. *arXiv preprint arXiv:1611.01734*.

Long Duong, Trevor Cohn, Steven Bird, and Paul Cook. 2015. Low resource dependency parsing: Cross-lingual parameter sharing in a neural network parser. In *Proceedings of the 53rd Annual Meeting of the Association for Computational Linguistics and the 7th International Joint Conference on Natural Language Processing (Volume 2: Short Papers)*, pages 845–850.

Agnieszka Falenska and Özlem Çetinoğlu. 2017. Lexicalized vs. delexicalized parsing in low-resource scenarios. In *Proceedings of the 15th International Conference on Parsing Technologies*, pages 18–24.

Ross Girshick. 2015. Fast r-cnn. In *Proceedings of the IEEE international conference on computer vision*, pages 1440–1448.

Raúl Gómez. 2018. Understanding categorical cross-entropy loss, binary cross-entropy loss, softmax loss, logistic loss, focal loss and all those confusing names. *URL: https://gombru. github. io/2018/05/23/cross_entropy_loss/(visited on 29/03/2019)*.

Joseph Greenberg. 1963. Some universals of grammar with particular reference to the order of meaningful elements. *In J. Greenberg, ed., Universals of Language. 73-113. Cambridge, MA*.

Jiang Guo, Wanxiang Che, David Yarowsky, Haifeng Wang, and Ting Liu. 2016. A representation learning framework for multi-source transfer parsing. In *Thirtieth AAAI Conference on Artificial Intelligence*.

Martin Haspelmath Harald Hammarstrom, Robert Forkel and Sebastian Bank. 2015. Glottolog 2.6.

Martin Haspelmath Hartmann, Iren and editors Bradley Taylor. 2013. Valency Patterns Leipzig.

Martin Haspelmath. 2009. *The typological database of the World Atlas of Language Structures*. Berlin: Walter de Gruyter.

Zuchao Li, Jiaxun Cai, Shexia He, and Hai Zhao. 2018. Seq2seq dependency parsing. In *Proceedings of the 27th International Conference on Computational Linguistics*, pages 3203–3214.

Patrick Littell, David R Mortensen, Ke Lin, Katherine Kairis, Carlisle Turner, and Lori Levin. 2017. Uriel and lang2vec: Representing languages as typological, geographical, and phylogenetic vectors. In *Proceedings of the 15th Conference of the European Chapter of the Association for Computational Linguistics: Volume 2, Short Papers*, pages 8–14.

Xiaodong Liu, Jianfeng Gao, Xiaodong He, Li Deng, Kevin Duh, and Ye-Yi Wang. 2015. Representation learning using multi-task deep neural networks for semantic classification and information retrieval.

Gary F. Simons M. Paul Lewis and Charles D. Fennig. 2015. Ethnologue: Languages of the World, Eighteenth edition.

Ian Maddieson, Sébastien Flavier, Egidio Marsico, Christophe Coupé, and François Pellegrino. 2013. Lapsyd: lyon-albuquerque phonological systems database. In *INTERSPEECH*, pages 3022–3026.

Chaitanya Malaviya, Graham Neubig, and Patrick Littell. 2017. Learning language representations for typology prediction. *arXiv preprint arXiv:1707.09569*.

Ryan McDonald, Slav Petrov, and Keith B Hall. 2011. Multi-source transfer of delexicalized dependency parsers.

Philippe Maurer Martin Haspelmath Michaelis, Susanne Maria and editors Magnus Huber. 2013. Atlas of Pidgin and Creole Language Structures Online.

Daniel McCloy Moran, Steven and editors Richard Wright. 2014. PHOBIA Online.

Phoebe Mulcaire, Jungo Kasai, and Noah A Smith. 2019. Low-resource parsing with crosslingual contextualized representations. *arXiv preprint arXiv:1909.08744*.

Tahira Naseem, Regina Barzilay, and Amir Globerson. 2012. Selective sharing for multilingual dependency parsing. The Association for Computational Linguistics.

Johanna Nichols. 1992. *Linguistic diversity in space and time*. University of Chicago Press.

Helen O'Horan, Yevgeni Berzak, Ivan Vulić, Roi Reichart, and Anna Korhonen. 2016. Survey on the use of typological information in natural language processing. *arXiv preprint arXiv:1610.03349*.

Robert Östling and Jörg Tiedemann. 2016. Continuous multilinguality with language vectors. *arXiv preprint arXiv:1612.07486*.

Edoardo Maria Ponti, Roi Reichart, Anna Korhonen, and Ivan Vulić. 2018. Isomorphic transfer of syntactic structures in cross-lingual nlp. In *Proceedings of the 56th Annual Meeting of the Association for Computational Linguistics (Volume 1: Long Papers)*, pages 1531–1542.

Mohammad Sadegh Rasooli and Michael Collins. 2017. Cross-lingual syntactic transfer with limited resources. *Transactions of the Association for Computational Linguistics*, 5:279–293.

Sebastian Ruder. 2017. An overview of multi-task learning in deep neural networks. *arXiv preprint arXiv:1706.05098*.

Ehsan Shareghi, Yingzhen Li, Yi Zhu, Roi Reichart, and Anna Korhonen. 2019. Bayesian learning for neural dependency parsing. In *Proceedings of the 2019 Conference of the North American Chapter of the Association for Computational Linguistics: Human Language Technologies, Volume 1 (Long and Short Papers)*, pages 3509–3519.

Oscar Täckström, Ryan McDonald, and Joakim Nivre. 2013. Target language adaptation of discriminative transfer parsers.

Clara Vania, Yova Kementchedjhieva, Anders Søgaard, and Adam Lopez. 2019. A systematic comparison of methods for low-resource dependency parsing on genuinely low-resource languages. *arXiv preprint arXiv:1909.02857*.

Ashish Vaswani, Noam Shazeer, Niki Parmar, Jakob Uszkoreit, Llion Jones, Aidan N Gomez, Łukasz Kaiser, and Illia Polosukhin. 2017. Attention is all you need. In *Advances in neural information processing systems*, pages 5998–6008.

David Vilares, Carlos Gómez-Rodríguez, and Miguel A Alonso. 2015. One model, two languages: training bilingual parsers with harmonized treebanks. *arXiv preprint arXiv:1507.08449*.

Dingquan Wang and Jason Eisner. 2016a. The galactic dependencies treebanks: Getting more data by synthesizing new languages. *Transactions of the Association for Computational Linguistics*, 4:491–505.

Dingquan Wang and Jason Eisner. 2016b. The galactic dependencies treebanks: Getting more data by synthesizing new languages. *Transactions of the Association for Computational Linguistics*, 4:491–505.

Dingquan Wang and Jason Eisner. 2017. Fine-grained prediction of syntactic typology: Discovering latent structure with supervised learning. *Transactions of the Association for Computational Linguistics*, 5:147–161.

Shijie Wu and Mark Dredze. 2019. Beto, bentz, becas: The surprising cross-lingual effectiveness of bert. *arXiv preprint arXiv:1904.09077*.

Yonghui Wu, Mike Schuster, Zhifeng Chen, Quoc V Le, Mohammad Norouzi, Wolfgang Macherey, Maxim Krikun, Yuan Cao, Qin Gao, Klaus Macherey, et al. 2016. Google's neural machine translation system: Bridging the gap between human and machine translation. *arXiv preprint arXiv:1609.08144*.

Daniel Zeman, Jan Hajic, Martin Popel, Martin Potthast, Milan Straka, Filip Ginter, Joakim Nivre, and Slav Petrov. 2018. Conll 2018 shared task: Multilingual parsing from raw text to universal dependencies. In *Proceedings of the CoNLL 2018 Shared Task: Multilingual parsing from raw text to universal dependencies*, pages 1–21.

Zhanpeng Zhang, Ping Luo, Chen Change Loy, and Xiaoou Tang. 2014. Facial landmark detection by deep multi-task learning. In *European conference on computer vision*, pages 94–108. Springer.

Identifying the Correlation Between Language Distance and Cross-Lingual Transfer in a Multilingual Representation Space

Fred Philippy[1,2*] and **Siwen Guo**[1] and **Shohreh Haddadan**[1]

[1]Zortify Labs, Zortify S.A.
19, rue du Laboratoire L-1911 Luxembourg
[2]SnT, University of Luxembourg
29, Avenue J.F Kennedy L-1359 Luxembourg
{fred, siwen, shohreh}@zortify.com

Abstract

Prior research has investigated the impact of various linguistic features on cross-lingual transfer performance. In this study, we investigate the manner in which this effect can be mapped onto the representation space. While past studies have focused on the impact on cross-lingual alignment in multilingual language models during fine-tuning, this study examines the absolute evolution of the respective language representation spaces produced by MLLMs. We place a specific emphasis on the role of linguistic characteristics and investigate their inter-correlation with the impact on representation spaces and cross-lingual transfer performance. Additionally, this paper provides preliminary evidence of how these findings can be leveraged to enhance transfer to linguistically distant languages.

1 Introduction

It has been shown that language models implicitly encode linguistic knowledge (Jawahar et al., 2019; Otmakhova et al., 2022). In the case of multilingual language models (MLLMs), previous research has also extensively investigated the influence of these linguistic features on cross-lingual transfer performance (Lauscher et al., 2020; Dolicki and Spanakis, 2021; de Vries et al., 2022). However, limited attention has been paid to the impact of these factors on the language representation spaces of MLLMs.

Despite the fact that state-of-the-art MLLMs such as mBERT (Devlin et al., 2019) and XLM-R (Conneau et al., 2020), use a shared vocabulary and are intended to project text from any language into a language-agnostic embedding space, empirical evidence has demonstrated that these models encode language-specific information across all layers (Libovický et al., 2020; Gonen et al., 2020). This leads to the possibility of identifying distinct monolingual representation spaces within the shared multilingual representation space (Chang et al., 2022).

Past research has focused on the cross-linguality of MLLMs during fine-tuning, specifically looking at the alignment of representation spaces of different language pairs (Singh et al., 2019; Muller et al., 2021). Our focus, instead, is directed towards the absolute impact on the representation space of each language individually, rather than the relative impact on the representation space of a language compared to another one. Isolating the impact for each language enables a more in-depth study of the inner modifications that occur within MLLMs during fine-tuning. The main objective of our study is to examine the role of linguistic features in this context, as previous research has shown their impact on cross-lingual transfer performance. More specifically, we examine the relationship between the impact on the representation space of a target language after fine-tuning on a source language and five different language distance metrics. We have observed such relationships across all layers with a trend of stronger correlations in the deeper layers of the MLLM and significant differences between language distance metrics.

Additionally, we observe an inter-correlation among language distance, impact on the representation space and transfer performance. Based on this observation, we propose a hypothesis that may assist in enhancing cross-lingual transfer to linguistically distant languages and provide preliminary evidence to suggest that further investigation of our hypothesis is merited.

2 Related Work

In monolingual settings, Jawahar et al. (2019) found that, after pre-training, BERT encodes different linguistic features in different layers. Merchant et al. (2020) showed that language models do not forget these linguistic structures during fine-tuning on a downstream task. Conversely, Tanti et al.

[*] Research was conducted at Zortify.

Proceedings of the 5th Workshop on Research in Computational Linguistic Typology and Multilingual NLP (SIGTYP 2023), pages 22–29
May 6, 2023 ©2023 Association for Computational Linguistics

(2021) have shown that during fine-tuning in multilingual settings, mBERT forgets some language-specific information, resulting in a more cross-lingual model.

At the representation space level, Singh et al. (2019) and Muller et al. (2021) studied the impact of fine-tuning on mBERT's cross-linguality layer-wise. However, their research was limited to the evaluation of the impact on cross-lingual alignment comparing the representation space of one language to another, rather than assessing the evolution of a language's representation space in isolation.

3 Methodology

3.1 Experimental Setup

In this paper, we focus on the effect of fine-tuning on the representation space of the 12-layer multilingual BERT model (`bert-base-multilingual-cased`). We restrict our focus on the Natural Language Inference (NLI) task and fine-tune on all 15 languages of the XNLI dataset (Conneau et al., 2018) individually. We use the test set to evaluate the zero-shot cross-lingual transfer performance, measured as accuracy, and to generate embeddings that define the representation space of each language. More details on the training process and its reproducibility are provided in Appendix A.

3.2 Measuring the Impact on the Representation Space

We focus on measuring the impact on a language's representation space in a pre-trained MLLM during cross-lingual transfer. We accomplish this by measuring the similarity of hidden representations of samples from different target languages before and after fine-tuning in various source languages. For this purpose, we use the Centered Kernel Alignment (CKA) method (Kornblith et al., 2019)[1]. When using a linear kernel, the CKA score of two representation matrices $X \in \mathbb{R}^{N\times m}$ and $Y \in \mathbb{R}^{N\times m}$, where N is the number of data points and m is the representation dimension, is given by

$$CKA(X,Y) = 1 - \frac{\|XY^{\intercal}\|_F^2}{\|XX^{\intercal}\|_F \|YY^{\intercal}\|_F}$$

where $\|\cdot\|_F$ is the Frobenius norm.

[1]CKA is invariant to orthogonal transformations and thus allows to reliably compare isotropic but language-specific subspaces (Chang et al., 2022).

Notation We define $H^i_{S\to T} \in \mathbb{R}^{N\times m}$ as the hidden representation[2] of N samples from a target language T at the i-th attention layer of a model fine-tuned in the source language S, where m is the hidden layer output dimension. Similarly, we denote the hidden representation of N samples from language L at the i-th attention layer of a pre-trained base model (i.e. before fine-tuning) as $H^i_L \in \mathbb{R}^{N\times m}$. More specifically, the representation space of each language will be represented by the stacked hidden states of its samples.

We define the impact on the representation space of a target language T at the i-th attention layer when fine-tuning in a source language S as follows:

$$\Phi^{(i)}(S,T) = 1 - CKA\left(H^i_T, H^i_{S\to T}\right)$$

3.3 Measuring Language Distance

In order to quantify the distance between languages we use three types of typological distances, namely the syntactic (SYN), geographic (GEO) and inventory (INV) distance, as well as the genetic (GEN) and phonological (PHON) distance between source and target language. These distances are pre-computed and are extracted from the URIEL Typological Database (Littell et al., 2017) using `lang2vec`[3]. For our study, such language distances based on aggregated linguistic features offer a more comprehensive representation of the relevant language distance characteristics. More information on these five metrics is provided in Appendix B.

4 Correlation Analysis

Relationship Between the Impact on the Representation Space and Language Distance. Given the layer-wise differences of mBERT's cross-linguality (Libovický et al., 2020; Gonen et al., 2020), we measure the correlation between the impact on the representation space and the language distances across all layers. Figure 1 shows almost no significant correlation between representation space impact and **inventory** or **phonological** distance. **Geographic** and **syntactic** distance mostly show significant correlation values at the last layers. Only the **genetic** distance correlates significantly across all layers with the impact on the representation space.

[2]We refer here to the hidden representation of the `[CLS]` token which is commonly used in BERT for classification tasks.

[3]`https://github.com/antonisa/lang2vec`

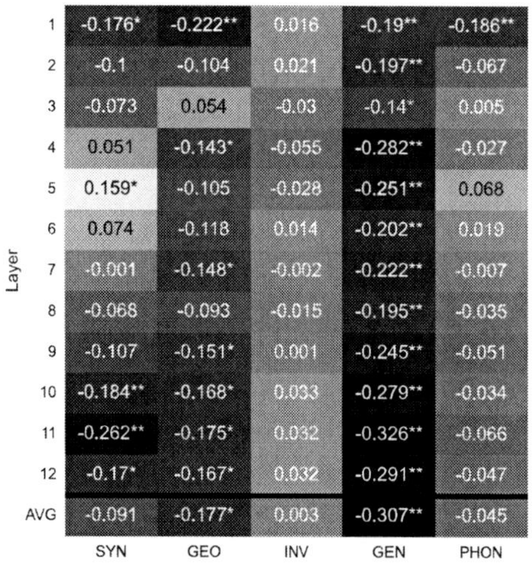

Figure 1: **Pearson correlation coefficient** between the **impact on a target language's representation space when fine-tuning in a source language** and different types of **linguistic distances between the source and target language** for each layer. Same source-target language pair data points were excluded in order to prevent an overestimation of effects. ($^{*}p < 0.05$, and $^{**}p < 0.01$, two-tailed).

Relationship Between Language Distance and Cross-Lingual Transfer Performance. Table 1 shows that all distance metrics correlate with cross-lingual transfer performance, which is consistent with the findings of Lauscher et al. (2020). Furthermore, we note that the correlation strengths align with the previously established relationship between language distance and representation space impact, with higher correlation values observed for syntactic, genetic, and geographic distance than for inventory and phonological distance. The exact zero-shot transfer results are provided in Figure 3 in Appendix C.

	Pearson	Spearman
SYN	-0.3193^{**}	-0.4683^{**}
GEO	-0.3178^{**}	-0.3198^{**}
INV	-0.1706^{*}	-0.1329^{*}
GEN	-0.3364^{**}	-0.3935^{**}
PHON	-0.2075^{**}	-0.2659^{**}

Table 1: Pearson and Spearman **correlation coefficients** quantifying the relationship between **zero-shot cross-lingual transfer performance** and different **language distance metrics**. ($^{*}p < 0.05$, and $^{**}p < 0.01$, two-tailed).

Relationship Between the Impact on the Representation Space and Cross-Lingual Transfer Performance. In general, cross-lingual transfer performance clearly correlates with impact on the representation space of the target language, but this correlation tends to be stronger in the deeper layers of the model (Table 2).

Layer	Pearson	Spearman
1	0.2779^{*}	0.3233^{*}
2	0.2456^{*}	0.2639^{*}
3	0.5277^{*}	0.5926^{*}
4	0.3585^{*}	0.3411^{*}
5	-0.009	0.0669
6	0.1033	0.1969
7	0.2945^{*}	0.3500^{*}
8	0.3004^{*}	0.3517^{*}
9	0.4209^{*}	0.4583^{*}
10	0.6088^{*}	0.6532^{*}
11	0.7110^{*}	0.7525^{*}
12	0.5731^{*}	0.5901^{*}
All	0.4343^{*}	0.5026^{*}

Table 2: **Pearson correlation** coefficients between **cross-lingual transfer performance** and the **impact on the representation space of the target language**. ($^{*}p < 0.01$, two-tailed).

5 Does Selective Layer Freezing Allow to Improve Transfer to Linguistically Distant Languages?

In the previous section we observed an inter-correlation between cross-lingual transfer performance, the linguistic distance between the target and source language, and the impact on the representation space. Given this observation, we investigate the possibility to use this information to improve transfer to linguistically distant languages. More specifically, we hypothesize that it may be possible to regulate cross-lingual transfer performance by selectively interfering with the previously observed correlations at specific layers. A straightforward strategy would be to selectively freeze layers, during the fine-tuning process, where a significant negative correlation between the impact on their representation space and the distance between source and target languages has been observed. By freezing a layer, we manually set the correlation between the impact on the representation space and language distance to zero, which may simultaneously reduce the significance of the

Exp.	Frozen Layers	SYN	GEO	INV	GEN	PHON	CLTP
		-0.7354	**-0.5109**	**-0.4907**	**-0.6116**	**-0.5776**	**66.70**
A	{2}	-0.7310	-0.5109	-0.4791	-0.6009	-0.5791	66.53
B	{5}	-0.7438	-0.5053	-0.4897	-0.6148	-0.5896	66.77
C	{1,2,6}	-0.7325	-0.5000	-0,4846	-0.6065	-0.5666	66.75

Table 3: Pearson **correlation coefficients** quantifying the relationship between **cross-lingual transfer performance** and different **language distance metrics** after freezing different layers during fine-tuning. The first row contains baseline values for full-model fine-tuning. The last column provides the average cross-lingual transfer performance (CLTP), measured as accuracy, across all target languages. English has been the only source language.

correlation between language distance and transfer performance.

Wu and Dredze (2019) already showed that freezing early layers of mBERT during fine-tuning may lead to increased cross-lingual transfer performance. With the same goal in mind, Xu et al. (2021) employ meta-learning to select layer-wise learning rates during fine-tuning. In what follows, we will, however, not focus on pure overall transfer performance. Our approach is to specifically target transfer performance improvements for target languages that are linguistically distant from the source language, rather than trying to achieve equal transfer performance increases for all target languages.

5.1 Experimental Setup

For our pilot experiments, we focus on English as the source language. Additionally, we choose to carry out our pilot experiments on layers 1, 2, 5, and 6, as the representation space impact at these layers exhibits low correlation values with transfer performance (Table 2) and high correlations with different language distances (Figure 2 in Appendix C). This decision is made to mitigate the potential impact on the overall transfer performance, which could obscure the primary effect of interest, and to simultaneously target layers which might be responsible for the transfer gap to distant languages. We conduct 3 different experiments aiming to regulate correlations between specific language distances and transfer performance. In an attempt to diversify our experiments, we aim to decrease the transfer performance gap for both a single language distance metric (Experiment **A**) and multiple distance metrics (Exp. **C**). Furthermore, in another experiment we aim at deliberately increasing the transfer gap (Exp. **B**).

5.2 Results

Table 3 provides results of all 3 experiments.

Experiment A. The 2nd layer shows a strong negative correlation (-0.66) between representation space impact and inventory distance to English. Freezing the 2nd layer during fine-tuning has led to a less significant correlation between inventory distance and transfer performance (+0.0116).

Experiment B. The 5th layer shows a strong positive correlation (0.499) between representation space impact and phonological distance to English. Freezing the 5th layer during fine-tuning has led to a more significant correlation between phonological distance and transfer performance (-0.012).

Experiment C. The 1st layer, 2nd layer and 6th layer show a strong negative correlation between the impact on the representation space and the syntactic (-0.618), inventory (-0.66) and phonological (-0.543) distance to English, respectively. Freezing the 1st, 2nd and 6th layer during fine-tuning has led to a less significant correlation of transfer performance with syntactic (+0.0029) and phonological (+0.011) distance.

6 Conclusion

In previous research, the effect of fine-tuning on a language representation space was usually studied in relative terms, for instance by comparing the cross-lingual alignment between two monolingual representation spaces before and after fine-tuning. Our research, however, focused on the absolute impact on the language-specific representation spaces within the multilingual space and explored the relationship between this impact and language distance. Our findings suggest that there is an intercorrelation between language distance, impact on the representation space, and transfer performance which varies across layers. Based on this finding, we hypothesize that selectively freezing layers during fine-tuning, at which specific inter-correlations are observed, may help to reduce the transfer performance gap to distant languages. Although our hypothesis is only supported by three pilot experiments, we anticipate that it may stimulate further research to include an assessment of our hypothesis.

Limitations

It is important to note that the evidence presented in this paper is not meant to be exhaustive, but rather to serve as a starting point for future research. Our findings are based on a set of 15 languages and a single downstream task and may not generalize to other languages or settings. Additionally, the proposed hypothesis has been tested through a limited number of experiments, and more extensive studies are required to determine its practicality and effectiveness.

Furthermore, in our study, we limited ourselves to using traditional correlation coefficients, which are limited in terms of the relationships they can capture, and it is possible that there are additional correlations that could further strengthen our results and conclusions.

Ethics Statement

This study was designed to minimize its environmental impact by reducing the amount of required computational resources to run our experiments. We are aware of the high energy consumption and carbon footprint associated with large-scale machine learning experiments and took steps to minimize these impacts.

Additionally, in this study, our objective was to address the performance gap in languages that are underrepresented in comparison to high-resource languages, rather than solely striving for performance enhancement.

References

Tyler Chang, Zhuowen Tu, and Benjamin Bergen. 2022. The Geometry of Multilingual Language Model Representations. In *Proceedings of the 2022 Conference on Empirical Methods in Natural Language Processing*, pages 119–136, Abu Dhabi, United Arab Emirates. Association for Computational Linguistics.

Chris Collins and Richard Kayne. 2011. *Syntactic Structures of the World's Languages*. New York University, New York.

Alexis Conneau, Kartikay Khandelwal, Naman Goyal, Vishrav Chaudhary, Guillaume Wenzek, Francisco Guzmán, Edouard Grave, Myle Ott, Luke Zettlemoyer, and Veselin Stoyanov. 2020. Unsupervised Cross-lingual Representation Learning at Scale. In *Proceedings of the 58th Annual Meeting of the Association for Computational Linguistics*, pages 8440–8451, Online. Association for Computational Linguistics.

Alexis Conneau, Ruty Rinott, Guillaume Lample, Adina Williams, Samuel Bowman, Holger Schwenk, and Veselin Stoyanov. 2018. XNLI: Evaluating Cross-lingual Sentence Representations. In *Proceedings of the 2018 Conference on Empirical Methods in Natural Language Processing*, pages 2475–2485, Brussels, Belgium. Association for Computational Linguistics.

Wietse de Vries, Martijn Wieling, and Malvina Nissim. 2022. Make the Best of Cross-lingual Transfer: Evidence from POS Tagging with over 100 Languages. In *Proceedings of the 60th Annual Meeting of the Association for Computational Linguistics (Volume 1: Long Papers)*, pages 7676–7685, Dublin, Ireland. Association for Computational Linguistics.

Jacob Devlin, Ming-Wei Chang, Kenton Lee, and Kristina Toutanova. 2019. BERT: Pre-training of Deep Bidirectional Transformers for Language Understanding. In *Proceedings of the 2019 Conference of the North American Chapter of the Association for Computational Linguistics: Human Language Technologies, Volume 1 (Long and Short Papers)*, pages 4171–4186, Minneapolis, Minnesota. Association for Computational Linguistics.

Błażej Dolicki and Gerasimos Spanakis. 2021. Analysing The Impact Of Linguistic Features On Cross-Lingual Transfer. ArXiv:2105.05975 [cs].

Matthew S. Dryer and Martin Haspelmath. 2013. *WALS Online*. Max Planck Institute for Evolutionary Anthropology, Leipzig.

Hila Gonen, Shauli Ravfogel, Yanai Elazar, and Yoav Goldberg. 2020. It's not Greek to mBERT: Inducing Word-Level Translations from Multilingual BERT. In *Proceedings of the Third BlackboxNLP Workshop on Analyzing and Interpreting Neural Networks for NLP*, pages 45–56, Online. Association for Computational Linguistics.

Harald Hammarström, Robert Forkel, Martin Haspelmath, and Sebastian Bank. 2015. *Glottolog 2.6*. Max Planck Institute for the Science of Human History, Jena.

Ganesh Jawahar, Benoît Sagot, and Djamé Seddah. 2019. What Does BERT Learn about the Structure of Language? In *Proceedings of the 57th Annual Meeting of the Association for Computational Linguistics*, pages 3651–3657, Florence, Italy. Association for Computational Linguistics.

Simon Kornblith, Mohammad Norouzi, Honglak Lee, and Geoffrey Hinton. 2019. Similarity of Neural Network Representations Revisited. In *Proceedings of the 36th International Conference on Machine Learning*, pages 3519–3529. PMLR.

Anne Lauscher, Vinit Ravishankar, Ivan Vulić, and Goran Glavaš. 2020. From Zero to Hero: On the Limitations of Zero-Shot Language Transfer with Multilingual Transformers. In *Proceedings of the 2020 Conference on Empirical Methods in Natural Language Processing (EMNLP)*, pages 4483–4499, Online. Association for Computational Linguistics.

M. Paul Lewis, Gary F. Simons, and Charles D. Fennig. 2015. *Ethnologue: Languages of the World, Eighteenth edition*. SIL International, Dallas, Texas.

Jindřich Libovický, Rudolf Rosa, and Alexander Fraser. 2020. On the Language Neutrality of Pre-trained Multilingual Representations. In *Findings of the Association for Computational Linguistics: EMNLP 2020*, pages 1663–1674, Online. Association for Computational Linguistics.

Patrick Littell, David R. Mortensen, Ke Lin, Katherine Kairis, Carlisle Turner, and Lori Levin. 2017. URIEL and lang2vec: Representing languages as typological, geographical, and phylogenetic vectors. In *Proceedings of the 15th Conference of the European Chapter of the Association for Computational Linguistics: Volume 2, Short Papers*, pages 8–14, Valencia, Spain. Association for Computational Linguistics.

Ilya Loshchilov and Frank Hutter. 2019. Decoupled Weight Decay Regularization.

Amil Merchant, Elahe Rahimtoroghi, Ellie Pavlick, and Ian Tenney. 2020. What Happens To BERT Embeddings During Fine-tuning? In *Proceedings of the Third BlackboxNLP Workshop on Analyzing and Interpreting Neural Networks for NLP*, pages 33–44, Online. Association for Computational Linguistics.

Steven Moran, Daniel McCloy, and (eds.). 2019. *PHOIBLE 2.0*. Max Planck Institute for the Science of Human History, Jena.

Benjamin Muller, Yanai Elazar, Benoît Sagot, and Djamé Seddah. 2021. First Align, then Predict: Understanding the Cross-Lingual Ability of Multilingual BERT. In *Proceedings of the 16th Conference of the European Chapter of the Association for Computational Linguistics: Main Volume*, pages 2214–2231, Online. Association for Computational Linguistics.

Yulia Otmakhova, Karin Verspoor, and Jey Han Lau. 2022. Cross-linguistic Comparison of Linguistic Feature Encoding in BERT Models for Typologically Different Languages. In *Proceedings of the 4th Workshop on Research in Computational Linguistic Typology and Multilingual NLP*, pages 27–35, Seattle, Washington. Association for Computational Linguistics.

Adam Paszke, Sam Gross, Francisco Massa, Adam Lerer, James Bradbury, Gregory Chanan, Trevor Killeen, Zeming Lin, Natalia Gimelshein, Luca Antiga, Alban Desmaison, Andreas Kopf, Edward Yang, Zachary DeVito, Martin Raison, Alykhan Tejani, Sasank Chilamkurthy, Benoit Steiner, Lu Fang, Junjie Bai, and Soumith Chintala. 2019. PyTorch: An Imperative Style, High-Performance Deep Learning Library. In *Advances in Neural Information Processing Systems*, volume 32. Curran Associates, Inc.

Jasdeep Singh, Bryan McCann, Richard Socher, and Caiming Xiong. 2019. BERT is Not an Interlingua and the Bias of Tokenization. In *Proceedings of the 2nd Workshop on Deep Learning Approaches for Low-Resource NLP (DeepLo 2019)*, pages 47–55, Hong Kong, China. Association for Computational Linguistics.

Marc Tanti, Lonneke van der Plas, Claudia Borg, and Albert Gatt. 2021. On the Language-specificity of Multilingual BERT and the Impact of Fine-tuning. In *Proceedings of the Fourth BlackboxNLP Workshop on Analyzing and Interpreting Neural Networks for NLP*, pages 214–227, Punta Cana, Dominican Republic. Association for Computational Linguistics.

Adina Williams, Nikita Nangia, and Samuel Bowman. 2018. A Broad-Coverage Challenge Corpus for Sentence Understanding through Inference. In *Proceedings of the 2018 Conference of the North American Chapter of the Association for Computational Linguistics: Human Language Technologies, Volume 1 (Long Papers)*, pages 1112–1122, New Orleans, Louisiana. Association for Computational Linguistics.

Thomas Wolf, Lysandre Debut, Victor Sanh, Julien Chaumond, Clement Delangue, Anthony Moi, Pierric Cistac, Tim Rault, Remi Louf, Morgan Funtowicz, Joe Davison, Sam Shleifer, Patrick von Platen, Clara Ma, Yacine Jernite, Julien Plu, Canwen Xu, Teven Le Scao, Sylvain Gugger, Mariama Drame, Quentin Lhoest, and Alexander Rush. 2020. Transformers: State-of-the-Art Natural Language Processing. In *Proceedings of the 2020 Conference on Empirical Methods in Natural Language Processing: System Demonstrations*, pages 38–45, Online. Association for Computational Linguistics.

Shijie Wu and Mark Dredze. 2019. Beto, Bentz, Becas: The Surprising Cross-Lingual Effectiveness of BERT. In *Proceedings of the 2019 Conference on Empirical Methods in Natural Language Processing and the 9th International Joint Conference on Natural Language Processing (EMNLP-IJCNLP)*, pages 833–844, Hong Kong, China. Association for Computational Linguistics.

Weijia Xu, Batool Haider, Jason Krone, and Saab Mansour. 2021. Soft Layer Selection with Meta-Learning for Zero-Shot Cross-Lingual Transfer. In *Proceedings of the 1st Workshop on Meta Learning and Its Applications to Natural Language Processing*, pages 11–18, Online. Association for Computational Linguistics.

A Technical Details

A.1 Data

We perform our experiments on the XNLI (Conneau et al., 2018) dataset[4]. The dataset contains 392.702 train, 2.490 validation and 5.010 test samples, derived from the English-only MultiNLI (Williams et al., 2018), which have been translated to Arabic (ar), Bulgarian (bg), German (de), Greek (el), Spanish (es), French (fr), Hindi (hi), Russian (ru), Swahili (sw), Thai (th), Turkish (tr), Urdu (ur), Vietnamese (vi) and Chinese (zh). The objective of the dataset is to evaluate a model's capability of classifying the relationship between two sentences, namely a premise and a hypothesis, as entailment, contradiction, or neutral.

The dataset has been released under a *Creative Commons Attribution Non Commercial 4.0 International*[5] license (CC BY-NC 4.0).

A.2 Model

We use the base cased multilingual BERT (Devlin et al., 2019) model, which has 12 attention heads and 12 transformer blocks with a hidden size of 768. The dropout probability is 0.1. The model has 110M parameters and covers 104 languages. Its vocabulary size is about 120k.

A.3 Training

We fine-tune the models using the HuggingFace Transformers (Wolf et al., 2020) and PyTorch (Paszke et al., 2019) frameworks. We use AdamW (Loshchilov and Hutter, 2019) as an optimizer, with $\beta_1 = 0.9$, $\beta_2 = 0.999$, $\epsilon = 1e^{-8}$. We train for 3 epochs with a batch size of 32 and an initial learning rate of $2e^{-5}$ with linear decay. Full model fine-tuning on a single language took about 2.5 hours on a single NVIDIA® V100 GPU. Total GPU hours for all 18 fine-tuned models (15 and 3 in Sections 4 and 5 respectively was about 45 hours.

In order to minimize computational costs and reduce our environmental impact, we chose not to conduct a full hyper-parameter search and instead used the fixed values reported in Section 3.1.

For reproducibility, our code is provided here: `https://anonymous.4open.science/r/sigtyp2023_workshop_paper-223F`.

[4] `https://github.com/facebookresearch/XNLI`

[5] `https://creativecommons.org/licenses/by-nc/4.0/`

B Additional Information on Language Distance Metrics

We used the following lang2vec distances:

1. **Syntactic Distance** is the cosine distance between the syntax feature vectors of languages, sourced from the World Atlas of Language Structures.[6] (WALS) (Dryer and Haspelmath, 2013), Syntactic Structures of World Languages[7] (SSWL) (Collins and Kayne, 2011) and Ethnologue[8] (Lewis et al., 2015).

2. **Geographic Distance** refers to the shortest distance between two languages on the surface of the earth's sphere, also known as the orthodromic distance.

3. **Inventory Distance** is the cosine distance between the inventory feature vectors of languages, sourced from the PHOIBLE[9] database (Moran et al., 2019).

4. **Genetic Distance** is based on the Glottolog[10] (Hammarström et al., 2015) tree of language families and is obtained by computing the distance between two languages in the tree.

5. **Phonological Distance** is the cosine distance between the phonological feature vectors of languages, sourced from WALS and Ethnologue.

The values range from 0 to 1, where 0 indicates the minimum distance and 1 indicates the maximum distance.

C Additional Figures

Figure 2 provides **Pearson correlation coefficients** between the **impact on the target language representation space** when fine-tuning in **English** and different types of **linguistic distances between English and the target language** for each layer. English-English data points were excluded in order to prevent an overestimation of effects.

Figure 3 contains the cross-lingual zero-shot transfer results. The numbers illustrated in the figure represent accuracies.

[6] `https://wals.info`

[7] `http://sswl.railsplayground.net/`

[8] `https://www.ethnologue.com/`

[9] `https://phoible.org/`

[10] `https://glottolog.org`

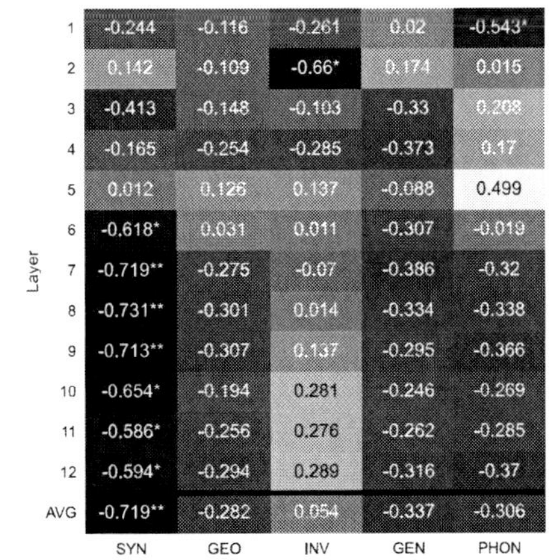

Figure 2: Pearson correlation coefficients between the impact on the representation space and different types of linguistic distances (with English as the only source language). ($^{*}p < 0.05$, and $^{**}p < 0.01$, two-tailed).

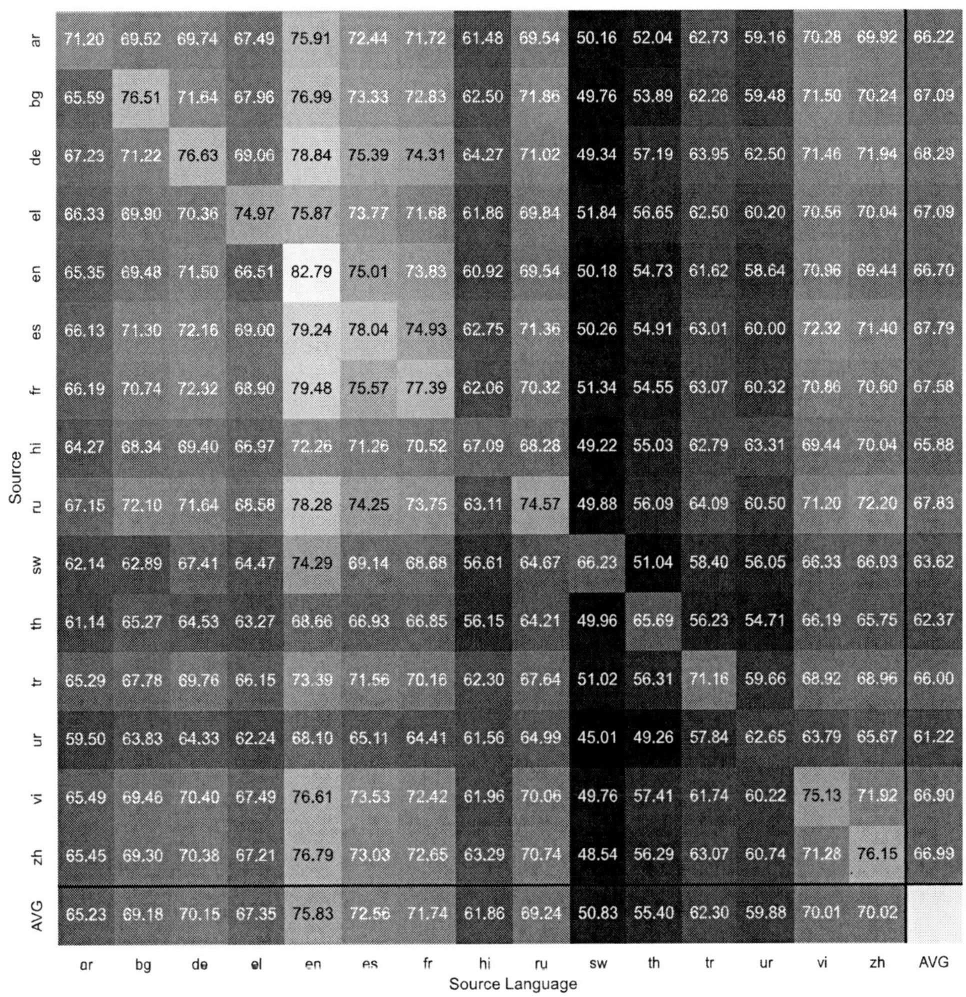

Figure 3: Cross-lingual zero-shot transfer results for XNLI

Using modern languages to parse ancient ones: a test on Old English

Luca Brigada Villa
University of Bergamo/Pavia
luca.brigadavilla@unibg.it

Martina Giarda
University of Bergamo/Pavia
martina.giarda@unibg.it

Abstract

In this paper we test the parsing performances of a multilingual parser on Old English data using different sets of languages, alone and combined with the target language, to train the models. We compare the results obtained by the models and we analyze more in deep the annotation of some peculiar syntactic constructions of the target language, providing plausible linguistic explanations of the errors made even by the best performing models.

1 Introduction

The performance of dependency parsing models for high-resource languages (HRLs) has improved significantly in recent years due to the availability of large annotated corpora and the advancement of deep learning techniques. Among others, models such as Stanza (Qi et al., 2020) and UDPipe (Straka, 2018) can achieve very high accuracy, with F1 scores approaching or even exceeding 0.90 on some treebanks datasets. This is true for some models for parsing data of (both modern and ancient) languages that have plenty of annotated resources, upon which is possible to train the models, while dependency parsing of low-resource languages (LRLs) is more problematic. The challenges that dependency parsing for LRLs has to face can be summarized as follows: a) data scarcity: LRLs often have limited annotated text corpora, which makes it difficult to train high-quality models and b) transfer learning limitations: transfer learning approaches that rely on models pre-trained on HRLs may not work well for LRLs due to the language-specificity of syntactic constructions.

As thoroughly discussed in Section 2.1, for what concerns dependency parsing, Old English (henceforth OE) can be considered a LRL, since the amount of annotated data available for this historical variety is scarce. Given these premises, we attempted an automatic parsing of OE, starting from the automatic conversion of the *York-Toronto-Helsinki Parsed Corpus of Old English Prose*[1] (henceforth YCOE) into a CoNLLU file, in which, however, the annotation is restricted to the sole morphological features retrievable from the YCOE annotation. Taking this as a starting point, we manually annotated 292 sentences, following the standards of Universal Dependencies (de Marneffe et al., 2021). Then we tested the results obtained training UUParser v2.4 (de Lhoneux et al., 2017b; Kiperwasser and Goldberg, 2016) on data coming from our set of annotated sentences in OE and a set of treebanks of three related languages, following Meechan-Maddon and Nivre's (2019) methodology, also followed by Karamolegkou and Stymne (2021) to test the performances of cross-lingual transfer learning for parsing Latin.

The paper is structured as follows: in Section 2 we introduce Old English providing a brief description of its history, developments, and typological features. In addition, we provide a brief survey of the main available resources for this language and introduce some issues that an automatic parsing of OE may face. In Section 3 we present our data and methodology. In Section 4 we overview the results of the parsing of OE data and discuss them. Finally, Section 5 concludes the paper and summarizes our findings.

2 Old English

Old English is a West-Germanic language, classified with Old Frisian and Old Saxon among the so-called Ingvaeonic languages. It was the language spoken in England after Angles, Saxons, Jutes and Frisians came to Britain and settled in the island in the 5th century. It is attested from the 7th century, except for some older brief runic inscriptions, whereas its ending point is conventionally established in 1066, date of the Norman Conquest of England (von Mengden, 2017b).

[1] https://www-users.york.ac.uk/~lang22/YCOE/YcoeHome.htm

Proceedings of the 5th Workshop on Research in Computational Linguistic Typology and Multilingual NLP (SIGTYP 2023), pages 30–41
May 6, 2023 ©2023 Association for Computational Linguistics

Typologically, OE shows a nominative-accusative alignment. Like other Indo-European languages, OE is a fusional language with inflectional word classes. Nouns are inflected by number and case, and follow three inflectional classes, depending on their original Proto-Germanic stem. After some merging processes, only four of the eight original Indo-European cases are found in OE: nominative, accusative, genitive, and dative. Some traces of the instrumental are present, but residual. Depending on the class, different cases can show syncretism. As other Germanic languages, OE has two main conjugational system: the so-called strong and weak verbs, the former building the preterit by means of apophony, i.e. the vowel alternation found in Present-Day English (PDE) irregular verbs, the latter with a dental suffix, just as PDE regular verb, whose past form is constructed with the *-ed* suffix. Finite OE verbs inflect for mood (indicative, subjunctive, imperative), tense (present and past), number, and person. Some forms show syncretism, in particular the plural in all moods and tenses, and the first and third person singular in the subjunctive (von Mengden, 2017a). Although some regularities may be found, word order in OE is not as rigid as in PDE (Mitchell and Robinson, 2012: 63-65), and it is still debated whether the basic word order was (S)VO or (S)OV. Like other ancient and modern Germanic languages, OE also exhibits V2, i.e. the tendency of the finite verb to follow the first constituent, regardless of its type. Concerning the order of other constituents, nouns are generally preceded by modifiers, e.g. demonstratives, adjectives, genitive complements. However the latter can follow the noun if another preceding modifier is present. In PPs, adpositions tend to precede a noun, but generally follow a pronoun; however, the opposite is also attested (Molencki, 2017). Contrary to PDE, OE allowed discontinuous constituents, above all in relative constructions.

2.1 Annotated resources for OE

Differently from other ancient languages, such as Latin or Ancient Greek,[2] and its contemporary counterpart, scholars have devoted little attention to the creation of resources to study Old English. The sole syntactically annotated resources for this language are the constituency treebank YCOE and its poetry counterpart, the *York-Helsinki Parsed Corpus of Old English Poetry*[3] (henceforth YCOEP), which follow the Penn style. Despite their value in size, these treebanks are hardly machine- nor user-friendly, have no interface and can only be investigated through their tool CorpusSearch2,[4] which require an intensive training in order to write even simple queries. There have been several attempts to convert constituency treebanks (particularly, Penn-style treebanks) into dependency-formats as the Estonian-EDT (Muischnek et al., 2014) and the Indonesian CSUI (Alfina et al., 2020), whereas, to our knowledge, no attempts in the opposite direction have been made.

2.2 Issues in automatically parsing OE data

An automatic parsing of such a free-ordered language can meet several problems. Regarding syntax, some problems may arise, given the freedom of word order and case syncretism, which may lead to a confusion, for instance, between subject and object constituents. Moreover, the use of both pre- and postpositions may result in erroneous annotation of oblique phrases. Another problematic issue is the parsing of relative clauses, which can be marked by a variety of means or even left unmarked, and often show non-projectivity.

3 Data and methods

3.1 Starting point and initial issues

Our data consist of two prose OE texts, *Adrian and Ritheus* and the first homily of Ælfric's *Supplemental Homilies*,[5] for a total of 292 sentences.[6] Both texts are written in the West-Saxon dialect and have religious content. First, the texts were coverted from the YCOE-format to a CoNLLU-file containing the POS and the morphological features retrievable from the YCOE annotation, i.e. case for nouns and adjectives, and mood and tense for verbs (when not ambiguous). Second, we manually annotated the remaining morphological fea-

[2]The latest release of UD (v2.11) includes 5 treebanks for Latin and 2 for Ancient Greek.

[3]https://www-users.york.ac.uk/~lang18/pcorpus.html

[4]https://corpussearch.sourceforge.net/CS.html.

[5]These are the first two texts in the YCOE treebank. *Adrian and Ritheus* is dialogue on several biblical issues (Cross and Hill, 1982 : 3-4). On the other hand, Ælfric's homily, *Nativitas Domini*, is a Christmas homily, with several expansions, consisting in scriptural elaborations (Pope, 1968 : 191-195).

[6]Data and scripts can be found at https://github.com/unipv-larl/wundorsmitha-geweorc/tree/main/paper_projects/parsing_oe_modern

tures, lemmatization and syntactic dependencies, following Universal Dependencies guidelines. This choice is due to these reasons: UD is the *de facto* standard for the annotation dependency treebanks; moreover, it allows for comparison, which is useful for both typological and historical analyses.

Some problematic issues derive from the conversion of texts itself: the YCOE tags as `P` both adpositions and subordinating conjunctions, which would be tagged, respectively, as `ADP` and `SCONJ` in Universal Dependencies. In the conversion, both options have been kept, to manually disambiguate them. Moreover, the verbs *beon* and *wesan* 'to be' and *weoṙþan* 'to become' have their specific tag in the YCOE annotation, i.e. `BE*`. Given the frequency of copular and passive constructions in which they appear, they have been all converted to `AUX`. However, this tagging disregards their occurrences as existential verbs, which should be tagged as `VERB`. As a general tendency, we chose not to include subtypes of the syntactic lables, except for the following cases:

- `advcl:relcl`, indicating a relative clause;
- the subtypes indicating a passive construction, i.e. `nsubj:pass`, `aux:pass` and `obl:agent`;
- `advmod:neg` for the negative particle and adverb *ne* and *na*,
- the specific `advmod:tmod` and `advmod:lmod` only when they were single-word adverbs, tagged in the YCOE as `ADV^L` and `ADV^T`;
- `obl:tmod` and `obl:lmod` have only been used when there was a unambiguous, not metaphorical interpretation.

3.2 Support languages

We used UUParser v2.4 (de Lhoneux et al., 2017b), a transition-based parser which is able to train multilingual models. Given the small amount of annotated sentences, we chose a multilingual parser, in order to test whether the inclusion of support languages in the training phase could have a beneficial impact on the parsing of OE sentences or not. To do so, we selected three languages related to OE since the addition of related languages has shown to be effective in the tests described in de Lhoneux et al. (2017a) and Meechan-Maddon and Nivre (2019).

While Meechan-Maddon and Nivre (2019) had three modern languages (Faroese, Upper Sorbian and North Saami) as target languages for the experiment, which resulted in an easier choice of languages to be used as support to train the models, our choice to focus on OE brings some issues in selecting the support languages. PDE has been excluded, due to its diachronic evolution: English has lost both nominal and verbal inflection, has developed a rigid SVO order, and its lexicon has been enriched by many French loanwords. Even though not part of the same sub-branch, i.e. Ingvaeonic, other modern Germanic languages present features that are closer to OE morphosyntax. In particular, we selected Modern Icelandic, Modern Swedish, and Modern German. The former two are part of the North-Germanic branch, whereas the latter is part of the West-Germanic branch, to which OE, too, belongs. Icelandic is considered the most archaic of Germanic languages, since it has retained many morphological and syntactical characteristics of Old Norse (Bandle et al., 2005: 1872). Some of its features compatible with OE are: a) prenominal definite determiners; b) pre- and post-nominal attributive genitive; c) the so-called "oblique objects" (i.e. impersonal constructions); d) the presence of verb-auxiliary constructions. The last feature is lost in Swedish, which has also undergone a process of morphological simplification. However Swedish features, as OE, prenominal possessive determiners, while Icelandic has mainly postnominal possessives (Bandle et al., 2005: 1874). Nonetheless, both Scandinavian languages show a fixed SVO order, which contrasts with the free OE word order. The Scandinavian languages, as well as German, are V2 languages, like OE. Regarding the West-Germanic branch, German is similar to OE in that it retains, at least in subordinate clauses, a verb-final order. Similarly to OE, it has both prepositions and postpositions. Both German and OE have prenominal definite determiners and attributive genitive both pre- and postnominal positions (Haider, 2010). Of the three support languages, Swedish shows the major innovations, whereas Icelandic and German may give better results.

3.3 Experimental setup

We split our sample of manually annotated OE sentences in three sets (see Table 1) and from Universal Dependencies v2.11 (de Marneffe et al., 2021), we selected one treebank for each of the support languages, namely UD Swedish-Talbanken (Nivre and Megyesi, 2007), UD Icelandic-Modern and

UD German-GSD (McDonald et al., 2013).

	train	dev	test	total
tokens	2673	1308	1334	5315
sentences	149	73	70	292

Table 1: The sets resulted from splitting OE data.

We reduced the treebanks of the support languages to 60k tokens to avoid the effect on the results that the size of the treebanks might have,[7] and we converted the characters which were not in the target language as shown in Table 6 in Appendix A.

Then, for each one of the combinations of the four languages (the target language and the three support languages), we performed the training of the models and, after the training phase, we used the best model to parse the OE test set. Our workflow followed these steps:

1. we used UUParser to train the model (30 epochs)
2. the epoch that had the best LAS on OE dev data was selected as the best model
3. we parsed the OE test data using the best model

The training phase did not take into account the part-of-speech tags, even if the parser is able to learn embeddings of POS tags if a specific option is given. We decided not to use that option since we wanted to test how well the model performed in a common situation when it comes to work with OE data, that is not having POS annotated texts.

In Section 4 we show the results achieved by each model and discuss them.

4 Results and discussion

Table 2 shows the accuracy reached by each model measured on the parsing of OE test data. At first glance, we can see that the model trained using only OE data significantly outperforms each of the models trained without OE data in the training set. This applies for both the monolingual and multilingual models and seems to confirm what was found by Meechan-Maddon and Nivre (2019).

Considering the metrics, the best-performing models were the ones trained with Icelandic and OE data, which achieved the best Unlabeled Attachment Score (UAS) and Labeled Attachment Score (LAS), together with the one trained with Icelandic, German and OE data, which achieved the best Label Accuracy (LA).[8]

Considering the UAS and the LAS achieved by the models, it is surprising to notice that the model that performed best was the one trained upon only Icelandic and target language data, since the Icelandic monolingual model was the one which obtained significantly worse results than the other monolingual models. For what concerns the LA, it seems reasonable to see a model trained on German data performing better that the others considering that the monolingual model trained upon German was the one that achieved the best scores among the monolingual models trained without OE data, even though such multilingual model was trained also upon Icelandic data. Finally, all models trained including the target language data achieved better results than their counterparts trained without having the target language data in the training set, even though the best performances are achieved combining Icelandic and German with OE data. This seems reasonable in light of what discussed in Section 3.2.

In the following sections we will analyze more in detail the output of the parsing phase of the two models which scored the highest metrics (is+target and de+is+target) and the monolingual model trained only upon OE data. We will focus on the deprels `advmod` and `obl` for the following reasons: the former showed unexpectedly low results for the OE model (as shown in Table 3); the latter allows investigating whether postpositions have been recognized and correctly annotated. We will also concentrate on `advcl:rel`, as relative clauses can be marked by different pronouns and can show non-projectivity. We will discuss and exemplify the output of the models for these constructions, using four erroneously annotated sentences. Finally, in Section 4.4, we will show some recurrent errors made by the models tagging the dependency relations and the impact of a rule we designed to correct the output of the parsing process.

[7]This is the main reason why we did not consider the Gothic PROIEL treebank (Haug and Jøhndal, 2008), even if its inclusion could have improved the parsing scores. In this work we decided to restrict the set of languages to be considered as support data for our models to the modern ones.

[8]The LA was measured dividing the number of token whose deprel was tagged correctly by the number of tokens in the test set.

	-Target			+Target		
	UAS	**LA**	**LAS**	**UAS**	**LA**	**LAS**
Old English				60.79	64.39	47.23
sv	27.06	24.44	9.45	65.07	73.61	57.20
de	32.91	25.34	10.12	65.82	72.19	56.45
is	20.31	22.64	4.57	**68.44**	73.76	**58.70**
sv+de	32.16	25.56	10.42	65.82	72.19	57.42
sv+is	26.39	23.76	9.45	64.62	70.09	54.42
de+is	30.73	27.74	11.17	66.34	**74.29**	57.42
sv+de+is	32.46	24.96	11.02	65.97	71.66	57.57

Table 2: UAS, LA and LAS of each model measured on the parsing of OE test data. -Target = cross-lingual models trained without target language data. +Target = models trained including target language data.

		`advmod`	`obl`	`acl:relcl`
oe	**P**	41.67	61.26	62.50
	R	35.71	80.95	52.63
oe-is	**P**	65.45	65.42	72.22
	R	51.43	83.33	86.67
oe-de-is	**P**	58.21	70.93	51.85
	R	55.71	72.62	63.64

Table 3: Precision (P) and Recall (R) for the dependency relations `advmod`, `obl` and `acl:relcl`.

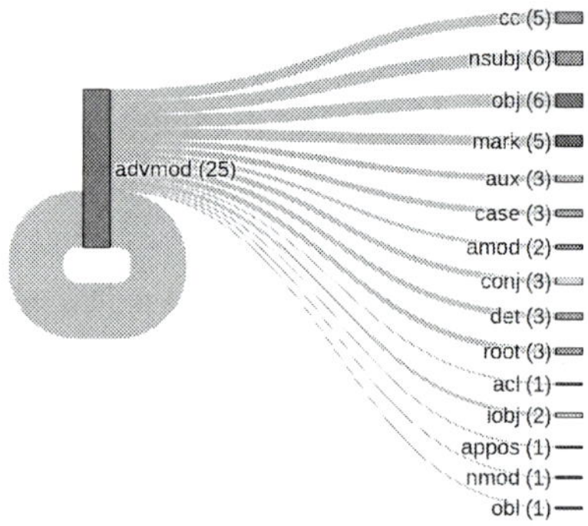

Figure 1: How oe model tagged tokens which had to be tagged as `advmod` (see Figures 9 and 10 in Appendix A for the other models).

4.1 The deprel `advmod`

As shown in Figure 1, no relevant patterns of error seem to be present. However, it is remarkable that many of the errors are found with the word *ne* 'not' and *swa* 'so'. Both can have several functions in the sentences: *ne* can either be a negative adverb or a negative conjunction, whereas *swa* can introduce a subordinate clause or function as an adverb. The different usages are distinguished in the UPOS, which however is not considered by the models, causing confusion in the syntactic annotation as well.

An interesting example is shown in Figure 2, where the adverb *swutelicor* 'more clearly' has been annotated by the three models as `obj` of the verb *cweðað* '(we) talk' in this context, but generally 'say'. This can be accounted for in light of the absence of a true direct object depending on the verb.

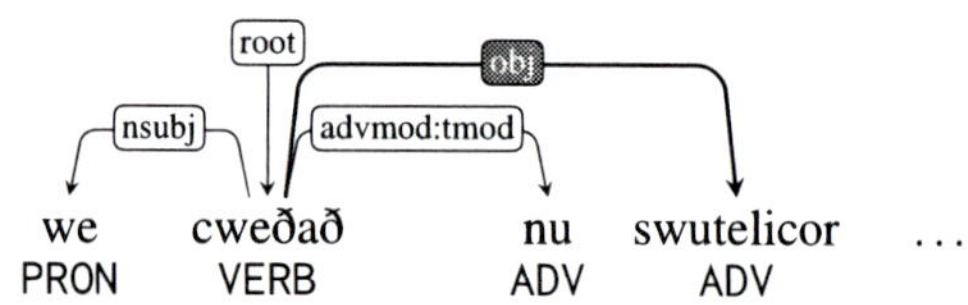

Figure 2: Dependecy tree of part of the sentence 'we cweðað nu swutelicor , on þam Godes wisdome , þe is witodlice lif , & cann wyrcan his weorc be his dihte' ('we now talk more clearly about God's wisdom, which truly is life, and can make his actions by his command'). Correct annotation in Figure 15 in Appendix B.

4.2 The deprel `obl`

As in 4.1, no significant patterns of error can be identified for the deprel `obl`. Remarkably, Figure 5 compared to Figures 11 and 12 in Appendix A shows that the best model in this respect is the one trained only on OE data.

One example of incorrect annotation is worth discussing: as touched upon in Section 2.2, the annotation of postpositions has been problematic. None of the three models could correctly recognize that the adposition *ongean* 'against, towards' depended on the preceding pronoun *hiom* 'them'. The OE model considered *hiom* as `case`, directly

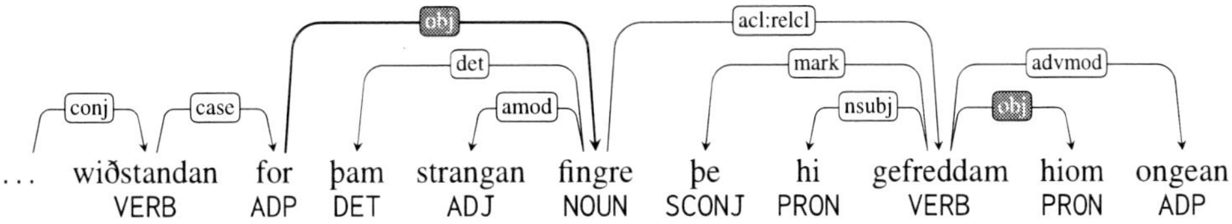

Figure 3: Dependency tree of '[... & hi ne mihton na leng Moyse] wiðstandan for þam strangan fingre þe hi gefreddan hiom ongean.' ('[and they could no longer] withstand [Moyses] for that strong finger that they felt against them '). This is the output of the oe-de-is model, see Figure 16 in Appendix B for the correct tree.

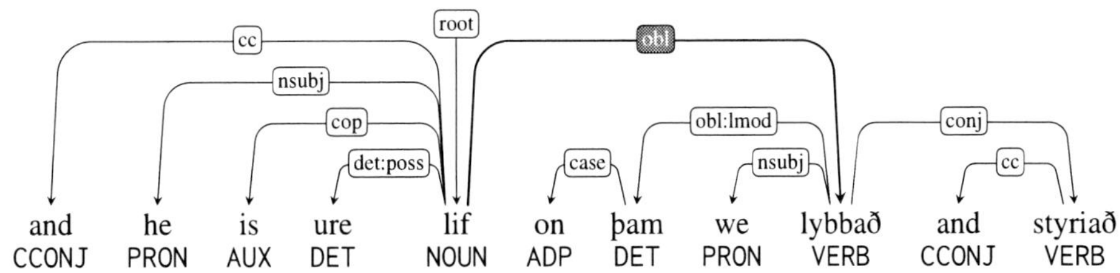

Figure 4: Dependency tree of part of the sentence '& he is ure lif on þam we lybbað & styriað, & on þam we syndon, swa swa us sæde Paulus.' ('and he is our life, in which we live and move, in which we are, so as Paul said to us'). This is the output of the oe-is model, see Figure 17 in Appendix B for the correct tree.

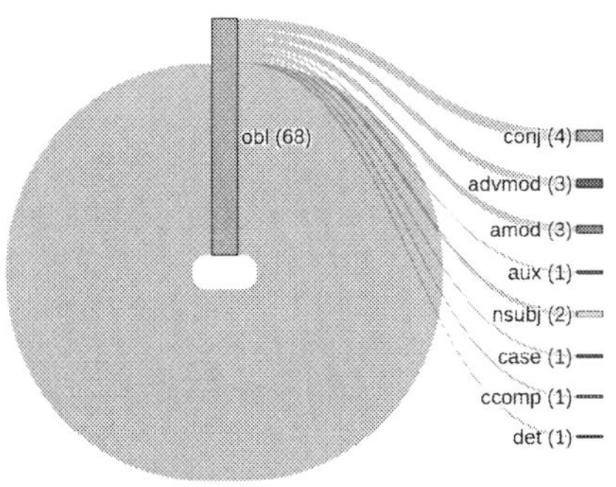

Figure 5: How oe model tagged tokens which had to be tagged as obl (see Figures 11 and 12 in Appendix A for the other models).

depending on the preceding verb *gefreddan* 'feel, perceive'. On the other hand, both multilingual models considered *hiom* as the object of *gefreddan* and *ongean* an adverb modifying the verb, as shown in Figure 3.

4.3 The deprel `acl:relcl`

Most problems in the annotation of relative clauses are: a) the great variability in the relative pronouns marking them, and b) non-projectivity. Concerning the point in a), OE has an invariable complementizer *þe*, which generally functions as a relative marker, at times accompanied by the determiner *se, seo, þæt*. However, the determiner can be found without the complementizer to mark relative clauses, above all when part of PPs, or relative clauses can simply be left unmarked. Other POS, e.g. locative adverbs, can function as relative pronouns. All three models tended to make the same errors, generally recognizing and annotating correctly only the sentences with *þe*, and making mistakes when this element did not occur.

An example of this is shown Figure 4, where the PP *on þam* 'in which' (lit. 'in the.DAT') was not recognized by the models as marking the relative clause. The sole model which recognized that this was a subordinate clause was the de-is-oe model, which annotated it as `advcl` correctly depending on the noun *lif* 'life', whereas the other models considered it a nominal constituent (either `conj` or `obl`). Another issue is that OE allowed for discontinuity in relative clauses, which could be separated from their antecedent by other constituents. Some of the errors are probably due to this, as shown in the sentence in Figure 6. This sentence shows how the relative clause *þe forlærdon Farao* 'which corrupted the Pharaoh', was not considered as depending on the noun *drymen* 'joys', given that the two constituents are separated by two PPs. What the multilingual model annotated as relative clause (erroneously, as it read the verb *forlærdon* as modifying *Farao*) is dependent on the nearest noun,

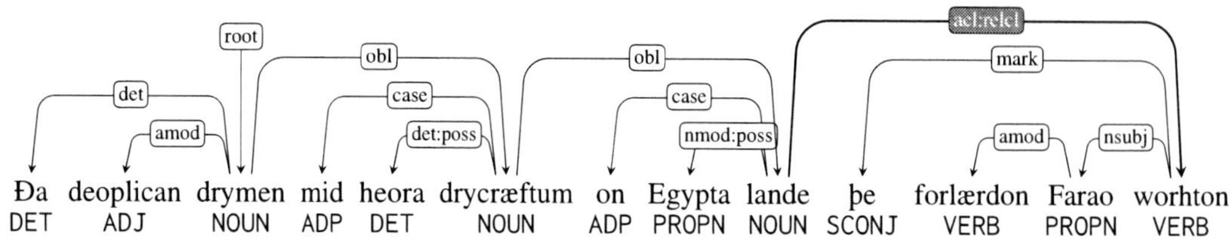

Figure 6: Dependency tree of 'Ða deoplican drymen mid heora drycræftum on Egypta lande þe forlærdon Farao worhton [tacna ongean Moysen of þam ylcan antimbre þe God ær gesceop...]' ('The deep joys, **which corrupted the Pharaoh** with their magical arts in the lands of Egypt, made...'). This is the output of the oe-de-is model, see Figure 18 in Appendix B for the correct tree.

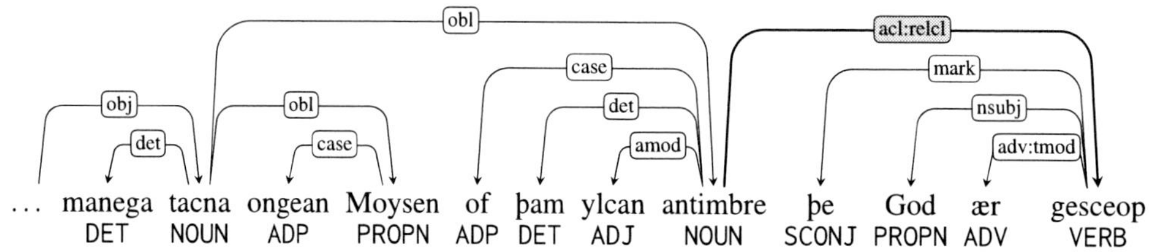

Figure 7: Dependency tree of '[Ða deoplican drymen mid heora drycræftum on Egypta lande þe forlærdon Farao worhton] tacna ongean Moysen of þam ylcan antimbre þe God ær gesceop...' ('...[made] towards Moyses many signs of the same substance, **which God had created before**...'). This is the output of the oe-de-is model, see Figure 19 in Appendix B for the correct tree.

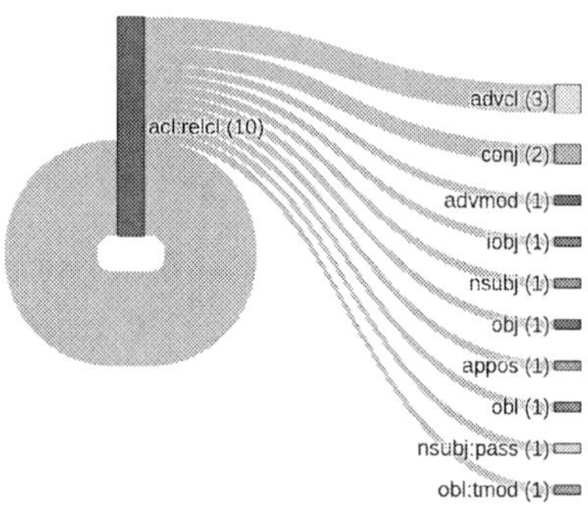

Figure 8: How oe model tagged tokens which had to be tagged as `acl:relcl` (see Figures 13 and 14 in Appendix A for the other models).

i.e. *lande* 'lands'. On the contrary, the following relative clause (Figure 7) *þe God ær gesceop* 'which God had created before', has been annotated correctly by all three models, as it is immediately preceded by its antecedent, *antimbre* 'substance'.

4.4 Recurrent erroneous dependency relations

During the manual check of the output generated by the models, we noticed some recurrent errors that the models could have avoided. These errors are due to the fact that the generated tree and the annotation of dependency relations do not take into account the POS of the tokens.

form	upos	xpos	deprel
ne	CCONJ	any	cc
ne	PART	any	advmod:neg
any	any	starts with MD	aux
any	any	ADV^L	advmod:lmod
any	any	ADV^T	advmod:tmod

Table 4: Deprel correction table (upos=universal part-of-speech; xpos=language-specific part-of-speech).

We decided to assign automatically a dependency relation to tokens which had certain features, as displayed in Table 4. As discussed in Section 4.1, the word *ne* 'not, nor' could function both as negative particle (in which case was assigned PART as universal POS), but also as a negative coordinative conjunction, thus assigned CCONJ as universal POS. Syntactically, the former function can be labeled only as `advmod:neg`, while the latter only as `cc`, whether it conjuncts two NPs/PPs or two clauses. For this reason, we automatically assigned the deprel `advmod:neg` to all the occurrences of *ne*, whose UPOS was PART, and the deprel `cc` to those tagged as CCONJ. Together with *ne*, we also mentioned *swa* 'so', as a frequent error in advmod. However, we could not proceed to an automatic correction of it, as we did with *ne*, since *swa* tagged as ADV can also appear in the fixed expression *swa swa* 'so, in the same way', introducing a subordinate clause. In this case, the first *swa*, whose UPOS is ADV, should be annotated as fixed, instead of advmod.

	before		after	
	LA	LAS	LA	LAS
oe	64.39	47.23	66.79	48.28
oe-is	73.76	58.70	75.34	59.30
oe-de-is	74.29	57.42	75.79	58.17

Table 5: Comparison between the LA and the LAS before and after the correction.

We also noticed many errors in the annotation of modals, which in the YCOE are all tagged as MD (and its variants, which show mood and tense). Following Universal Dependencies guidelines, they should all be annotated as aux, making an automatic correction of these errors possible. The original YCOE annotation is useful also with temporal and spatial adverbs. They were originally tagged as ADV^L and ADV^T, which can easily be automatically converted, respectively, in advmod:lmod and advmod:tmod, correcting both main deprel and the subtype.

Our correction affected the label accuracy of the treebanks resulting on an increase of 1 or 2 points depending on the model, which had an impact also on the LAS, as shown in Table 5.

5 Conclusion

In this paper we tested the dependency parsing performances of four monolingual models and seven multilingual models on Old English data. We showed that the model trained just using data of the target language achieved far better results than the models (both monolingual and multiliguals) trained without target language data and that, out of the three support languages we selected, Icelandic and German combined better than Swedish according to the scores reached parsing OE test data. As discussed in 3.2, we expected this result given the fact that Modern Icelandic and Modern German retained many morphosyntactic features similar to those of the target language.

Then, we also discussed some cases of problematic annotation: in Sections 4.1, 4.2, 4.3 we gave some linguistic explanations of the errors made by the best models, which include advmod, obl and acl:relcl showing that some poor results might be due to the peculiarity of such constructions in OE. Finally, in 4.4, we discussed the impact which the correction of the dependency relation annotation using some rules based on the word forms, the universal parts-of-speech and the language-specific parts-of-speech had on the results achieved by the best models. This errors might have been avoided if we had used the option to force the models to learn embeddings for the parts-of-speech during the training phase, which would have made the parsing process aware of the already annotated parts-of-speech. The situation in which the POSs are annotated, though, is not so usual for OE, except for the above-mentioned YCOE and YCOEP treebanks.

Our test, following the methodology described in Meechan-Maddon and Nivre (2019), led to the same conclusions in terms of the benefits that support languages have on the parsing scores when combined to OE data during the training phase. In particular this is true when the support languages are related to the target language or, at least, share a significant number of features with the target language.

This approach has proven useful for our broader twofold aim: a) having an alternative to a rule-based conversion of the YCOE(P) treebanks and b) developing a tool to annotate other OE texts, which are not included in the above-mentioned treebanks. Despite the challenges, using this approach to parse historical languages can accelerate the process of creating new resources and produce outputs that, while not perfect, are satisfactory in terms of dependency parsing.

Aknowledgments

We would like to thank the anonymous reviewers who provided great insights and suggestions. We also thank Chiara Zanchi and Luigi Talamo for their precious comments and Andrew Dyer for the suggestions which led to this paper. The paper is the result of close collaboration between the two authors. For academic purposes, Luca Brigada Villa is responsible of training the models and parsing the data, and of Sections 1, 3.3, 4, 5. Martina Giarda is responsible of the manual annotation, and of Sections 2, 3, 3.1, 3.2, 4.1, 4.2, 4.3, 4.4.

References

Ika Alfina, Daniel Zeman, Arawinda Dinakaramani, Indra Budi, and Heru Suhartanto. 2020. Selecting the ud v2 morphological features for indonesian dependency treebank. In *2020 International Conference on Asian Language Processing (IALP)*, pages 104–109.

Oscar Bandle, Kurt Braunmüller, Ernst Hakon Jahr, Allan Karker, Hans-Peter Naumann, Ulf Telemann, Lennart Elmevik, and Gun Widmark. 2005. *The Nordic Languages*, volume 2. De Gruyter, Berlin,Boston.

James E. Cross and Thomas D. Hill. 1982. *The Prose Solomon and Saturn and Adrian and Ritheus*. University of Toronto Press, Toronto.

Miryam de Lhoneux, Yan Shao, Ali Basirat, Eliyahu Kiperwasser, Sara Stymne, Yoav Goldberg, and Joakim Nivre. 2017a. From raw text to Universal Dependencies - look, no tags! In *Proceedings of the CoNLL 2017 Shared Task: Multilingual Parsing from Raw Text to Universal Dependencies*, pages 207–217, Vancouver, Canada. Association for Computational Linguistics.

Miryam de Lhoneux, Sara Stymne, and Joakim Nivre. 2017b. Arc-hybrid non-projective dependency parsing with a static-dynamic oracle. In *Proceedings of the The 15th International Conference on Parsing Technologies (IWPT).*, Pisa, Italy.

Marie-Catherine de Marneffe, Christopher D. Manning, Joakim Nivre, and Daniel Zeman. 2021. Universal Dependencies. *Computational Linguistics*, 47(2):255–308.

Hubert Haider. 2010. *The Syntax of German*. Cambridge University Press, Cambridge.

Dag T. T. Haug and Marius L. Jøhndal. 2008. Creating a parallel treebank of the old indo-european bible translations. In *Proceedings of the Second Workshop on Language Technology for Cultural Heritage Data (LaTeCH 2008)*, pages 27–34.

Antonia Karamolegkou and Sara Stymne. 2021. Investigation of transfer languages for parsing Latin: Italic branch vs. Hellenic branch. In *Proceedings of the 23rd Nordic Conference on Computational Linguistics (NoDaLiDa)*, pages 315–320, Reykjavik, Iceland (Online). Linköping University Electronic Press, Sweden.

Eliyahu Kiperwasser and Yoav Goldberg. 2016. Simple and accurate dependency parsing using bidirectional LSTM feature representations. *TACL*, 4:313–327.

Ryan McDonald, Joakim Nivre, Yvonne Quirmbach-Brundage, Yoav Goldberg, Dipanjan Das, Kuzman Ganchev, Keith Hall, Slav Petrov, Hao Zhang, Oscar Täckström, Claudia Bedini, Núria Bertomeu Castelló, and Jungmee Lee. 2013. Universal Dependency annotation for multilingual parsing. In *Proceedings of the 51st Annual Meeting of the Association for Computational Linguistics (Volume 2: Short Papers)*, pages 92–97, Sofia, Bulgaria. Association for Computational Linguistics.

Ailsa Meechan-Maddon and Joakim Nivre. 2019. How to parse low-resource languages: Cross-lingual parsing, target language annotation, or both? In *Proceedings of the Fifth International Conference on Dependency Linguistics (Depling, SyntaxFest 2019)*, pages 112–120, Paris, France. Association for Computational Linguistics.

Bruce Mitchell and Fred C. Robinson. 2012. *A guide to Old English. Eighth edition*. John Wiley & Sons, Malden, Oxford.

Rafał Molencki. 2017. Syntax. In Laurel J. Brinton and Alexander Bergs, editors, *The History of English. Old English*, volume 2, chapter 5, pages 100–124. De Gruyter Mouton, Berlin, Boston.

Kadri Muischnek, Kaili Müürisep, Tiina Puolakainen, Eleri Aedmaa, Riin Kirt, and Dage Särg. 2014. Estonian Dependency Treebank and its annotation scheme. In *Proceedings of the 13th Workshop on Treebanks and Linguistic Theories (TLT13)*, pages 285–291, Tübingen, Germany.

Joakim Nivre and Beata Megyesi. 2007. Bootstrapping a swedish treebank using cross-corpus harmonization and annotation projection. In *Proceedings of the 6th international workshop on treebanks and linguistic theories*, pages 97–102. Association for Computational Linguistics Pennsylvania, PA.

John C. Pope. 1968. *Homilies of Ælfric: a Supplementary Collection*. Early English Society, Oxford University Press, London.

Peng Qi, Yuhao Zhang, Yuhui Zhang, Jason Bolton, and Christopher D. Manning. 2020. Stanza: A Python natural language processing toolkit for many human languages. In *Proceedings of the 58th Annual Meeting of the Association for Computational Linguistics: System Demonstrations*.

Milan Straka. 2018. UDPipe 2.0 prototype at CoNLL 2018 UD shared task. In *Proceedings of the CoNLL 2018 Shared Task: Multilingual Parsing from Raw Text to Universal Dependencies*, pages 197–207, Brussels, Belgium. Association for Computational Linguistics.

Ferdinand von Mengden. 2017a. Morphology. In Laurel J. Brinton and Alexander Bergs, editors, *The History of English. Old English*, volume 2, chapter 5, pages 73–99. De Gruyter Mouton, Berlin, Boston.

Ferdinand von Mengden. 2017b. Old english: Overview. In Laurel J. Brinton and Alexander Bergs, editors, *The History of English. Old English*, volume 2, chapter 3, pages 32–49. De Gruyter Mouton, Berlin, Boston.

A Additional tables and figures

character	conversion
ä	æ
ö	o
ü	u
Ä	A
Ö	O
Ü	U
ß	ss
á	a
é	e
í	i
ó	o
ú	u
ý	y
Á	A
É	E
Í	I
Ó	O
Ú	U
Ý	Y
å	a
Å	A

Table 6: The character conversion table.

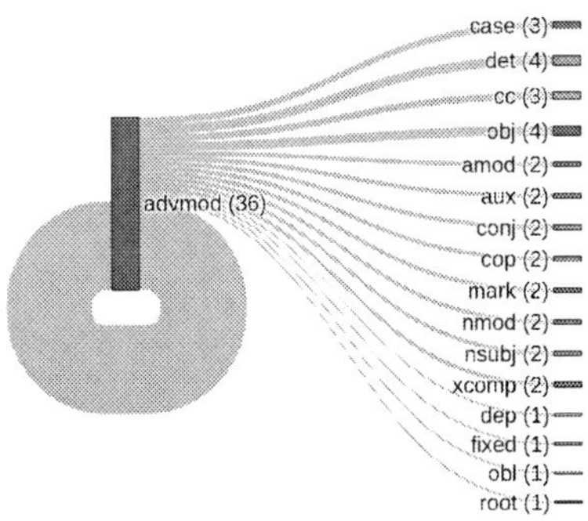

Figure 9: How oe-is model tagged tokens which had to be tagged as `advmod`.

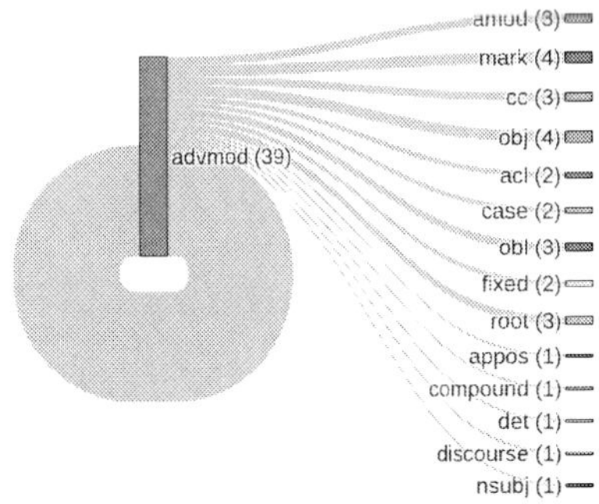

Figure 10: How oe-de-is model tagged tokens which had to be tagged as `advmod`.

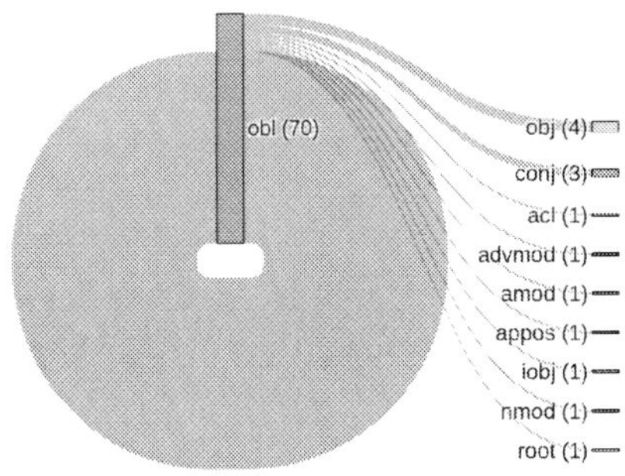

Figure 11: How oe-is model tagged tokens which had to be tagged as `obl`.

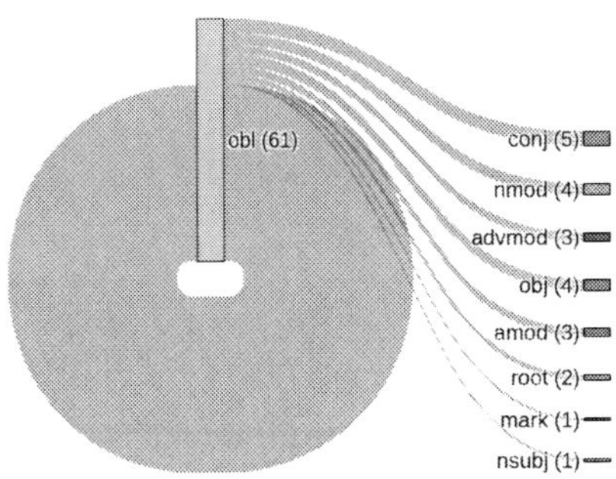

Figure 12: How oe-de-is model tagged tokens which had to be tagged as `obl`.

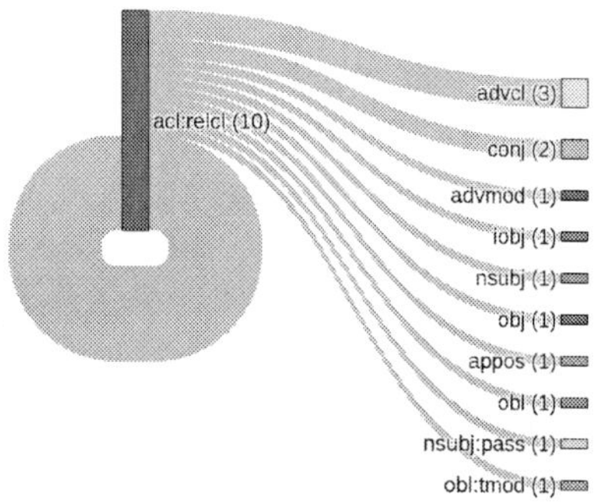

Figure 13: How oe-is model tagged tokens which had to be tagged as `acl:relcl`.

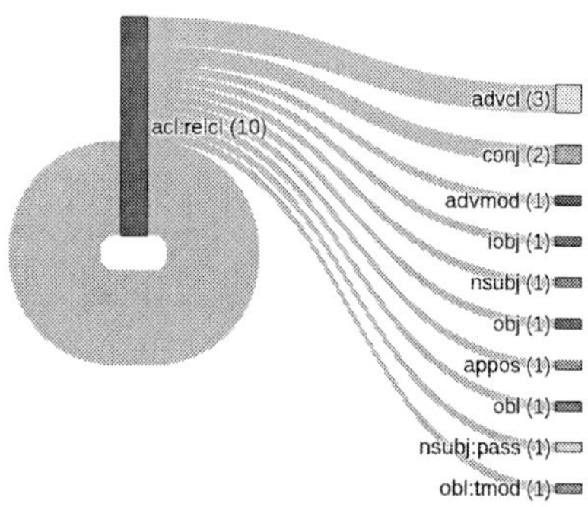

Figure 14: How oe-de-is model tagged tokens which had to be tagged as `acl:relcl`.

B Additional trees

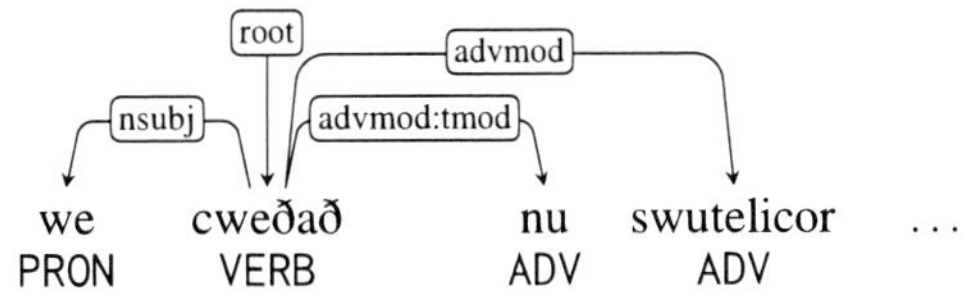

Figure 15: Correct version of the dependency tree in Figure 2.

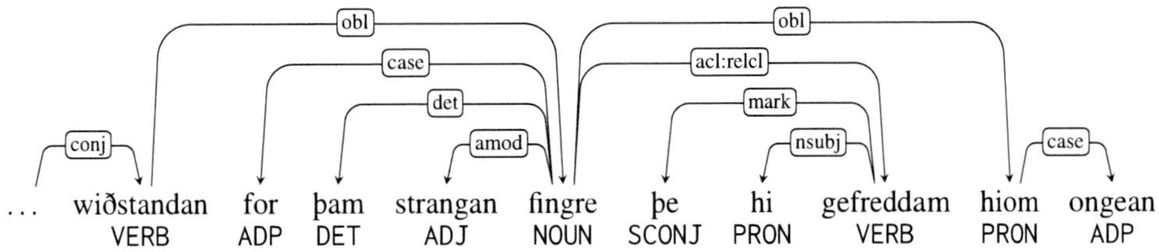

Figure 16: Correct version of the dependency tree in Figure 3.

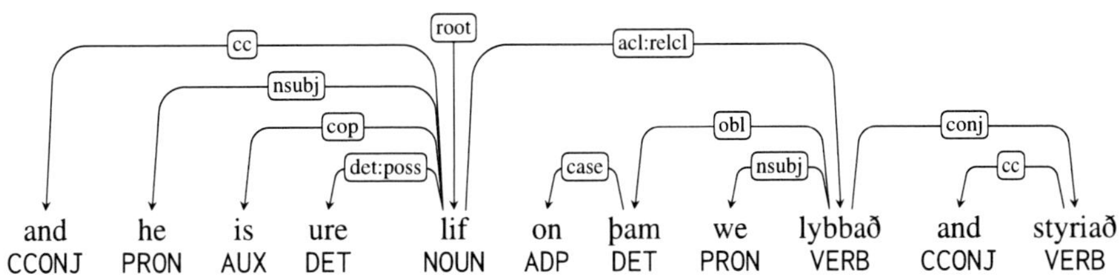

Figure 17: Correct version of the dependency tree in Figure 4.

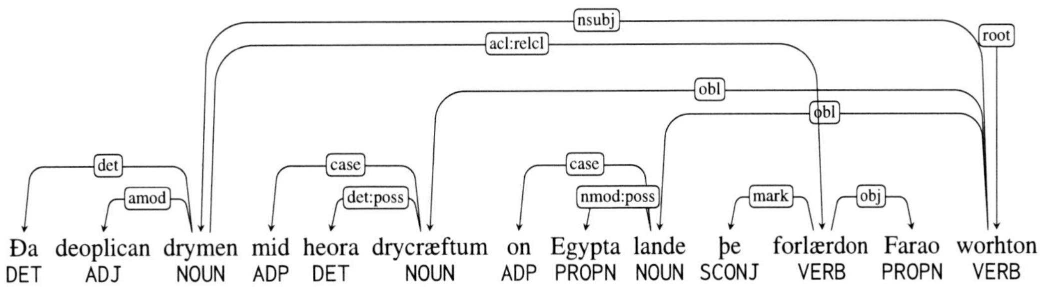

Figure 18: Correct version of the dependency tree in Figure 6.

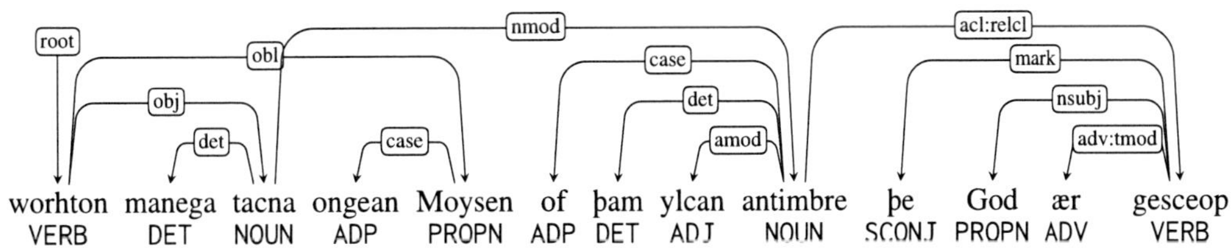

Figure 19: Correct version of the dependency tree in Figure 7.

The Denglisch Corpus of German-English Code-Switching

Doreen Osmelak
Language Science and Technology
Saarland University, Germany
s9doosme@stud.uni-saarland.de

Shuly Wintner
Department of Computer Science
University of Haifa, Israel
shuly@cs.haifa.ac.il

Abstract

When multilingual speakers involve in a conversation they inevitably introduce *code-switching (CS)*, i.e., mixing of more than one language between and within utterances. CS is still an understudied phenomenon, especially in the written medium, and relatively few computational resources for studying it are available.

We describe a corpus of German-English code-switching in social media interactions. We focus on some challenges in annotating CS, especially due to words whose language ID cannot be easily determined. We introduce a novel schema for such word-level annotation, with which we manually annotated a subset of the corpus. We then trained classifiers to predict and identify switches, and applied them to the remainder of the corpus. Thereby, we created a large-scale corpus of German-English mixed utterances with precise indications of CS points.

1 Introduction

Multilinguality is becoming more and more ubiquitous, to the extent that psycholinguists increasingly acknowledge that bilingualism is the rule and not the exception (Harris and McGhee Nelson, 1992). Grosjean (2010, p. 16) stated that "bilingualism is a worldwide phenomenon, found on all continents and in the majority of the countries of the world" and Grosjean and Li (2013) assessed that more than half the world's population is multilingual.

Multilingual speakers have two or more language systems active in their minds, and they tend to use them interchangeably, especially when communicating with other multilinguals. This process of mixing two or more languages within a discourse or even within a single utterance is called *code-switching (CS)*. In order to understand and produce natural language, NLP systems need to cope with this phenomenon, but today's language technology still cannot efficiently process CS, partly due to lacunae in our understanding of the factors driving CS, and partly due to lack of resources.

We introduce a corpus of German-English CS in spontaneous written communication.[1] We discuss challenges in determining the language ID of tokens in multilingual texts in Section 4, and present our novel annotation scheme in Section 5. We describe the corpus in Section 6, and then describe classifiers (Section 7) that accurately identify the language ID of tokens in the corpus, thereby allowing us to effectively identify switch points in unseen texts. We conclude with suggestions for future research.

2 Background and Related Work

The Phenomenon of CS Code-switching is the process of mixing two or more languages within a discourse or even within a single utterance, where the mixed words or fragments do not suffer any syntactic or phonological alternation. CS can happen on various linguistic levels (phonological, morphological, lexical, syntactic), and can be *intra-sentential* (the switch occurs within the boundaries of a sentence or utterance), or *inter-sentential* (the switch occurs between two sentences or utterances). There are two competing theories on how this process works: as a symmetric relation or as an asymmetric relation. In the *symmetric approach* both languages are equally dominant, and any lexical items from either language can be replaced by the corresponding items of the other language, as long as the switch happens at syntactic boundaries that are shared by both languages. The monolingual fragments conform to the grammar of the corresponding language they are taken from (Poplack, 1980). In the *asymmetric approach* one of the languages is more dominant than the other, and only content morphemes can be taken from both languages, whereas late system morphemes indicating grammatical relations can only be taken from the subordinate language. The dominant language

[1] All the data and code developed in this work are available at https://github.com/HaifaCLG/Denglisch.

Proceedings of the 5th Workshop on Research in Computational Linguistic Typology and Multilingual NLP (SIGTYP 2023), pages 42–51
May 6, 2023 ©2023 Association for Computational Linguistics

from which the grammatical framework is taken is called the *Matrix Language*, and the subordinate language that is mixed into it is called the *Embedded Language* (Joshi, 1982).

Oral CS CS in oral communication has been studied extensively. It interacts with speakers' proficiency as well as style and content of the utterances, serving several, partly contradicting, purposes, such as compensating for words the speaker does not know in one language or expressing nuanced meanings that cannot be expressed precisely with the other language (Gardner-Chloros, 2009). But CS can also serve sociolinguistic purposes such as conveying identity, interpersonal relations and formality. Conclusions from past research have differed greatly in whether CS is a strategy used by highly adaptive speakers to convey very subtle meaning differences between words of different languages (Kootstra et al., 2012), or a strategy used by speakers less familiar with one of the languages to overcome lexical deficiencies (Poulisse, 1990).

Written CS CS in written communication has not drawn much attention in research so far. Written communication differs significantly from spoken interaction, especially in formality and spontaneity: e.g., literary texts undergo an inherent process of conscious reflection, correction, editing and review. Findings thus far have differed on whether oral and written CS behave in the same manner and serve the same purposes. Written CS in literary texts does partially serve the same purposes as in spoken CS (Gardner-Chloros and Weston, 2015), but there are additional functions and purposes that are not found in spontaneous oral speech, such as serving as a poetic device (Chan, 2009).

Online Forums With the increasing ubiquity of online discussion platforms, there are large amounts of written communication reflecting more spontaneous speech productions than classical written texts, thereby constituting a hybrid between speech and formal writing. Research on CS in online forums has so far mainly focused on computational challenges for NLP algorithms (Çetinoğlu et al., 2016). Sociolinguistic aspects of the communicative purpose of CS in these settings are severely understudied. Most sociolinguistic works mainly focused on very limited data of a small number of language-pairs or authors (Sebba et al., 2011).

Rabinovich et al. (2019) developed a large-scale corpus of written CS data from Reddit posts containing various languages switched with English, but not including the German-English pair that we focus on here. They compared monolingual and code-switched posts, finding that there are topical and stylistic distinctions, as well as a difference in the proficiency of speakers. Shehadi and Wintner (2022) compiled an Arabizi corpus from Twitter and Reddit posts which contains CS between Arabic, English and French, and trained classifiers to identify switches.

Annotating CS Language annotation of bilingual data is not always trivial (Clyne, 2003; Alvarez-Mellado and Lignos, 2022), especially when borrowings and named entities are involved. Borrowing is a continuous process, with different stages, where a word is first introduced as a completely foreign sounding word and is then phonologically and morphologically adapted to the borrowing language, until it becomes a common word of the language's lexicon. Clear cuts on when a word is still to be considered a foreign word or already a common word of the language are hard to make. Due to the geographical and phylogenetic closeness of German and English and their common cultural and religious roots, it is often hard to determine whether a word is borrowed, adapted, foreign or native to the language. Alvarez-Mellado and Lignos (2022) added a "language" tag, BOR, to indicate recent borrowings, in addition to a tag for named entities. Shehadi and Wintner (2022) proposed the use of a *shared* category for words that can be used in both languages. We further refine their annotation scheme and the definition of the *shared* category. For a different approach to language ID annotation of multilingual texts, see Zhang et al. (2018).

Predicting CS Points CS is influenced by various sociolinguistic characteristics, such as topic and setting or the speakers involved in the conversation and their level of familiarity. It can serve several sociopragmatic functions such as direct quotation, emphasis, clarification, parenthetical comments, etc. Several linguistic features can be exploited for predicting CS points. Soto et al. (2018) showed that POS-tags, cognates, and entrainment of a word can trigger switches on the succeeding word, but not on the preceding word. This suggests that predicting CS points from the previous words alone is possible. Solorio and Liu (2008) predicted CS points using lexical and syntactic features, such as tokens, part-of-speech (POS) tags, and tree tags. Recent works show that the strong relationship between CS and cognate words, as proposed by Clyne (1967, 1980, 2003) in the *Triggering Hypothesis*, can be used to improve language models (Solorio and Liu, 2008; Soto and Hirschberg, 2019).

It is important to note that predicting CS is a difficult task because CS is a subjectively motivated process, subject to the speaker's preferences and background. Clearly, bilingual speakers do not *have* to code-switch, as by definition they can converse in any of their two languages. Understanding when and where they do code-switch is an ultimate goal of our research program, but undoubtedly some degree of arbitrariness is inherent to the phenomenon. Solorio and Liu (2008) therefore proposed the use of human judgments additionally to standard statistical evaluation measures.

3 Experimental Setup

Data *Reddit* is a large-scale social news and discussion platform, with several hundreds of thousands of sub-categories (*sub-reddits*) on different topics, and over 100 million new posts a year. There are many region-based sub-reddits, which attract large bilingual communities. The posts and comments are length-unlimited, and unlike in lab-settings the interlocutors produce language spontaneously, which allows us to analyze natural conversation flow.

German is one of the most widely-used languages in the world. With approximately 100 million native speakers, it is the most prevalent mother-tongue and, after English, the most widely understood language in Europe.[2] Since English is the world's main lingua franca, that non-native speakers across Europe use on a regular basis, German speakers are constantly exposed to English (through movies, music, the Internet, etc.) and CS exists in their daily life. It is thus worthwhile to investigate CS in German-English. However, to the best of our knowledge, no corpus or any work on written German-English CS is available, although a German-Turkish corpus of Twitter posts does exist (Çetinoğlu, 2016).

Most existing CS corpora and studies on CS use language pairs in communities where both languages are either co-official or co-native to the community (e.g., Hindi-English, where English is an official language and a lingua franca throughout India (Ganji et al., 2019); Maltese-English, where Malta as a former British colony maintained English as a lingua franca (Camilleri Grima, 2013); Turkish-German in the German-Turkish community (Çetinoğlu, 2016); etc.) Here, we address CS in a country that is officially monolingual (German) and neither has a major community of English-natives nor uses English as a lingua franca.

We investigate German-English CS using country-specific sub-reddits for German-speaking countries/regions, like `r/Germany` or `r/DE`. Since these sub-reddits contain discussions about region-based topics, we expect authors in these communities to be speakers of both German and English.

Statistical Classification We use (supervised) statistical classification in order to identify CS points. *Statistical classification* is the problem of identifying to which of at least two categories a given observation belongs. A classifier is trained on labeled examples, i.e., instances of which the classification is known a priori. Each instance is represented by a set of features, to which the classifier assigns weights during training. Given that the chosen features are actually relevant for the classification and given that the training set is large enough, the classifier can then predict the category of a new unseen instance. We use *Conditional Random Fields (CRF)* for the classification (Lafferty et al., 2001); CRF is a sequence to sequence classifier that uses its predictions on the previous instance in order to predict the label of the current instance.

Linguistic interpretation of the results can help us extend our knowledge of CS. By predicting CS points, we can learn about the specific features of language that trigger CS or discourage it. Such linguistic insights into the CS process can be used to build NLP systems that better cope with CS and multilingual discourse.

4 Shared Lexicon

The key to identifying CS points is precise annotation of the language ID of each token in the text. In multilingual texts, this problem is non-trivial (Alvarez-Mellado and Lignos, 2022). We now discuss some of its challenges. We provide examples from German-English, but most of the observations are valid for any language pair.

Many words are shared across the German and English lexicons. We differentiate between *inher-*

[2] https://en.wikipedia.org/wiki/List_of_European_languages_by_number_of_speakers

ited words, or *cognates*, which developed from words in an earlier stage of the language, and *borrowed words*, which are taken from or developed from words of another language. Borrowing is a continuous process with different stages: words are first introduced into the language as a completely foreign sounding word; they are gradually adapted to the phonological and morphological rules of the borrowing language until eventually they are considered to be common words of the language (Haspelmath, 2009; Grant, 2015; Campbell, 2020).

Loan words are fully integrated borrowings, i.e., fully adapted to the borrowing language in flexion, phonology and orthography. Borrowings without (or with minimal) adaptions are called *foreign words*. A *pseudo-borrowing* is a word created from elements of a borrowing language, but which does not exist in the donor language (e.g., *Handy–cellphone*) (Bussmann, 2008; Campbell, 2020).

The reasons that words are borrowed or shared across languages include geographical language contact, phylogenetic closeness, and common cultural background (Haspelmath, 2009; Grant, 2015; Campbell, 2020). It is not always easy to tell whether a word is borrowed, native, or a switch.

German and English are both Germanic languages, which share a common ancestral lexicon and many similar-looking words. Both languages were religiously and culturally influenced by Greek and Latin. Nevertheless, words can be marked by native morphology or orthography and some of these adaptions may intuitively look more German than others (e.g., *-ieren*, which is usually used on long integrated Latin words instead of *-en*). Further, not all of these words are actually shared. Many Latinate words entered English through Old French and by today either displaced their Germanic equivalents or shifted their meaning.

Many cultural terms are borrowed into other languages as full new concepts without translations. This is the case for modern inventions, but many everyday words entered the German lexicon centuries ago, and native speakers are often unaware of their foreign roots (e,g, *meschugge, Schal, cotton, assassin*).

Named entities are usually borrowed without translation, but they may take different forms: they can be shared completely or adapted orthographically, phonologically, and morphologically, sometimes with very distant looking forms, or even be taken from different etymological roots. Additionally, they can take derivational or inflectional morphemes of the borrowing language or even be used in compounds with native words.

Additional challenges are due to the fact that some very high-frequency words share spelling with a word of the other language (e.g., *was, die*) although they are totally unrelated. Furthermore, words can be composed of components of two different languages (e.g., *Pushnachrichten–push notifications*).

Using English entities like *Fifth Avenue*, or untranslatable terms like *hamburger*, in a German sentence cannot be considered a regular switch, since there is no actual German equivalent for such terms. Nevertheless, the use of these terms might activate the English lexicon and trigger a future switch. The extent of such triggering may be reduced for entities or terms that are adapted to German in orthography and morphology. These considerations are the motivating principles for our annotation scheme, which we now present.

5 Annotation Scheme

We introduce a novel, highly-detailed annotation scheme that reflects the observations of Section 4 above. We present the scheme in Section 5.1, and then propose a flattened version of it in Section 5.2. Crucially, while we define the schemes and exemplify annotated instances in terms of English and German, the schemes are applicable to any language pair.

5.1 Detailed Annotation Scheme

The annotation scheme is summarized in Table 1. We defined the following basic categories:

English (1): pure/regular English words.

German (2): pure/regular German words.

Overlap (3): words that belong to both mental lexicons, including shared and adapted named entities (3a), borrowed words (3), language-mixed words (3c), and words that overlap in the given context (3b).

Neutral (4): tokens that are language universal, including numbers (4b), emoticons (4c), interjections (4d), and words of other languages than English and German (4a).

In addition, we sometimes add the origin of the word to the tag, as a suffix `-E` for English, `-D` for German, and `-O` for other. We now explain how we assign labels to the problematic cases described in Section 4.

1	English						
2	German						
3	Overlaps						
3a	Named Entities	3c	Merge-Words			3b	Ambiguous Words
3a-E	English Origin	3c-C	Compounds				
3a-D	German Origin	3c-M	Morphology			3-E	Untranslatable English
3a-AE	Adapted to English	3c-EC	Entity Compounds			3-D	Untranslatable German
3a-AD	Adapted to German	3c-EM	Entity Morphology			3-O	Untranslatable Other
4	Neutral						
4a	Foreign	4b	Numbers	4d	Interjections	<url>	URL
		4b-E	English only	4d-E	English only	<punct>	Punctuation
		4b-D	German only	4d-D	German only	<EOS>	End of Sentence
		4c	Smiley	4e-E	English abbr.	<EOP>	End of Paragraph

Table 1: Detailed Annotation Scheme.

Named Entities are often borrowed and shared across languages. They can be adapted to the borrowing language on all linguistic levels. We introduce the following subcategories: *NE of German Origin* (3a-D), *NE of English Origin* (3a-E), *NE Adapted to German* (3a-AD), *NE Adapted to English* (3a-AE), *NE of Other origin* (3a). We differentiate among the following adaption cases:

Unadapted entities: entities that do not show any kind of adaption to the borrowing language or are native to the language (*Paris, Berlin*) are tagged according to their origin (3a-E for English, 3a-D for German, 3a for Other).

Translated entities: entities that are full translations (*United Kingdom–Vereiniges Königreich*) or stem from different etymologies (*Germany–Deutschland*) are considered regular words (1 / 2).

Orthographic adaptions: entities that have only spelling differences due to orthographical rules (English */c/* vs. German */k/*) or pronunciation are tagged equally to the original name.

Morphologic adaptions: major phonological and morphological adaptions in the entity itself affect the annotation in case they identify one of the languages (*Kalifor**nien**–California*, where *-ien* is a German location morpheme). Such entities are tagged as Adapted Entities (3a-AE for adapted to English, 3a-AD for adapted to German). Entities that show case or plural markings (*Münchens*, where *-s* is a genitive morpheme) are also Adapted Entities.

Lexical adaptions entities containing translated word parts (***New** Zealand–**Neu**seeland*) are considered Adapted Entities. Prefixes of other languages than German and English ('*anti-*') were not relevant for the annotation.

We consider the following to be NEs: geographical location as well as their demonyms, including religious and ethnic or tribal groups, as well as language communities, persons, companies and organizations, names of weekdays and months, units, and measures. The origin of an entity was identified by etymological roots, and phonetic, phonological and lexical features of the word.

Borrowings Often, words are borrowed as new concepts without any native translation. This is especially the case for modern inventions (*Smartphone*) and cultural terms related to food (*Döner*), religion (*Hijab*), festive activities and traditions (*Oktoberfest*) and philosophy/ideology (*LGBTQ, Feng Shui*), including academic and honorific titles (*Tsar, Shah*).

We differentiate among the following cases:

Established untranslatables: well-established cultural and technological terms without native translations are tagged as 3-E/D/O according to their origin.

Unestablished untranslatables: unestablished technical terms common only to certain groups (*Blockchain*) and terms that only recently entered the lexicon (*Lockdown*) are tagged as regular English words (1).

Translatables: Borrowings that have translation equivalents that could have been chosen instead (*Bildschirm–Display*), are tagged as regular words (1 / 2).

Integrated old loans: Words that originate from a third language, e.g., Old French, Latin, Greek, Arabic, or Persian, and have been fully integrated in the language (e.g., *cemetery, origin, assassin, coffee, cotton*), including Greek or Latin prefixes, are considered regular words (1 / 2).

Unintegrated old loans: Many unintegrated Latin words are found in abbreviations (e.g., *PS*) and were tagged as 4a. Those Latin abbreviations that are spelled out with English words and are not used in German (*e.g.*) are tagged as English (1).

Neologisms and pseudoborrowings: Borrowed Greek and Latin neologisms (*video*) are tagged as 3-O. Pseudo-borrowings (*Handy*) are tagged as 3-E.

Mixes Borrowed words can be compounded with native words (***Wohlstands**bubble*) or morphologically adapted to the borrowing language (***ge**sterotyped*). Such words contain intra-word switches. We differentiate:

Compounding: Compounds of an English and a German word are tagged 3c-C.

Flexion: English words with German flexion morphemes are tagged 3c-M.

The same is possible with borrowed NE:

Entity Compounds: Borrowed English entities (3a-E, 3a-AE) with German flexion (*google**n***) or vice versa are tagged as 3c-EM.

Inflected Entities: English Entities compounded with German words (*NRA-**mäßig***) are tagged as 3c-EC.

Compounds and flexion on NEs of the same or a third language are tagged as Adapted Entities.

Ambiguous Cases Words that cannot be identified as German or English in the given context due to overlapping spelling and meaning and switches occurring around them (*taxes with a **separate** Einnahmen-Überschussrechnung **plus** Umsatzsteuererklärung*) are tagged as 3b.

Language Markings on Neutral Items Neutral language-universal tokens like numbers and interjections can bear cues to the active language lexicon (*90s–90er, 10th–10ter, ähm–erm, achso*). Those tokens that are specific to one lexicon are tagged as *English/German use only* (4b-E/D, 4d-E/D), those used in both languages as 4b, 4d. English language abbreviations that are used as interjections across languages (*lol, rofl*) are tagged 4e-E.

5.2 Collapsed Annotation Scheme

These categories were over-refined, and some of them had relatively few occurrences in our corpus. We therefore defined a collapsed version of the scheme, as shown in Table 2.

English (E): all English words (1), English numbers and interjections (4b-E, 4d-E).

German (D): all German words (2), German numbers and interjections (4b-D, 4d-D).

Mix (M): words containing properties of both languages, including intra-word switches (3c-(E)M/(E)C).

Shared English (SE): all English words that are used in both languages (3a-(A)E, 3-E, 4e-E).

Shared German (SD): all German words that are used in both languages (3a-(A)D, 3-D).

Shared Other (SO): all words of other origin that are used in both languages (3a, 3-O, 4a), including shared interjections (4d) and other overlaps (3, 3b).

Other (O): all tokens that are language independent, including neutral number constructions, emoticons, and punctuation (4b, 4c, <punct>, <url>, 4).

E	English	1, 4b-E, 4d-E
D	German	2, 4b-D, 4d-D
M	Mix	3c, 3c-C, 3c-M, 3c-EC, 3c-EM
SE	Shared English	3a-E, 3a-AE, 3-E, 4e-E
SD	Shared German	3a-D, 3a-AD, 3-D
SO	Shared Other	3, 3a, 3b, 3-O, 4a, 4d
O	Other	4, 4b, 4c, <punct>, <url>

Table 2: Collapsed Annotation Scheme.

6 Corpus Creation

We used a modified version of the method used by Rabinovich et al. (2019) to collect and extract our data. We downloaded approximately 17 million comments from the German-language sub-reddits *r/DE, r/Deutschland, r/Germany, r/Berlin* using the Pushshift Reddit API. We extracted 10,000 comments that potentially contained CS using the Polyglot language detector. We[3] annotated 950 of the extracted comments manually following the detailed scheme of Section 5. These contained over 75,000 tokens in 4,200 sentences, of which 1,250 contained intra-sentential switches. We then generated a version with the collapsed annotation scheme.

We then downloaded another set of 25.5 million comments from German-language sub-reddits, including also sub-reddits dedicated to cities and regions in Austria and Switzerland, as well as a few general topics. Of those, 21,500 comments were extracted as potentially including switches. These comments, together with the remainder of the initially downloaded comments, were used to create a larger automatically annotated corpus. The data for the automatic annotation thus consists of 31,500

[3]All annotation was done by the first author. We therefore cannot report inter-annotator agreement.

comments containing 230,000 sentences with over 5 million tokens.

To identify code-switches in the automatically-tagged corpus we use two different criteria. The *strict* definition requires a sentence to contain at least one word annotated "pure English" (1), and at least one tagged as "pure German" (2). The *relaxed* definition only requires a token tagged as English-origin, excluding named entities (1,4b-E,4d-E,3-E) and a token similarly annotated as German-origin, excluding NEs (2,4b-D,4d-D,3-D), or a token tagged as Merge-Word, excluding NE-Merger (3c-M,3c-C). Table 3 lists data on the manually-tagged and automatically-tagged corpora. It reports the total number of sentences in each corpus, the number of sentences containing CS (both strict and relaxed), and the number of posts containing CS (for posts, the strict and relaxed numbers are almost identical).

We now provide some observations on the manually-annotated portion of the corpus.

Amount of Switches The portion of bilingual posts was very small, only 0.62‰ of the downloaded comments. A considerable amount of the bilingual raw data contained the second language only as citations or as titles (of books, movies, songs, etc.)

Types of Switches Many of the extracted posts contained switches on sentence boundaries. Intra-sentential switches were often *insertional*, i.e., comprised of only a single switched word or construct of a few switched words in an otherwise monolingual sentence. Intra-word switches do exist, especially as German flexion and derivation on English words and entities.

Topics A few topical peculiarities were striking: computer and gaming related terms as well as social media related terms were often switched to English in otherwise German comments; terms related to politics, authorities, law or regulations were often switched to German in otherwise English comments.

7 Identifying Switches

In order to identify switches in an unseen utterance, we need to identify the language ID tag of the words in the sentence. We now describe a classifier that establishes this task.

7.1 Word-Level Classification

We used CRF to train a sequence to sequence classifier, using various features we list below. We opted for more traditional, statistical classification rather than neural classification both because we were interested in interpreting the features and because Shehadi and Wintner (2022), on a very similar task, report that both methods yielded almost identical accuracy.

Orthography: the word in lower case; whether the word is in upper, lower or all-upper case; whether the word is is an emoji or emoticon; whether it contains digits, punctuation, or special German letters (*ü, ö, ä, ß*).

N-Grams: whether the word contains one of the most frequent English or German letter bi- and trigrams; 400 most frequent n-grams in the corpus as separate features.

Morphology: whether the word contains German or English derivational or inflexional affixes, including common verbal prefixes and noun and adjective suffixes.

Function Words: whether the word is included in German or English lists of function words.[4]

Frequency: whether the word is in the 207 most frequent German words, or the 5050 most frequent English words, taken from the one billion word Corpus of Contemporary American English.

Lexical Components: whether the word contains lexical parts that are regularly used in German or English named entities, e.g., *weiler, burg, neu; borough, dale, port.*

Word Lists: several word lists for named entities and cultural terms, e.g., the names of the biggest German cities or companies.

We used 10-fold cross-validation for evaluation. The evaluation results are listed in Table 4, reflecting an overall accuracy of 0.965.

7.2 Sentence-Level Classification

Following Shehadi and Wintner (2022) we combined the results of the word level annotation to form bit-vector annotations for sentences. Each sentence is thus associated with a single bit-vector indicating which of the language category tags are present in it. We then trained a classifier to predict the full bit-vectors at the sentence level. The results, reflecting the accuracy of the sentence-level classifier on each category, are presented in Table 5.

[4]We compiled these lists and will make them available.

Corpus	Sentences	Strict CS	Relaxed CS	Posts with CS
Manually-tagged	4,200	1,250	1,400	950
Automatically-tagged	228,800	72,250	74,000	30,150
Total	233,000	73,500	75,400	31,100

Table 3: Statistics of the corpora: the total number of sentences in each corpus, the number of sentences containing CS (both strict and relaxed), and the number of posts containing CS.

Tag	Prc	Rcl	F1	Support
English	0.97	0.98	0.98	29918
German	0.96	0.98	0.97	29730
Mix	0.50	0.19	0.28	246
Shared English	0.82	0.55	0.66	699
Shared German	0.78	0.54	0.64	807
Shared Other	0.75	0.50	0.60	1108
Other	0.99	0.98	0.99	12505
Micro Avg	0.96	0.96	0.96	75013
Macro Avg	0.82	0.68	0.74	75013
Weighted Avg	0.96	0.96	0.96	75013

Table 4: Results: Word-Level Classification.

The overall accuracy of predicting the full bit-array of a sentence correctly is 0.764.

Tag	Acc	Prc	Rcl	F1
English	0.95	0.96	0.96	0.96
German	0.96	0.97	0.98	0.97
Mix	0.96	0.59	0.26	0.36
Shared English	0.95	0.86	0.68	0.76
Shared German	0.95	0.81	0.65	0.72
Shared Other	0.92	0.83	0.61	0.70
Other	1.00	1.00	1.00	1.00

Table 5: Results: Sentence-Level Classification.

7.3 Analysis

Mix Many of the words classified as Mix were seen in the training corpus. Some of the misclassifications of `3c-M` and `3c-C` on full-German words (*ge**back**en–baked*, *Krisenter**mine**–crisis dates*) indicate that the classifier actually learns to classify words as Mixed that could be decomposed to parts reflecting both languages.

Untranslatables Identifying untranslatables works relatively well even with only few training instances, probably due to the word lists. Most of the words tagged as `3-E/D/O` were actually contained in the word lists.

NEs Most of the words classified as Adapted Entities contain one of the derivation suffixes (*-ish*, *-ian*, etc.) Many words classified as `3a-D` contained lexical features of the Lexical Components lists, this was not observed for `3a-E`. This might be due to the training corpus containing several German person and town names, but not many English ones.

Ambiguous The classification of ambiguous words is rather poor, probably because identifying whether the word can be disambiguated in the context is a very subjective feature and only very few examples were seen in training. It mainly classifies some of the instances of the words seen as `3b` in training as `3b`.

8 Conclusion

We presented a corpus of German-English code-switched utterances from user generated social media content, which contains precise language annotation indicating code switches. Our corpus is partly hand-annotated and partly automatically annotated. We addressed some challenges in annotation of multilingual data by introducing various types of shared and mixed categories. We trained classifiers to predict our word-level annotation and switch-points. First experimental results from the prediction of switch-points indicate that properties of shared and mixed words are relevant factors for CS. This encourages us to use our corpus as a basis for further sociolinguistic research on spontaneous written CS, specifically for studying the use and effects of Shared and Mixed words on switches in German-English and how these compare to other language pairs. Such work is currently underway.

Ethical considerations

This research was approved by the University of Haifa IRB. We collected data from a social media outlet, Reddit, in compliance with its terms of service. For anonymity, we systematically replaced all user IDs by unique IDs; we do not have, and therefore do not distribute, any personal information of the authors. With this additional level of anonymization, we anticipate very minimal risk of abuse or dual use of the data.

Limitations

Like any other dataset, the corpus we report on here is not representative. In particular, it probably includes German as used mainly by users highly fluent in English. It is very likely unbalanced in terms of any demographic aspect of its authors. Clearly, the automatic annotation of language IDs is not perfect, and may introduce noise, especially on the smaller and more subjective categories (e.g., 3b, M). Further, when extracting the comments for the final corpus, very short comments were not included and comments with only a single switch or borrowed word might have been skipped, due to the rather low sensitivity of the language detector. Use of this corpus for linguistic research must therefore be done with caution. Nevertheless, we trust that the sheer size of the dataset would make it instrumental for research on code-switching in general and in German-English in particular.

Acknowledgements

We are grateful to Yuli Zeira and Safaa Shedahi for great ideas and fruitful discussions, and to the anonymous reviewers for their constructive comments. This work was supported in part by grant No. 2019785 from the United States-Israel Binational Science Foundation (BSF), and by grants No. 2007960, 2007656, 2125201 and 2040926 from the United States National Science Foundation (NSF).

References

Elena Alvarez-Mellado and Constantine Lignos. 2022. Borrowing or codeswitching? Annotating for finer-grained distinctions in language mixing. In *Proceedings of the Thirteenth Language Resources and Evaluation Conference*, pages 3195–3201, Marseille, France. European Language Resources Association.

Hadumod Bussmann. 2008. *Lexikon der Sprachwissenschaft*. Alfred Kröner Verlag, Stuttgart.

Antoinette Camilleri Grima. 2013. Challenging Code-Switching in Malta. *Revue Française de Linguistique Appliquée*, 18:45–61.

Lyle Campbell. 2020. *Historical Linguistics - An Introduction*, fourth edition. Edinburgh University Press.

Özlem Çetinoğlu. 2016. A Turkish-German code-switching corpus. In *Proceedings of the Tenth International Conference on Language Resources and Evaluation (LREC'16)*, pages 4215–4220, Portorož, Slovenia. European Language Resources Association (ELRA).

Özlem Çetinoğlu, Sarah Schulz, and Ngoc Thang Vu. 2016. Challenges of computational processing of code-switching. In *Proceedings of the Second Workshop on Computational Approaches to Code Switching*, pages 1–11, Austin, Texas. Association for Computational Linguistics.

Brian Hok-Shing Chan. 2009. English in Hong Kong Cantopop: Language choice, code-switching and genre. *World Englishes*, 28(1):107–129.

Michael G. Clyne. 1967. *Transference and triggering: Observations on the language assimilation of post-war German-speaking migrants in Australia*. Martinus Nijhoff, The Hague, Netherlands.

Michael G. Clyne. 1980. Triggering and language processing. *Canadian Journal of Psychology*, 34(34):400–406.

Michael G. Clyne. 2003. *Dynamics of language contact*. Cambridge University Press, Cambridge, UK.

Sreeram Ganji, Kunal Dhawan, and Rohit Sinha. 2019. IITG-HingCoS Corpus: A Hinglish Code-Switching Database for Automatic Speech Recognition. *Speech Communication*, 110:76–89.

Penelope Gardner-Chloros. 2009. *Code-Switching*. Cambridge University Press.

Penelope Gardner-Chloros and Daniel Weston. 2015. Code-Switching and Multilingualism in Literature. *Language and Literature*, 24(3):182–193.

Anthony P. Grant. 2015. Lexical Borrowing. In *The Oxford Handbook of the Word*. Oxford University Press.

François Grosjean. 2010. *Bilingual: Life and Reality*. Harvard University Press.

François Grosjean and Ping Li. 2013. *The Psycholinguistics of Bilingualism*. Wiley-Blackwell.

Richard Jackson Harris and Elizabeth Marie McGhee Nelson. 1992. Bilingualism: Not the exception any more. In Richard Jackson Harris, editor, *Cognitive Processing in Bilinguals*, volume 83 of *Advances in Psychology*, pages 3–14. North-Holland.

Martin Haspelmath. 2009. Lexical Borrowing: Concepts and issues. In *Loanwords in the World's Languages: A Comparative Handbook*. De Gruyter Mouton.

Aravind K. Joshi. 1982. Processing of sentences with intra-sentential code-switching. In *Coling 1982: Proceedings of the Ninth International Conference on Computational Linguistics*.

Gerrit J. Kootstra, Janet G. van Hell, and Ton Dijkstra. 2012. Priming of Code-Switches in Sentences: The Role of Lexical Repetition, Cognates, and Language Proficiency. *Bilingualism: Language and Cognition*, 15(4):797–819.

John D. Lafferty, Andrew McCallum, and Fernando C. N. Pereira. 2001. Conditional random fields: Probabilistic models for segmenting and labeling sequence data. In *Proceedings of the Eighteenth International Conference on Machine Learning*, ICML '01, pages 282–289, San Francisco, CA, USA. Morgan Kaufmann Publishers Inc.

Shana Poplack. 1980. Sometimes I'll start a sentence in spanish Y TERMINO EN ESPAÑOL: toward a typology of code-switching 1. *Linguistics*, 18(7-8):581–618.

Nanda Poulisse. 1990. *The Use of Compensatory Strategies by Dutch Learners of English*, volume 8 of *Studies on Language Acquisition*. Cambridge University Press.

Ella Rabinovich, Masih Sultani, and Suzanne Stevenson. 2019. CodeSwitch-Reddit: Exploration of written multilingual discourse in online discussion forums. In *Proceedings of the 5th Workshop on Noisy User-generated Text (W-NUT 2019)*, page 446, Hong Kong, China. Association for Computational Linguistics.

Mark Sebba, Shahrzad Mahootian, and Carla Jonsson. 2011. *Language Mixing and Code-Switching in Writing: Approaches to Mixed-Language Written Discourse*. Routledge.

Safaa Shehadi and Shuly Wintner. 2022. Identifying code-switching in Arabizi. In *Proceedings of the The Seventh Arabic Natural Language Processing Workshop (WANLP)*, pages 194–204, Abu Dhabi, United Arab Emirates (Hybrid). Association for Computational Linguistics.

Thamar Solorio and Yang Liu. 2008. Learning to predict code-switching points. In *Proceedings of the 2008 Conference on Empirical Methods in Natural Language Processing*, pages 973–981, Honolulu, Hawaii. Association for Computational Linguistics.

Victor Soto, Nishmar Cestero, and Julia Hirschberg. 2018. The Role of Cognate Words, POS Tags and Entrainment in Code-Switching. In *Proceedings of Interspeech 2018*, pages 1938–1942, Hyderabad, India. ISCA.

Victor Soto and Julia Hirschberg. 2019. Improving Code-Switched Language Modeling Performance Using Cognate Features. In *Proceedings of Interspeech 2019*, pages 3725–3729, Graz, Austria.

Yuan Zhang, Jason Riesa, Daniel Gillick, Anton Bakalov, Jason Baldridge, and David Weiss. 2018. A fast, compact, accurate model for language identification of codemixed text. In *Proceedings of the 2018 Conference on Empirical Methods in Natural Language Processing*, pages 328–337, Brussels, Belgium. Association for Computational Linguistics.

Trimming Phonetic Alignments Improves the Inference of Sound Correspondence Patterns from Multilingual Wordlists

Frederic Blum
DLCE
MPI-EVA
Leipzig, Germany
frederic_blum@eva.mpg.de

Johann-Mattis List
Chair of Multil. Comput. Linguistics / DLCE
University of Passau / MPI-EVA
Passau / Leipzig, Germany
mattis.list@uni-passau.de

Abstract

Sound correspondence patterns form the basis of cognate detection and phonological reconstruction in historical language comparison. Methods for the automatic inference of correspondence patterns from phonetically aligned cognate sets have been proposed, but their application to multilingual wordlists requires extremely well annotated datasets. Since annotation is tedious and time consuming, it would be desirable to find ways to improve aligned cognate data automatically. Taking inspiration from trimming techniques in evolutionary biology, which improve alignments by excluding problematic sites, we propose a workflow that trims phonetic alignments in comparative linguistics prior to the inference of correspondence patterns. Testing these techniques on a large standardized collection of ten datasets with expert annotations from different language families, we find that the best trimming technique substantially improves the overall consistency of the alignments. The results show a clear increase in the proportion of frequent correspondence patterns and words exhibiting regular cognate relations.

1 Introduction

With the introduction of automated methods for the inference of correspondence patterns from multilingual wordlists (List, 2019), computational historical linguistics has acquired a new technique with multiple applications in the field. Correspondence patterns have been used to identify problematic cognate judgments in individual datasets (List, 2019) or to assess their general characteristics (Wu et al., 2020), they have been used as the basis to predict cognate reflexes (Bodt and List, 2022; List et al., 2022c; Tresoldi et al., 2022) or to reconstruct protoforms (List et al., 2022b). They have also shown to be useful to compare different cognate judgments with respect to the overall regularity they introduce in a multilingual dataset (Greenhill et al., 2023).

While machine-readable correspondence patterns have already shown to be useful for various tasks in historical linguistics, their basic properties have so far not yet been thoroughly investigated. Thus, although we can easily see that correspondence patterns show long-tail distributions with respect to the number of alignment sites that individual patterns reflect in multilingual datasets, no closer investigations of these patterns have been carried out so far. Here, historical linguistics can learn from evolutionary biology, where specific characteristics of alignments of DNA or protein sequences have been investigated for several decades now. Scholars have also looked into the characteristics of those alignment sites that turn out to be problematic when it comes to phylogenetic reconstruction and similar secondary tasks (Talavera and Castresana, 2007; Dress et al., 2008). In order to handle these "irregular" sites, biologists have proposed methods to *trim* alignments by removing sites that contradict more general evolutionary tendencies. This allows scholars to reduce the amount of artifacts in the data and retrieve more accurate information about the evolutionary processes behind the alignments.

In computational historical linguistics, *trimming* of alignments has so far been ignored. In classical historical language comparison, however, the practice of ignoring specific sites in the alignment of cognate words has been practiced for a long time. When arguing for particular sound changes or correspondence patterns, scholars routinely consider only the supposed *root* of a cognate set (Trask, 2000, 290), ignoring inflectional and derivational markers or irregular parts of individual cognate reflexes. While this is a common procedure for the comparative method, it is seldom made explicit. One of the few cases where this process *is* made explicit is offered by Payne (1991). Here, the author provides an alignment matrix where all the non-cognate material is set into brackets, distin-

Proceedings of the 5th Workshop on Research in Computational Linguistic Typology and Multilingual NLP (SIGTYP 2023), pages 52–64
May 6, 2023 ©2023 Association for Computational Linguistics

guishing them from the true alignment sites. This step is accompanied by a detailed discussion of the morphemic elements and its implication for reconstructing the proto-forms, a step that is rarely put into such detail. The importance of this practice is also reflected in tools that allow for the manual correction of alignments, like EDICTOR (List, 2017a) and RefLex (Segerer and Flavier, 2015) which offer options to flag alignment sites as problematic (or important). Specifically the trimming facility of the EDICTOR tool has also been used to increase the transparency of cognate sets in studies devoted to phylogenetic reconstruction (Sagart et al., 2019; Cayón and Chacon, 2022).

Given the highly skewed distributions of alignment sites over correspondence patterns in computational comparative linguistics and the practice of human annotators to regularly ignore certain parts of phonetically aligned cognate sets in historical linguistics, it would be beneficial to find automated ways to *trim* phonetic alignments in multilingual wordlists. Trimmed alignments could either form the basis of a more extensive annotation of phonetic alignments in a computer-assisted setting (List, 2017b), or they could serve as the basis of extensive cross-linguistic, typologically oriented studies devoted to the regularity of sound change and sound correspondence patterns. For example, correspondence patterns have already been used in typological studies investigating the history of pronoun systems in South America (Rojas-Berscia and Roberts, 2020), or for studies with simulated data that use phonetic alignments to construct artificial cognate sets (Wichmann and Rama, 2021).

In the following, we will provide a first framework for the trimming of phonetic alignments and test it on ten datasets from typologically diverse language families. Our experiments show that trimming increases the overall regularity of the correspondence patterns – even when using very rudimentary strategies– and thus shrinks the long tail of their distributions over alignment sites. The closer inspection of individual trimmed alignments, however, also shows that our methods still have a lot of room for improvement. We conclude by pointing to various techniques that could enhance the trimming of phonetic alignments in the future.

2 Background

Sound correspondences are the core of the comparative method. They form the basis for proving genetic relationship between languages, for establishing the internal classification of language families, as well as for the reconstruction of proto-languages. Sets of sound correspondences are commonly analyzed as *correspondence patterns*. A crucial component of correspondence patterns in contrast to sound correspondences is that the correspondence set is not defined on the basis of language pairs, but rather as a pattern shared between several languages (List, 2019, 141). In other words, a correspondence pattern is defined as the set of sounds in any number of daughter languages that derive from the same phoneme of the ancestral language in a specific environment (Hoenigswald, 1960; Anttila, 1972).

In order to qualify as a *pattern*, sound correspondences must be backed by many examples. Examples are drawn from concrete cognate sets that need to be phonetically aligned in order to reveal which sounds correspond with each other. In order to constitute a valid pattern that would be accepted as a *regular* or *systematic* sound correspondence (Trask, 2000, 336f), a considerably large amount of examples backing a certain pattern must be assembled from the data. This step is necessary to avoid chance similarities resulting from erroneous cognate judgments or undetected scarce borrowings. While the minimum number of examples is not universally agreed upon, most scholars tend to accept two or three examples as sufficient to consider a pattern as regular.

Correspondence patterns are typically represented with the help of a matrix, in which the rows correspond to individual languages and the columns correspond to patterns, with cell values indicating the sounds (the *reflexes*) of individual language varieties in individual patterns (Clackson, 2007, 307). Correspondence patterns are traditionally inferred by manually inspecting phonetic alignments of cognate sets, trying to identify individual columns (*alignment sites*) in the alignments that are compatible with each other (Anttila, 1972; List, 2019). Figure 1 illustrates this process with phonetic alignments of fictitious words from fictitious languages. In order to reconstruct the ancestral form underlying a cognate set, it is common to ignore certain sites in the alignment that are considered as difficult to align. Problems of alignability (Schweikhard and List, 2020, 10) usually result from the fact that words in a cognate set are not entirely, but only partially cognate. This can be

	I		II			II		I	
Language A	t	a	h	e		h	i	t	u
Language B	tʰ	a	x	e		x	u	tʰ	i
Language C	t	a	x	e		x	u	t	i
Language D	ts	a	x	e		x	u	ts	i

Figure 1: Corresponding alignment sites in a set of four fictitious languages.

Pacaraos	w	a	ɲ	u	+	k	u
Napo	w	a	ɲ	u	+	n	a
Pastaza	w	a	ɲ	u	+	n	a
Ayacucho	w	a	ɲ	u			
Jauja	w	a	ɲ	u			
Lamas	w	a	ɲ	u			

Figure 2: Trimming morphemes in Quechua. The root is combined with different morphemes in some varieties.

due to processes of word formation or inflection in individual language varieties (Wu and List, 2023), as illustrated in Figure 2 with data from Quechua (Blum et al., forthcoming).

3 Materials and Methods

3.1 Materials

We use ten freely available datasets from typologically diverse language families, taken from the Lexibank collection (List et al., 2022a). This collection contains datasets that were (retro)standardized following the recommendations of the Cross-Linguistic Data Formats initiative (CLDF, https://cldf.clld.org, Forkel et al. 2018). One core aspect of CLDF is to make active use of *reference catalogs* like Glottolog (https://glottolog.org, Hammarström et al. 2022) and Concepticon (https://concepticon.clld.org), List et al. 2023). Reference catalogs in this context are metadata collections that provide extensive information on very general linguistic constructs, such as languages, concepts, or speech sounds. By linking the languages in a given dataset to Glottolog, by providing Glottocodes for individual language varieties, one guarantees the comparability of the language varieties with other datasets which have also been linked to Glottolog. By mapping concepts in multilingual wordlists to Concepticon, one guarantees the comparability of the concepts with other datasets that have also been linked to Concepticon. Apart from Glottolog and Concepticon, many datasets from the Lexibank collection offer standardized phonetic transcriptions following the Cross-Linguistic Transcription Systems reference catalog (CLTS, https://clts.clld.org, List et al. 2021, see Anderson et al. 2018). In this reference catalog, more than 8000 different speech sounds are defined and can be distinguished with the help of distinctive features. At the same time, new, so far unseen sounds can be derived using a specific parsing algorithm underlying the PyCLTS software package (List et al., 2020). As a result, the Lexibank collection of multilingual wordlists offers a large number of multilingual datasets that have been standardized with respect to languages, concepts, and transcriptions.

Apart from offering standardized phonetic transcriptions, all datasets also offer cognate judgments provided by experts. Alignments were computed automatically, using the SCA method for multiple phonetic alignments (List, 2012, 2014) in its default settings. Of the ten datasets, two (CROSSANDEAN and WALWORTHPOLYNESIAN) were reduced to 20 language varieties in order to have datasets of comparable sizes. While the datasets differ with respect to the number of language varieties and time depth of the families in question, they are all large enough to allow us to infer a substantial amount of frequent sound correspondence patterns.

3.2 Methods

3.2.1 Trimming Phonetic Alignments

The main purpose of trimming is to remove problematic alignments and increase the potential of retrieving relevant information from the remaining sites. In biology, trimming of sequence alignments is primarily performed to improve phylogenetic inference. The goal is to reduce the noise in the data in order to get a clearer picture of the actual phylogenetic information contained in DNA sequences (Talavera and Castresana, 2007). Despite the removal of some data, the accuracy of phylogenetic trees inferred from the data often improves. To assure that enough relevant information is maintained after trimming, trimmed alignments need to have some minimal length. Several tools for automated trimming have been developed in evolutionary biology. Some of them select the most reliable columns and remove sparse alignments that consists mainly of gaps (Capella-Gutiérrez et al., 2009), while other tools focus on entropy values and evaluate whether a site is expected or not (Criscuolo and Gribaldo, 2010). The most ambiguous and divergent sites

Data set	Lang.	Concepts	Cog.-Sets	Words	Source
CONSTENLACHIBCHAN	25	106	213	1216	Constenla Umaña (2005)
CROSSANDEAN	20	150	223	2789	Blum et al. (forthcoming)
DRAVLEX	20	100	179	1341	Kolipakam et al. (2018)
FELEKESEMITIC	21	150	271	2622	Feleke (2021)
HATTORIJAPONIC	10	197	235	1710	Hattori (1973)
HOUCHINESE	15	139	228	1816	Hóu (2004)
LEEKOREANIC	15	206	233	2131	Lee (2015)
ROBINSONAP	13	216	253	1424	Robinson and Holton (2012)
WALWORTHPOLYNESIAN	20	205	383	3637	Walworth (2018)
ZHIVLOVOBUGRIAN	21	110	182	1974	Zhivlov (2011)

Table 1: Number of languages, concepts, non-singleton cognate sets and total entries across the different datasets

are removed in this approach, arguing that they might result from erroneous judgements of homology (Steenwyk et al., 2020).

In contrast to the trimming of DNA sequences in biology, the main goal of trimming alignments in linguistics is not to infer phylogenetic trees, but to make the alignments more useful for secondary use in computing sound correspondences and helping phonological reconstruction. Each cognate set is reduced to a 'core' alignment, which can then later be reconstructed as approximating the *root* in the proto-language of the respective cognate set.

Our initial trimming strategies focus on the presence of gaps in the alignment sites. For this purpose, we compute the proportion of gaps in each site and evaluate whether this proportion is above or below a certain threshold (*gap threshold*). All sites which are above the threshold are identified as *candidates* for trimming. The default value for the gap threshold in our implementation is 0.5, which means that we *could* trim all sites in which the majority of sounds is a gap.

However, since a naive trimming of all alignment sites exceeding our gap threshold might well lead to the trimming of all sites in an alignment and therefore discard the corresponding cognate set in its entirety, we define a minimal skeleton of alignment sites that should not be touched by the trimming procedure (similar to the minimal sequence length in DNA trimming). This skeleton is based on consonant-vowel profiles of the alignments and defaults to CV and VC. The preference of minimal CV/VC skeletons for aligned cognate sets is justified by linguistic practice (Tian et al., 2022) and can be adjusted to account for extended root structures, such as, for example, CVC . This means that only those results of the trimming procedure are accepted that leave a core alignment of at least one consonant and one vowel, ignoring their particular order. In order to make sure that the core is preserved, we first define an ordered list of candidate sites that could be removed and then start removing them site after site, checking after each removal whether the core skeleton has been left untouched. When only the core skeleton is left, trimming is stopped.

Based on this general procedure of trimming until a core skeleton defined by the user is reached, we test two detailed strategies for trimming. In the first strategy, we only trim *consecutive* gaps occurring in the beginning or the end of the alignment, a strategy that is also used in the context of sequence comparison in biology (Raghava and Barton, 2006). This *core-oriented* strategy allows us to drop spurious prefixes and suffixes occurring in some language varieties in individual alignments. In order to create our ordered list of candidate sites, we start from the right-most sites in our alignment and combine them with the left-most sites. In the second strategy, we trim all sites where the frequency of gaps exceeds our threshold, regardless of their position. This *gap-oriented* strategy would also trim gapped sites occurring in the beginning and the end of an alignment, but may additionally trim gapped sites regardless of their position. In order to create our ordered list of candidate sites, we sort all sites exceeding the gap threshold by the proportion of gaps in reversed order. Figure 3 illustrates the calculation of gap profiles and the trimming using the two strategies defined here for a toy example of fictitious words from fictitious languages.

Language	Core-oriented							Gap-oriented						
Language A	s	-	t	e	r	b	-	s	-	t	e	r	b	-
Language B	m	e	t^h	e	-	-	-	m	e	t^h	e	-	-	-
Language C	-	a	t	e	-	b	u	-	a	t	e	-	b	u
Language D	-	-	t	e	-	b	-	-	-	t	e	-	b	-
Gap proportion	0.5	0.5	0.0	0.0	0.75	0.25	0.75	0.5	0.5	0.0	0.0	0.75	0.25	0.75

Figure 3: Artificial example for the computation of gap profiles followed by trimming using the *core-oriented* (left) and the *gap-oriented* strategy (right).

3.2.2 Evaluating Cognate Set Regularity

With the method by List (2019), correspondence patterns can be inferred from phonetically aligned cognate sets with the help of an iterative partitioning strategy which clusters the individual alignment sites. The resulting patterns are reflected by varying amounts of alignment sites, which we can use to compute certain statistics, building on earlier work by Greenhill et al. (2023). In a first step, we can compare the number of frequently recurring patterns with the number of patterns that do not recur frequently in the data. Based on this comparison, we can compute the proportion of alignment sites that are assigned to a frequently recurring pattern. This comes close to the notion of "regular" correspondence patterns in traditional historical linguistics, with the difference that we need to choose a concrete threshold by which a pattern recurs in our data (the *pattern threshold*, which is set to 3 by default). By defining frequently recurring patterns as *regular*, we can now assess for individual cognate sets how many of the alignment sites reflect regular patterns and how many reflect irregular patterns. This allows us to distinguish *regular* from *irregular* cognate sets by calculating the proportion of alignment sites reflecting regular correspondence patterns and setting some threshold beyond which we consider a cognate set as irregular (the *cognate threshold*, which is set to 0.75 by default). Having identified regular cognates in a given wordlist, we can contrast them with irregular cognates and calculate the proportion of *reflexes* (words in individual cognate sets) that appear in regular cognate sets. Given that this proportion gives us an idea of how many of the words in our data that appear in cognate relations can be assigned to some regular cognate set via regular sound correspondences, we interpret this proportion of *regular words* as the *overall regularity* of the dataset.

Selecting meaningful thresholds is not an easy task, specifically when calculations depend on multiple parameters as in our case. We decided to take a conservative pattern threshold of 3, which means that a pattern to be considered as regular must at least recur across three alignment sites in a given dataset. For the regularity of cognate sets, we decided for an even more conservative threshold of 0.75, which means that three quarters of the alignment sites in a given cognate set must reflect correspondence patterns that recur three or more times in the data.

3.2.3 Evaluating Trimmed Alignments

We make use of this interpretation of frequency as regularity in order to evaluate the success of our trimming operations. In order to check to which degree the trimming of phonetic alignments leads to an increase of overall regularity, modeled by taking the frequency of correspondence patterns into account, we compare three different constellations, namely (a) no trimming, (b) core-oriented trimming, and (c) gap-oriented trimming. We compare the three methods by computing the *proportion of regular correspondence patterns* and the *proportion of regular words* in all datasets, as outlined in the previous section. A successful trimming strategy should lead to an increase of both measures.

For further evaluation, we implement a random model that compares our targeted trimming strategies with a random strategy for trimming. To account for this, we randomly delete the same amount of alignment sites from each alignment as we did with the gap- or core-oriented strategies, while preserving the ratio of consonantal and vocalic alignment sites. With this step we assure that the resulting randomly trimmed alignment preserves the minimal CV/VC skeleton. For each dataset and trimming-strategy, we run the random model 100 times and analyze how many times the random model surpasses the results of the targeted model with respect to the proportion of regular words. This error analysis helps us to assess whether a trimming strategy systematically outperforms the random model.

3.2.4 Implementation

The new methods for the trimming of phonetic alignments are implemented in Python in the form of a plugin to the LingRex software package (https://pypi.org/project/lingrex, List and Forkel 2022, Version 1.3.0). LingRex itself extends LingPy (https://pypi.org/project/lingpy, List and Forkel 2021, Version 2.6.9) – which we use for phonetic alignments – by providing the method for correspondence pattern detection which we use to evaluate the consequences of trimming our alignments. For the handling of the cross-linguistic datasets provided in CLDF, CLDFBench (https://pypi.org/project/cldfbench, Forkel and List 2020, Version 1.13.0) is used with the PyLexibank plugin (https://pypi.org/project/pylexibank, Forkel et al. 2021, Version 3.4.0).

4 Results

4.1 General Results

The two trimming strategies were applied to all datasets in our sample and regularity scores for the proportion of regular sound correspondence patterns and the proportion of regular words were computed. Given that the trimming strategies might reduce alignments only to a core skeleton (CV/VC), only those cognate sets whose alignments consist of at least one vocalic and one consonantal site were considered in this comparison. Phonetic alignments were carried out with the help of the default settings of the SCA method (List, 2012). Correspondence patterns were computed with the help of the method by List (2019). The results of our general comparison of different trimming strategies are presented in Table 2. For both the proportion of regular correspondence patterns and the proportion of regular words, the best result for each dataset is highlighted in the table. Without exception, the gap-oriented trimming strategy yields the highest proportion of regular correspondence patterns and the highest proportion of regular words. The core-orientied trimming strategy outperforms the baseline without trimming in some cases, but not consistently, often only leading to minimal improvements over the baseline. Random tests confirm this trend for both trimming strategies.

The reduction of alignment sites generally leads to a reduced number of correspondence patterns inferred from the individual datasets, no matter which trimming procedure is applied. This holds in all settings for both irregular and regular correspondence patterns (see Appendix A for details). Gap-oriented trimming removes more patterns than core-oriented trimming, which is also expected, given that in the latter setting we preserve some sites in the core that would otherwise have been trimmed. Figure 4 visualizes the reduction of correspondence patterns and alignment sites for all ten datasets in our sample. This analysis allows us to make two

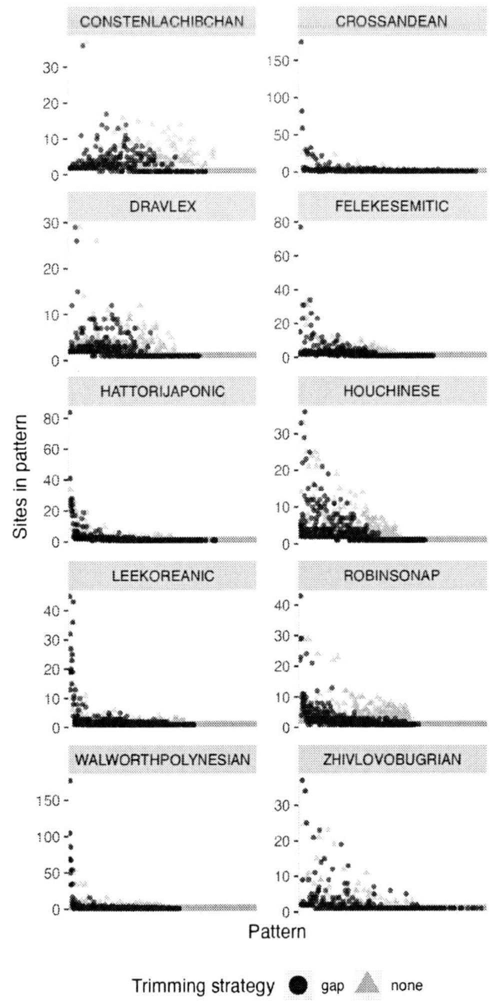

Figure 4: Distribution of alignment sites per pattern with gap-oriented trimming and without. Each point on the x-axis represents one correspondence pattern, its value on the y-axis reflects the number of alignment sites it contains. The patterns are sorted on the x-axis by their number of alignment sites. Gap-oriented trimming and the baseline are distinguished by shape and color.

	Original		Core		Gap	
Dataset	P	W	P	W	P	W
CONSTENLACHIBCHAN	0.71	0.50	0.69/ 0.70	0.46/ 0.47	**0.76**/ 0.70	**0.51**/ 0.43
CROSSANDEAN	0.73	0.58	0.74/ 0.73	0.60/ 0.59	**0.75**/ 0.73	**0.64**/ 0.59
DRAVLEX	0.56	0.23	0.57/ 0.55	0.27/ 0.23	**0.61**/ 0.55	**0.31**/ 0.24
FELEKESEMITIC	0.55	0.22	0.58/ 0.56	0.25/ 0.24	**0.62**/ 0.56	**0.29**/ 0.25
HATTORIJAPONIC	0.58	0.33	0.57/ 0.58	0.33/ 0.33	**0.59**/ 0.58	**0.38**/ 0.34
HOUCHINESE	0.65	0.40	0.65/ 0.65	0.42/ 0.40	**0.69**/ 0.64	**0.45**/ 0.35
LEEKOREANIC	0.44	0.21	0.47/ 0.45	0.20/ 0.21	**0.52**/ 0.47	**0.22**/ 0.20
ROBINSONAP	0.64	0.36	0.65/ 0.63	0.37/ 0.47	**0.67**/ 0.63	**0.41**/ 0.35
WALWORTHPOLYNESIAN	0.66	0.40	0.66/ 0.65	0.40/ 0.39	**0.72**/ 0.66	**0.48**/ 0.39
ZHIVLOVOBUGRIAN	0.57	0.24	0.58/ 0.57	0.26/ 0.25	**0.61**/ 0.58	**0.28**/ 0.26

Table 2: Proportion of regular correspondence patterns (P) and regular words (W) across all datasets after trimming. The numbers after the slashes provide the average from 100 iterations of the random model.

general observations. First, frequently recurring correspondence patterns tend to grow with respect to the number of alignment sites in which they recur after trimming. We attribute this to the greedy nature of the correspondence pattern inference procedure. Second, the long tail of correspondence patterns with very few alignment sites is substantially shortened in almost all languages. This provides yet another perspective on the necessity of trimming in linguistics. Many of the patterns with a low amount of alignment sites do indeed seem to contain erroneous alignment judgements, and trimming them successfully improves the distribution of sites across the patterns. The two datasets where the tail does not seem substantially shortened, CROSSANDEAN and ZHIVLOVOBUGRIAN, are also the ones with the lowest gain in the proportion of regular correspondence patterns. While there are still small improvements, it does seem that in those cases the gap-oriented trimming does not seem as effective as for other datasets.

One likely explanation for this observation is the fact that both datasets, as well as HATTORIJAPONIC, include language varieties that are closely related to each other. ZHIVLOVOBUGRIAN includes data from one subgroup of the Uralic language family, while the Quechua languages from CROSSANDEAN are generally considered to be quite similar to each other and of shallow time-depth. In those cases, we expect many forms that are (nearly) identical to each other. This would directly result in correspondence patterns of high frequency, from which not too many sites are trimmed. Especially for CROSSANDEAN, this is reflected by the fact that it has the highest proportion of regular words across all the datasets, pointing to a very regular set of lexical items.

Table 3 shows the results of our error analysis, comparing in how many out of 100 trials for each trimming strategy the proportion of regular words was higher in the random trial than in the concrete trimming method. As we can see from the table, the random-deletion model often outperforms the core-oriented trimming strategy, while it performs consistently worse than the gap-oriented trimming strategy. This clearly shows that it is not enough to trim alignment sites at random in order to reduce the noise in the data. As can be expected due to traditional theories on the regularity of sound change, specific sites, which reflect irregular correspondence patterns, must be targeted. For some datasets, the random model does surprisingly well in the core-oriented setting, and in some cases, it is even consistently better than the targeted core-strategy. This can be explained by the fact that the random trimming might also trim sites within the core – sites that apparently are very irregular in some languages – and hence improve the model in comparison to a trimming-model where a certain core is always preserved. Given that the model performs worse than the gap-oriented trimming in all languages, it seems recommendable to trim all sites above the gap-threshold, regardless of their position in the alignment. The successful trimming of sites that include a majority of gaps shows that those sites contain many irregular correspondences, and removing them improves our measures of regularity. We are now able to explain more words in the dataset with a lower number of regular correspondence patterns.

Dataset	Core	Gap
CONSTENLACHIBCHAN	0.58	0.00
CROSSANDEAN	0.02	0.00
DRAVLEX	0.00	0.00
FELEKESEMITIC	0.17	0.01
HATTORIJAPONIC	0.40	0.00
HOUCHINESE	0.05	0.00
LEEKOREANIC	0.54	0.06
ROBINSONAP	0.34	0.00
WALWORTHPOLYNESIAN	0.11	0.00
ZHIVLOVOBUGRIAN	0.12	0.05

Table 3: Percentage of models with random deletion of alignment sites that achieved higher regularity than the respective trimming model.

Boruca	-	-	b	ɾ	u	-	ŋ	-	-	-
Cabecar	-	-	b	-	u	-	ɹ	i	t	u
Chimila	-	-	b	-	u	h	ŋ	a	ʔ	-
Malayo	-	-	b	-	ɨ	-	n	-	-	-
Ngabere	ŋ	ɯ	b	ɾ	ɯ	-	-	-	-	-
Proto-Chibchan			^{m}b		ũ		^{n}d			

Figure 5: Gap-oriented trimming for the cognate words of ASHES in Chibchan languages

Boruca	d	i	ʔ
Bribri	d	i	ʔ
Buglere	tʃ	i	-
Cogui	n	i	-
Ngabere	ɲ	ɤ	-
Proto-Chibchan	^{n}d	i	ʔ

Figure 6: Trimming for the cognate words of WATER in Chibchan

Further experimentation will have to be done with respect to different gap thresholds. Our initial threshold of 0.5 reflects the fact that we did not want to search for the threshold with the highest number of regularity, but rather to account heuristically for sites that include more gaps than reflexes of sound. Furthermore, the optimal threshold might well be different for each language family, given that correspondence patterns can differ greatly across languages. For example, patterns of change in which sounds are lost in certain positions might be very frequent for one language family, but not in another, leading to a different role of gaps in the correspondence patterns.

4.2 Success and Failure of Trimming

Our implementation is fully compatible with computer-assisted workflows (List, 2017b). We output all data in a way that experts can check them, and make both the trimmed sites as well as the resulting (ir)regular correspondence patterns explicit. This makes it possible to use the output of our method in various tasks in historical linguistics. Figure 5 provides one example from the CONSTENLACHIBCHAN dataset of the output that our trimming provides. The figure presents a subset of cognate words for the concept ASHES, including all gaps in the original alignment from the selected languages. All alignment sites which featured mostly gaps were successfully trimmed from the alignment and are displayed as greyed out in the example. Three alignment sites remain, which pattern well with the reconstruction of ASHES in Proto-Chibchan as provided by Pache (2018, 41). If the core-oriented trimming were performed instead, five instead of three alignment sites would have remained in the final alignment, as the two sites represented by the fourth and sixth column are within the preserved core. This case illustrates the advantage of the gap-oriented trimming strategy, as all spurious alignment sites are trimmed from the data, regardless of their position.

The closer inspection of individual trimmed alignments shows that our methods still have a lot of room for improvement. One major problem lies in the nature of the gap-oriented trimming. As we remove all sites which include mostly gaps, we might lose relevant correspondence patterns in which the gaps do not constitute an erroneous alignment, but rather an actual case of gaps in the pattern. It is a very reasonable assumption that there are language families in which merger with zero occurred for some correspondence pattern in the majority of languages. One such example can be found in Figure 6, where the trimmed alignments for the concept WATER in several Chibchan languages can be found. Again, we add to the data from the CONSTENLACHIBCHAN-dataset the reconstruction as provided by Pache (2018, 235). As we can see, the alignment site which includes the reflexes the glottal stop as reconstructed for Proto-Chibchan contains gaps in most languages. With the current methodology which focuses exclusively on gaps, this pattern will be trimmed from the alignment, despite reflecting relevant information. This is paralleled by discussions in biology, where gaps might contain phylogenetically relevant information (Tan et al., 2015). This opens up the question whether we will be able to feed such information into the trimming algorithm, and preserve certain patterns that we know of that would otherwise be trimmed.

What remains to be done in future studies is to manually evaluate trimmed correspondence patterns. This is a general task for historical language comparison, as linguists often base their reconstruction judgements on impressionistic statements of regularity or only report the most frequent correspondence patterns.

5 Conclusion

We introduce the concept of trimming multiple sequence alignments, originally developed for applications in evolutionary biology, to the field of historical linguistics. Trimming as such is already practiced implicitly in the comparative method, but as of yet, there are no computational implementations for the procedure. Our trimming algorithms provide considerable improvements compared to state-of-the-art alignment methods. By trimming the alignment sites down to a subsequence without gaps, we achieve a higher number of regular correspondence patterns and cognate sets than without trimming. Even though our technique is merely a very preliminary approximation to the classical workflow of the comparative method, the average regularity of correspondence patterns across data sets is improved in all settings analyzed. Our study thus shows that automated trimming is both achievable and worthwhile in computational historical linguistics.

The main target of our trimming-strategies were alignment sites that included more gaps than defined in a certain threshold. Our model comparison shows that the best results are achieved when all such sites are trimmed, rather than only those at the periphery of stable alignment sites. Similar to biology, we find that alignment sites with many gaps contain divergent information, and trimming them improves the accuracy of our methods. It is also not sufficient to trim sites at random, since in that case we lose correspondence patterns that explain the data well. The examples we provide show both the potential of trimming alignment sites and their methodological limitations. The success of our strategy varies considerably between the datasets. A closer analysis of those cases where improvements are considerably small could provide valuable information for improved trimming strategies to be implemented in the future.

Limitations

In addition to the already discussed problems related to the exclusive focus on gaps, we have only tested the trimming with respect to a generalized function of regularity in each dataset. It is not yet clear whether this actually improves the computational success of secondary tasks like reconstructions or new methods of cognate detection.

Ethics Statement

Our data are taken from publicly available sources. For this reason, we do not expect that there are ethical issues or conflicts of interest in our work.

Supplementary Material

The supplementary material accompanying this study contains the data and code needed to replicate the results reported here, along with detailed information on installing and using the software. It is curated on GitHub (`https://github.com/pano-tacanan-history/trimming-paper`, Version 1.1) and has been archived with Zenodo (`https://doi.org/10.5281/zenodo.7780719`).

Acknowledgements

This research was supported by the Max Planck Society Research Grant *CALC³* (FB, JML, `https://digling.org/calc/`) and the ERC Consolidator Grant *ProduSemy* (JML, Grant No. 101044282, see `https://doi.org/10.3030/101044282`). Views and opinions expressed are however those of the authors only and do not necessarily reflect those of the European Union or the European Research Council Executive Agency (nor any other funding agencies involved). Neither the European Union nor the granting authority can be held responsible for them. We thank Nathan W. Hill and Thiago C. Chacon and the anonymous reviewers for helpful comments. We are grateful to all people who share their data openly.

References

Cormac Anderson, Tiago Tresoldi, Thiago Costa Chacon, Anne-Maria Fehn, Mary Walworth, Robert Forkel, and Johann-Mattis List. 2018. A cross-linguistic database of phonetic transcription systems. *Yearbook of the Poznań Linguistic Meeting*, 4(1):21–53.

Raimo Anttila. 1972. *An Introduction to Historical and Comparative Linguistics*. The Macmillan Company, New York.

Frederic Blum, Carlos Barrientos, Adriano Ingunza, and Zoe Poirier. forthcoming. A phylolinguistic classification of the Quechua language family. *Indiana*, 0(0):1–20.

Timotheus Adrianus Bodt and Johann-Mattis List. 2022. Reflex prediction. a case study of western kho-bwa. *Diachronica*, 39(1):1–38.

Salvador Capella-Gutiérrez, José M. Silla-Martínez, and Toni Gabaldón. 2009. trimAl: a tool for automated alignment trimming in large-scale phylogenetic analyses. *Bioinformatics*, 25(15):1972–1973.

Luis Cayón and Thiago Chacon. 2022. Diversity, multilingualism and inter-ethnic relations in the long-term history of the Upper Rio Negro region of the Amazon. *Interface Focus*, 13(1).

James Clackson. 2007. *Indo-European linguistics*. Cambridge University Press, Cambridge.

Adolfo Constenla Umaña. 2005. ¿Existe relación genealógica entre las lenguas misumalpas y las chibchenses? *Estudios de Lingüística Chibcha*, 14:7–85.

Alexis Criscuolo and Simonetta Gribaldo. 2010. BMGE (block mapping and gathering with entropy): a new software for selection of phylogenetic informative regions from multiple sequence alignments. *BMC Evolutionary Biology*, 10(1):210.

Andreas W. Dress, Christoph Flamm, Guido Fritzsch, Stefan Grünewald, Matthias Kruspe, Sonja J. Prohaska, and Peter F. Stadler. 2008. Noisy: Identification of problematic columns in multiple sequence alignments. *Algorithms for Molecular Biology*, 3(1).

Tekabe Legesse Feleke. 2021. Ethiosemitic languages: Classifications and classification determinants. *Ampersand*, page 100074.

Robert Forkel, Simon J Greenhill, Hans-Jörg Bibiko, Christoph Rzymski, Tiago Tresoldi, and Johann-Mattis List. 2021. lexibank/pylexibank: pylexibank for clts 1.x.

Robert Forkel and Johann-Mattis List. 2020. Cldfbench. give your cross-linguistic data a lift. In *Proceedings of the Twelfth International Conference on Language Resources and Evaluation*, pages 6997–7004, Luxembourg. European Language Resources Association (ELRA).

Robert Forkel, Johann-Mattis List, Simon J. Greenhill, Christoph Rzymski, Sebastian Bank, Michael Cysouw, Harald Hammarström, Martin Haspelmath, Gereon A. Kaiping, and Russell D. Gray. 2018. Cross-Linguistic Data Formats, advancing data sharing and re-use in comparative linguistics. *Scientific Data*, 5(180205):1–10.

Simon Greenhill, Hannah Haynie, Robert Ross, Angela Chira, Johann-Mattis List, Lyle Campbell, Carlos Botero, and Russell Gray. 2023. A recent northern origin for the Uto-Aztecan family. *Language*.

Harald Hammarström, Robert Forkel, Martin Haspelmath, and Sebastian Bank. 2022. *Glottolog*. Max Planck Institute for Evolutionary Anthropology, Leipzig.

Shirō Hattori. 1973. Japanese dialects. In Henry M. Hoenigswald and Robert H. Langacre, editors, *Diachronic, areal and typological linguistics*, number 11 in Current Trends in Linguistics, pages 368–400. Mouton, The Hague and Paris.

Henry M. Hoenigswald. 1960. *Language Change and Linguistic Reconstruction*. The University of Chicaco Press, Chicago.

Jīngyī Hóu, editor. 2004. *Xiàndài Hànyǔ fāngyán yīnkù [Phonological database of Chinese dialects]*. Shànghǎi Jiàoyù, Shànghǎi.

Vishnupriya Kolipakam, Fiona M. Jordan, Michael Dunn, Simon J. Greenhill, Remco Bouckaert, Russell D. Gray, and Annemarie Verkerk. 2018. A bayesian phylogenetic study of the Dravidian language family. *Royal Society Open Science*, 5(3):171504.

Sean Lee. 2015. A sketch of language history in the Korean Peninsula. *PLOS ONE*, 10(5):e0128448.

Johann-Mattis List. 2012. SCA: Phonetic alignment based on sound classes. In Marija Slavkovik and Dan Lassiter, editors, *New directions in logic, language, and computation*, pages 32–51. Springer, Berlin and Heidelberg.

Johann-Mattis List. 2014. *Sequence comparison in historical linguistics*. Düsseldorf University Press, Düsseldorf.

Johann-Mattis List. 2017a. A web-based interactive tool for creating, inspecting, editing, and publishing etymological datasets. In *Proceedings of the 15th Conference of the European Chapter of the Association for Computational Linguistics. System Demonstrations*, pages 9–12, Valencia. Association for Computational Linguistics.

Johann-Mattis List. 2017b. *Computer-Assisted Language Comparison. Reconciling Computational and Classical Approaches in Historical Linguistics [Research Project, 2017–2022]*. Max Planck Institute for Evolutionary Anthropology, Leipzig.

Johann-Mattis List. 2019. Automatic inference of sound correspondence patterns across multiple languages. *Computational Linguistics*, 45(1):137–161.

Johann-Mattis List, Cormac Anderson, Tiago Tresoldi, and Robert Forkel. 2020. PYCLTS. A Python library for the handling of phonetic transcription systems.

Johann-Mattis List, Cormac Anderson, Tiago Tresoldi, and Robert Forkel. 2021. CLTS. Cross-Linguistic Transcription Systems.

Johann-Mattis List and Robert Forkel. 2021. *LingPy. A Python library for quantitative tasks in historical linguistics [Book Library, Version 2.6.8]*. Max Planck Institute for Evolutionary Anthropology, Leipzig.

Johann-Mattis List and Robert Forkel. 2022. Lingrex. linguistic reconstruction with lingpy.

Johann-Mattis List, Robert Forkel, Simon J. Greenhill, Christoph Rzymski, Johannes Englisch, and Russell D. Gray. 2022a. Lexibank, a public repository of standardized wordlists with computed phonological and lexical features. *Scientific Data*, 9(316):1–31.

Johann-Mattis List, Nathan W. Hill, and Robert Forkel. 2022b. A new framework for fast automated phonological reconstruction using trimmed alignments and sound correspondence patterns. In *Proceedings of the 3rd Workshop on Computational Approaches to Historical Language Change*, pages 89–96, Dublin. Association for Computational Linguistics.

Johann Mattis List, Annika Tjuka, Mathilda van Zantwijk, Frederic Blum, Carlos Barrientos Ugarte, Christoph Rzymski, Simon Greenhill, and Robert Forkel, editors. 2023. *CLLD Concepticon 3.1.0*. Max Planck Institute for Evolutionary Anthropology, Leipzig.

Johann-Mattis List, Ekatarina Vylomova, Robert Forkel, Nathan Hill, and Ryan D. Cotterell. 2022c. The SIGTYP shared task on the prediction of cognate reflexes. In *Proceedings of the 4th Workshop on Computational Typology and Multilingual NLP*, pages 52–62, Seattle. Association for Computational Linguistics, Max Planck Institute for Evolutionary Anthropology.

Matthias Pache. 2018. *Contributions to Chibchan Historical Linguistics*. Ph.D. thesis, Universiteit Leiden.

David L. Payne. 1991. A Classification of Maipuran (Arawakan) Languages Based on Shared Lexical Retentions. In Desmond C. Derbyshire and Geoffrey K. Pullum, editors, *Handbook of Amazonian Languages*. Mouton De Gruyter, Berlin, New York.

G. P. S. Raghava and Geoffrey J. Barton. 2006. Quantification of the variation in percentage identity for protein sequence alignments. *BMC Bioinformatics*, 7(415).

Laura C Robinson and Gary Holton. 2012. Internal classification of the Alor-Pantar language family using computational methods applied to the lexicon. *Language Dynamics and Change*, 2(2):123–149.

Luis Miguel Rojas-Berscia and Sean Roberts. 2020. Exploring the history of pronouns in South America with computer-assisted methods. *Journal of Language Evolution*, 5(1):54–74.

Laurent Sagart, Guillaume Jacques, Yunfan Lai, Robin Ryder, Valentin Thouzeau, Simon J. Greenhill, and Johann-Mattis List. 2019. Dated language phylogenies shed light on the ancestry of Sino-Tibetan. *Proceedings of the National Academy of Science of the United States of America*, 116:10317–10322.

Nathanael E. Schweikhard and Johann-Mattis List. 2020. Developing an annotation framework for word formation processes in comparative linguistics. *SKASE Journal of Theoretical Linguistics*, 17(1):2–26.

Guillaume Segerer and S. Flavier. 2015. Reflex: Reference lexicon of africa.

Jacob L. Steenwyk, Thomas J. Buida, Yuanning Li, Xing-Xing Shen, and Antonis Rokas. 2020. ClipKIT: A multiple sequence alignment trimming software for accurate phylogenomic inference. *PLOS Biology*, 18(12):e3001007.

Gerard Talavera and Jose Castresana. 2007. Improvement of phylogenies after removing divergent and ambiguously aligned blocks from protein sequence alignments. *Systematic Biology*, 56(4):564–577.

Ge Tan, Matthieu Muffato, Christian Ledergerber, Javier Herrero, Nick Goldman, Manuel Gil, and Christophe Dessimoz. 2015. Current methods for automated filtering of multiple sequence alignments frequently worsen single-gene phylogenetic inference. *Systematic Biology*, 64(5):778–791.

Zheng Tian, Yuxin Tao, Kongyang Zhu, Guillaume Jacques, Robin J. Ryder, José Andrés Alonso de la Fuente, Anton Antonov, Ziyang Xia, Yuxuan Zhang, Xiaoyan Ji, Xiaoying Ren, Guanglin He, Jianxin Guo, Rui Wang, Xiaomin Yang, Jing Zhao, Dan Xu, Russell D. Gray, Menghan Zhang, Shaoqing Wen, Chuan-Chao Wang, and Thomas Pellard. 2022. Triangulation fails when neither linguistic, genetic, nor archaeological data support the transeurasian narrative. *bioRxiv*.

Robert L. Trask, editor. 2000. *The dictionary of historical and comparative linguistics*. Edinburgh University Press, Edinburgh.

Tiago Tresoldi, Christoph Rzymski, Robert Forkel, Simon Greenhill, Johann-Mattis List, and Russell D. Gray. 2022. Managing historical linguistic data for computational phylogenetics and computer-assisted language comparison [with accompanying tutorial]. In Andrea Berez-Kroeker, Bradley McDonnell, Eve Koller, and Lauren B. Collister, editors, *Open Handbook of Linguistic Data Management*, pages 345–354. MIT Press, Massachusetts.

Mary Walworth. 2018. Polynesian segmented data.

Søren Wichmann and Taraka Rama. 2021. Testing methods of linguistic homeland detection using synthetic data. *Philosophical Transactions of the Royal Society B: Biological Sciences*, 376(1824).

Mei-Shin Wu and Johann-Mattis List. 2023. Annotating cognates in phylogenetic studies of Southeast Asian languages. *Language Dynamics and Change*, pages 1–37.

Mei-Shin Wu, Nathanael E. Schweikhard, Timotheus A. Bodt, Nathan W. Hill, and Johann-Mattis List. 2020. Computer-assisted language comparison. state of the art. *Journal of Open Humanities Data*, 6(2):1–14.

Mikhail Zhivlov. 2011. Annotated Swadesh wordlists for the Ob-Ugrian group (Uralic family). In George S. Starostin, editor, *The Global Lexicostatistical Database*. RGGU, Moscow.

A Table of Results for Individual Datasets

Analysis	Frequ. Pat.	Rare Pat.	All Pat.	Reg. Words	Irr. Words	All Words
constenlachibchan	884	355	1239	607	609	1216
constenlachibchan/gap	593	188	781	622	594	1216
constenlachibchan/gap/r	549	232	781	517	699	1216
constenlachibchan/core	680	304	984	563	653	1216
constenlachibchan/core/r	693	291	984	572	644	1216
crossandean	781	296	1077	1624	1165	2789
crossandean/gap	724	243	967	1777	1012	2789
crossandean/gap/r	708	259	967	1660	1129	2789
crossandean/core	769	276	1045	1667	1122	2789
crossandean/core/r	760	285	1045	1634	1155	2789
dravlex	665	515	1180	312	1029	1341
dravlex/gap	494	311	805	415	926	1341
dravlex/gap/r	439	366	805	317	1024	1341
dravlex/core	591	442	1033	359	982	1341
dravlex/core/r	566	466	1033	306	1035	1341
felekesemitic	928	755	1683	579	2043	2622
felekesemitic/gap	824	504	1328	773	1849	2622
felekesemitic/gap/r	743	585	1328	643	1979	2622
felekesemitic/core	860	632	1492	654	1968	2622
felekesemitic/core/r	838	654	1492	632	1990	2622
hattorijaponic	812	580	1392	562	1148	1710
hattorijaponic/gap	620	424	1044	644	1066	1710
hattorijaponic/gap/r	600	444	1044	587	1123	1710
hattorijaponic/core	707	534	1241	569	1141	1710
hattorijaponic/core/r	721	520	1241	568	1142	1710
houchinese	1329	726	2055	723	1093	1816
houchinese/gap	1020	453	1473	819	997	1816
houchinese/gap/r	940	533	1473	640	1176	1816
houchinese/core	1212	646	1858	756	1060	1816
houchinese/core/r	1201	657	1858	723	1093	1816
leekoreanic	603	764	1367	441	1690	2131
leekoreanic/gap	524	480	1004	464	1667	2131
leekoreanic/gap/r	467	537	1004	433	1698	2131
leekoreanic/core	543	623	1166	434	1697	2131
leekoreanic/core/r	521	645	1166	440	1691	2131
robinsonap	1094	616	1710	518	906	1424
robinsonap/gap	742	358	1100	584	840	1424
robinsonap/gap/r	693	407	1100	498	926	1424
robinsonap/core	877	479	1356	532	892	1424
robinsonap/core/r	861	495	1356	523	901	1424
walworthpolynesian	1568	820	2388	1472	2165	3637
walworthpolynesian/gap	1187	470	1657	1746	1891	3637
walworthpolynesian/gap/r	1094	563	1657	1414	2223	3637
walworthpolynesian/core	1377	708	2085	1452	2185	3637
walworthpolynesian/core/r	1357	728	2085	1415	2222	3637
zhivlovobugrian	469	355	824	482	1492	1974
zhivlovobugrian/gap	414	265	679	546	1428	1974
zhivlovobugrian/gap/r	393	286	679	506	1468	1974
zhivlovobugrian/core	420	307	727	505	1469	1974
zhivlovobugrian/core/r	413	314	727	494	1480	1974

Table 4: Full results with information on all patterns and words

A Crosslinguistic Database for Combinatorial and Semantic Properties of Attitude Predicates

Deniz Özyıldız
Universität Konstanz
deniz.ozyildiz@uni-konstanz.de

Ciyang Qing
University of Edinburgh
cqing@ed.ac.uk

Floris Roelofsen
Universiteit van Amsterdam
f.roelofsen@uva.nl

Maribel Romero
Universität Konstanz
maribel.romero@uni-konstanz.de

Wataru Uegaki
University of Edinburgh
w.uegaki@ed.ac.uk

Abstract

We introduce a crosslinguistic database for attitude predicates, which references their combinatorial (syntactic) and semantic properties. Our data allows assessment of crosslinguistic generalizations about attitude predicates as well as discovery of new typological/crosslinguistic patterns. This paper highlights empirical and theoretical issues that our database will help to address, motivates the predicate sample and the properties that it references, as well as our methodological choices. Two case studies illustrate how the database can be used to assess the validity of crosslinguistic generalizations.

1 Introduction

Attitude predicates are natural language expressions characterized by the fact that they combine with sentential complements and that they ascribe to their subject an attitude. They are used to talk about what people believe, wonder, hope, or say. These predicates exhibit a variety of combinatorial restrictions in terms of the types of clauses they can combine with. For example, they can be distinguished into three classes based on whether they are compatible with declarative or question complements: *Antirogatives* like *believe* combine only with declaratives, in (1a). *Rogatives* like *wonder* combine only with interrogatives, in (1b). And *responsives* like *know* combine with either, in (1c).

(1) a. Al believes that/*whether Jo is Dutch.
b. Al wonders *that/whether Jo is Dutch.
c. Al knows that/whether Jo is Dutch.

Other instances of combinatorial restrictions include responsive predicates that are compatible with constituent questions (*who*, *what*, *which*, etc.) while being incompatible with *whether* questions, e.g., *be amazed* or *be surprised*, and predicates that differ in terms of whether they are compatible with indicative or subjunctive complements in languages that make the distinction.

In a tradition tracing back at least to Frege (1898 [1948]), attitude ascriptions have been studied extensively in the philosophical and the linguistic literature. One recent strand of research argues that differences in the combinatorial properties of attitude predicates, rather than being accidental and idiosyncratic facts, can be explained generally on the basis of their semantic properties (Zuber, 1982; Egré, 2008; Mayr, 2019; Theiler et al., 2019; Uegaki and Sudo, 2019). We elaborate on some of these semantic properties and how they might relate to attitude verbs' combinatorial properties in Section 2. A second, intimately connected strand of research aims to uncover semantic properties that classes of attitude predicates have in common (in addition to places of variation), within a given language's lexicon and across languages, i.e., crosslinguistic universals in the attitude domain (White and Rawlins, 2016; Roelofsen and Uegaki, 2020; Steinert-Threlkeld, 2019; Maldonado et al., 2022).

In this paper, we present a database that will allow researchers to address these questions and explore other linguistic properties of attitude predicates in a crosslinguistic way. The database references a sample of semantic and combinatorial properties of approximately 50 attitude predicates from 15 languages. The values of these properties are based on introspective judgments of native speakers of each language, and are collected by means of a questionnaire. They are summarized in tables in CSV format, one per language and speaker, which are accompanied by text documents that contain the linguistic examples that motivate the speaker's responses and reference additional facts about the data (e.g., the variety of the language spoken by the native speaker consultant, particular clause type distinctions available in the language, etc.).

This resource adds to a set of existing databases about the properties of attitude predicates: The *Mega* databases MegaAcceptability (White and Rawlins, 2016), MegaVeridicality (White and

Proceedings of the 5th Workshop on Research in Computational Linguistic Typology and Multilingual NLP (SIGTYP 2023), pages 65–75
May 6, 2023

Rawlins, 2018), MegaNegRaising (An and White, 2020), MegaIntensionality (Kane et al., 2021) and MegaOrientation (Moon and White, 2020), as well as the ZAS Database of Clause-embedding Predicates (Stiebels et al., 2018). The contribution of our database is novel in at least three respects. First, it enables a *crosslinguistic* exploration of the properties of attitude predicates. This is important because generalizations that concern these predicates are often formulated on the basis of a single language and yet, given their nature, are expected to hold crosslinguistially. Second, it is the same speakers that provide the introspective judgments that underlie the semantic and combinatorial properties that are tested. To the extent that we can assume that these judgments come from the same source grammar, within speaker and within language comparisons can be made consistently. It has been shown that speakers may differ from one another in terms of how strongly a linguistic expression displays some property, and that correlations between syntactic or semantic properties may ultimately depend on this gradient perception (Chemla et al., 2011; Tonhauser et al., 2018). Third, the quantitative component of the database (the summary tables in CSV format) is supported by a qualitative component (the text documents with examples and other considerations supporting/qualifying the consultant's judgments). This makes it possible not only to draw broad generalizations, but also to examine the properties of specific predicates in more depth. We would finally like to highlight that the dataset may be used for a broad range of applications in NLP, including but not limited to improving and evaluating the performance of natural language understanding and machine translation systems. This, we believe, is particularly valuable in that our dataset references several 'low resource' languages, for which such systems might perform poorly.

Outline Section 2 of this paper presents the semantic properties of attitude predicates included in our database and how these have been argued to relate to these predicates' combinatorial properties. Section 3 references the predicates that we have included, as well as the response categories that were used to elicit these predicates' semantic and combinatorial properties. Section 4 contains practical information about how the database is formatted, can be accessed, and further contributed to. Section 5 presents two case studies illustrating how the database can be used to test generalizations concerning attitude predicates. Section 6 concludes. (We draw attention to Limitations in the Appendix.)

2 Semantic Properties

This section introduces the semantic properties of attitude predicates included in our database and relevant generalizations about them in the literature.

A predicate V is *veridical* iff *x Vs that S* entails S. For instance, *know* is veridical, but *be certain* is not: (2) entails that it is raining but (3) does not.

(2) Alice knows that it is raining.

(3) Alice is certain that it is raining.

Veridicality is argued to correlate with the ability to take interrogative complements (e.g., Egré, 2008).

A predicate is *projective under negation* (or *projective* for short) if one can infer the complement when the predicate is negated. For instance, *be happy* and *be surprised* are projective (4).

(4) Alice isn't happy/surprised that it is raining
$\rightsquigarrow$ It is raining

A predicate V is *neg-raising* if *not V S* is interpreted as *V not S*. For instance, *think* and *believe* are neg-raising (5), whereas *know* and *be sure* are not (6).

(5) Alice does not think/believe it is raining
$\approx$ Alice thinks/believes it is not raining.

(6) Alice doesn't know/isn't sure it is raining
$\not\approx$ Alice knows/is sure it is not raining.

It has been suggested that neg-raising predicates are generally anti-rogative, and several theoretical explanations for this have been proposed (Zuber, 1982; Mayr, 2019; Theiler et al., 2019).

Many predicates, such as *be happy* and *hope*, have meanings that intuitively involve a notion of preference. Several formal semantic accounts characterize *preferentiality* in terms of *focus sensitivity* and *gradability* (Villalta, 2008; Romero, 2015; Uegaki and Sudo, 2019). A predicate V is *focus sensitive* if its truth conditions can be influenced by the placement of focus in the embedded clause. For instance, *be happy* and *hope* are focus sensitive because the two sentences in (7) need not be true at the same time: Mary might be the best among syntax teachers, but syntax might not be the best among subjects Mary can teach.

(7) a. Alice is happy/hopes that

MARY will teach syntax.

b. Alice is happy/hopes that Mary will teach SYNTAX.

In contrast, *know* and *think* are not focus sensitive. If one sentence in (8) is true of Alice's epistemic/doxastic state, the other must be true as well.

(8) a. Alice knows/thinks that MARY will teach syntax.

b. Alice knows/thinks that Mary will teach SYNTAX.

A predicate is *gradable* if it can participate in degree constructions, e.g., intensification (9) or comparison (10).

(9) Alice is very happy that Mary is here.

(10) Alice hopes that it is raining more than Bob does.

Karttunen (1977) observes that a certain class of preferential predicates, which he calls *emotive factives*, can take *wh*-questions but not *whether* questions (11) (see Section 5.1 for further discussion, and Saebø (2007) and Abenina-Adar (2019) for challenges). Uegaki and Sudo (2019) suggest that non-veridical preferential predicates such as *hope* cannot take embedded questions altogether (12).

(11) It is amazing what they serve for breakfast / *whether they serve breakfast.

(12) *Alice hopes whether Bob left / who left.

There is no consensus on exactly how to characterize emotive factives (see, e.g., Egré, 2008, for discussion), but it is uncontroversial that when they take a declarative complement, the attitude holder must believe that the complement is true (13).

(13) Alice is happy/surprised that it is raining
$\Rightarrow$ Alice believes that it is raining

There is a complication, however. It is unclear what level of credence *believe* corresponds to, since this attitude predicate can often be used when the subject is not fully certain that the complement is true (e.g., Hawthorne et al., 2016). Therefore, in our database we instead directly test the compatibility between a predicate and various levels of credence. For instance, a predicate *V always implies likelihood* if *x Vs that S* entails that *x* considers *S* more likely than *not S*.

For question-embedding predicates, one important semantic property is what can be inferred about the relation between the subject's belief and possible answers to the embedded question. Some predicates, such as *know*, entail that there is a possible answer to the embedded question that the subject believes (14). Such predicates are *belief-implying*. Some predicates, such as *wonder*, entail that there is no possible answer that the subject believes (15). Such predicates are *ignorance-implying*. Other predicates, such as *care*, are *neutral wrt belief and ignorance*. *Alice cares (about) who won* can be true with or without Alice having a belief as to who won (Elliott et al., 2017).

(14) Alice knows whether Bob left.
$\Rightarrow$ Alice believes that Bob left or she believes that Bob didn't leave.

(15) Alice wonders whether Bob left.
$\Rightarrow$ Alice neither believes that Bob left nor does she believe that Bob didn't leave.

Ciardelli and Roelofsen (2015) use the fact that predicates such as *wonder* entail ignorance to explain their rogativity.

For a responsive predicate V, an important question is how the meanings of their declarative-embedding use *x Vs that S* and their interrogative-embedding use *x Vs Q* are related. V is *Q-to-P veridical* if *x Vs Q* entails *x Vs that p*, where *p* is the true answer to Q. For instance, if *Alice knows which player won* and in fact *Bob won*, then it follows that *Alice knows that Bob won.*

V is *Q-to-P distributive* if *x Vs Q* entails *x Vs that p* for some *p* that is a potential answer to Q. For instance, if *Alice is certain (about) which player won*, then there must be some player *y* such that *Alice is certain that y won.* Note that Q-to-P veridical predicates must be Q-to-P distributive but not vice versa. For instance, *be certain* is Q-to-P distributive but not Q-to-P veridical.

Finally, V is *P-to-Q distributive* if *x Vs that p*, where *p* is a possible answer to a question Q, entails *x Vs Q*. For instance, *Alice is certain that Bob won* entails *Alice is certain (about) which player won.*

Spector and Egré (2015) propose that responsive predicates are all Q-to-P distributive, whereas Roelofsen and Uegaki (2020) propose, instead, that they are all P-to-Q distributive (see Section 5.2 for further discussion).

Before concluding this section, we note that the semantic properties described here can in principle be applied to predicates in any language. Similarly,

Class	Verbs
Communication	*accept, announce, argue, assert, claim, complain, deny, explain, inform, tell, whisper, write*
Doxastic	*agree, assume, believe, (be) certain, (be) convinced, doubt, expect, forget, know, learn, prove, (be) right, suspect, think, (be) unaware, (be) wrong*
Perception	*see*
Directive	*decide, demand, order, propose*
Emotive	*fear, (be) happy, hope, pray, prefer, regret, (be) surprised, want, (be) worried*
Inquisitive	*ask, (be) curious, inquire, investigate, wonder*
Relevance	*care*

Table 1: Verb classes and verbs included in the database

the empirical generalizations proposed in the literature make crosslinguistic predictions, even though they were typically motivated by data from English or a few well-studied languages. Testing such predictions in a wider range of languages is crucial to assess the validity of existing proposals.

3 Design of the Crosslinguistic Database

Our database is designed to assess empirically the kinds of crosslinguistic generalizations described in Section 2. Furthermore, it will possibly enable discovery of previously unnoticed correlations, in particular ones involving interactions between multiple properties. In this section, we introduce the general design of the database. We will also briefly discuss practical aspects of data collection.

3.1 The properties and sample predicates

The database contains information about ~50 clause-embedding predicates in each language. Each predicate is annotated with respect to ~15 semantic properties and ~12 combinatorial properties. The numbers are approximate because in some languages there are multiple attitude predicates corresponding to just one predicate in another language, and certain languages make more clause type distinctions than others. In the English database there are 48 predicates, listed in Table 1. The semantic and combinatorial properties considered are listed in Table 2.

Semantic properties The semantic properties are annotated based on inferential diagnostics and acceptability judgments. For example, the property of Veridicality is annotated based on the following inferential test:

Veridicality test Consider:

(16) Ann *V*s that it is raining.

Does this sentence always imply that it is raining? If not, does it always imply that it is not raining?

Marking instructions

- If you answered *yes* to the first question, please mark *V* as **always veridical**.
- If you answered *yes* to the second question, please mark *V* as **always anti-veridical**.
- If you answered *no* to both questions, but you feel that the sentence typically implies that it is raining, please mark *V* as **typically veridical**.
- Similarly, if you answered *no* to both questions, but you feel that the sentence typically implies that it is not raining, please mark *V* as **typically anti-veridical**.
- Otherwise, please mark *V* as **neither**.

An example of a semantic property annotated based on acceptability judgments rather than an inferential test is Gradability. Specifically, this property is annotated based on the acceptability of sentences like (9) and (10) above. For some predicates, the judgments can be unclear, in which case the option *undecided* is used.

Combinatorial properties Combinatorial properties are annotated based on whether the predicate can take specific clause types. The relevant clause types for English are listed in the last row of Table 2, and those for other languages contain corresponding information with respect to syntactic equivalents of these clause types. Some languages involve further clause-type distinctions. For example, the data for Catalan, French, Italian, and Spanish involve an indicative/subjunctive mood distinction and the data for Greek, Hungarian, Japanese, and Turkish involve complementizer and other clause-type distinctions.

Predicate sample The sample of 48 English predicates in Table 1 has been selected from various classes of predicates investigated in the theoretical literature and cover a wide range of combinations of semantic and combinatorial properties. For languages other than English, we initially ask consul-

Semantic properties	**Response options**
Veridicality†	veridical, anti-veridical, neither
Conjunction with negation of the complement	contradictory, redundant, neither
Conjunction with the complement	contradictory, redundant, neither
Complement projection/reversal through negation†	projective, reversive, neither
Neg-raising†	neg-raising, non-neg-raising
Subject's { likelihood / unlikelihood / equal likelihood } estimation towards complement	always implies, typically implies, compatible, incompatible
Subject's { certainty / counter-certainty / uncertainty } towards complement	always implies, typically implies, compatible, incompatible
Subject's { preference / opposition / indifference } towards complement	always implies, typically implies, compatible, incompatible
Focus sensitivity	focus-sensitive, non-focus-sensitive
Grammatical gradability with declaratives	gradable, non-gradable, undecided
Belief/ignorance implications w.r.t. interrogatives†	belief-, ignorance-implying, neutral
Grammatical gradability w.r.t. interrogatives	gradable, non-gradable, undecided
Q-to-P veridicality†	veridical, anti-veridical, neither
Q-to-P distributivity†	distributive, non-distributive
P-to-Q distributivity†	distributive, non-distributive
Combinatorial properties	**Response options**
Finite & non-finite declaratives; Finite & non-finite interrogatives (polar, alternative, *which*, *who/what*); Concealed questions; Intransitive use	acceptable, unacceptable, degraded (from ? to ???), [preposition/particle/etc.] required, undecided

Table 2: All of the properties included in the questionnaire, where † indicates properties for which a graded response was elicited, e.g., *typically* or *always* veridical.

tants to provide direct translations of the English predicates, to the extent that such translations exist. If a direct translation does not exist, consultants are encouraged to consider predicates that are similar in meaning to the original English predicate and comment on the extent to which they are comparable in the text document. We further discuss this translation-based method of sampling predicates across languages in the Limitations section.

3.2 Annotation

The annotation instructions are collated in a questionnaire format, with accompanying predicate-specific notes that discuss certain confounding factors that need to be controlled for on a predicate-specific basis. Both documents are accessible at `https://osf.io/vd8mg/`. Data were annotated by native speakers with a background in linguistics (at least an undergraduate degree). Each consultant spent 60 to 100 hours (distributed over 3 to 4 months) on completing their dataset, and consulted regularly with at least one of the authors during this process in order to clarify difficult judgments or resolve possible complications. Annotation was performed across all properties by a single consultant for each language. This design allows a within-subject testing of possible correlations between different properties. At the same time, since the format of our database tracks consultant IDs for each data point, our design of the database does not preclude addition of data based on annotation from other speakers in the future.

4 Practical Details about the Database

4.1 Format

The database is located at `https://wuegaki.ppls.ed.ac.uk/mecore/mecore-databases/`. Each language has its own folder containing the following documents: (i) a README file containing basic information about the language, the list of language-specific semantic and combinatorial properties, and the data collection process, (ii) a table (a CSV file) in wide format, where each row corresponds to a predicate and each column to a combinatorial or semantic property (see Table 3), (iii) the corresponding text document containing the linguistic examples used in determining the properties and relevant discussions.

The tables are in wide format so that it is easy to visually inspect them, which is useful when one is casually exploring the database. However, as discussed in the previous section, different languages have different sets of properties. For instance, Mandarin Chinese has two negation markers which can lead to different interpretations. As a result, each negation-related property corresponds to two columns in the Mandarin table but only one in other languages. Therefore it is impossible to directly aggregate tables in wide format from different languages. They need to be converted to long format tables first to be appended to one another. In this case, the long format includes an additional column called NegationMarker. For a negation-related property, the value of this column is the negation marker under consideration. If the property does not involve negation, the value is NONE.

Other language-specific distinctions are, e.g., *mood* (for Romance languages) and *complementizer* (for Japanese, Greek, Turkish and Hungarian). Information about such distinctions is stated in the README file for the relevant languages.

4.2 Snapshot

At the time of writing, the database contains 15 languages: Catalan, Dutch, English, French, German, Greek, Hebrew, Hindi, Italian, Japanese, Kĩĩtharaka, Mandarin, Spanish, Swedish and Turkish. For two of the languages, German and Polish, a detailed report on the process of creating a first version of the dataset (superseded by the version that we currently release) is available as Master's theses (Naehrlich, 2022; Klochowicz, 2022).

4.3 Contributing to the database

Researchers are welcome to contribute to the database. The simplest way is to use our questionnaire and predicate-specific notes to collect data on (possibly a subset of) the translations of the 48 English predicates in the current database (as part, for example, of a student's research project or internship). While the questionnaire and predicate-specific notes are designed for trained linguists as consultants, they can be adapted to a fieldwork setup for consultants with no training in linguistics.

We emphasize that the additional data need not be about a new language. Due to intra-language variation, it is also valuable to have judgments from multiple speakers of the same language.

One can also apply the questionnaire to predicates beyond the ones in the current database. In this case, contributors are encouraged to provide predicate-specific notes on the additional predicates to faciliate future crosslinguistic investigations.

5 Two case studies

We discuss two case studies using our database. Although strong conclusions cannot be drawn from the limited sample we currently have, as a proof of concept, they show how our database informs debates about crosslinguistic generalizations.

5.1 Emotive factives and whether questions

The first case study concerns the relation between combinatorial and semantic properties. Recall that Karttunen (1977) observes that emotive factives cannot take *whether* questions (11). We aim to evaluate this generalization crosslinguistically.

In line with how this class of predicates is generally thought of in the literature, we adopt the following criteria. A predicate is emotive factive if it is (i) typically or always veridical, (ii) typically or always projective, (iii) focus sensitive, (iv) gradable, and (v) it entails that the subject believes the complement—which we operationalize as implying that, according to the subject, the complement is more likely than its negation (e.g., Egré, 2008; Villalta, 2008; Romero, 2015). In our database for English, 4 predicates satisfy these criteria: *be happy*, *be surprised*, *regret*, and *care*. The first three are indeed canonical examples of emotive factives, and intuitively *care* is an emotive predicate and shares the semantic properties listed above, e.g., it is typically veridical and projective (17).

Predicate	English translation	Veridicality/ Anti-veridicality	...	Finite declaratives	Finite *which* interrogatives	...
vergeten	*forget*	always veridical	...	acceptable	acceptable	...
ongelijk hebben	*be wrong*	always anti-veridical	...	acceptable	acceptable	...
geloven	*believe*	neither	...	acceptable	unacceptable	...
zich afvragen	*wonder*	NA	...	unacceptable	acceptable	...
...	...	...	...	...	...	

Table 3: Part of the Dutch predicate table in wide format

(17) Alice cares/does not care that Bob won
$\rightsquigarrow$ Bob won

But, while the first three predicates indeed cannot take *whether* questions, *care* can (18), which makes it a potential counterexample to the generalization.

(18) Ann cares whether Bob or Charles won.

However, note that the meaning of (18) is different from what one would expect when an emotive factive predicate takes a question complement. For instance, (19) entails that there is an answer p to the embedded question such that the subject is surprised that p. That is, canonical emotive factives are Q-to-P distributive. In contrast, (18) does not have such an entailment (20). This is because *Alice cares that x won* entails that Alice believes that x won, but (18) can be true even if Ann does not have a belief about who won at all (Elliott et al., 2017).

(19) Alice is surprised (about) who won.
$\Rightarrow \exists x$. Alice is surprised that x won.

(20) Alice cares whether Bob or Charles won.
$\not\Rightarrow \exists x$. Alice cares that x won.

This observation allows us to refine the original generalization by Karttunen. A predicate cannot take *whether* questions if it is an emotive factive (as operationalized above) *and Q-to-P distributive*.

This refined generalization is highly robust crosslinguistically. When the counterparts of canonical emotive factives *be happy*, *be surprised* and *regret* take *whether* questions, the results are consistently judged unacceptable or highly marked. The counterparts of *care* consistently lack Q-to-P distributivity and can take *whether* questions.

It is worth looking into Kĩĩtharaka *rigara*, offered by our consultant as the translation of English *be surprised*, in some more detail. This predicate has two senses. When it takes a declarative complement, it is translated as *be surprised*. When it takes a *wh*-question, it can mean that there is an answer p to the question such that the subject is surprised that p. In this respect *rigara* is an emotive factive predicate just like *be surprised*. However, when *rigara* takes a question, it can also be translated as *wonder*. Crucially, although *rigara* can take *whether* questions, it can only be translated as *wonder* in such cases. In particular, *Bill rigara whether Mary left* means that Bill wonders whether Mary left, and crucially, it does not entail that either *Bill rigara that Mary left* or *Bill rigara that Mary did not leave* must be true. Thus, when *rigara* takes *whether*-complements, it is not Q-to-P distributive.

There are further cases of predicates that satisfy the criteria of emotive factives while lacking Q-to-P distributivity. For instance, Swedish *vara orolig över*, unlike its English counterpart *be worried*, is always veridical (therefore a more accurate translation would be *it worries x that*). It is not Q-to-P distributive and can take *whether* questions.

This case study lends support for a modified version of Karttunen's generalization: if a predicate is an emotive factive and Q-to-P distributive, it is incompatible with *whether* questions. It also highlights the utility of our database in the investigation of crosslinguistic correlations between semantic and combinatorial properties of attitude predicates. Without the type of data available in the current database, it would be difficult to empirically assess the relevance of Q-to-P distributivity to Karttunen's original observation in a crosslinguistic context.

5.2 P-to-Q distributivity

The second case study concerns the crosslinguistic validity of the generalization that all responsive attitude predicates satisfy P(roposition)-to-Q(uestion) distributivity (Roelofsen and Uegaki, 2020). To illustrate, from (21a), we may infer (21b) and (21c), where the embedded declarative in (21a) ("P") is one of the possible answers to the embedded interrogatives in (21b) and (21c) ("Q").

(21) a. Al knows/cares that Jo is Dutch.

b. Al knows/cares whether Jo is Dutch.
c. Al knows/cares where Jo is from.

Roelofsen and Uegaki identify three classes of potential counter-examples to P-to-Q distributivity, without drawing definite conclusions. First, some predicates are non-veridical with declarative complements, but veridical with interrogative complements (Q-to-P veridical). A prototypical example is *tell* (Karttunen, 1977). Examples like (22) do not entail the embedded clause, suggesting non-veridicality with declaratives, but the conjunction of (23a) and (23b) is often judged to entail (23c), suggesting that *tell* might be Q-to-P veridical. (Note, however, that the predicate is not considered Q-to-P veridical by everyone—see Tsohatzidis 1993; Holton 1997; Spector and Egré 2015, a.o.)

(22) Al told Jo that Sue won. $\not\to$ Sue won.

(23) a. Al told Jo which runner won.
b. Zoe won.
c. ∴ Al told Jo that Zoe won.

If this is correct, *tell* cannot be P-to-Q distributive as (23a) does not follow from (22) in situations where Sue did not win.

Second, there are predicates similar to Kĩĩtharaka *rigara*, which alternate between *surprise*- and *wonder*-like interpretations. Third, predicates like English *explain* alternate between 'explanans' ('that which explains') and 'explanandum' ('that which is explained') interpretations (Pietroski, 2000; Elliott, 2017; Bondarenko, 2021). What unifies these predicates is that they have qualitatively different meanings across declarative and interrogative embedding.

Our sample corroborates that there is a general tendency for responsive predicates to be P-to-Q distributive, but also that the identified classes of counter-examples are crosslinguistically attested: Speakers of some languages in our sample judged that every predicate obeys the property (Dutch, English, Greek, Kĩĩtharaka and Mandarin); for others there was a variable, but small number of exceptions (Catalan, Italian, Hebrew, Hindi, Japanese, Polish, Spanish, Swedish and Turkish). Among these exceptions, we first find communicative and doxastic predicates that are non-veridical in declarative, but veridical in interrogative embedding. Some examples include Turkish *bildir-* 'inform' and Polish *wyjaśniać* 'explain' (see also Özyıldız 2019, Bondarenko 2020, Jeong 2020).

Second, we find predicates like Swedish *tänka på*, which roughly translates sentences of the form '*think about* the fact that x won' with declaratives, and ones like '*think about* which runner won' with questions. Importantly, the former is reported to entail the belief that x won, and the latter, ignorance about which runner won. As belief is incompatible with ignorance in this situation, P-to-Q distributivity fails. One way of identifying this kind of predicate involves comparing their values for likelihood and certainty implications with the one for belief/ignorance implications w.r.t. interrogatives. Mismatching values here will point towards a shift in meaning across declarative and interrogative embedding. Among this class of predicates, we also find the counterparts of 'think' in Catalan, Spanish and Turkish, *surprise/wonder*-type predicates in Japanese, Spanish and Swedish, and a third set of predicates instantiated by Turkish communicatives *de-*, *yaz-* and *fısılda-* ('say,' 'write,' and 'whisper'). With declaratives, these Turkish predicates imply that their subject linguistically produced the declarative (e.g., *Al said: "Jo won."*), but with interrogatives, that the subject produced the interrogative (e.g., *Al said: "Which runner won?").* Hence, P-to-Q distributivity fails for them as well.

This case study confirms a general tendency for predicates to be P-to-Q distributive, but also reveals variation, both within and across languages. Its results are consistent with debates in the literature, e.g., regarding the properties of *tell* and *explain.* Some exceptions to the general tendency are better understood (e.g., veridicality alternating predicates) than others (e.g., the class of *surprise/wonder* predicates). This, in turn, paves the way for new empirical and theoretical research.

6 Conclusions

We have presented our crosslinguistic database for combinatorial and semantic properties of attitude predicates. As our case studies show, the database enables assessment of two types of crosslinguistic generalisations: one concerning correlations between semantic and combinatorial properties of attitude predicates and the other concerning general semantic constraints on attitude predicates. The database complements existing resources due to three features: (i) crosslinguistic data; (ii) enabling within-subject comparison across properties, and (iii) accompanying text documents that allow fine-grained qualitative assessment of data.

Limitations

The data collection process was time-intensive. Each language required a total of 60 to 100 hours of work by a native speaker with a background in linguistics, typically over the course of 3 to 4 months with regular consultation sessions with one of the authors of the present paper. Because of this, the current database for the most part only features introspective judgments coming from a single speaker per language (although occasionally informants would consult other native speakers and/or corpora when they were uncertain). While this is a good place to start, the database is not yet equipped to address issues pertaining to within and across speaker variability. For the same reason, we have had to limit the number of attitude predicates that we tested to a manageable number. While we believe that our sample covers much of the logical space of possibilities for the meaning of attitude predicates, the number of predicates remains small (especially in comparison with the *Mega* datasets). The fact that our initial survey is translation based makes it also possible that certain predicates of interest in the target languages were missed.

The languages that were included in the database are typologically diverse, but they do not cover all known language families and are currently restricted to the spoken modality. There is nothing, however, that prevents the inclusion of other languages, including sign languages, and we are hopeful that our database will expand in these directions.

Regarding the tests that we have used to elicit semantic and combinatorial properties, while some are relatively easy to transpose into other languages (e.g., conjunction with the (negation of the) complement), others are harder, and their results might be less reliable. For example, the question about neg-raising is currently eliciting an inference which might be driven by factors other than the predicate actually being neg-raising. An alternative, arguably more reliable test would make use of strict Negative Polarity Items (NPIs), but identifying NPIs in a given language requires detailed knowledge of the language and may only be possible for languages the researcher is familiar with or has conducted extensive fieldwork on.

Regarding the consistency of the data, there are some values that some of the properties cannot jointly take. For example, a predicate cannot at the same time be less than always veridical, always Q-to-P veridical and always P-to-Q distributive. However, this particular combination of values has been observed for certain predicates in our sample. We have attempted to minimize such inconsistencies by conducting follow-up interviews with our speakers, and making sure that they assessed the predicates in all relevant contexts of use. Rather than being a problem, however, this can be seen as a feature of our method, as it allows us to identify strong tendencies in how speakers interpret attitude ascriptions.

Finally, we note that, while the tables that are included in the database are machine readable, the supporting text documents are currently not. They have to be processed directly by the interested researcher. We are working towards making the text documents machine readable as well.

Ethics Statement

The data collection process, described in Section 3.2, and the projected or otherwise possible applications of our data have been approved by the ethics committees of the institutions funding and hosting this research, and they conform to the ACL Ethics Policy. The language consultants who have provided their introspective judgments have been compensated in accordance with the laws in place in the UK and in Germany. The database only contains anonymized consultant IDs, and our consultants have been offered the option of remaining anonymous, or of being authors on or being acknowledged by name in relevant publications—the latter two options being relevant for the academic recognition of some of our consultants, who are also professional linguists.

Acknowledgements

We thank our consultants: Aayush Bagchi, Sjaak de Wit, Rebecka Elm, Clara Giralt, Nori Hayashi, Patrick Kanampiu, Tomasz Klochowicz, Sarah Molina Raith, Flavia Naehrlich, Aviv Schoenfeld, Anastasis Stefas, Yingyu Su, Ilaria Venagli, Caitlin Wilson, and one anonymous consultant. We thank two additional consultants, Nana Kwame and Eszter Ótott-Kóvacs, who we are still working with on collecting data for two additional languages. The results will be added to the database once the data collection is complete.

We also thank Kajsa Djärv, Jenny Doetjes, Despina Oikonomou, Jakub Szymanik and Malte Zimmermann for helping with data collection and discussion of methodological issues at various stages of the project.

This paper is a part of the project 'MECORE: A cross-linguistic investigation of meaning-driven combinatorial restrictions in clausal embedding', supported by the AHRC-DFG Collaborative Grant in Humanities (AHRC reference: AH/V002716/1; DFG reference: RO 4247/5-1).

References

Maayan Abenina-Adar. 2019. Surprising. In *Proceedings of the 36th West Coast Conference on Formal Linguistics*, pages 41–47. Somerville, MA: Cascadilla Proceedings Project.

Hannah Youngeun An and Aaron Steven White. 2020. The Lexical and Grammatical Sources of Neg-Raising Inferences. In *Proceedings of the Society for Computation in Linguistics 3*, pages 220–233.

Tatiana Bondarenko. 2020. Factivity from pre-existence: Evidence from Barguzin Buryat. *Glossa: a journal of general linguistics*, 5:1–35.

Tatiana Bondarenko. 2021. Two paths to explain: clausal embedding with verbs of speech. Manuscript, MIT.

Emmanuel Chemla, Vincent Homer, and Daniel Rothschild. 2011. Modularity and intuitions in formal semantics: the case of polarity items. *Linguistics and Philosophy*, 34:537–570.

Ivano Ciardelli and Floris Roelofsen. 2015. Inquisitive dynamic epistemic logic. *Synthese*, 192(6):1643–1687.

Paul Egré. 2008. Question-embedding and factivity. In F. Lihoreau, editor, *Grazer Philosophische Studien 77*, pages 85–125.

Patrick Elliott. 2017. *Elements of clausal embedding*. Ph.D. thesis, UCL.

Patrick D. Elliott, Nathan Klinedinst, Yasutada Sudo, and Wataru Uegaki. 2017. Predicates of relevance and theories of question embedding. *Journal of Semantics*, 34(3):547–554.

Gottlob Frege. 1898 [1948]. Sense and reference. *The philosophical review*, 57(3):209–230.

John Hawthorne, Daniel Rothschild, and Levi Spectre. 2016. Belief is weak. *Philosophical Studies*, 173(5):1393–1404.

Richard Holton. 1997. Some telling examples: A reply to tsohatzidis. *Journal of pragmatics*, 28(5):625–628.

Sunwoo Jeong. 2020. Prosodically-conditioned Factive Inferences in Korean: An Experimental Study. In *Semantics and Linguistic Theory 30 (SALT 30)*.

Benjamin Kane, William Gantt, and Aaron Steven White. 2021. Intensional gaps: Relating doxasticity, bouleticity, veridicality, factivity, and neg-raising. In *Proceedings of Semantics and Linguistic Theory 31*.

Lauri Karttunen. 1977. Syntax and semantics of questions. *Linguistics and Philosophy*, 1:3–44.

Tomasz Klochowicz. 2022. Investigation semantic and selectional properties of clause-embedding predicates in Polish. MSc in Logic thesis, Universiteit van Amsterdam.

Mora Maldonado, Jennifer Culbertson, and Wataru Uegaki. 2022. Learnability and constraints on the semantics of clause-embedding predicates. In *Proceedings of the Annual Meeting of the Cognitive Science Society*.

Clemens Mayr. 2019. Triviality and interrogative embedding: Context sensitivity, factivity and neg-raising. *Natural Language Semantics*, 27.

Ellise Moon and Aaron Steven White. 2020. The Source of Nonfinite Temporal Interpretation. In *Proceedings of the 50th Annual Meeting of the North East Linguistic Society*, pages 11–24. Amherst, MA: GLSA Publications.

Flavia Naehrlich. 2022. Semantic and selectional properties of clause-embedding predicates in German. MSc in Logic thesis, Universiteit van Amsterdam.

Deniz Özyıldız. 2019. Potential answer readings expected, missing. In *Proceedings of Tu+ 4*.

Paul M. Pietroski. 2000. On explaining that. *The Journal of philosophy*, 97(12):655–662.

Floris Roelofsen and Wataru Uegaki. 2020. Searching for a universal constraint on the denotations of clause-embedding predicates. In *Proceedings of Semantics and Linguistic Therory 30*.

Maribel Romero. 2015. Surprise-predicates, strong exhaustivity and alternative questions. In *Semantics and Linguistic Theory*, volume 25, pages 225–245.

Kjell Johan Saebø. 2007. A whether forecast. In B.D. ten Cate and H.W. Zeevat, editors, *TbiLLC 2005*, pages 189–199. Springer-Verlag Berlin Heidelberg.

Benjamin Spector and Paul Egré. 2015. A uniform semantics for embedded interrogatives: an answer, not necessarily the answer. *Synthèse*, 192(6):1729–1781.

Shane Steinert-Threlkeld. 2019. An Explanation of the Veridical Uniformity Universal. *Journal of Semantics*, 37(1):129–144.

Barbara Stiebels, Thomas McFadden, Kerstin Schwabe, Torgrim Solstad, Elisa Kellner, Livia Sommer, and Katarzyna Stoltmann. 2018. Zas database of clause-embedding predicates, release 1.0. OWIDplus, hg. v. Institut für Deutsche Sprache, Mannheim, http://www.owid.de/plus/zasembed.

Nadine Theiler, Floris Roelofsen, and Maria Aloni. 2019. Picky predicates: Why believe doesn't like interrogative complements, and other puzzles. *Natural Language Semantics*, 27(2):95–134.

Judith Tonhauser, David I Beaver, and Judith Degen. 2018. How Projective is Projective Content? Gradience in Projectivity and At-issueness. *Journal of Semantics*, 35(3):495–542.

Savas L Tsohatzidis. 1993. Speaking of truth-telling: The view from wh-complements. *Journal of pragmatics*, 19(3):271–279.

Wataru Uegaki and Yasutada Sudo. 2019. The *hope-wh puzzle. *Natural Language Semantics*, 27:323–356.

Elisabeth Villalta. 2008. Mood and gradability: An investigation of the subjunctive mood in Spanish. *Linguistics and Philosophy*, 31(4):467–522.

Aaron Steven White and Kyle Rawlins. 2016. A computational model of S-selection. In *Proceedings of Semantics and Linguistic Theory 26*, pages 641–663.

Aaron Steven White and Kyle Rawlins. 2018. The role of veridicality and factivity in clause selection. In *Proceedings of the 48th Annual Meeting of the North East Linguistic Society*, volume 3, pages 221–234. Amherst, MA: GLSA Publications.

Richard Zuber. 1982. Semantic restrictions on certain complementizers. In *Proceedings of the 12th International Congress of Linguists, Tokyo*, pages 434–436.

Corpus-based Syntactic Typological Methods for Dependency Parsing Improvement

Diego Alves
Faculty of Humanities and
Social Sciences - University of Zagreb
dfvalio@ffzg.hr

Božo Bekavac
Faculty of Humanities and
Social Sciences - University of Zagreb
bbekavac@ffzg.hr

Daniel Zeman
Faculty of Mathematics and Physics
Charles University
zeman@ufal.mff.cuni.cz

Marko Tadić
Faculty of Humanities and
Social Sciences - University of Zagreb
marko.tadic@ffzg.hr

Abstract

This article presents a comparative analysis of four different syntactic typological approaches applied to 20 different languages to determine the most effective one to be used for the improvement of dependency parsing results via corpora combination. We evaluated these strategies by calculating the correlation between the language distances and the empirical LAS results obtained when languages were combined in pairs. From the results, it was possible to observe that the best method is based on the extraction of word order patterns which happen inside subtrees of the syntactic structure of the sentences.

1 Introduction

Dependency parsing is a Natural Processing Processing (NLP) task that concerns the process of determining the grammatical structure of a sentence by examining the syntactic relations between its linguistic units. In other words, it consists of the identification of heads and dependents as well as the type of relationship between them (Jurafsky and Martin, 2009).

From 2015 onward, the usage of deep learning techniques has been dominant in studies regarding the dependency parsing task. Although it has provided a great improvement in overall results even for under-resourced languages (Otter et al., 2018), it requires a large amount of annotated data which can be problematic, particularly in terms of cost (Guillaume et al., 2016).

To overcome the problem of lack of data, cross-lingual parsing strategies using typological methods have been proposed to determine which languages can be combined for effective improvement of dependency parsing results (Ponti et al., 2019b). Most of these studies rely on the usage of information provided by typological databases such as WALS (Dryer and Haspelmath, 2013) sometimes combined with n-grams analysis extracted from corpora. On the other hand, the usage of corpus-based typology for this aim is still incipient.

Moreover, most studies focus on the obtained improvement, without analyzing the existence of a proper correlation between the typological features involved in the process with the overall synergy regarding the impact on the dependency parsing results.

Therefore, our aim in this paper is to propose an examination of several corpus-based typological methods in terms of correlation between language distances and dependency parsing scores. The paper is composed as follows: Section 2 presents an overview of the related work to this topic. In Section 3, we describe the campaign design: language and data-sets selection, corpus-based typological characterization, dependency parsing experiments, and correlation measures; Section 4 presents the obtained results which are discussed in Section 5. In Section 6 we provide conclusions and possible future directions for research.

2 Related Work

The WALS database is one of the most used typological resources in NLP studies (Ponti et al., 2019a). It contains phylogenetic, phonological, morphosyntactic, and lexical information for a large number of languages that can be used for a large variety of linguistic studies (Dryer and Haspelmath, 2013). Along with that, the URIEL Typological Compendium was conceived as a meta-repository that is composed of numerous databases (WALS included) and is the base of the lang2vec tool (Littell et al., 2017). This tool is a powerful resource that allows languages to be characterized as vectors composed of typological features associated with specific values. Users can choose the type of features (i.e.: genealogical, phonological, syntactic, etc) according to their precise needs. While proposing an effective way to compare languages typologically, this tool does not characterize all lan-

Proceedings of the 5th Workshop on Research in Computational Linguistic Typology and Multilingual NLP (SIGTYP 2023), pages 76–88
May 6, 2023

guages homogeneously as it depends on the availability of linguistic descriptions provided by its sources. Thus, low-resourced languages usually have less information. For example, it is not possible to compare all 24 European Union languages as there are no common features with valid values for all of them. Furthermore, typological databases usually fail to illustrate the variations that can occur within a single language (i.e.: in general, only the most frequent phenomena are reported in the literature, and not all attested ones).

In terms of corpus-based typological studies, a broad survey was provided by Levshina (2022). The author showed that while several authors quantitively analyzed specific word-order patterns (e.g.: subject, verb, and object position (Östling, 2015), and verb and locative phrases (Wälchli, 2009)), other researchers have focused on quantitative analyses regarding language complexity (e.g.: (Hawkins, 2003) and (Sinnemäki, 2014)). On the other hand, the concept of Typometrics was introduced by Gerdes et al. (2021). The focus of their research was to extract rich details from corpora for testing typological implicational universals and explored new kinds of universals, named quantitative ones. Thus, different word-order phenomena were analyzed quantitatively (i.e.: the distribution of their occurrences in annotated corpora) to identify the ones present in all or most languages.

Thus, it is possible to notice that most studies regarding quantitative typology focus either on the analysis of specific linguistic phenomena or on the identification of universals. Our approach differs from theirs as our aim is to compare languages (i.e.: language vectors) using quantitative information concerning all syntactic structures extracted from corpora to obtain a more general syntactic overview of the elements in our language set and use the results as strategies to improve dependency parsing results.

An interesting method concerning the extraction and comparison of syntactic information from tree-banks was developed by Blache et al. (2016a). The MarsaGram tool is a resource that allows syntactic information (together with its statistics) to be extracted from annotated corpora by inferring context-free grammars from the syntactic structures. MarsaGram allows the extraction of linear patterns (i.e.: if a specific part-of-speech precedes another one inside the same subtree ruled by a determined head). The authors conducted a cluster analysis comparing 10 different languages and showed the potential in terms of typological analysis of this resource. However, the results were only compared to the genealogical classification of the selected languages and did not provide any comparison to other corpus-based methods. Moreover, the authors did not use the obtained classification with the perspective of improvement of dependency parsing systems via corpora-combination.

One example of effective usage of typological features (from URIEL database) to improve results of NLP methods was presented by Üstün et al. (2020). The authors developed the UDapter tool that uses a mix of automatically curated and predicted typological features as direct input to a neural parser. The results showed that this method allows the improvement of the dependency parsing accuracy for low-resourced languages. A similar study, using a different deep-learning architecture was conducted by Ammar et al. (2016), however, in both cases, there is no detailed analysis of which features were the most relevant.

Furthermore, Lynn et al. (2014) proposed a study concerning the Irish language using delexicalized corpora. The authors performed a series of cross-lingual direct transfer parsing for the Irish language and the best results were achieved with a model trained with the Indonesian corpus, a language from the Austronesian language family. The authors proposed some analysis considering similarities between the treebanks of both languages in terms of dependency parsing labels, however, a detailed statistical analysis of corpora and a complete comparison of specific typological features were not carried out.

While some papers focus on genealogical features, others consider syntactic ones. For example, Alzetta et al. (2020) presented a study whose aim was to identify cross-lingual quantitative trends in the distribution of dependency relations in annotated corpora from distinct languages by using an algorithm (LISCA - LInguiStically- driven Selection of Correct Arcs) (Dell'Orletta et al., 2013) which detects patterns of syntactic structures in tree-banks. However, only four Indo-European languages were scrutinized but some interesting insights concerning language peculiarities were observed.

Thus, studies regarding corpus-based typology and dependency parsing are usually presented without a specific comparison to other existing approaches or to the classic one concerning typological databases. That is why in this article the idea is to analyse possible quantitative typological methods in terms of correlation with the improvement obtained regarding dependency parsing results when corpora from different languages are combined.

3 Campaign Design

In this section, a brief overview of the selected data-sets is provided, followed by a description of selected the corpus-based syntactic typological approaches. Moreover, we detail the dependency parsing experiments and the correlation measures that were chosen for the analysis of the results.

3.1 Parallel Corpora

For the ensemble of experiments presented in this paper, we decided to use the Parallel Universal Dependencies (PUD) compilation that was created for the CoNLL 2017 shared task on Multilingual Parsing from Raw Text to Universal Dependencies (Zeman et al., 2018).

Levshina (2022) showed the benefit of using parallel corpora in typological studies, as the bias regarding size and content is avoided. Especially in this case, the usage of parallel sentences allows the focus to be on the syntactic strategies that are used by each language to express the same meaning.

The PUD collection provides 1,000 parallel sentences from news sources and Wikipedia annotated following Universal Dependencies guidelines (De Marneffe et al., 2021) in the CoNLL-U format for twenty languages[1]: Arabic, Chinese, Czech, English, Finnish, French, German, Hindi, Icelandic, Indonesian, Italian, Japanese, Korean, Polish, Portuguese, Russian, Spanish, Swedish, Thai, and Turkish. The PUD corpora are composed of translations from English (750 sentences), German (100), French (50), Spanish (50), and Italian (50). Although avoiding some biases linked to size and genre, these data-sets may contain some "translationese" ones, phenomena described by Volansky et al. (2015). Dependency parsing annotations were done automatically and, then, verified manually.

The list of PUD languages together with their ISO 639-3 codes and their genealogical information[2] is provided in Table 1. Although the total number of languages is limited to 20, the PUD collection provides, at least, some variety in terms of genealogy (i.e.: most languages belong to the Indo-European family, but 8 other different linguistic families are also present in this data-set).

The PUD Collection used in this article corresponds to the one available in the Universal Dependencies[3] data-set v.2.7 (November 2020).

3.2 Corpus-based Typological Approaches

Four different quantitative approaches were selected:

- MarsaGram all properties
- MarsaGram linear properties
- Head and dependent relative order
- Verb and object relative order

Each method is fully described in the subsections below. In the results section, these strategies are compared to the typological classification obtained with lang2vec tool (Littell et al., 2017): PUD languages are represented as language vectors composed of 41 syntactic features with valid values (i.e.: 0.0, 0.33, 0.66, and 1.0). The total number of syntactic features in this tool is 103, but only 41 are common to all PUD languages.

For each typological method, first, we generated the language vectors by extracting the syntactic information from the data-sets. Then, dissimilarity matrices were calculated using Euclidean and cosine distances (using R scripts). Thus, for each strategy, two matrices were obtained. The distance information between the languages is one of the inputs for the correlation analysis.

3.2.1 MarsaGram all properties

MarsaGram is a tool for exploring treebanks, it extracts context-free grammars (CFG) from annotated data-sets that can be used for statistical comparison between languages as proposed by Blache et al. (2016b). We have used the latest release of this software downloaded from the ORTOLANG platform of linguistic tools and resources[4].

This software identifies four types of properties from the corpora:

[1]Originally it was composed of fewer languages. Polish and Icelandic were added after the shared task, for example.

[2]Although the existence of the Altaic family has been challenged by some experts as detailed by Norman (2009), WALS database consider it in its genealogical classification.

[3]https://universaldependencies.org/

[4]https://www.ortolang.fr/market/tools/ortolang-000917

Language	ISO 639-3	Family	Genus
Arabic	arb	Afro-Asiatic	Semitic
Chinese	cmn	Sino-Tibetan	Chinese
Czech	ces	Indo-European	Slavic
English	eng	Indo-European	Germanic
Finnish	fin	Uralic	Finnic
French	fra	Indo-European	Romance
German	deu	Indo-European	Germanic
Hindi	hin	Indo-European	Indic
Icelandic	isl	Indo-European	Germanic
Indonesian	ind	Austronesian	Malayo-Sumbawan
Italian	ita	Indo-European	Romance
Japanese	jpn	Japanese	Japanese
Korean	kor	Korean	Korean
Polish	pol	Indo-European	Slavic
Portuguese	por	Indo-European	Romance
Russian	rus	Indo-European	Slavic
Spanish	spa	Indo-European	Romance
Swedish	swe	Indo-European	Germanic
Thai	tha	Tai-Kadai	Kam-Tai
Turkish	tur	Altaic	Turkic

Table 1: List of languages inside PUD collection, their respective ISO 639-3 three-character code, and their genealogical information according to WALS.

- Precede or Linear: It describes the relative position of two elements (A precedes B) inside a subtree governed by a specific head. Each element is described by its part-of-speech (POS) and dependency relation (deprel) in the syntactic tree. Although being part of the same subtree, elements A and B are not necessarily syntactically linked. An example of a sentence with this property is presented in the Annex section (Figure 1).
- Require: This property describes the cases where the presence of an element A requires the existence of an element B inside the subtree. An example of a sentence with this property is presented in the Annex section (Figure 2).
- Unicity: an element A has this property if inside the subtree it occurs only once (i.e.: no other element with the same part-of-speech and dependency label is attested). In the Annex section, one example of a sentence with this property is presented (Figure 3).
- Exclude: In this case, the presence of element A excludes the occurrence of element B inside the subtree.

Property	Number of Patterns	%
Linear	21,242	13.38
Require	6,189	3.90
Unicity	2,144	1.35
Exclude	129,180	81.37

Table 2: Distribution of extracted features using MarsaGram in terms of properties.

Of the four properties described above, only the linear one is directly linked to word-order patterns on the surface level of the sentence. In total 158,755 patterns were extracted from the PUD corpora. The distribution in terms of types of property is presented in table 2.

Each language vector regarding the MarsaGram all properties strategy is composed of these features associated with the value corresponding to its frequency of occurrence inside the corpus.

3.2.2 MarsaGram linear properties

As previously explained, the patterns with the linear property extracted with the MarsaGram tool are the ones that correspond to word-order phenomena inside subtrees. Thus, it seems pertinent to analyze them separately from the patterns regarding other properties, especially because when all phenomena are considered, the large majority correspond to the "exclude" property as presented in Table 2.

Thus, by extracting just linear patterns from PUD corpora, we generated language vectors composed of 21,242 features.

3.2.3 Head and dependent relative order

Besides the typological analysis provided from the data extracted using the MarsaGram tool, we also propose a quantitative approach concerning syntax, more specifically the head directionality parameter (i.e.: whether the heads precede the dependents (right-branching) or follow them (left-branching) in the surface-level of the sentence (Fábregas et al., 2015).

Hence, the attested head and dependent relative position patterns (and their frequency) in the different PUD corpora were extracted using a Python script. All observed features extracted from the PUD corpora (2,890 in total) have been included in the language vectors. From this total, 1,374 features (47.5%) correspond to cases where the dependent precedes the head, and 1,516 (52.5%) to right-branching patterns. In the cases where a feature was not observed in a determined language, the value 0 was attributed to it.

Two examples of head and dependent relative position patterns are presented below:

- ADV_advmod_precedes_ADJ - head-final or left-branching - It means that the dependent, which is an adverb (ADV) precedes the head which is an adjective (ADJ) and has the syntactic function of an adverbial modifier (advmod). The dependent can be in any position of the sentence previous to the head, not necessarily right before. An example of a sentence with this pattern is presented in the Appendix section (Figure 4).

- NOUN_obl_follows_VERB - head-initial or right-branching - In this case, the dependent (NOUN), comes after the head, which is a verb, and has the function of oblique nominal (obl). The dependent can be in any position after the head, not necessarily being right next to it. An example of a sentence representing this pattern is presented in the Appendix (Figure 5).

This specific analysis of the head and dependent relative position corresponds to a quantitative interpretation of the Head and Dependent theory (Hawkins, 1983) which considers that there is a tendency of organizing head and dependents in homogeneous word ordering. This author proposed a set of language types according to attested word-order phenomena concerning a limited list of elements as heads and dependents. In this article, we decided to consider all possible head and dependent pairs to conduct our analysis to have a more global overview of these ordering phenomena.

3.2.4 Verb and object relative order

Inside the ensemble of features extracted for the analysis of the head and dependent relative position, it is possible to extract the ones regarding verbs and direct objects (deprel: "obj") for a specific analysis of these phenomena. We decided to examine the position of these two elements in detail as they are key in typological studies such as the one proposed by Dryer (1992) where correlations are defined according to whether the verb comes before or after the object.

Thus, to compose the language vectors we extracted the head and dependent patterns which concern verbs and objects only (not only nominal but all other possible ones). We have decided to consider all the direct objects as if only nominal ones were analysed, the obtained classification would be similar to the general one available in databases (VO or OV languages), thus, not allowing us to differentiate in detail all PUD languages. In total, 13 OV and 12 VO features were attested in the PUD collection, allowing us to generate a 25-dimension language vector for each language.

3.3 Dependency parsing experiments

For the ensemble of experiments regarding dependency parsing, we used the UDify tool (Kondratyuk and Straka, 2019) which proposes an architecture aimed at PoS-MSD and dependency parsing tagging of tokenized texts integrating Multilingual BERT language model (104 languages) (Pires et al., 2019). It can be fine-tuned using specific corpora (mono or multilingual) to enhance overall results. This tool was selected as it presents state-of-the-art algorithms concerning the specific task of dependency parsing annotation.

Training parameters were defined as:

- Number of epochs: 80

- Warmup: 500

Other parameters remained the same as proposed by the authors. To calculate the statistical significance of the results, for each training corpus, we conducted 6 experiments with different values of random seeds, allowing us to calculate the mean value of the labeled attachment score (LAS) and its standard deviation.

The baseline regarding dependency parsing results consists of LAS values obtained with monolingual-trained models of PUD languages. For each experiment, 600 sentences were used for training, 200 for validation, and 200 for testing. Regarding the multilingual experiments, we combined PUD languages in pairs (concatenation of the training corpora). Thus, a total of 380 models were trained. Validation and test sets were the same ones as those used for the baseline experiments (monolingual ones).

With the baseline scores and the results obtained with the multilingual language pairs, we were able to calculate deltas to quantify the existing synergy between languages when corpora are combined for dependency parsing improvement. The deltas were obtained with:

$$Delta = LAS_{lang\_1\_and\_2} - LAS_{lang\_1} \quad (1)$$

The deltas were considered statistically significant if the p-value calculated between the two LAS scores was lower than 0.01.

3.4 Correlation calculation

The main focus of this study is to check whether the language distances obtained from the corpus-based typological approaches correlate with the LAS deltas (i.e., with the synergy between the languages when combined in dependency parsing experiments with deep-learning tools).

Two different correlation coefficients were chosen as they represent different ways that variables can correlate: Pearson's and Spearman's. The first one corresponds to the measure of linear correlation between two variables (Pearson, 1895), while the second determines how well the relationship between two variables can be defined as a monotonic function (Lehman, 2005).

Correlation values vary from -1 to 1. In our case, we expect negative values as we hypothesize that languages distances and deltas are inversely correlated (i.e.: the higher the distance between the languages, the lower will be the delta).

Language	LAS	Std. Dev.
tha	74.68	0.13
cmn	74.84	0.56
tur	76.68	0.21
hin	77.46	0.35
isl	78.90	0.16
fin	82.46	0.28
arb	83.34	0.24
swe	84.69	0.26
ind	85.72	0.19
kor	85.99	0.20
eng	86.63	0.15
ces	86.80	0.40
pol	86.88	0.21
rus	88.42	0.15
ita	89.48	0.14
deu	89.55	0.17
por	89.65	0.16
fra	91.20	0.21
spa	91.24	0.09
jpn	91.57	0.20

Table 3: LAS results obtained using UDify tool and PUD corpora using monolingual models.

4 Results

In the following subsections, we present the baseline results regarding the dependency parsing experiments together with an overview of the LAS values obtained when languages were associated. Then, the correlation analyses are displayed.

4.1 Dependency parsing baseline

As previously explained, the baseline consists of the LAS values obtained when monolingual training corpora were used to train the models using UDify tool. The PUD corpora were divided into train, development, and test sets (with 600, 200, and 200 sentences respectively). For each dataset, we conducted 6 experiments varying the random seed value for the calculation of the standard deviation and p-values. The results are presented in Table 3.

It is possible to notice that LAS results vary from 74.68 (for the Thai language) to 91.57 (for Japanese), almost 17 points of difference. Moreover, besides Japanese, all Romance languages also have rather high scores. The German language appears in between the ones of the Romance group, while other Germanic languages have lower scores (below Slavic languages). English and Swedish

Language	Positive deltas	Negative deltas
hin	0	0
jpn	0	6
kor	0	14
ind	1	1
tha	1	6
arb	2	0
fra	3	0
cmn	4	0
tur	4	1
deu	6	0
pol	9	0
ita	10	0
por	11	0
spa	11	0
ces	12	0
eng	14	0
isl	14	0
swe	14	0
rus	15	0
fin	16	0

Table 4: Number of positive and negative deltas concerning the LAS scores of the language combination experiments with the UDify tool (p-value < 0.01).

have quite similar results, however, Icelandic is positioned with the languages with the lowest scores (below 80) which are: Thai, Chinese, Turkish, and Hindi.

It has been shown by Alves et al. (2022) that these results are moderately correlated with the size of the language representation inside the language model (mBERT) present in the UDify architecture. However, it does not mean that this is the only parameter with a major influence on the results. Languages with more strict word order configurations tend to have higher LAS.

4.2 Dependency parsing multilingual results

In Table 4, we present the overall synergy results regarding the association of PUD corpora in terms of the number of cases, per language, where the combination of corpora provided statistically positive and negative deltas. For these experiments, each PUD language was combined in pairs with all the others (i.e.: the training sets were merged, a total of 1.200 sentences, and the development and test sets remained monolingual).

It is possible to observe that the group of languages with more than 10 cases of language combination with positive deltas is composed of Finnish, some Slavic, Germanic, and Romance languages. Nevertheless, not all PUD languages from these genera have the same positive tendency: it is the case of Polish, German, and French, all of them with less than 10 positive deltas. The Finnish language is the most favored one in terms of LAS when combined with other languages (i.e.: statistically relevant positive delta in 84% of the cases).

On the other hand, Japanese, Korean, and Thai do not obtain considerable improvement when combined with other PUD languages in terms of LAS but present many combinations which implicate a decrease in this score when compared to the baseline. Other non-Indo-European languages, such as Indonesian, Chinese, Thai, and Arabic do not benefit much from the language combinations but, at least, do not present negative synergies.

4.3 Correlations

As previously described, we calculated Pearson's and Spearman's correlation for each PUD language and for each typological strategy using the language distances from the dissimilarity matrices and the LAS deltas obtained when the languages were combined. All the correlation coefficients are displayed in the Appendix section (Tables 7 and 8)

When the obtained correlation value was between -0.7 and -0.5, it was considered a moderate inverse correlation, and a strong one for values below -0.7. In Tables 5 and 6, we present the overall results concerning the number of cases presenting either moderate or strong inverse correlation per typological strategy (Pearson's and Spearman's correlations respectively).

From the results displayed in table 5, the typological approach which provides the language classification which correlates the most with the empirical improvement in terms of LAS is the MarsaGram linear one concerning cosine distances. This approach presents a moderate or strong correlation for half of all PUD languages. It indicates that the linear order of components inside the same subtree is one of the relevant factors that may affect deep-learning systems. However, since the correlation is not observed for all languages, further research is necessary to verify the extent of this influence.

The classic classification using lang2vec syntactic features only shows a strong or moderate correlation for 7 out of the 20 PUD languages. This score is even lower than other new methods such as Head and Dependent (cosine) and MarsaGram

	Msg. all Euc.	Msg. all cos	Msg. lin. Euc.	Msg. lin. cos	HD Euc.	HD cos	VO Euc.	VO cos	L2v Euc.	L2v cos
Strong	0	0	0	0	0	1	1	2	1	1
Moderate	3	8	3	10	7	7	5	2	6	5
Total	3	8	3	**10**	7	8	6	4	7	6

Table 5: Number of Pearson's correlations (moderate and strong) regarding all 20 PUD languages. In bold is highlighted the highest value regarding the total number.

	Msg. all Euc.	Msg. all cos	Msg. lin. Euc.	Msg. lin. cos	HD Euc.	HD cos	VO Euc.	VO cos	L2v Euc.	L2v cos
Strong	0	1	0	0	1	2	2	0	1	1
Moderate	3	2	3	7	6	5	5	5	5	5
Total	3	3	3	**7**	**7**	**7**	**7**	5	6	6

Table 6: Number of Spearman's correlations (moderate and strong) regarding all 20 PUD languages. In bold is highlighted the highest value regarding the total number.

all properties (cosine).

5 Discussion

The results displayed in Table 4 show that as it is described in the literature, combining corpora is an effective way to improve dependency parsing scores. In our experiments, we showed that the simple association of corpora allowed us to improve significantly the LAS score for 17 out of the 20 selected languages. The ones which did not present any improvement are from linguistic families which are not well represented in the language sample. It is important to mention that all experiments were conducted in a low-resourced scenario (i.e.: corpora composed of 1,000 sentences) even though the majority of the selected languages have other annotated corpora. The idea was to find the best typological method which could be used for under-resourced languages which are the ones with the lowest LAS scores in the literature.

Moreover, from tables 5 and 6, it is possible to notice that the method with the highest number of inverse correlations is the MarsaGram linear one with language distances calculated with the cosine measure. The scores were either moderate or strong for half of the languages in the PUD collection. This specific corpus-based approach seems to be more effective than the state-of-the-art one (i.e.: using features from the lang2vec tool). Moreover, since the highest values were obtained with Pearson's correlations, it is possible to say that what is observed is a linear inverse correlation between the distances and the deltas.

However, even though the MarsaGram linear (cosine) strategy provides the most optimized results, it fails to explain the LAS values for 10 PUD languages. For Icelandic, Indonesian, and Turkish, the Pearson's correlation coefficient of this strategy is lower than -0.2, which indicates, at least, a low correlation, while for Italian, this coefficient is lower than -0.10 but higher than -0.20. On the other hand, for Chinese, Japanese, German, and Russian, this coefficient is very close to 0.00 (i.e.: no correlation). And, for Korean and Hindi, values are positive.

With the values from the dissimilarity matrix obtained using the MarsaGram linear method, it is possible to generate a dendrogram with the hclust() function using R. The classification in clusters is presented in the Annex (Figure 6). It is possible to notice some similarities with the languages' genealogy (e.g.: Romance languages in the same cluster) and with other typological classifications (e.g. OV languages on the same side of the dendrogram), however not all languages are classed following these expected configurations.

6 Conclusion and Perspectives

In this paper, we presented four corpus-based typological approaches and evaluated them in comparison with the state-of-the-art method consisting of using syntactic information from databases. First, we described these new strategies followed by the results of the dependency parsing experiments via corpora association.

We showed that the combination of corpora is an effective way to improve LAS results in low-resourced scenarios and that the typological approach concerning the order of elements inside subtrees (MarsaGram linear) is the one with the highest number of moderate and strong correlations for the languages in the PUD collection. In the future, we aim to analyze in detail the languages for which this method was not effective. Moreover, we intend to increase the number of languages to have a more homogeneous language-set in terms of the number of languages per linguistic family as well as conduct tests with non-parallel corpora. Another perspective for future work is to optimize Marsagram linear method defining weights for the features as the extracted patterns may influence the results differently.

7 Acknowledgements

The work presented in this paper has received funding from the European Union's Horizon 2020 research and innovation program under the Marie Skłodowska-Curie grant agreement no. 812997 and under the name CLEOPATRA (Cross-lingual Event-centric Open Analytics Research Academy).

References

Diego Alves, Marko Tadić, and Božo Bekavac. 2022. Multilingual comparative analysis of deep-learning dependency parsing results using parallel corpora. In *Proceedings of the BUCC Workshop within LREC 2022*, pages 33–42.

Chiara Alzetta, Felice Dell'Orletta, Simonetta Montemagni, Petya Osenova, Kiril Simov, and Giulia Venturi. 2020. Quantitative linguistic investigations across universal dependencies treebanks. In *Proceedings of the Seventh Italian Conference on Computational Linguistics, CLiC-it 2020, Bologna, Italy, March 1-3, 2021*, volume 2769 of *CEUR Workshop Proceedings*. CEUR-WS.org.

Waleed Ammar, George Mulcaire, Miguel Ballesteros, Chris Dyer, and Noah A. Smith. 2016. Many languages, one parser. *Transactions of the Association for Computational Linguistics*, 4:431–444.

Philippe Blache, Stéphane Rauzy, and Grégoire Montcheuil. 2016a. Marsagram: an excursion in the forests of parsing trees. In *Language Resources and Evaluation Conference*, 10, page 7.

Philippe Blache, Stéphane Rauzy, and Grégoire Montcheuil. 2016b. MarsaGram: an excursion in the forests of parsing trees. In *Proceedings of the Tenth International Conference on Language Resources and Evaluation (LREC'16)*, pages 2336–2342, Portorož, Slovenia. European Language Resources Association (ELRA).

Marie-Catherine De Marneffe, Christopher D Manning, Joakim Nivre, and Daniel Zeman. 2021. Universal dependencies. *Computational linguistics*, 47(2):255–308.

Felice Dell'Orletta, Giulia Venturi, and Simonetta Montemagni. 2013. Linguistically–driven selection of correct arcs for dependency parsing. *Computación y Sistemas*, 17.

Matthew S Dryer. 1992. The greenbergian word order correlations. *Language*, 68(1):81–138.

Matthew S. Dryer and Martin Haspelmath, editors. 2013. *WALS Online*. Max Planck Institute for Evolutionary Anthropology, Leipzig.

Antonio Fábregas, Jaume Mateu, and Michael T. Putnam. 2015. *Contemporary Linguistic Parameters: Contemporary Studies in Linguistics*. Bloomsbury Academic, London.

Kim Gerdes, Bruno Guillaume, Sylvain Kahane, and Guy Perrier. 2021. Starting a new treebank? go SUD! In *Proceedings of the Sixth International Conference on Dependency Linguistics (Depling, SyntaxFest 2021)*, pages 35–46, Sofia, Bulgaria. Association for Computational Linguistics.

Bruno Guillaume, Karën Fort, and Nicolas Lefèbvre. 2016. Crowdsourcing Complex Language Resources: Playing to Annotate Dependency Syntax. In *International Conference on Computational Linguistics (COLING)*, Proceedings of the 26th International Conference on Computational Linguistics (COLING), Osaka, Japan.

John A Hawkins. 1983. *Word order universals*, volume 3. Elsevier.

John A Hawkins. 2003. Efficiency and complexity in grammars: Three general principles. *The nature of explanation in linguistic theory*, 121:152.

Dan Jurafsky and James H. Martin. 2009. *Speech and language processing : an introduction to natural language processing, computational linguistics, and speech recognition*. Pearson Prentice Hall, Upper Saddle River, N.J.

Dan Kondratyuk and Milan Straka. 2019. 75 languages, 1 model: Parsing universal dependencies universally.

A Lehman. 2005. Jmp for basic univariate and multivariate statistics: a step-by-step guide. 481p.

Natalia Levshina. 2022. Corpus-based typology: applications, challenges and some solutions. *Linguistic Typology*, 26(1):129–160.

Patrick Littell, David R Mortensen, Ke Lin, Katherine Kairis, Carlisle Turner, and Lori Levin. 2017. Uriel and lang2vec: Representing languages as typological, geographical, and phylogenetic vectors. In *Proceedings of the 15th Conference of the European Chapter of the Association for Computational Linguistics: Volume 2, Short Papers*, pages 8–14.

Teresa Lynn, Jennifer Foster, Mark Dras, and Lamia Tounsi. 2014. Cross-lingual transfer parsing for low-resourced languages: An Irish case study. In *Proceedings of the First Celtic Language Technology Workshop*, pages 41–49, Dublin, Ireland. Association for Computational Linguistics and Dublin City University.

Jerry Norman. 2009. A new look at altaic. *Journal of the American Oriental Society*, 129(1):83–89.

Robert Östling. 2015. Word order typology through multilingual word alignment. In *Proceedings of the 53rd Annual Meeting of the Association for Computational Linguistics and the 7th International Joint Conference on Natural Language Processing (Volume 2: Short Papers)*, pages 205–211.

Daniel W. Otter, Julian R. Medina, and Jugal K. Kalita. 2018. A survey of the usages of deep learning in natural language processing. *CoRR*, abs/1807.10854.

Karl Pearson. 1895. Vii. note on regression and inheritance in the case of two parents. *proceedings of the royal society of London*, 58(347-352):240–242.

Telmo Pires, Eva Schlinger, and Dan Garrette. 2019. How multilingual is multilingual BERT? In *Proceedings of the 57th Annual Meeting of the Association for Computational Linguistics*, pages 4996–5001, Florence, Italy. Association for Computational Linguistics.

Edoardo Maria Ponti, Helen O'Horan, Yevgeni Berzak, Ivan Vulić, Roi Reichart, Thierry Poibeau, Ekaterina Shutova, and Anna Korhonen. 2019a. Modeling language variation and universals: A survey on typological linguistics for natural language processing. *Computational Linguistics*, 45(3):559–601.

Edoardo Maria Ponti, Helen O'horan, Yevgeni Berzak, Ivan Vulić, Roi Reichart, Thierry Poibeau, Ekaterina Shutova, and Anna Korhonen. 2019b. Modeling language variation and universals: A survey on typological linguistics for natural language processing. *Computational Linguistics*, 45(3):559–601.

Kaius Sinnemäki. 2014. Complexity trade-offs: A case study. In *Measuring grammatical complexity*, pages 179–201. Oxford University Press.

Ahmet Üstün, Arianna Bisazza, Gosse Bouma, and Gertjan van Noord. 2020. UDapter: Language adaptation for truly Universal Dependency parsing. In *Proceedings of the 2020 Conference on Empirical Methods in Natural Language Processing (EMNLP)*, pages 2302–2315, Online. Association for Computational Linguistics.

Vered Volansky, Noam Ordan, and Shuly Wintner. 2015. On the features of translationese. *Digital Scholarship in the Humanities*, 30(1):98–118.

Bernhard Wälchli. 2009. Data reduction typology and the bimodal distribution bias. 13(1):77–94.

Daniel Zeman, Jan Hajic, Martin Popel, Martin Potthast, Milan Straka, Filip Ginter, Joakim Nivre, and Slav Petrov. 2018. Conll 2018 shared task: Multilingual parsing from raw text to universal dependencies. In *Proceedings of the CoNLL 2018 Shared Task: Multilingual parsing from raw text to universal dependencies*, pages 1–21.

A Appendix

```
# text = Each map in the exhibition tells its own story, not all factual.
1   Each    each    DET DT  _   2   det 2:det   _
2   map map NOUN    NN  Number=Sing 6   nsubj   6:nsubj _
3   in  in  ADP IN  _   5   case    5:case  _
4   the the DET DT  Definite=Def|PronType=Art   5   det 5:det   _
5   exhibition  exhibition  NOUN    NN  Number=Sing 2   nmod    2:nmod:in   _
6   tells   tell    VERB    VBZ Mood=Ind|Number=Sing|Person=3|Tense=Pres|VerbForm=Fin   0   root    0:root  _
7   its its PRON    PRP$    Gender=Neut|Number=Sing|Person=3|Poss=Yes|PronType=Prs  9   nmod:poss   9:nmod:poss _
8   own own ADJ JJ  Degree=Pos  9   amod    9:amod  _
9   story   story   NOUN    NN  Number=Sing 6   obj 6:obj   SpaceAfter=No
10  ,   ,   PUNCT   ,   _   6   punct   6:punct _
11  not not ADV RB  Polarity=Neg    12  advmod  12:advmod   _
12  all all DET DT  _   13  nsubj   13:nsubj    _
13  factual factual ADJ JJ  Degree=Pos  6   parataxis   6:parataxis SpaceAfter=No
14  .   .   PUNCT   .   _   6   punct   6:punct _
```

Figure 1: Example of a sentence with the pattern NOUN_precede_DET-det_NOUN-nmod rom the PUD English corpus. The determiner (DET) on line 4 has the incoming relation det. It precedes the noun (NOUN) on line 5, which has the incoming relation nmod. Both appear in the subtree headed by a NOUN (the first tag in the pattern description); in this case, it is again the noun on line 5.

```
# sent_id = w02015088
# text = The ruins were later built over.
1   The the DET DT  Definite=Def|PronType=Art   2   det 2:det   _
2   ruins   ruin    NOUN    NNS Number=Plur 5   nsubj:pass  5:nsubj:pass    _
3   were    be  AUX VBD Mood=Ind|Tense=Past|VerbForm=Fin    5   aux:pass    5:aux:pass  _
4   later   later   ADV RB  _   5   advmod  5:advmod    _
5   built   build   VERB    VBN Tense=Past|VerbForm=Part    0   root    0:root  _
6   over    over    ADP RP  _   5   compound:prt    5:compound:prt  SpaceAfter=No
7   .   .   PUNCT   .   _   5   punct   5:punct
```

Figure 2: Example of a sentence with the pattern VERB_require_NOUN-nsubj:pass_AUX-aux:pass from the PUD English corpus. The noun (NOUN) on line 2 has the incoming relation nsubj:pass. It requires the auxilary (AUX) on line 3, which has the incoming relation aux:pass. Both appear in the subtree headed by a VERB (token "built" on line 5).

```
# sent_id = n01011004
# text = She has also been charged with trying to kill her two-year-old daughter.
1   She she PRON    PRP Case=Nom|Gender=Fem|Number=Sing|Person=3|PronType=Prs   5   nsubj:pass  5:nsubj:pass    _
2   has have    AUX VBZ Mood=Ind|Number=Sing|Person=3|Tense=Pres|VerbForm=Fin   5   aux 5:aux   _
3   also    also    ADV RB  _   5   advmod  5:advmod    _
4   been    be  AUX VBN Tense=Past|VerbForm=Part    5   aux:pass    5:aux:pass  _
5   charged charge  VERB    VBN Tense=Past|VerbForm=Part    0   root    0:root  _
6   with    with    SCONJ   IN  _   7   mark    7:mark  _
7   trying  try VERB    VBG VerbForm=Ger    5   advcl   5:advcl:with    _
8   to  to  PART    TO  _   9   mark    9:mark  _
9   kill    kill    VERB    VB  VerbForm=Inf    7   xcomp   7:xcomp _
10  her she PRON    PRP$    Gender=Fem|Number=Sing|Person=3|Poss=Yes|PronType=Prs   16  nmod:poss   16:nmod:poss    _
11  two two NUM CD  NumType=Card    15  nummod  15:nummod   SpaceAfter=No
12  -   -   PUNCT   HYPH    _   15  punct   15:punct    SpaceAfter=No
13  year    year    NOUN    NN  Number=Sing 15  obl:npmod   15:obl:npmod    SpaceAfter=No
14  -   -   PUNCT   HYPH    _   15  punct   15:punct    SpaceAfter=No
15  old old ADJ JJ  Degree=Pos  16  amod    16:amod _
16  daughter    daughter    NOUN    NN  Number=Sing 9   obj 9:obj   SpaceAfter=No
17  .   .   PUNCT   .   _   5   punct   5:punct _
```

Figure 3: Example of a sentence with the pattern ADJ_unicity_NOUN-obl:npmod from the PUD English corpus. The head of the subtree is the token "old" (ADJ) on line 15. The element on line 13 ("year") has the part-of-speech of noun (NOUN) and the dependency relation of obl:npmod and no other element with the same characteristics can be found inside the same subtree.

```
# text = These are not very popular due to the often remote and roadless locations.
1   These   these   PRON    DT  Number=Plur|PronType=Dem    5   nsubj   5:nsubj _
2   are be  AUX VBP Mood=Ind|Tense=Pres|VerbForm=Fin    5   cop 5:cop   _
3   not not PART    RB  Polarity=Neg    5   advmod  5:advmod    _
4   very    very    ADV RB  _   5   advmod  5:advmod    _
5   popular popular ADJ JJ  Degree=Pos  0   root    0:root
6   due due ADP IN  _   13  case    13:case _
7   to  to  ADP IN  _   6   fixed   6:fixed _
8   the the DET DT  Definite=Def|PronType=Art   13  det 13:det  _
9   often   often   ADV RB  _   10  advmod  10:advmod   _
10  remote  remote  ADJ JJ  Degree=Pos  13  amod    13:amod _
11  and and CCONJ   CC  _   12  cc  12:cc   _
12  roadless    roadless    ADJ JJ  Degree=Pos  10  conj    10:conj:and|13:amod _
13  locations   location    NOUN    NNS Number=Plur 5   obl 5:obl:due_to    SpaceAfter=No
14  .   .   PUNCT   .   _   5   punct   5:punct _
```

Figure 4: Example of a sentence with two occurrences of the pattern ADV_advmod_precedes_ADJ. The adverb (ADV) on line 9 has the incoming relation advmod. It precedes the adjective (ADJ) on line 10. And, the adverb (ADV) on line 4 has the incoming relation advmod. It precedes the adjective (ADJ) on line 5.

```
# text = The new spending is fueled by Clinton's large bank account.
1   The the DET DT  Definite=Def|PronType=Art   3   det 3:det   _
2   new new ADJ JJ  Degree=Pos  3   amod    3:amod  _
3   spending    spending    NOUN    NN  Number=Sing 5   nsubj:pass  5:nsubj:pass    _
4   is  be  AUX VBZ Mood=Ind|Number=Sing|Person=3|Tense=Pres|VerbForm=Fin   5   aux:pass    5:aux:pass  _
5   fueled  fuel    VERB    VBN Tense=Past|VerbForm=Part    0   root    0:root  _
6   by  by  ADP IN  _   11  case    11:case _
7   Clinton Clinton PROPN   NNP Number=Sing 11  nmod:poss   11:nmod:poss    SpaceAfter=No
8   's  's  PART    POS _   7   case    7:case  _
9   large   large   ADJ JJ  Degree=Pos  11  amod    11:amod _
10  bank    bank    NOUN    NN  Number=Sing 11  compound    11:compound _
11  account account NOUN    NN  Number=Sing 5   obl 5:obl:by    SpaceAfter=No
12  .   .   PUNCT   .   _   5   punct   5:punct _
```

Figure 5: Example of a sentence with the pattern NOUN_obl_follows_VERB. The noun (NOUN) on line 11 has the incoming relation obl. It comes after the verb (VERB) on line 5.

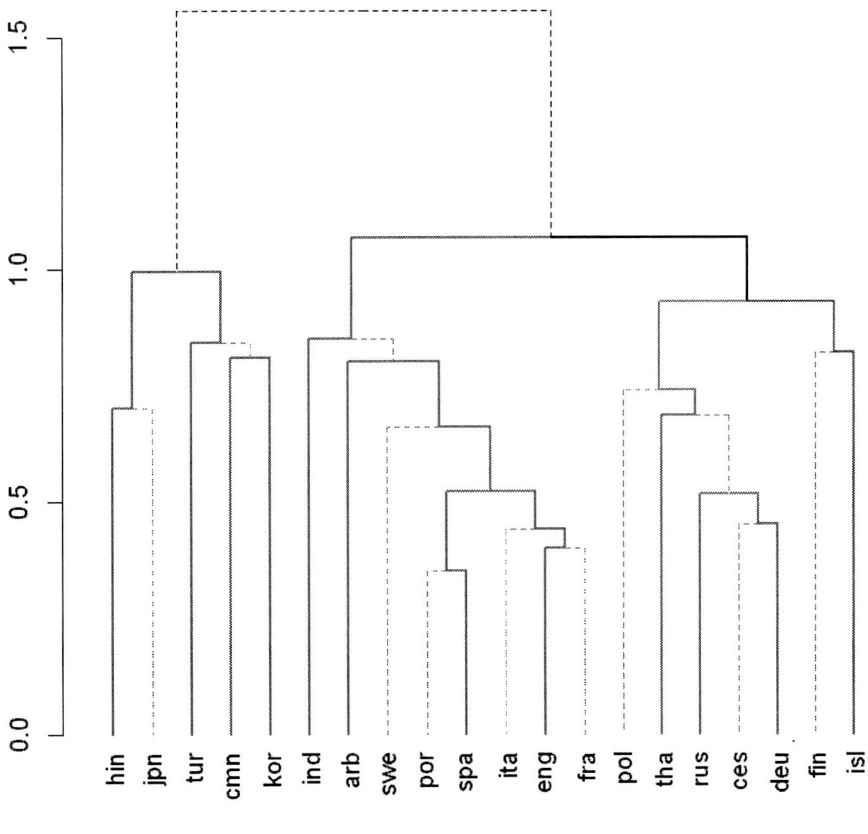

Figure 6: Marsagram Linear cosine Dendrogram

	Msg. all Euc.	Msg. all cos	Msg. lin. Euc.	Msg. lin. cos	HD Euc.	HD cos	VO Euc.	VO cos	L2v Euc.	L2v cos
arb	-0.11	-0.52	-0.03	-0.57	-0.54	-0.65	-0.59	-0.47	-0.59	-0.55
cmn	0.19	-0.11	-0.26	0.00	0.25	0.15	-0.06	-0.21	0.01	-0.03
ces	-0.25	-0.60	-0.28	-0.57	-0.65	-0.67	-0.57	-0.57	-0.36	-0.28
eng	-0.34	-0.53	-0.21	-0.59	-0.41	-0.49	-0.35	-0.16	-0.36	-0.41
fin	-0.16	-0.52	-0.46	-0.63	-0.46	-0.44	-0.71	-0.72	-0.10	-0.01
fra	-0.50	-0.51	-0.52	-0.62	-0.62	-0.59	-0.38	-0.31	-0.50	-0.47
deu	-0.48	-0.11	-0.22	-0.03	-0.23	-0.22	0.03	0.46	-0.03	-0.02
hin	-0.36	-0.27	0.05	0.40	0.12	0.41	0.56	0.50	0.44	0.46
isl	0.18	-0.19	-0.26	-0.36	-0.12	-0.31	-0.49	-0.44	-0.40	-0.42
ind	0.23	-0.30	0.20	-0.21	0.12	0.05	0.00	0.05	-0.21	-0.11
ita	-0.21	-0.23	-0.02	-0.13	-0.14	-0.17	-0.30	-0.16	-0.10	-0.17
jpn	-0.18	0.06	-0.15	-0.05	0.38	0.35	0.02	0.07	0.40	0.50
kor	0.30	0.29	0.08	0.38	0.42	0.49	0.41	0.47	0.43	0.37
pol	-0.23	-0.37	-0.50	-0.62	-0.13	-0.34	-0.51	-0.40	-0.37	-0.34
por	-0.64	-0.52	-0.39	-0.61	-0.64	-0.53	-0.45	-0.40	-0.57	-0.50
rus	-0.16	-0.08	0.17	0.03	-0.27	-0.24	-0.46	-0.28	-0.15	-0.17
spa	-0.59	-0.45	-0.57	-0.51	-0.53	-0.50	-0.43	-0.38	-0.60	-0.55
swe	-0.48	-0.59	-0.31	-0.64	-0.58	-0.63	-0.59	-0.49	-0.70	-0.68
tha	0.26	-0.59	-0.22	-0.62	-0.64	-0.88	-0.60	-0.80	-0.76	-0.81
tur	-0.09	0.10	-0.34	-0.25	-0.45	-0.53	-0.42	-0.56	-0.61	-0.60

Table 7: Pearson's correlation values regarding all 20 PUD languages.

	Msg. all Euc.	Msg. all cos	Msg. lin. Euc.	Msg. lin. cos	HD Euc.	HD cos	VO Euc.	VO cos	L2v Euc.	L2v cos
arb	-0.05	-0.33	-0.09	-0.53	-0.55	-0.66	-0.65	-0.52	-0.70	-0.69
cmn	0.24	-0.15	-0.12	-0.08	0.36	0.18	0.03	-0.12	-0.02	-0.03
ces	-0.14	-0.54	-0.31	-0.49	-0.51	-0.48	-0.52	-0.57	-0.31	-0.31
eng	-0.38	-0.59	-0.27	-0.48	-0.49	-0.52	-0.46	-0.02	-0.37	-0.38
fin	-0.20	-0.48	-0.41	-0.60	-0.35	-0.44	-0.74	-0.66	-0.09	-0.06
fra	-0.50	-0.48	-0.55	-0.59	-0.57	-0.56	-0.47	-0.26	-0.50	-0.53
deu	-0.52	-0.28	-0.22	-0.03	-0.30	-0.29	0.05	0.44	-0.09	-0.08
hin	-0.31	-0.23	0.06	0.32	-0.05	0.34	0.68	0.60	0.43	0.44
isl	0.24	-0.19	-0.21	-0.46	-0.03	-0.20	-0.50	-0.26	-0.43	-0.44
ind	0.13	-0.27	0.02	-0.22	0.04	0.01	-0.16	-0.24	-0.29	-0.23
ita	-0.23	-0.31	-0.02	-0.11	-0.16	-0.15	-0.24	0.12	-0.20	-0.20
jpn	0.08	0.16	-0.01	-0.26	0.45	0.52	-0.10	-0.16	0.50	0.49
kor	0.52	0.34	0.13	0.52	0.18	0.53	0.22	0.17	0.24	0.27
pol	-0.29	-0.44	-0.67	-0.62	-0.23	-0.42	-0.55	-0.48	-0.31	-0.31
por	-0.42	-0.29	-0.23	-0.37	-0.41	-0.42	-0.49	-0.47	-0.48	-0.47
rus	-0.01	-0.14	0.16	0.07	-0.08	-0.09	-0.46	-0.06	-0.08	-0.06
spa	-0.51	-0.45	-0.55	-0.55	-0.56	-0.53	-0.50	-0.55	-0.67	-0.66
swe	-0.46	-0.73	-0.38	-0.68	-0.70	-0.74	-0.80	-0.40	-0.64	-0.63
tha	0.25	-0.49	-0.19	-0.62	-0.51	-0.81	-0.36	-0.69	-0.68	-0.70
tur	0.09	-0.15	-0.26	-0.18	-0.59	-0.69	-0.15	-0.31	-0.59	-0.57

Table 8: Spearman's correlation values regarding all 20 PUD languages.

Cross-lingual Transfer Learning with Persian

Sepideh Mollanorozy
University of Malta
University of Groningen
sepid.mnorozy@gmail.com

Marc Tanti
University of Malta
marc.tanti@um.edu.mt

Malvina Nissim
University of Groningen
m.nissim@rug.nl

Abstract

The success of cross-lingual transfer learning for POS tagging has been shown to be strongly dependent, among other factors, on the (typological and/or genetic) similarity of the low-resource language used for testing and the language(s) used in pre-training or to fine-tune the model. We further unpack this finding in two directions by zooming in on a single language, namely Persian. First, still focusing on POS tagging we run an in-depth analysis of the behaviour of Persian with respect to closely related languages and languages that appear to benefit from cross-lingual transfer with Persian. To do so, we also use the World Atlas of Language Structures to determine which properties are shared between Persian and other languages included in the experiments. Based on our results, Persian seems to be a reasonable potential language for Kurmanji and Tagalog low-resource languages for other tasks as well. Second, we test whether previous findings also hold on a task other than POS tagging to pull apart the benefit of language similarity and the specific task for which such benefit has been shown to hold. We gather sentiment analysis datasets for 31 target languages and through a series of cross-lingual experiments analyse which languages most benefit from Persian as the source. The set of languages that benefit from Persian had very little overlap across the two tasks, suggesting a strong task-dependent component in the usefulness of language similarity in cross-lingual transfer.

1 Introduction and Background

Cross-lingual transfer learning consists in using a (usually high resource) language for fine-tuning a pre-trained model for a given task, but then using such model to obtain predictions for a different (usually low-resourced) language. This is advantageous if the lesser-resourced language lacks enough resources for training. While in early work on transfer learning English has often been used as source language, due to its high availability, more recent research has shown that this might not be the optimal choice. For example, de Vries et al. (2021) show that for POS tagging language similarity has a great impact on the success of transfer learning, and even with a small amount of data, one can achieve high accuracy.de Vries et al. (2022) expands this study by doing cross-lingual transfer learning between over 100 languages, in search of good combinations of source and target languages. They find that there is no single language that is a good source language for cross-lingual transfer learning with all other languages. Besides, the target language being included in the model pre-training is the most effective factor on performance of the model which does not play a role in low-resource settings. The next best predictor found for finding a good performing source-target language pair is the LDND distance (Wichmann et al., 2010) between them, considered as the language similarity measure. This measure is based on the Levenshtein distance between a set of selected words in two languages.

As a contribution to a better understanding of the properties of source and target languages towards successful transfer learning, and towards better processing for low-resource languages, we investigate cross-lingual transfer learning with a focus on Persian. We analyze the results of de Vries et al. (2022) experiments that include Persian as either the source or the target language to find the languages that are a good match with Persian for POS tagging. To explain the potential reasons for the results, we use the linguistic features from World Atlas of Language Structures (WALS).

We also examine the performance of ParsBERT, the pre-trained monolingual Persian model, in comparison to XLM-RoBERTa, a pre-trained multilingual model, for the POS tagging task.

Finally, we investigate whether the language pairs with Persian in the POS tagging are generalizable to other NLP tasks or not. We perform cross-

Proceedings of the 5th Workshop on Research in Computational Linguistic Typology and Multilingual NLP (SIGTYP 2023), pages 89–95
May 6, 2023

lingual transfer learning for sentiment analysis as there is Persian dataset available for this task and this task is a high-level NLP task compared to POS tagging as a low-level NLP task. This combination of tasks has been of interest for cross-lingual transfer learning in other studies as well (Dat, 2021).

We gather sentiment analysis datasets from various resources and carry out experiments using the pre-trained multilingual XLM-RoBERTa language model. We fine-tune this model using Persian data and then test it with other languages. In the end, we compare the best target languages with Persian as source in sentiment analysis and POS tagging.

Persian language is the official language of Iran, Afghanistan and Tajikestan. The variety of Persian in these countries is Iranian Persian (main and official variety of Persian), Dari, and Tajik. The writing system of Iranian Persian and Dari are the same, using Persian alphabet, whereas, the Tajik variety has a different writing system. Figure 1 shows the geographical location of people whose mother tongue is Persian.

Persian is an Indo-European language, with a subject-object-verb word order, and it has words borrowed from French and English. Additionally, its grammar is similar to many Indo-European languages. But also it has many words in common with Arabic, as Iran has Iraq as one of its neighbour countries and the official religious book for both countries is in Arabic.

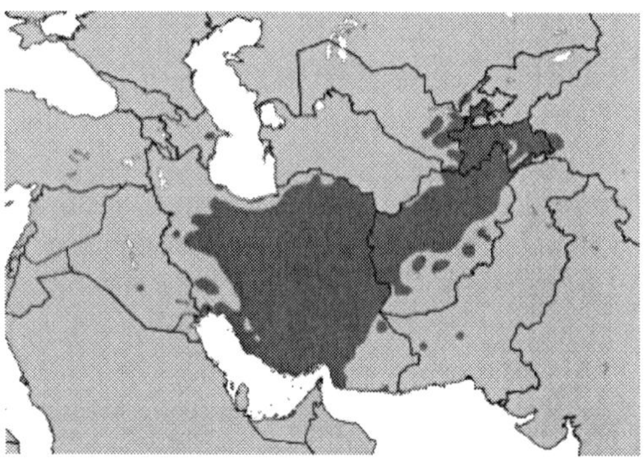

Figure 1: Regions that the majority of people's mother tongue is Persian (Commons, 2021b)

Considering Iran's population of 85 million people, the number of Persian speakers is considerably large. According to Figure 2, Persian speakers are widely spread around the world. These observations show the importance of research with Persian language as it is used by a lot of people around the world, and it can result in applications benefiting a large group of people.

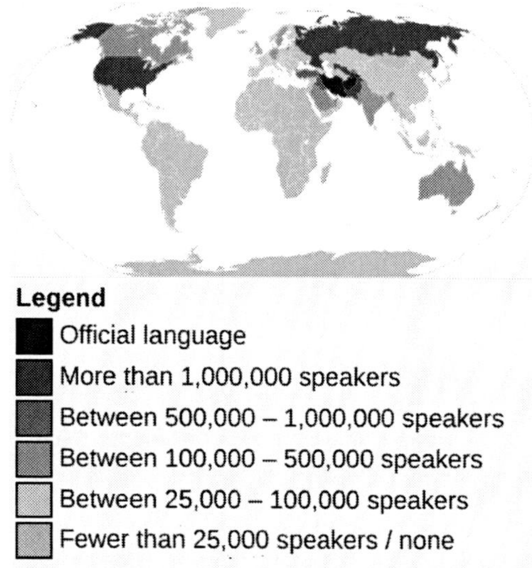

Figure 2: Persian speakers spread around the world (Commons, 2021a)

2 Experimental Setup

2.1 Datasets

For the POS tagging analysis, we a subset of the Universal Dependencies (UD) dataset as de Vries et al. (2022)[1] that has a tag set of 17 tags. There are 105 languages in this dataset in total, all having at least 10 samples as test data that we consider as target language in our analysis. Among them, 65 languages also have at least 25 samples as train data which we consider as source languages. We also obtained the accuracy scores of these 6825 different source-target language pairs using the XLM-RoBERTa model from de Vries et al. (2022).

We use the LDND distance measure between 90 different languages from the ASJP database[2] (Wichmann et al., 2022) as a measure of language similarity. In addition, we use the WALS dataset (wal, 2013)[3] including 192 different phonological, grammatical, and lexical properties of 2 676 unique languages. The number of common linguistics features is the second language similarity measure that we use in our analysis.

A multilingual sentiment analysis dataset containing all the languages that exist in UD dataset for

[1] https://huggingface.co/datasets/wietsedv/udpos28

[2] https://asjp.clld.org/

[3] https://www.kaggle.com/datasets/rtatman/world-atlas-of-language-structures

POS tagging does not exist. The largest one that we found contains negative and positive tagged data including 23 languages[4] as follows: Algerian, Arabic, Basque, Bulgarian, Cantonese, Chinese, Croatian, English, Finnish, German, Greek, Hebrew, Indonesian, Japanese, Korean, Maltese, Norwegian, Russian, Slovak, Spanish, Thai, Turkish, and Vietnamese. In addition, we gather data for 8 languages namely Persian, Urdu, Hindi, Welsh, Polish, Romanian, Bambara, and Uyghur from multiple resources, resulting in 31 languages in total. Details about the datasets is provided in appendix A. We converted all of them to the same structure and only kept the positive and negative data entries [5].

2.2 Methods

For POS tagging analysis, we analyze the results of experiments that de Vries et al. (2022) did with Persian and other languages. In each experiment, de Vries et al. (2022) fine-tuned the XLM-RoBERTa model with a source language and then tested it with a target language. We focus on the result of experiments that have Persian as the source or target language and attempt to find languages that result in a high score with Persian in each scenario. We find the target languages that have Persian as one of their top 10 source languages based on accuracy score. Then, we consider Persian as the target language, and find the source languages that have Persian as one of their top 10 target languages.

We also explore the linguistic features of the languages that are a good pair with Persian using the WALS data. We get all the features of the languages and measure their Hamming distance to the Persian features.

In our last experiment for POS tagging, we fine-tune the ParsBERT language model for 3 epochs with Persian data. At this stage, we achieved a high performance with an accuracy score of 95.99% on the validation set. As this score is higher than the XLM-RoBERTa Persian monolingual score, we kept this model and did not continue the training procedure. Then, we test this model with Persian and other languages that are a good match with it for POS tagging.

For the sentiment analysis experiments, we use the XLM-RoBERTa[6] pre-trained model, the same model that is used by de Vries et al. (2022) for the POS tagging experiments. We fine-tune the model with Persian data for 10 epochs with the best score occurring at the 5th epoch, yielding an accuracy of 87.21%. Model fine-tuning details are provided in appendix A. We take the model checkpoint at epoch 5 and test it with Persian and other target languages to predict the sentiment of the input text as positive or negative.

3 Results and discussion

3.1 POS-tagging

Using the XLM-RoBERTa model, the monolingual Persian experiment [7] has the highest accuracy of 91.43%. Considering Persian as the target language, Persian itself is the best source language, as the accuracy score drops under 81% in other experiments. Only two languages: Gothic and Arabic have Persian as one of their top 10 target languages but with low accuracies of 53.12% and 76.08%. Therefore, for POS tagging, Persian as target does not benefit from other languages as the source language. Details of source languages and scores is provided in appendix3

Nevertheless, considering Persian as the source language yields interesting results. The list of languages that have Persian as one of their top 10 source languages is as follows: Akkadian (low resource), Assyrian (low resource), Bambara (low resource), Bhojpuri (low resource), Hindi, Kurmanji (low resource), Persian, Tagalog (low resource), Urdu, Uyghur, and Welsh. Among these 11 languages, 6 languages are low resource languages which draw our interest. For Tagalog (78.96%) and Kurmanji (78.90%) we observe a score of roughly 79%, which is higher than the other low-resource languages. In addition, among the languages resulting in a high accuracy for Kurmanji listed in appendix 4, Persian is the most similar language to it regarding the LDND distance measure. Also from another perspective to assess languages similarity, we use the linguistic features from WALS dataset. We observe that for Kurmanji there are only 12 features in WALS and 10 of them are shared with Persian. Therefore, we propose that Persian is a good source languages for Kurmanji. Besides, Persian and Kurmanji are spoken in close geographical locations (Iran, Turkey, Iraq, Syria).

[4]https://github.com/jerbarnes/typology_of_crosslingual

[5]The whole dataset is accessible from https://huggingface.co/sepidmnorozy

[6]xlm-roberta-base

[7]The source language and the target language are the same

For languages that have Persian as one of their top 10 source languages, we provide the number of features available for each language in WALS and the number of common ones with Persian in appendix 6. According to this table, first Hindi and second Tagalog have the most common features with Persian. Although Tagalog is a low-resource language, it has 145 features listed in WALS. Besides, Persian has 147 features and has 54 features in common with Tagalog. In addition, among the list of top 10 source languages for Tagalog shown in appendix 5, Persian has the lowest LDND distance. Therefore we propose Persian as a potential source language for Tagalog in other cross-lingual tasks.

Using the Pars-BERT model, fine-tuning it with Persian as source, and test it with Persian and others as target, Persian as target has a score of 95.99% which is higher than the monolingual Persian experiment with XLM-RoBERTa. However, only with Persian Pars-BERT outperforms XLM-RoBERTa. Therefore, the monolingual Persian model is not enough for transfer learning and other languages' existence in the pre-training of the model has a significant effect on both high-resource and low-resource languages.

3.2 Sentiment analysis

The evaluation metrics for top 10 languages based on the accuracy score are shown in figure 3. Surprisingly the accuracy of the monolingual Persian experiment is only 87.69%, and Persian is not on the top of the list. However, Slovak has the highest accuracy of 93.38% occupying the first rank.

In this binary sentiment analysis task, most of the languages shown in Figure 3 have higher precision than recall. High precision values show that the model is not labeling negative samples as positive. The opposite case happens for Polish and sharply for German. For these two languages, the model has a higher recall, better at predicting the positive case and performs poorly on negative samples.

Considering Persian as the source language, the target languages that have a high score for POS tagging (listed in appendix7) and for sentiment analysis (listed in figure 3) only have two languages in common: "Polish" and "Bulgarian" Therefore, based on our results, cross-lingual transfer learning with Persian is task-dependent, and not the same group of languages appeared for both tasks.

4 Conclusion

All in all, we analyse the result of previous experiments for POS tagging and investigate whether having Persian as source or target language in cross-lingual transfer learning would be beneficial for Persian and other languages. We observe that Persian is the best source for itself as target and achieves a score of 91.43% for POS tagging. Besides, it can serve as a good source for 6 low-resource languages. We use LDND distance measure and linguistic features from WALS to reason that Persian can be a potential good source for Kurmanji and Tagalog for other tasks than POS tagging as well. Lastly for POS tagging, we observe that ParsBERT outperforms XLM-RoBETa only for monolingual Persian experiment and achieves a score of 96%. Then, we gather data and perform sentiment analysis to investigate whether the same target languages found for POS tagging would also benefit from Persian as the source language for sentiment analysis. We observe different target languages from the POS tagging results and only two languages: Polish and Bulgarian appear for both tasks. In addition, monolingual Persian experiment does not achieve the highest accuracy and Slovak is the best performing target. Therefore, we conclude that cross-lingual transfer learning with Persian is task dependent.

5 Limitations

The main challenge of this work was to find sentiment analysis dataset for various languages, especially the low-resource ones.

References

2013. Wals online.

2021. *Evaluating morphological typology in zero-shot cross-lingual transfer*. Association for Computational Linguistics, Online.

Wikimedia Commons. 2021a. File:map of persian speakers.svg — wikimedia commons, the free media repository. [Online; accessed 13 February 2022].

Wikimedia Commons. 2021b. File:persian language location map.svg — wikimedia commons, the free media repository. [Online; accessed 13-February-2022].

Wietse de Vries, Martijn Bartelds, Malvina Nissim, and Martijn Wieling. 2021. Adapting monolingual models: Data can be scarce when language similarity is high. *Findings of the Association for Computational Linguistics: ACL-IJCNLP 2021*.

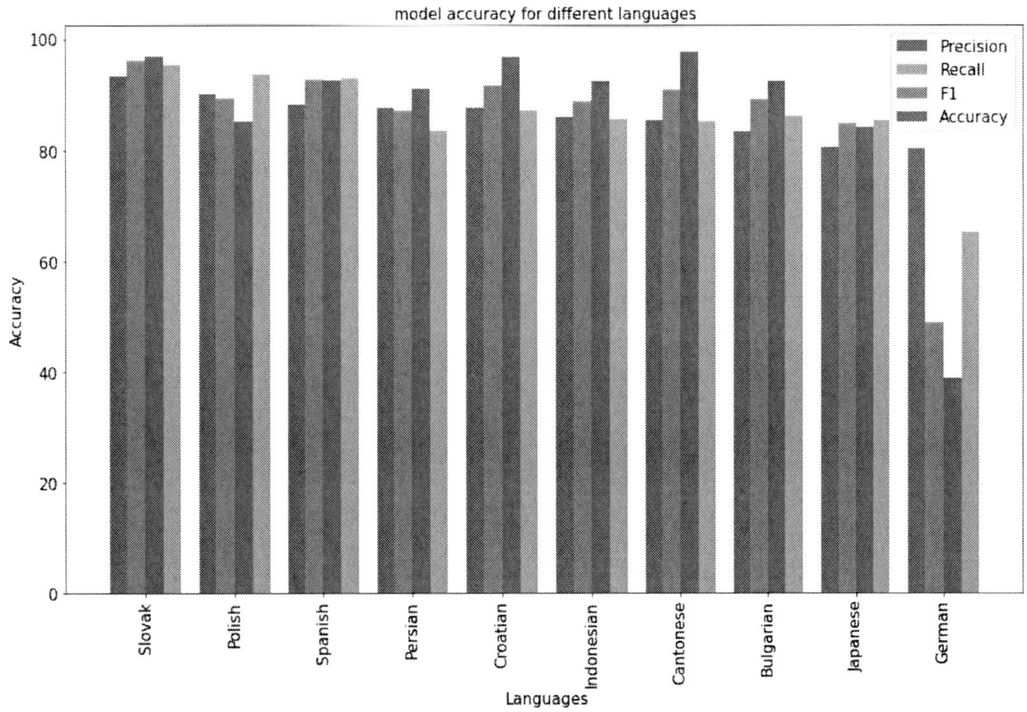

Figure 3: Evaluation metrics for sentiment analysis testing

Wietse de Vries, Martijn Wieling, and Malvina Nissim. 2022. Make the best of cross-lingual transfer: Evidence from POS tagging with over 100 languages. In *Proceedings of the 60th Annual Meeting of the Association for Computational Linguistics (Volume 1: Long Papers)*, pages 7676–7685, Dublin, Ireland. Association for Computational Linguistics.

Mountaga Diallo, Chayma Fourati, and Hatem Haddad. 2021. Bambara language dataset for sentiment analysis.

Luis Espinosa-Anke, Geraint Palmer, Padraig Corcoran, Maxim Filimonov, Irena Spasic, and Dawn Knight. 2021. English–welsh cross-lingual embeddings. *Applied Sciences*, 11:6541.

Mehrdad Farahani, Mohammad Gharachorloo, Marzieh Farahani, and Mohammad Manthouri. 2020. Parsbert: Transformer-based model for persian language understanding.

Muhammad Yaseen Khan and Muhammad Suffian Nizami. 2020. Urdu sentiment corpus (v1.0): Linguistic exploration and visualization of labeled datasetfor urdu sentiment analysis. In *2020 IEEE 2nd International Conference On Information Science Communication Technology (ICISCT)*. IEEE.

Jan Kocoń, Piotr Miłkowski, and Monika Zaśko-Zielińska. 2019. Multi-level sentiment analysis of PolEmo 2.0: Extended corpus of multi-domain consumer reviews. pages 980–991.

Siyu Li, Kui Zhao, Jin Yang, Xinyun Jiang, Zhengji Li, and Zicheng Ma. 2022. Senti-exlm: Uyghur enhanced sentiment analysis model based on xlm. *Electronics Letters*, 58.

Søren Wichmann, Eric W. Holman, Dik Bakker, and Cecil H. Brown. 2010. Evaluating linguistic distance measures. *Physica A: Statistical Mechanics and its Applications*, 389(17):3632–3639.

Søren Wichmann, Eric W. Holman, and Cecil H. Brown. 2022. The ASJP Database.

A Sentiment Analysis Details

Table 1 shows the details of different datasets we gathered for sentiment analysis. Table 2 shows the evaluation metrics while fine-tuning the XLM-RoBERTa model for sentiment analysis.

B POS Tagging Details

Table 3, table 4, and table 5 show the top 10 source languages for target languages Persian, Kurmanji, and Tagalog respectively. Table 6 shows the number of features from WALS dataset for languages that have Persian as one of their top 10 source languages. Table 7 shows the languages achieving the highest accuracies when Persian is the source.

Lang	#pos	#neg	content	source	#train	#val	#test
Persian	35k	35k	food reviews	(Farahani et al., 2020)	56.7k	6.3k	7k
Urdu	500	480	political tweets	Khan and Nizami (2020)	685	-	294
Hindi			movie reviews	Kaggle	513	115	-
Welsh	25k	25k	movie reviews	Espinosa-Anke et al. (2021)	25k	-	25k
Polish	1762	2455	school, products, medicine, hotels reviews	Kocoń et al. (2019)	3737	-	480
Romanian	17271	11675	products and movie reviews	Huggingface	17941	-	11005
Bambara	1663	579	sports, politics, music, etc Common-crawl	Diallo et al. (2021)	1569	-	673
Uyghur	2450	353		Li et al. (2022)	1962	-	841

Table 1: Details of sentiment analysis data

Epoch	Training Loss	Validation Loss	Accuracy	F1	Precision	Recall
1	0.3645	0.4315	0.8603	0.8466	0.9386	0.7711
2	0.374	0.4015	0.8713	0.8648	0.9105	0.8235
3	0.3363	0.4772	0.8705	0.8615	0.9256	0.8057
4	0.3131	0.4579	0.8702	0.8650	0.9007	0.8321
5	0.3097	0.4160	0.8721	0.8663	0.9069	0.8292
6	0.2921	0.4638	0.8673	0.8630	0.8917	0.8362
7	0.272	0.5183	0.8654	0.8602	0.8947	0.8283
8	0.2481	0.5846	0.8649	0.8624	0.8787	0.8467
9	0.192	0.6481	0.8610	0.8596	0.8680	0.8514
10	0.1945	0.7030	0.8603	0.8585	0.8699	0.8473

Table 2: XLM-RoBERTa fine-tuning results for sentiment analysis

Idx	Source	Target	Score	dist
1	Persian	Persian	91.43	nan
2	Urdu	Persian	80.63	78.87
3	Czech	Persian	80.09	94.62
4	Irish	Persian	79.73	98.25
5	Croatian	Persian	79.39	93.12
6	Armenian	Persian	79.23	98.0
7	Romanian	Persian	79.05	92.91
8	Galician	Persian	78.88	92.96
9	Welsh	Persian	78.7	97.71
10	Russian	Persian	78.7	93.02

Table 3: Top 10 best source languages for Persian as target

Idx	Source	Target	Score	Dist
1	Romanian	Kurmanji	79.52	89.76
2	Galician	Kurmanji	79.38	93.39
3	Czech	Kurmanji	79.28	95.59
4	Persian	Kurmanji	78.9	79.4
5	French	Kurmanji	78.88	90.9
6	Icelandic	Kurmanji	78.56	95.49
7	Croatian	Kurmanji	78.51	93.89
8	Bulgarian	Kurmanji	78.47	93.55
9	Dutch	Kurmanji	78.32	90.39
10	Italian	Kurmanji	78.24	89.86

Table 4: Top 10 best source languages for Kurmanji as target

Idx	Source	Target	Score	Dist
1	Bulgarian	Tagalog	81.56	102.73
2	Russian	Tagalog	80.91	101.1
3	Polish	Tagalog	80.17	98.98
4	Icelandic	Tagalog	79.98	100.87
5	Hebrew	Tagalog	79.24	101.8
6	Persian	Tagalog	78.96	96.05
7	Urdu	Tagalog	78.49	99.32
8	Serbian	Tagalog	77.47	97.51
9	Faroese	Tagalog	76.07	102.85
10	Spanish	Tagalog	74.39	96.76

Table 5: Top 10 best source languages for Tagalog as target

Idx	Lang	#features	#Common
0	Persian	147	147
1	Hindi	144	71
2	Tagalog	145	54
3	Bambara	90	33
4	Welsh	69	28
5	Urdu	42	20
6	Bhojpuri	36	17
7	Uyghur	35	11
8	Kurmanji	12	10
9	Arabic	30	10
10	Assyrian	3	2

Table 6: WALS features for languages related to Persian

idx	Lang	Score	Mono score	Dist
1	Hebrew	89.58	93.75	99.16
2	Marathi	84.05	88.96	91.65
3	Estonian	83.52	96.80	100.19
4	Bulgarian	83.452	99.30	97.11
5	Polish	82.692	98.22	91.71
6	Serbian	82.472	99.06	93.93
7	Icelandic	82.32	95.64	98.67
8	Telugu	82.11	94.87	98.47
9	Tamil	82.00	85.64	97.17
10	Arabic	81.70	75.93	97.46

Table 7: Top 10 target languages for Persian as Source language based on POS tagging score

Information-Theoretic Characterization of Vowel Harmony: A Cross-Linguistic Study on Word Lists

Julius Steuer[υ] **Badr M. Abdullah**[υ] **Johann-Mattis List**[Υ] **Dietrich Klakow**[υ]
[υ]Language Science and Technology (LST), Saarland University
[Υ]MPI-EVA, Univ. of Passau
{ jsteuer, babdullah, dietrich }@lsv.uni-saarland.de, mattis.list@uni-passau.de

Abstract

We present a cross-linguistic study that aims to quantify vowel harmony using data-driven computational modeling. Concretely, we define an information-theoretic measure of harmonicity based on the predictability of vowels in a natural language lexicon, which we estimate using phoneme-level language models (PLMs). Prior quantitative studies have relied heavily on inflected word-forms in the analysis of vowel harmony. We instead train our models using cross-linguistically comparable lemma forms with little or no inflection, which enables us to cover more under-studied languages. Training data for our PLMs consists of word lists with a maximum of 1000 entries per language. Despite the fact that the data we employ are substantially smaller than previously used corpora, our experiments demonstrate the neural PLMs capture vowel harmony patterns in a set of languages that exhibit this phenomenon. Our work also demonstrates that word lists are a valuable resource for typological research, and offers new possibilities for future studies on low-resource, under-studied languages.

1 Introduction

1.1 Vowel Harmony

Many of the world's languages exhibit vowel harmony – a phonological co-occurrence constraint whereby vowels in polysyllabic words have to be members of the same natural class (Ohala, 1994). Natural classes of vowels are defined with respect to polar phonological features such as vowel backness (±BACK) and roundedness (±ROUND). In a prototypical language with backness, or ±BACK harmony, all vowels within a word tend to share the ±BACK feature, i.e. they are either all front (−BACK) or back (+BACK). Table 1 illustrates vowel harmony in Turkish, one of the languages best known to have this feature. In Table 1, the nominative plural and genitive plural are examples of −BACK harmony, while the genitive singular column of +BACK harmony. In the case of Turkish, vowel harmony can be defined as a constraint applying to almost all words and the entire inflectional system. In other languages vowel harmony may be restricted to the inflectional system, or even only a subset of inflectional suffixes. For example, In Estonian there are vestiges of vowel harmony in lexical items and it is absent from the inflectional system, while in Bislama it only occurs in a single suffix marking transivity (Crowley, 2014). Between these extremes of Turkish and Bislama lie languages such as Finnish and Hungarian, with intermediate vowel harmony systems where not all vowels participate in vowel harmony to the same extent. Both languages have ±BACK harmony, but a subset of the −BACK vowels allow +BACK harmony to spread: In a word like [ɑtikːo] 'box' (not [lɑtikːø]), +BACK harmony is not violated, whereas a word containing only neutral vowels triggers −BACK harmony, as in [merkitys] 'meaning' where the +BACK disharmonic form [merkitus] is not possible.

The rather broad application of the term has made it increasingly difficult to define it as a phonological process (cf. Anderson 1980). If vowel harmony is used as a typological feature to group languages into phylogenetic families, this broad application becomes perilous to the researcher since they have to be aware of the the degree of vowel harmonicity in the individual languages. Instead of searching for a necessarily complex definition of vowel harmony, research has consequentially concentrated on a quantitative description.

1.2 Prior Work and Scope

Prior approaches to a quantitative description of vowel harmony have mostly focused on strictly local harmony processes. Mayer et al. (2010) used vowel succession counts derived from corpora of inflected word-forms to quantify vowel harmony in a large number of languages in terms of χ^2-values,

Proceedings of the 5th Workshop on Research in Computational Linguistic Typology and Multilingual NLP (SIGTYP 2023), pages 96–109
May 6, 2023 ©2023 Association for Computational Linguistics

	Nom. Sg.	Gen. Sg.	Nom. Pl.	Gen. Pl.	Gloss
−BACK/−ROUND	[ip]	[ip-in]	[ip-lɛr]	[ip-lɛr-in]	'string'
+BACK/−ROUND	[kɯz]	[kɯz-ɯn]	[kɯz-lar]	[kɯz-lar-ɯn]	'girl'
−BACK/+ROUND	[jyz]	[jyz-yn]	[jyz-lɛr]	[jyz-lɛr-in]	'face'
+BACK/+ROUND	[pul]	[pul-un]	[pul-lar]	[pul-lar-ɯn]	'stamp'

Table 1: Illustration of the Turkish vowel harmony system following Polgárdi (1999). The first vowel of a word form determines the harmony type. If the first vowel is +BACK, the vowels of the following suffixes must agree w. r. t. the +BACK feature. ±ROUND harmony applies only in suffixes that have separate forms for this feature: The genitive suffix takes both ±BACK and ±ROUND forms, while the plural suffix varies only for ±BACK.

while Ozburn (2019) used count data to estimate succession probabilities and calculate the relative risk of encountering an harmonic vowel in a word form. These two approaches treated all positions in a word form identically. Goldsmith and Riggle (2012) argued that vowel harmony involves at least one type of non-local dependency, since it operates over consonants intervening between adjacent vowels. They employed a simple n-gram language model to learn the phonology of Finnish and calculated pointwise mutual information of vowel-vowel and consonant-vowel pairs based on the phoneme probabilities predicted by the language model, finding evidence for consonant-vowel harmony besides the expected ±BACK harmony, with a small bias towards +BACK harmony. However, n-gram language models are limited by their predefined context size. A language model with a left-hand context of $n = 3$ cannot capture the effect of vowel harmony if it operates over a neutral vowel intervening between two harmonic vowels. While this effect could be mitigated by allowing by allowing for a larger or flexible n, estimating probabilities from corpora becomes increasingly difficult with higher values of n. In this study we aim to improve over these methods by quantifying vowel harmony with a information-theoretic measure based on *surprisal*, capturing the relative strength of vowel harmony in language in terms of the likelihood of a vowel in a word to share a specific feature with preceding vowels. To do so, we employ neural recurrent language models with variable-length preceding phoneme context that are trained on cross-linguistically comparable lexical data. While some previous work on modeling vowel harmony with language models has been carried out (Rodd, 1997), finding evidence for Turkish vowel harmony in the hidden activations of a simple neural language model, it seems that this topic has not been further explored since then. In the following section, we first introduce feature surprisal as an information-theoretic measure of vowel harmony (§2). We then present our computational experiments with the introduced measure of vowel harmony and discuss the results of their application to a large collection of cross-linguistic lexical data (§3, §4). We conclude by discussing the implications of our study for future studies on vowel harmony in classical and computational studies (§5).

2 Quantifying Vowel Harmony

2.1 Phoneme-Level Language Models

Preliminaries and Notations. To quantify vowel harmony in our study, we make use of phoneme-level language models (PLMs). Consider a natural language with a lexicon $\mathcal{L}$ and a phoneme inventory $\boldsymbol{\Phi}$ (using IPA symbols). Using a cross-linguistic word list, we obtain K samples from the lexicon $\mathcal{D} = \{\boldsymbol{w}^k\}_{k=1}^K \sim \mathcal{L}$ where each sample is a word-form that is transcribed as a phoneme sequence $\boldsymbol{w} = (\varphi_1, \cdots, \varphi_{|\boldsymbol{w}|}) \in \boldsymbol{\Phi}^*$. Given this sample of word-forms as training data, a PLM can be trained to estimate a probability distribution over $\boldsymbol{\Phi}$ by maximizing the term

$$\begin{aligned} J(\theta, \mathcal{D}) &= \sum_{\boldsymbol{w} \in \mathcal{D}} p(\boldsymbol{w}; \theta) \\ &= \sum_{\boldsymbol{w} \in \mathcal{D}} \prod_{t \in \{1, \cdots, |\boldsymbol{w}|\}} p(\varphi_t | \boldsymbol{\varphi}_{<t}; \theta) \end{aligned} \tag{1}$$

Here, θ are the parameters of the model that are learned by maximizing the objective function above. Once a PLM has been trained, it can be used to compute the probability of unseen, held-out word-forms (i.e, word-forms that were not observed in the training data). Ideally, a PLM should assign a higher probability mass to plausible word-forms given the phonotactic rules of the language of the train data, and lower probability to implausible word-forms.

Recurrent PLMs. Although different architectures can be used to build a PLM, we choose to employ a recurrent architecture based on unidirectional long short-term memory (LSTM) cell (Hochreiter and Schmidhuber, 1997). Given a word-form as a sequence of phonemes $\boldsymbol{w} = (\varphi_1, \cdots, \varphi_{|\boldsymbol{w}|})$, each phoneme is first projected into a continuous-vector phoneme representation using an embedding matrix as $\mathbf{E}(\varphi_t) = \mathbf{x}_t \in \mathbb{R}^d$. Then, the LSTM takes as input the sequence at each position t within the word-form to compute the hidden state representation

$$\mathbf{h}_t = \mathcal{F}_{\text{LSTM}}(\mathbf{x}_t, \mathbf{h}_{t-1}) \in \mathbb{R}^h \tag{2}$$

To obtain a probability distribution over the phoneme inventory, a linear transformation is applied on the hidden state vector followed by a softmax function to obtain a probability vector as

$$p(\varphi_t|\boldsymbol{\varphi}_{<t}) = \text{SOFTMAX}(\mathbf{W}\mathbf{h}_t + \mathbf{b}) \tag{3}$$

Here, $\mathbf{W} \in \mathbb{R}^{|\boldsymbol{\Phi}| \times h}$ is a projection matrix at the network output and $\mathbf{b} \in \mathbb{R}^{|\boldsymbol{\Phi}|}$ is a bias term.

Nevertheless, we make a few (trivial) design modifications to the vanilla LSTM-based PLMs to make them more suitable for our study. First, since our main interest is to model the predictability of the vowels, we confine the output probability distribution to be over the set of vocalic segments, which is a subset of the phoneme inventory $\mathcal{V} \subset \boldsymbol{\Phi}$. Second, we train and evaluate our PLMs to predict the next vowel only in the intra-word positions where we know that the next phoneme is indeed a vowel, given a preceding phoneme context that contains at least one vowel. While the output in this modified PLM is over the set $\mathcal{V}$, the word-forms remain sequences in $\boldsymbol{\Phi}^*$. That is, both consonants and vowels could appear in the preceding context.

Note that we do not employ fixed-length context n-gram PLMs in our study since we aim to account for non-local phoneme dependencies within a word-form. Given that word-forms within a lexicon have arbitrary lengths, restricting the preceding context to a fixed number of phonemes does not enable us to model vowel harmony across variable-length contexts beyond phoneme n-grams. On the other hand, we do not employ more powerful architectures such as a transformer (Vaswani et al., 2017) or a bidirectional LSTM (Graves and Schmidhuber, 2005) on grounds of suitability for the task: (1) the dependencies between vowels are relatively short (the domain of vowel harmony is the phonological word), (2) vowel harmony is a progressive phenomenon (i.e., operates from left to right–unlike its regressive counterpart *umlaut*), and (3) the training sets of the individual languages in our study are likely too small to train a large transformer model. Moreover, several prior studies within the information-theoretic approaches to investigate phonological structure have also employed LSTM-based PLMs (e.g., Pimentel et al., 2020, 2021a).

2.2 Harmony as Surprisal

Given that our phoneme-level language model that was trained on a set of word-forms sampled from a natural language lexicon, we can quantify the vowel harmony phenomenon using Shannon's information content, or **surprisal**. Given a non-initial vocalic position t after a phoneme context $\boldsymbol{\varphi}_{<t}$, vowel surprisal is

$$\eta(v, t) = -\log_2 p(v \mid t, \boldsymbol{\varphi}_{<t}) \tag{4}$$

which is measured in bits. Note that surprisal is maximal when the preceding context tells us nothing about which vowels are more likely to occur. That is, if the vowels are sampled from a uniform distribution over the vowel inventory $\mathcal{V}$, then $\eta(v, t) = \log_2|\mathcal{V}|$ (bits). Therefore, surprisal in our case is mainly a metric of how "predictable" a vowel is in a given context. Now consider a set of vowels $\mathcal{H} \in \mathcal{V}$ that share a phonological feature. For a given vowel $v \in \mathcal{H}$, we refer to the set $\mathcal{H}$ as a harmonic group, while its disharmonic counterpart $\neg\mathcal{H} \in \mathcal{V} \setminus \mathcal{H}$ as a disharmonic group with respect to the vowel v. For example, consider the front vowel [i] in Turkish that has the feature −BACK. With respect to [i], the front vowels in the Turkish vowel inventory $\mathcal{H} = \{$[i], [e], [y], [œ]$\}$ make a harmonic group since they all share the feature −BACK, while the rest of the vowels make a disharmonic group $\neg\mathcal{H} = \{$[ɯ], [a], [u], [o]$\}$ since they all lack the feature −BACK. Given a phoneme context that contains at least one vowel v such that $v \in \mathcal{H}$, we compute the surprisal of a harmonic group at position t in a word-form by summing over the vowels in $\mathcal{H}$, i.e.

$$\eta(\mathcal{H}, t) = -\log_2 \sum_{\pi \in \mathcal{H}} p(\pi \mid t, \boldsymbol{\varphi}_{<t}) \tag{5}$$

We refer to the quantity $\eta(\mathcal{H}, t)$ as **feature surprisal**, since all members of the harmonic group

Language	Harmonic Groups		
Finnish	−BACK {y, ø, æ}	+BACK {u, o, ɑ}	BACK neutral {e, i}
Hungarian	−BACK {y, ø}	+BACK {u, o, ɒ}	BACK neutral {e, i}
Manchu	−BACK {e/ɤ}	+BACK {ɑ, ɔ}	BACK neutral {i, u}
Khalkha Mongolian	−ATR {e, u, ɔ} −ROUND {e, a, i}	+ATR {a, ɒ, o} +ROUND {o}	ATR neutral {i} ROUND neutral {u, ʊ}
Turkish	−BACK {i, e, y, œ} −ROUND {i, e, u, o}	+BACK {ɯ, a, u, o} +ROUND {ɯ, a, y, œ}	
Arabic, Ainu, Armenian, Basque, Estonian†	−	−	−

Table 2: Languages from NorthEuraLex used in our sample along with their harmonic groups. Khalkha Mongolian has a special type of vowel harmony involving the placement of the tongue root: +ATR codes an advanced position of the tongue root in the vocal tract, while −ATR encodes an retracted or further back position. Languages in our sample that do not exhibit vowel harmony are marked with the symbol (†).

$\mathcal{H}$ share one phonological feature. Likewise, we compute the surprisal of a disharnomic group by summing over the vowels in $\neg\mathcal{H}$ as

$$\eta(\neg\mathcal{H}, t) = -\log_2 \sum_{\pi \in \neg\mathcal{H}} p(\pi \mid t, \varphi_{<t}) \quad (6)$$

Assuming that a PLM has learned the vowel harmony constraints of a language from the training word-forms, we expect the model to predict that vowels in $\mathcal{H}$ are more likely to co-occur in a single word-form. By implication, we expect the model to "disfavour" the occurrence of a vowel in $\neg\mathcal{H}$ when observing members of $\mathcal{H}$ in the context. That is, in a language that exhibits this linguistic phenomenon, word-forms that conform to vowel harmony should be assigned a higher probability than word-forms that do not. For example, the Finnish word form [s i l m æ s ae] is expected to be assigned a high probability by our model since the sequence of vowels [i], [ae], [ae] is −BACK harmonic, and its disharmonic counterpart [s i l m æ s o] is expected to be assigned a lower probability.

Note in equations (5) and (6) we compute the surprisal at a single vocalic position in a given word-form. To quantify harmonic group surprisal across a set of held-out word-forms $\mathcal{W}$, we compute the quantity

$$\overline{\eta}(\mathcal{H}) = -\frac{1}{|\mathcal{W}|} \sum_{w \in \mathcal{W}} \sum_{t \in \{\tau, \cdots, T\}} \eta(\mathcal{H}, t) \quad (7)$$

which is the average feature surprisal. Here, the outer sum $\sum_{w \in \mathcal{W}}$ iterates over all word-forms in $\mathcal{W}$, while the inner sum $\sum_{t \in \{\tau, \cdots, T\}}$ iterates over non-initial vocalic positions within the word-form w. The feature surprisal of a disharmonic group $\overline{\eta}(\neg\mathcal{H})$ is computed in the same way as in equation (7) but summing over the term $\eta(\neg\mathcal{H}, t)$ instead.

Finally, we quantify the strength of a vowel harmony constraint in a language as the difference of feature surprisal of the harmonic and disharmonic vowels

$$\Delta_\eta = \overline{\eta}(\mathcal{H}) - \overline{\eta}(\neg\mathcal{H}) \quad (8)$$

If feature surprisal in harmonic phoneme sequences is lower than feature surprisal in disharmonic phoneme sequences, Δ_η is negative, indicating that harmonic sequences are assigned higher probability. It is worth pointing out that our grouping of the vowels into harmonic groups is only used to obtain feature surprisal values from the model after it has been trained. That is, our PLMs for all languages in our study are trained without an explicit signal that informs the model about the features of the vowels.

3 Experimental Data and Setup

3.1 Data

Previous research has made use of large corpora of inflected word-forms (Goldsmith and Riggle, 2012) or running text (Mayer et al., 2010) to infer vowel harmony patterns. This is mainly because vowel harmony constraints often surface in inflectional suffixes, especially in highly agglutinating languages such as Finnish, Hungarian or Turkish. Though this approach is not in itself problematic, it relies on data that may not exist for the majority of the world's languages. It is also not applicable for languages that have a different grammatical structure, for example, reduced or fusional morphology. On the other hand, if a language has vowel harmony as a phonologically conditioned rather than a purely grammatical phenomenon, the relevant vowel harmony patterns should also be recoverable from lexical data with little or no inflection at all.

We use parts of the NorthEuraLex database (`http://www.northeuralex.org/`, Dellert et al.

	Maximum	Minimum	Average	Median
Phoneme inventory size	72 (Skolt Sami)	23 (Turkish)	38.9	37
Number of word-forms	1513 (Manchu)	677 (Italian)	1136.6	1142

Table 3: Inventory sizes and word list lengths in the data sampled from NorthEuraLex.

2020) as experimental data to train our phoneme language models and quantify the effect of vowel harmony in languages that are known to exhibit this linguistic phenomenon. NorthEuraLex offers a large multilingual word list consisting of 1005 concepts translated into 107 language varieties from North Eurasia with translations provided in a unified transcription following the International Phonetic Alphabet (IPA). Moreover, NorthEuraLex contains a larger number of diverse language varieties from various language families that are known to exhibit vowel harmony, as well as language varieties that are known to lack the phenomenon.

As there is no clear definition of what constitutes vowel harmony in languages, and linguistic resources such as the World Atlas of Language Structures (Dryer et al., 2014) do not provide this information, we concentrate on a subset of 10 language varieties from NorthEuraLex, with five varieties traditionally known to exhibit vowel harmony, and five known to not exhibit the phenomenon. When selecting the languages, we tried to obtain a rather diverse sample of languages from different language families. Table 2 gives an overview over the languages and their active harmony processes (where present).

The NorthEuraLex data is available in the form of Cross-Linguistic Data Formats (CLDF `https://cldf.clld.org`, Forkel et al. 2018), following the recommendations underlying Lexibank (List et al., 2022a), a large collection of lexical word lists (`https://github.com/lexibank/northeuralex`). A core feature of CLDF is the integration of *reference catalogs*. Reference catalogs are metadata collections that offer basic information on major linguistic constructs, such as languages (Glottolog, `https://glottolog.org`, Hammarström et al. 2022) or concepts (Concepticon, `https://concepticon.clld.org`, List et al. 2022b). In addition to offering word lists standardized with respect to language names and concept elicitation glosses, Lexibank offers standardized phonetic transcriptions as specified by Cross-Linguistic Transcription Systems (CLTS, `https://clts.clld.org`, List et al. 2021), a reference catalog that offers a transcription system that conforms to the IPA but resolves ambiguities encountered in the original IPA specification (Anderson et al., 2018).

Since NorthEuraLex is available in CLDF, this means that we have direct access to standardized phonetic transcriptions segmented into individual sounds in each word form along with an underlying set of distinctive features provided by CLTS. The resulting data set provides on average 1136 unique word-forms per language (with several concepts having two or more word-forms as translational equivalents), with larger differences between individual languages. We decided against downsampling word lists to a common size due to the already small number of samples. The word list sizes range from 971 (Ainu) to 1513 (Manchu).

3.2 Preprocessing

For each of the languages, identical word-forms are collapsed to a single item, such that each sequence of phonemes is presented only once to the model. In addition, word-forms which are a substring of another word form are also ignored. Thus, if the word list of a language contains the sequences { [s i l m æ], [s i l m æ], [s i l m æ sː æ], [s i l m æ d æ] }, only the latter two sequences are kept: { [s i l m æ sː æ], [s i l m æ d æ] }. This procedure ensures that only unique sequences are presented to the model, and that train and test splits do not contain identical forms, which might otherwise lead to unjustified higher weights for sound sequences recurring across the vocabulary of individual language varieties.

3.3 Training

For each language, we randomly split the data into 60%, 10% and 30% subsets for train, validation and test splits respectively. The models were trained with the Adam optimizer (Kingma and Ba, 2015) on the task of minimizing the cross entropy of the predicted distribution and the true probability distributions over the vowel inventory. This is equivalent to minimizing the negative log-likelihood of the true phoneme at each position. 25% of the inputs were randomly replaced by a mask token to prevent overfitting on the relatively small sample. Note that the output probability distribution of the model is restricted to the vowel inventory of the language plus the end-of-sequence token, since only the vowel positions are of interest for the analysis.

A separate model was trained for each language in our subset of 10 languages from NorthEuraLex. The same hyperparameters were used for training as in Pimentel et al. (2021b), with batch size reduced to 32 since NorthEuraLex wordlists are considerably smaller than the datasets used in that paper. Table 4 in Appendix A shows the exact configuration of the hyperparameters. After each epoch the models were evaluated on a validation set, and all models were trained until validation loss converged. Training the models on unique sequences derived from word lists ensures that the model sees each sequence only once per epoch, and minimizes overlaps between train, test and validation set.

3.4 Significance Tests

As the expected behavior of vowel harmony languages is that the vowels are not evenly distributed over their words, average feature surprisal is likely to not be normally distributed. The Shapiro-Wilk test (Shapiro and Wilk, 1965) was used to check whether the surprisal values for every comparison. For every pairing of conditions at least one of them was not normally distributed with $p < 0.01$. Thus, the Wilcoxon signed-rank test was conducted to test the significance of a paired contrast (as in the example above). Effect size was calculated as the rank-biserial coefficient using the common language effect size $f = \frac{U}{n_1 \cdot n_2}$ as $r = f - (1 - f)$, with U being the test statistic and $n_1 \cdot n_2$ being the number of possible comparisons between two conditions. For an unpaired contrast (e.g. the contrast between average feature surprisal for $+$ROUND after a $-$ROUND vowel and average feature surprisal for $+$BACK after a $-$BACK vowel) a Mann-Whitney U-test was conducted, with effect size calculated as the rank-biserial coefficient using the T statistic and the sum of ranks S as $r = \frac{T}{S}$. All significance tests were conducted using the SciPy Python package (Virtanen et al., 2020).

3.5 Implementation

The methods described here are implemented in Python. The PyTorch library (Paszke et al., 2019) is used to train and evaluate our neural models. CLDF data are accessed with the help of CL Toolkit (`https://pypi.org/project/cltoolkit`, List and Forkel 2021), a Python package that provides convenient access to lexical word lists in CLDF.

4 Experimental Results

4.1 Feature Surprisal

All vowel harmony languages show significant differences in feature surprisal between harmonic and disharmonic conditions with negative Δ_η; individual results can be retrieved from the result tables 6-10 in Appendix C. Feature surprisal in the $+$BACK disharmonic condition was found to be higher than feature surprisal in the $-$BACK disharmonic condition for Finnish ($\Delta_\eta = -0.2148$, $p < 0.01$), Hungarian ($\Delta_\eta = -1.0806$, $p < 0.01$) and Turkish ($\Delta_\eta = -0.8602$, $p < 0.01$), which confirms the findings of Goldsmith (1985). Note that if the $+$BACK and $-$BACK harmony were equally strong, one would expect no difference in surprisal if the harmony is violated. Three out of four languages with $\pm$BACK harmony show this tendency, indicating that the relative strength of $+$BACK harmony over $-$BACK harmony is the usual case rather than an exception. A possible explanation for this difference in strength is the existence of neutral vowels, with 3 of the 4 $\pm$BACK harmony languages in our sample having at least one neutral vowel, and Turkish, the only language without neutral vowels, also showing the largest difference between the two disharmonic conditions . The probabilities of the neutral vowels are not included in the feature surprisal calculation, causing feature surprisal to be higher in the $+$BACK disharmonic condition while lowering feature surprisal in the $-$BACK disharmonic condition. For Hungarian feature surprisal was lowest in the neutral harmonic condition, meaning that neutral vowels are most likely to occur after another neutral vowel. Even though Hungarian neutral vowels trigger $-$BACK harmony, the low number of forms containing both $-$BACK vowels and neutral vowels makes it difficult for the neural language model to learn the pattern, leading to the highest feature surprisal occurring in the harmonic condition (i.e. for the $-$BACK feature). Figure 1 gives an overview of the relative strength of vowel harmony for all languages and harmonic features in the sample used in this study. For this figure the sign of Δ_η was reversed in order to quantify the reduction of feature surprisal in the harmonic sequences as compared to the dishar-

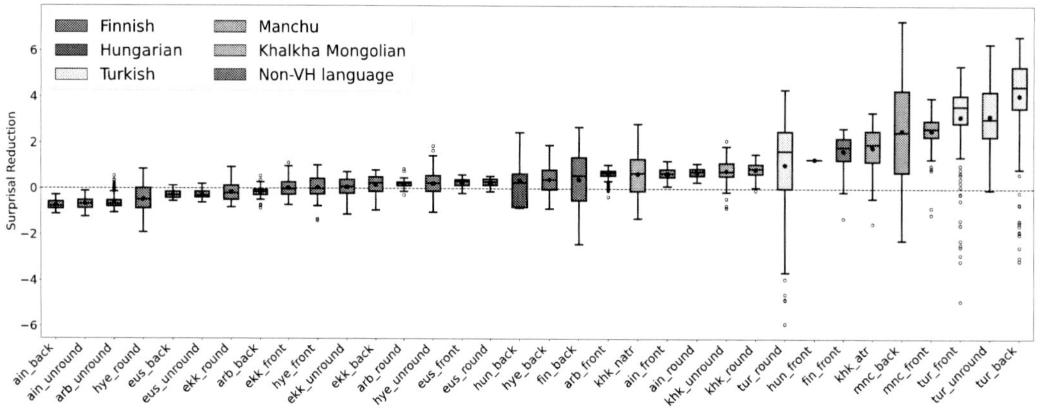

Figure 1: Surprisal reduction for the 10 varieties from NorthEuraLex. Best viewed in color.

monic sequences for each combination of feature and language. The boxplots of languages without vowel harmony are located towards the left of the plot with small differences between harmonic and disharmonic sequences, with some vowel harmony languages showing similar, yet still positive surprisal reduction (e.g. Finnish +BACK vowels, Hungarian +BACK vowels)

4.2 The Case of Turkish

For Turkish the difference in feature surprisal between harmonic and disharmonic conditions was large. Figure 2 shows that for both the ±BACK and ±ROUND conditions, the disharmonic condition displays a much higher surprisal value as compared to the harmonic condition ($\Delta_\eta = -3.6816$, $p < 0.01$ and $\Delta_\eta = -2.7061$, $p < 0.01$ respectively). A small but significant bias towards +BACK harmony was detected ($\Delta_\eta = -0.8602$, $p < 0.01$). There is one obvious reason for the relative strength of ±BACK harmony over ±ROUND, namely the parasitic nature of ±ROUND harmony in Turkish: while all morphemes have different forms for ±BACK, allowing for ±ROUND disharmony, only a subset also has separate forms for ±ROUND (Tab. 1). Thus, there are more instances of ±BACK harmony to be observed by the model, and this is expected to result in higher surprisal values for the ±BACK disharmonic conditions.

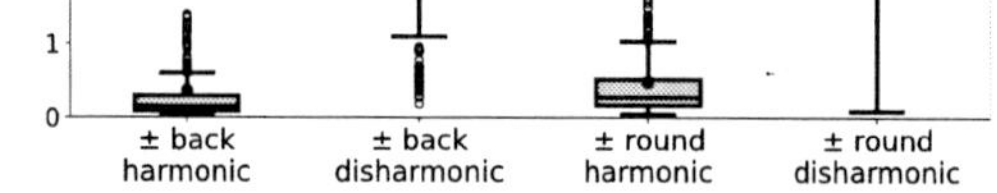

Figure 2: Feature surprisal for Turkish back harmonic/disharmonic sequences (left) and round harmonic/disharmonic sequences (right). The difference between harmonic and disharmonic conditions is significant with $p < 0.01$ in both cases.**: $p < 0.01$, *: $p < 0.05$, **ns**: $p > 0.05$

After ±ROUND vowels feature surprisal was also much higher in the disharmonic conditions, with feature surprisal in the round disharmonic condition being higher than in the unrounded disharmonic condition ($\Delta_\eta = -1.5827$, $p < 0.01$). In other words, +ROUND harmony seems to be stronger than −ROUND harmony in Turkish. When combining the disharmonic conditions within a harmonic feature and comparing them to the disharmonic conditions in the other harmonic feature, the combined back disharmonic condition (both front disharmonic and back disharmonic) yields slightly higher feature surprisal than the combined rounded disharmonic condition ($\Delta_\eta = 0.8555$, $p < 0.01$); see Table 8 in the appendix. This is in line with earlier research (Baker, 2009) that found a bias towards ±BACK harmony over ±ROUND harmony. This is also the expected result when taking into account that many suffixes do not have +ROUND forms and therefore introduce noise to the data.

4.3 Neutral Vowels

Learning vowel dependencies across neutral vowels turned out to be difficult: For Manchu and

Khalkha Mongolian the number of test items in this category was so low that no meaningful result could be produced. This is again caused by the nature of the data which consists of lemma forms. For Finnish and Hungarian the number of items was sufficient to conduct the appropriate significance tests, but the numbers are still small (102 and 63 respectively). The neural language model did not learn the association of neutral vowels with −BACK as assumed for Finnish and Hungarian, with significant $\Delta_\eta > 0$ between the neutral harmonic and neutral disharmonic condition only for Khalkha Mongolian and ±ATR sequences. In Hungarian, neutral vowels are most likely to occur after other neutral vowels, but this is not the case for Finnish, Manchu and Khalkha Mongolian. On the other hand, Turkish as the only language in the sample without neutral vowels showed the largest difference between harmonic and disharmonic conditions for both ±BACK and ±ROUND (see App. C for results).

It may be noted that Turkish, the language with the strongest vowel harmony effect in terms of Δ_η, has no neutral vowels both for ±BACK and ±ROUND harmony. This could have facilitated the generalization on the ±BACK and ±ROUND harmony patterns for the neural language model, at least proving that the neural language model does indeed assign higher surprisal to disharmonic sequences, since there the harmony system is symmetrical and the number of vowels is the same for each feature.

5 Discussion and Conclusion

Prior work in the (computational) linguistics community has adopted information theory as a framework for the study of human language structure across different linguistic levels including phonology (e.g., Pimentel et al., 2020, 2021c), morphology (e.g., Rathi et al., 2021; Wu et al., 2019), and syntax (e.g., Hahn et al., 2018; Futrell et al., 2015). Following the same spirit, we have introduced an information-theoretic metric to quantify vowel harmony based on feature surprisal. Our experiments have demonstrated that feature surprisal is a good indicator of whether a certain feature participates in vowel harmony patterns in a language, producing significant differences between harmonic and disharmonic conditions for most harmonic features in five vowel harmony languages. The effect was found on a very small sample of lemma forms with little to no morphological information, showing that large amounts of inflectional data are not necessary to identify some, but not all vowel harmony constraints. When calculated for ±BACK and ±ROUND features for five non-vowel harmony languages, the difference in surprisal was close to zero, meaning the neural language model did not detect any preference for harmony constraints in the languages evaluated.

We showed that neural language models can capture non-local harmony constraints over neutral vowels, which is not possible with count-based methods as employed by Mayer et al. (2010) or bigram models as in (Goldsmith and Riggle, 2012). Here the resolution of the analysis is more fine-grained with respect to the features underlying the harmonic groups. The advantage of the modeling approach presented here over both count-based and probabilistic models is that it can be used with a small dataset (word lists of about 1000 word-forms, of which ca. 300 are in the test set as the basis of the actual analysis).

The analysis presented could be extended to other types of phonological constraints, since neural language models in theory are able to learn all types of dependencies over sequences of arbitrary length. However, analysing Finnish, Hungarian, Manchu and Khalkha Mongolian required prior knowledge about harmonic vowels and the split of vowels into harmonic groups, either because the groups are not defined by the value of a feature as is the case for languages with neutral vowels, or because the feature representation in our standardized data itself might not describe a sound with the feature that is assumed to participate in vowel harmony.

If it is not known which vowels participate in vowel harmony, it seems best to use information on distinctive features in the data in order to find out which effects can be observed. However, if the vowel harmony patterns are as complex as in Khalkha Mongolian, the approach presented here would probably find its limits in corpus size. Identifying the approximate number of distinct word-forms needed to infer vowel harmony systems of individual language varieties (similar to previous studies inferring the number of words needed to get an approximate account of phoneme numbers, Dockum and Bowern 2019) would be an interesting topic for future analysis.

Limitations

The limiting factor in the analysis of Hungarian and Khalkha Mongolian was the low number of items with more than two vowels in the test data. Although this was less of a problem in the other three languages (Finnish, Turkish and Manchu all have 400+ items with three or more vowels), this is likely the case for many of the languages in NorthEuraLex. Figure 3 in Appendix B shows that many languages have an even lower number of items with more than three vowels than Finnish and Khalkha Mongolian. Given a train-valid-test split of 60%-10%-30%, the number of items available to the analysis of long-range dependencies (including, but not restricted to, the operation of vowel harmony across neutral vowels) will be very low for these languages. This is an inherent property of the data, and could only be amended by using larger word lists or a larger corpora that are not restricted to lemma forms.

Ethics Statement

The authors foresee no ethical concerns about the work presented in the paper.

Supplementary Material

The supplementary material accompanying this study was archived with Zenodo (`https://doi.org/10.5281/zenodo.7782090`). It contains all data and code needed to replicate this study, along with extensive instructions.

Acknowledgements

We thank the anonymous reviewers for their constructive comments. This research was supported by the Deutsche Forschungsgemeinschaft (DFG, German Research Foundation), Project ID 232722074 – SFB 1102 (Julius Steuer, Badr Abdullah), by the Max Planck Society Research Grant *CALC³* (JML, `https://digling.org/calc/`), and the ERC Consolidator Grant *ProduSemy* (JML, Grant No. 101044282, see `https://doi.org/10.3030/101044282`). Views and opinions expressed are however those of the authors only and do not necessarily reflect those of the European Union or the European Research Council Executive Agency (nor any other funding agencies involved). Neither the European Union nor the granting authority can be held responsible for them.

References

Cormac Anderson, Tiago Tresoldi, Thiago Costa Chacon, Anne-Maria Fehn, Mary Walworth, Robert Forkel, and Johann-Mattis List. 2018. A cross-linguistic database of phonetic transcription systems. *Yearbook of the Poznań Linguistic Meeting*, 4(1):21–53.

Stephen R. Anderson. 1980. Problems and perspectives in the description of vowel harmony. In Robert M. Vago, editor, *Issues in Vowel Harmony*, volume 6, pages 1–48. John Benjamins Publishing Company, Amsterdam.

Adam C. Baker. 2009. Two statistical approaches to finding vowel harmony. Technical report, University of Chicago.

Terry Crowley. 2014. *Bislama reference grammar*. University of Hawaii Press.

Johannes Dellert, Thora Daneyko, Alla Münch, Alina Ladygina, Armin Buch, Natalie Clarius, Ilja Grigorjew, Mohamed Balabel, Hizniye Isabella Boga, Zalina Baysarova, Roland Mühlenbernd, Johannes Wahle, and Gerhard Jäger. 2020. NorthEuraLex: a wide-coverage lexical database of Northern Eurasia. *Language Resources and Evaluation*, 54(1):273–301.

Rikker Dockum and Claire Bowern. 2019. Swadesh lists are not long enough: Drawing phonological generalizations from limited data. *Language Documentation and Description*, 16:35–54.

Matthew Dryer, Martin Haspelmath, and Robert Forkel. 2014. *WALS Online [Dataset, Version 2014.2]*. Zenodo, Geneva.

Robert Forkel, Johann-Mattis List, Simon J. Greenhill, Christoph Rzymski, Sebastian Bank, Michael Cysouw, Harald Hammarström, Martin Haspelmath, Gereon A. Kaiping, and Russell D. Gray. 2018. Cross-Linguistic Data Formats, advancing data sharing and re-use in comparative linguistics. *Scientific Data*, 5(180205):1–10.

Richard Futrell, Kyle Mahowald, and Edward Gibson. 2015. Quantifying word order freedom in dependency corpora. In *Proceedings of the Third International Conference on Dependency Linguistics (Depling 2015)*, pages 91–100, Uppsala, Sweden. Uppsala University, Uppsala, Sweden.

John Goldsmith. 1985. Vowel harmony in Khalkha Mongolian, Yaka, Finnish and Hungarian. *Phonology Yearbook*, 2(1):253–275.

John Goldsmith and Jason Riggle. 2012. Information theoretic approaches to phonological structure: the case of Finnish vowel harmony. *Natural Language & Linguistic Theory*, 30(3):859–896.

Alex Graves and Jürgen Schmidhuber. 2005. Framewise phoneme classification with bidirectional LSTM networks. In *Proceedings. 2005 IEEE International*

Joint Conference on Neural Networks, 2005., volume 4, pages 2047–2052, Montreal, Que., Canada. IEEE.

Michael Hahn, Judith Degen, Noah Goodman, Daniel Jurafsky, and Richard Futrell. 2018. An information-theoretic explanation of adjective ordering preferences. In *Proceedings of the 40th Annual Meeting of the Cognitive Science Society*, pages 1766–1772, Madison, WI. Cognitive Science Society.

Harald Hammarström, Robert Forkel, Martin Haspelmath, and Sebastian Bank. 2022. *Glottolog [Dataset, Version 4.7]*. Zenodo, Geneva.

Sepp Hochreiter and Jürgen Schmidhuber. 1997. Long short-term memory. *Neural computation*, 9(8):1735–1780.

Diederik P. Kingma and Jimmy Ba. 2015. Adam: A method for stochastic optimization. In *3rd International Conference on Learning Representations, ICLR 2015, San Diego, CA, USA, May 7-9, 2015, Conference Track Proceedings*.

Johann-Mattis List, Cormac Anderson, Tiago Tresoldi, and Robert Forkel. 2021. *Cross-Linguistic Transcription Systems [Dataset, Version 2.1.0]*. Max Planck Institute for the Science of Human History, Jena.

Johann-Mattis List and Robert Forkel. 2021. *CL Toolkit. A Python library for the processing of cross-linguistic data [Software package, Version 0.1.1]*. Max Planck Institute for Evolutionary Anthropology, Leipzig.

Johann-Mattis List, Robert Forkel, Simon J. Greenhill, Christoph Rzymski, Johannes Englisch, and Russell D. Gray. 2022a. Lexibank, a public repository of standardized wordlists with computed phonological and lexical features. *Scientific Data*, 9(1):316.

Johann-Mattis List, Annika Tjuka, Christoph Rzymski, Simon J. Greenhill, and Robert Forkel. 2022b. *CLLD Concepticon [Dataset, Version 3.0.0]*. Max Planck Institute for Evolutionary Anthropology, Leipzig.

Thomas Mayer, Christian Rohrdantz, Miriam Butt, Frans Plank, and Daniel A. Keim. 2010. Visualizing vowel harmony. *Linguistic issues in language technology*, 4(2):1–33.

John J. Ohala. 1994. Towards a universal, phonetically-based, theory of vowel harmony. In *3rd International Conference on Spoken Language Processing (ICSLP 1994)*, pages 491–494. ISCA.

Avery Ozburn. 2019. A segment-specific metric for quantifying participation in harmony. *Proceedings of the Annual Meetings on Phonology*, 7.

Adam Paszke, Sam Gross, Francisco Massa, Adam Lerer, James Bradbury, Gregory Chanan, Trevor Killeen, Zeming Lin, Natalia Gimelshein, Luca Antiga, Alban Desmaison, Andreas Kopf, Edward Yang, Zachary DeVito, Martin Raison, Alykhan Tejani, Sasank Chilamkurthy, Benoit Steiner, Lu Fang, Junjie Bai, and Soumith Chintala. 2019. Pytorch: An imperative style, high-performance deep learning library. In H. Wallach, H. Larochelle, A. Beygelzimer, F. d'Alché-Buc, E. Fox, and R. Garnett, editors, *Advances in Neural Information Processing Systems 32*, pages 8024–8035. Curran Associates, Inc.

Tiago Pimentel, Ryan Cotterell, and Brian Roark. 2021a. Disambiguatory signals are stronger in word-initial positions. In *Proceedings of the 16th Conference of the European Chapter of the Association for Computational Linguistics: Main Volume*, pages 31–41, Online. Association for Computational Linguistics.

Tiago Pimentel, Ryan Cotterell, and Brian Roark. 2021b. Disambiguatory signals are stronger in word-initial positions. In *Proceedings of the 16th Conference of the European Chapter of the Association for Computational Linguistics: Main Volume*, pages 31–41, Online. Association for Computational Linguistics.

Tiago Pimentel, Clara Meister, Elizabeth Salesky, Simone Teufel, Damián Blasi, and Ryan Cotterell. 2021c. A surprisal–duration trade-off across and within the world's languages. In *Proceedings of the 2021 Conference on Empirical Methods in Natural Language Processing*, pages 949–962, Online and Punta Cana, Dominican Republic. Association for Computational Linguistics.

Tiago Pimentel, Brian Roark, and Ryan Cotterell. 2020. Phonotactic Complexity and Its Trade-offs. *Transactions of the Association for Computational Linguistics*, 8:1–18.

Krisztina Polgárdi. 1999. Vowel harmony and disharmony in Turkish. *The Linguistic Review*, 16(2):187–204.

Neil Rathi, Michael Hahn, and Richard Futrell. 2021. An information-theoretic characterization of morphological fusion. In *Proceedings of the 2021 Conference on Empirical Methods in Natural Language Processing*, pages 10115–10120, Online and Punta Cana, Dominican Republic. Association for Computational Linguistics.

Jennifer Rodd. 1997. Recurrent neural-network learning of phonological regularities in Turkish. In *CoNLL97: Computational Natural Language Learning*.

Sam S. Shapiro and Martin B. Wilk. 1965. An analysis of variance test for normality (complete samples). *Biometrika*, 52(3-4):591–611.

Ashish Vaswani, Noam Shazeer, Niki Parmar, Jakob Uszkoreit, Llion Jones, Aidan N Gomez, Łukasz Kaiser, and Illia Polosukhin. 2017. Attention is all you need. In *Advances in Neural Information Processing Systems*, volume 30. Curran Associates, Inc.

Pauli Virtanen, Ralf Gommers, Travis E. Oliphant, Matt Haberland, Tyler Reddy, David Cournapeau, Evgeni Burovski, Pearu Peterson, Warren Weckesser, Jonathan Bright, Stéfan J. van der Walt, Matthew

Brett, Joshua Wilson, K. Jarrod Millman, Nikolay Mayorov, Andrew R. J. Nelson, Eric Jones, Robert Kern, Eric Larson, C J Carey, Ilhan Polat, Yu Feng, Eric W. Moore, Jake VanderPlas, Denis Laxalde, Josef Perktold, Robert Cimrman, Ian Henriksen, E. A. Quintero, Charles R. Harris, Anne M. Archibald, Antônio H. Ribeiro, Fabian Pedregosa, Paul van Mulbregt, SciPy 1.0 Contributors, Aditya Vijaykumar, Alessandro Pietro Bardelli, Alex Rothberg, Andreas Hilboll, Andreas Kloeckner, Anthony Scopatz, Antony Lee, Ariel Rokem, C. Nathan Woods, Chad Fulton, Charles Masson, Christian Häggström, Clark Fitzgerald, David A. Nicholson, David R. Hagen, Dmitrii V. Pasechnik, Emanuele Olivetti, Eric Martin, Eric Wieser, Fabrice Silva, Felix Lenders, Florian Wilhelm, G. Young, Gavin A. Price, Gert-Ludwig Ingold, Gregory E. Allen, Gregory R. Lee, Hervé Audren, Irvin Probst, Jörg P. Dietrich, Jacob Silterra, James T Webber, Janko Slavič, Joel Nothman, Johannes Buchner, Johannes Kulick, Johannes L. Schönberger, José Vinícius de Miranda Cardoso, Joscha Reimer, Joseph Harrington, Juan Luis Cano Rodríguez, Juan Nunez-Iglesias, Justin Kuczynski, Kevin Tritz, Martin Thoma, Matthew Newville, Matthias Kümmerer, Maximilian Bolingbroke, Michael Tartre, Mikhail Pak, Nathaniel J. Smith, Nikolai Nowaczyk, Nikolay Shebanov, Oleksandr Pavlyk, Per A. Brodtkorb, Perry Lee, Robert T. McGibbon, Roman Feldbauer, Sam Lewis, Sam Tygier, Scott Sievert, Sebastiano Vigna, Stefan Peterson, Surhud More, Tadeusz Pudlik, Takuya Oshima, Thomas J. Pingel, Thomas P. Robitaille, Thomas Spura, Thouis R. Jones, Tim Cera, Tim Leslie, Tiziano Zito, Tom Krauss, Utkarsh Upadhyay, Yaroslav O. Halchenko, and Yoshiki Vázquez-Baeza. 2020. SciPy 1.0: fundamental algorithms for scientific computing in Python. *Nature Methods*, 17(3):261–272.

Shijie Wu, Ryan Cotterell, and Timothy O'Donnell. 2019. Morphological irregularity correlates with frequency. In *Proceedings of the 57th Annual Meeting of the Association for Computational Linguistics*, pages 5117–5126, Florence, Italy. Association for Computational Linguistics.

A LSTM Hyperparameters

Hyperparameter	Value
Embedding Size	32
Hidden Size	256
LSTM Layers	2
Dropout	0.33
Batch Size	32

Table 4: Model and Training Hyperparameters as taken from (Pimentel et al., 2021b)

B Abbreviations of Harmonic Features

Abbreviation	Feature	
b	back	$+$BACK
f	front	$-$BACK
r	round	$+$ROUND
u	unround	$-$ROUND
atr	advanced tongue root	$+$ATR
natr	retracted tongue root	$-$ATR
n	neutral	
h	harmonic	
dish	disharmonic	

Table 5: Explanation of the abbreviations used in the result tables. The condition column refers to the type of harmony tested, with vowel successions abbreviated in the way described in this table. The sequence "f_n_f" represents sequences starting with a front/$-$BACK vowel, followed by a neutral/BACK neutral vowel and another front/BACK vowel. If more than one harmonic feature is present (as in Turkish, Manchu and Khalkha Mongolian), the magnitude of the effect on feature surprisal is compared between the two features in the disharmonic condition only (compare row "f_r/dish" in Table 8).

C Result Tables

Table 6: P-values, Δ_η and effect size for Finnish feature surprisal

Condition	Δ_η	Statistic	p-value	Effect Size	Test
f_f/f_b	-0.8298	71.0	2.e-12	0.0263	Wilcoxon
b_b/b_f	-0.8469	415.0	3.8e-17	0.0572	Wilcoxon
n_f/n_b	0.0009	4800.0	0.1723	0.4353	Wilcoxon
f_b/b_f	-0.2148	3148.0	0.001	-0.2813	Mann-Whitney
f_n_f/f_n_b	-0.563	59.0	7.57e-05	0.1052	Wilcoxon
b_n_b/b_n_f	-0.6077	236.0	0.0009	0.2183	Wilcoxon
n_n_f/n_n_b	-0.1206	85.0	0.1114	0.308	Wilcoxon
f_n_b/b_n_f	-0.1188	688.0	0.4834	-0.0935	Mann-Whitney

Table 7: P-values, Δ_η and effect size for Hungarian feature surprisal

Condition	Δ_η	Statistic	p-value	Effect Size	Test
f_f/f_b	-0.0917	270.0	0.64	0.4538	Wilcoxon
b_b/b_f	-2.1995	2.0	9.46e-21	0.0003	Wilcoxon
n_f/n_b	0.7951	1270.0	2.47e-14	0.1287	Wilcoxon
f_b/b_f	-1.0806	364.0	5.36e-13	-0.8154	Mann-Whitney
f_n_f/f_n_b	0.0864	27.0	1.0	0.4909	Wilcoxon
b_n_b/b_n_f	-1.6036	0.0	0.0078	0.0	Wilcoxon
n_n_f/n_n_b	0.4453	243.0	0.0019	0.2348	Wilcoxon
f_n_b/b_n_f	-0.674	24.0	0.1728	-0.4	Mann-Whitney

Table 8: P-values, Δ_η and effect size for Turkish feature surprisal

Condition	Δ_η	Statistic	p-value	Effect Size	Test
f_f/f_b	-3.1502	429.0	1.65e-29	0.0244	Wilcoxon
b_b/b_f	-4.0729	258.0	4.25e-42	0.008	Wilcoxon
f_b/b_f	-0.8602	14301.0	9.15e-13	-0.3978	Mann-Whitney
r_r/r_u	-1.0516	1107.0	1.8e-06	0.2236	Wilcoxon
u_u/u_r	-3.185	10.0	9.0e-58	0.0002	Wilcoxon
r_u/u_r	-1.5827	6339.0	2.48e-21	-0.6256	Mann-Whitney
f_h/dish	-3.6816	1348.0	4.71e-70	0.0138	Wilcoxon
r_h/dish	-2.7061	3473.0	4.5e-64	0.0356	Wilcoxon
f/r_dish	0.8555	132794.0	5.55e-21	0.3656	Mann-Whitney

Table 9: P-values, Δ_η and effect size for Manchu feature surprisal

Condition	Δ_η	Statistic	p-value	Effect Size	Test
f_f/f_b	-2.5563	6.0	1.68e-24	0.0006	Wilcoxon
b_b/b_f	-3.4993	209.0	1.16e-20	0.0253	Wilcoxon
n_f/n_b	0.354	14803.0	0.0086	0.4076	Wilcoxon
f_b/b_f	0.1359	9167.0	0.6778	0.0305	Mann-Whitney
f_n_f/f_n_b	-1.3331	43.0	3.58e-05	0.0814	Wilcoxon
b_n_b/b_n_f	-1.5021	259.0	1.61e-11	0.0743	Wilcoxon
n_n_f/n_n_b	0.1291	3941.0	0.7673	0.4849	Wilcoxon
f_n_b/b_n_f	-0.0086	1273.0	0.7338	-0.0414	Mann-Whitney

Table 10: P-values, Δ_η and effect size for Khalkha Mongolian feature surprisal

Condition	Δ_η	Statistic	p-value	Effect Size	Test
atr_atr/atr_natr	-1.8211	27.0	1.55e-13	0.0095	Wilcoxon
natr_natr/natr_atr	-0.6621	1819.0	2.55e-12	0.1672	Wilcoxon
n_atr/n_natr	-0.6531	91.0	0.0185	0.2407	Wilcoxon
atr_natr/natr_atr	-1.5526	7395.0	3.21e-05	0.3415	Mann-Whitney
r_r/r_u	-1.8211	2.0	4.37e-07	0.0034	Wilcoxon
u_u/u_r	-0.6621	2.0	8.35e-13	0.0009	Wilcoxon
n_r/n_u	-0.6531	371.0	0.148	0.3747	Wilcoxon
r_u/u_r	-1.5526	170.0	2.64e-12	-0.8529	Mann-Whitney
atr_h/dish	-1.0537	2337.5	1.09e-25	0.0944	Wilcoxon
r_h/dish	-1.6815	6.0	2.18e-18	0.0011	Wilcoxon
atr/r_dish	-0.3697	8941.0	0.0024	-0.2103	Mann-Whitney

D Vowel Counts in Test Set

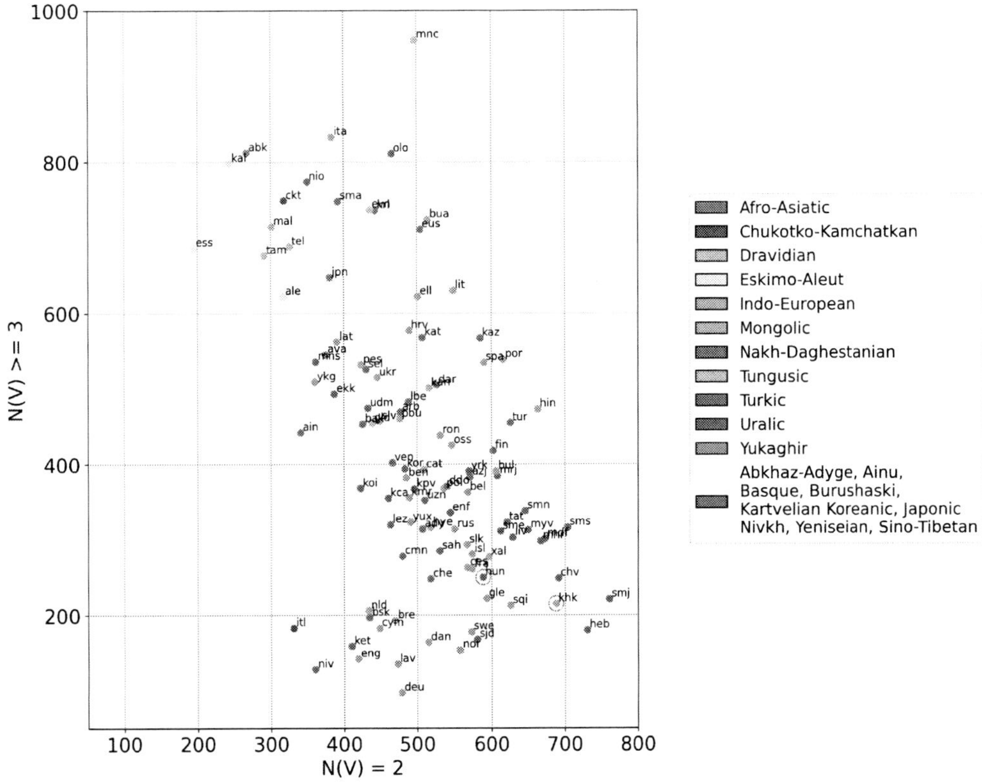

Figure 3: Number of items with 2 vowels (x-axis) and 3 or more vowels (y-axis) in all languages in NorthEuraLex. Hungarian and Khalkha Mongolian in red circles. Languages were coded for language family (see legend) and identified by ISO codes. For a mapping of ISO codes to language see the NorthEuraLex website `http://www.northeuralex.org/languages`.

Revisiting dependency length and intervener complexity minimisation on a parallel corpus in 35 languages

Andrew Dyer
Saarland University
Language Science & Technology
andrew.dyer@uni-saarland.de

Abstract

In this replication study of previous research into dependency length minimisation (DLM), we pilot a new parallel multilingual parsed corpus to examine whether previous findings are upheld when controlling for variation in domain and sentence content between languages. We follow the approach of previous research in comparing the dependency lengths of observed sentences in a multilingual corpus to a variety of baselines: permutations of the sentences, either random or according to some fixed schema. We go on to compare DLM with intervener complexity measure (ICM), an alternative measure of syntactic complexity. Our findings uphold both dependency length and intervener complexity minimisation in all languages under investigation. We also find a markedly lesser extent of dependency length minimisation in verb-final languages, and the same for intervener complexity measure. We conclude that dependency length and intervener complexity minimisation as universals are upheld when controlling for domain and content variation, but that further research is needed into the asymmetry between verb-final and other languages in this regard.

1 Introduction

Efficiency in language production and processing is widely held as a universal, underpinning various aspects of human language evolution and use. (Levshina and Moran, 2021). Within syntax, an expression of this is found in the theory of Dependency Locality (Gibson, 1998): the principle that syntactically related information should appear in close proximity in a sentence, so as to minimise the memory load required to parse it. Its observable effect is dependency length minimisation (DLM): the ordering of a sentence such that the sum distance of dependencies in sentences is minimised (Gibson). This effect has been well studied cross-lingually (Gildea and Temperley, 2010; Liu, 2008), and is widely held to be a universal of syntax, with the study of Futrell et al. (2015) finding evidence of the effect in all languages in a sample of 37 languages in Universal Dependencies (Nivre et al., 2016), among other such cross-lingual studies.[1]

There remain, however, inconsistencies and asymmetries in how and where DLM is applied, within languages and within sentence structures. For example, a common finding is that DLM is less pronounced or even absent in head-final languages when controlling for various factors such as sentence type, and when looking only at lexical tokens. Jing et al. (2022) find a negative association between head-finality and dependency length when controlling for harmony and considering only lexical dependencies, an effect that they find to be robust against multiple random baselines. Liu (2021) also finds mixed evidence for the correlation between dependency length and ordering choices for pre-verbal arguments in head-final languages; whereas argument ordering choice is more clearly associated with dependency length in languages with post-verbal arguments. These findings point to a more nuanced picture of DLM, where the effect is asymmetric in terms of word order, more clearly pronounced in head-initial languages (Yadav et al., 2020).

Another question is the extent to which DLM exists as an independent effect, as opposed to being a function of other constraints. Yadav et al. (2022) propose the alternative measure of sentence complexity, Intervener Complexity Measure (ICM), which measures not the number of tokens between dependants and their heads, but the number of syntactic heads between them, suggesting optimisation for ICM underlies the observed DLM effect.

As a first step in investigating these questions, our replication study revisits the work of Futrell and Gibson (2015) to broadly replicate this study on a new corpus, with some additions in light of

[1] https://universaldependencies.org/

Proceedings of the 5th Workshop on Research in Computational Linguistic Typology and Multilingual NLP (SIGTYP 2023), pages 110–119
May 6, 2023

subsequent research. We seek to reevaluate the following questions:

1. Does the observation of DLM in all languages hold when languages contain loosely parallel data?
2. To what extent is DLM achieved by word order variation, as opposed to canonical word order constraints?
3. Do we see the same asymmetry between verb-final and non-final languages as in previous works?
4. How does DLM compare to ICM minimization across languages?

Our study pilots a new corpus: the Corpus of Indo-European Prose Plus, or CIEP+ (Talamo and Verkerk, 2022). CIEP+ is a parallel corpus of translated works of modern prose in several languages, syntactically annotated under the Universal Dependencies[2] framework. The translated texts are drawn from the most widely translated works of prose in the world. While the corpus originated as a means of comparative study of Indo-European languages, and these languages make up the majority of its data, it also contains translations in some non-Indo-European languages.

The use of parallel corpora is beneficial in making language data more comparable between languages, controlling for domain differences and the natural variation of communicative intent in sentences (Dahl, 2007). However, most currently available parallel corpora suffer either from limited size and language coverage (e.g. Parallel Universal Dependencies), or from being drawn from highly specific lects that do not reflect common language use (e.g. parallel Bible corpora, UN Declaration of Human Rights).

A related problem in parallel corpora is the phenomenon of *Translationese* (Gellerstam, 1986): the effect whereby translated texts are identifiable by certain characteristics that are atypical in the target language, caused by language-specific or universal effects of the translation process (Koppel and Ordan, 2011).

Fictional and non-fictional prose are not immune to the effects of Translationese (Puurtinen, 2003; Popescu, 2011). Nevertheless, since the goal of translated prose is entertainment rather than exactitude, we expect that translators will use stylistic translations that may be closer to the conventions of the target language, thus mitigating this concern.[3]

The books that we use are large, containing thousands of sentences. And, though we do not escape the bias of translations mostly being available in a small set of languages, we nevertheless manage a decent coverage of 35 languages, with at least 20,000 sentences in each.

Our use of this corpus addresses a potentially confounding issue in Futrell et al. (2015) and other corpus-based studies: the variation in domain coverage across the UD corpora. With a parallel corpus, we once again put these findings to the test.

2 Background

Word ordering with respect to phrase heaviness has long been a topic of interest in constituency-based syntax (Arnold et al., 2000), and has been adapted to a dependency grammar framework as dependency length (Gildea and Temperley, 2010).

Since the inception of Universal Dependencies (Nivre et al., 2016) and other consistently annotated multilingual corpora, more multilingual studies of DLM have been carried out. Futrell and Gibson (2015) compare the sum dependency lengths of observed sentences in 37 languages in Universal Dependencies to random baselines of sentences permuted to random orders. They find that in all 37 languages, dependency length as a function of sentence length shows a consistently slower increase than would be expected in random word order baselines, whether free or fixed.

Yu et al. (2019) extend this study to probe the impacts of canonical word order constraints versus variability on DLM. Building on the setup of Futrell and Gibson (2015), they use randomly permuted baselines with *same valency* (i.e. all heads in the permuted sentence must have the same number of dependants on each side) and *same side* (i.e. dependants must be on the same side of their head) constraints, and find that each baseline shows a reduction in dependency length, and that atypical orderings in a language usually contribute to this.

In several studies, Liu (2020, 2021, 2022) probes the DLM effect with regard to ordering flexibility and pre- and postverbal argument domains. Among her findings is that while dependency length minimisation is well-correlated with phrase ordering

[2]https://universaldependencies.org

[3]We are unaware of any quantitative evaluation of the prevalence of Translationese in prose compared to other genres of translation, such as legal, technical and political translations. Such research would be very valuable.

choices in postverbal languages (e.g. English, Bulgarian, Dutch), this effect is much weaker or nonexistent in preverbal languages (e.g. Japanese, Persian), suggesting that the relevance of DLM depends greatly on word ordering constraints, among other pressures.

Intervener Complexity Measure is introduced by Yadav et al. (2022). They operationalise the complexity of intervening information in long dependencies as Intervener Complexity Measure, which counts the number of syntactic heads between a dependant and its head. By comparing random permutations of trees alternately matched for dependency length or intervener complexity, they find that random linear arrangements matched for dependency length tend to have very close ICM to the original sentence, but that the inverse effect is not as strong. Though Yadav et al. (2022) perform their experiments using several languages in Surface Universal Dependencies (Gerdes et al., 2018), accounting for language as a random effect, we are unaware of any multilingual study so far that has directly measured the extent of intervener complexity minimisation per language.

Most prior large cross-lingual studies of dependency length minimisation have used Universal Dependencies or Surface Universal Dependencies corpora, or other dependency corpora pre-dating UD (Liu, 2008), without control for domain and sentence variation. However, there are some that have used parallel corpora. For example, Jiang and Liu (2015) compare effects of sentence length and dependency direction in a parallel English-Chinese corpus; and Ferrer-i Cancho (2017) use the Parallel Universal Dependencies (PUD) corpora. We are unaware of any previous work with parallel corpora of the same size as CIEP+.

3 Method

In our investigation, we broadly replicate the experimental setup of Futrell and Gibson (2015).

The dependency length of a token in a sentence is defined as the number of tokens between it and its head in the linear surface order, including itself (i.e. a minimum of 1). The dependency length of a sentence is then the sum of dependency lengths for each token, excluding the root.

We compare the dependency lengths of observed sentences to a set of random baselines: reorderings of the sentences in the corpora with the same underlying tree structure but a different linear surface order of tokens. These baselines are:

1. **RandomFree** Random projective permutations of the sentence retaining the same structure.
2. **RandomFixed** Permutations according to a randomly generated grammar.
3. **FittedGrammar** Permutations of each sentence to strictly follow an approximation of the language's canonical word order.
4. **OptimalOrder** Permutation of each sentence to optimise for minimum dependency length.

Of these, FittedGrammar is introduced by our study, while the others are also used by Futrell and Gibson (2015). We briefly describe and motivate each permutation method in Section 3.1.

After creating permutations of each sentence in each book in each language, we use a linear mixed-effects model to estimate the rate at which dependency lengths increase as a function of sentence length. The response variable of the model is sentence dependency length, while the fixed variables are the interaction between sentence length (in number of tokens) and permutation mode: the baseline that produced the sentence (including the unaltered original sentence).

We use sentence ID as a random effect in the model. Sentence ID is shared across all permutations of a sentence, and including it accounts for the effect of the variance in sentence structure. This random effect is simplified compared to Futrell and Gibson's, which groups permutations by sentence ID. We found that doing this caused singular fits in the model.

Performing this separately for each language in the corpus, we use the coefficient of the model fit as the measure of a language's rate of dependency length increase. The higher the coefficient, the greater the dependency lengths we can expect to see as sentence length increases. The model gives us a separate fit for each of the baselines, and so we are able to compare the true rate of increase to what we could expect to see in each of the baseline conditions. If the true rate of increase is not lower from the random baseline, for example, then we do not see DLM in the language.

We use the same approach to measure intervener complexity minimisation. The intervener complexity of a token is defined by Yadav et al. (2022) as the number of syntactic heads that come between it and its own head; including the token's head itself, meaning that for each token the minimum intervener complexity is one. The Intervener Complexity Measure of a sentence is then the sum of tokenwise intervener complexities in the sentence. Fig. 1 shows an example of Intervener Complexity Measure for a sentence in contrast to dependency length.

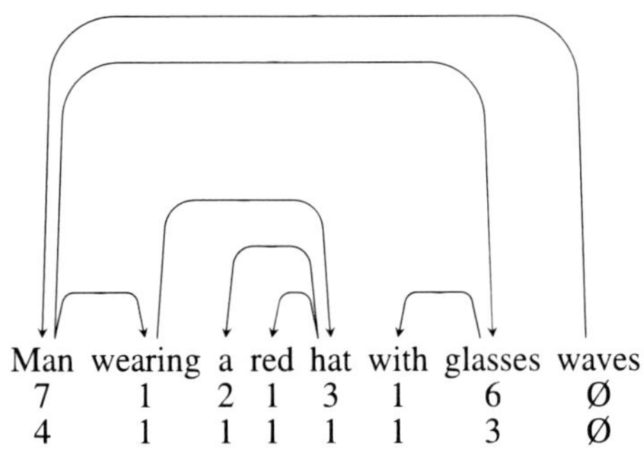

Figure 1: A demonstration of the difference between dependency length and intervener complexity. The top layer of numbers is dependency length; the bottom layer is intervener complexity.
For example. there are seven tokens between *waves* and its syntactic head *Man*, but only three heads between them (*wearing*, *hat* and *glasses*).
The ICM of this sentence is 12, compared to 21 for dependency length.

3.1 Permutation baselines

RandomFree

In the RandomFree baseline, we recursively permute each subtree within a sentence tree such that the children of any head may appear in any order before or after the head. The same underlying tree structure is retained, but the linear surface order is random with the sole constraint that the resulting tree is projective. We perform this procedure 10 times for each sentence in the corpus.[4]

If DLM holds, then the observed dependency lengths should be consistently below what we would expect to see in random linear arrangements of the same sentence.

RandomFixed

We use the term *grammar* throughout this paper to refer to a lookup table for a determinate position of each dependency relation with respect to its head.

For each dependency relation, we assign a lookup value in the range [-1,1]. For each recursive subtree in the corpus, the dependants are rearranged according to the lookup value of their dependency relation. Dependencies whose label has a negative lookup value go to the left of their head; those with a positive value go to the right. The higher the absolute value, the further the sentence is from the head in the new sentence permutation.

As in the RandomFixed baseline, we produce 10 random grammars in total, and permute each sentence according to each of these grammars.

This baseline is a more conservative variant of the random free baseline, taking into account that all languages have at least some degree of fixedness in their word order, the regularity of which is hypothesised to reduce dependency length on average.

FittedGrammar

The fitted grammar for each language is a count-based estimation of the majority position for each dependency relation. For each dependency relation, we assign two parameters: $sign$ - an integer -1 or 1, depending on whether the dependency relation most often appears on the left (-1) or the right (1) of its head; and $distance'$ - a float of the mean log distance of the dependency relation from its head (relative to other dependants) when on the side indicated by $sign$. The final parameter $position$ is then the product of $sign \times distance'$: a positive or negative real number. As in the random fixed baseline, all dependants are then ordered according to this lookup value. Fig. 2 shows an example of how such a grammar would assign the order of dependants.

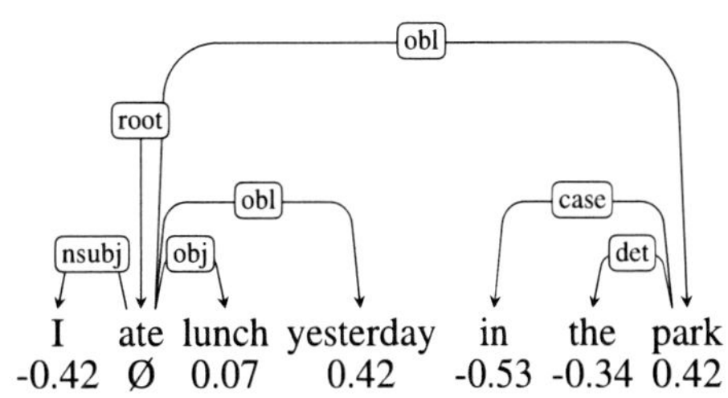

Figure 2: An example of how a grammar might assign the positions of dependants. Below each word is the position lookup value for its dependency relation. For example, `nsubj` has a $position$ value of -0.42. When two dependants have the same lookup value (as in *yesterday* and *park* here) the ordering of the two is arbitrary. The lookup values in this example are taken from the fitted grammar for English.

The fitted grammar is used as a rough measure

[4] Futrell and Gibson's setup calls for 100 random permutations. We find that this number quickly becomes intractable for storage and processing with our larger corpus size.

of the extent to which DLM is achieved through language users' choice of sentence orderings as opposed to the canonical word order constraints of the language. We find that the lookup values obtained by this method generally match with canonical word order classifications.

For example, Table 1 shows some lookup values for `nsubj`, `obj` and `obl` relations in four languages. In each of these languages, the relative lookup values correspond with the orderings of subject, object, and verb (SOV) (Dryer, 2013) and oblique, object and verb (XOV) (Dryer and Gensler, 2013) in WALS. Though we cannot fully model the canonical word order rules of a language with only the basic relations of UD, we can at least provide an approximation that is comparable between languages.

	nsubj	obj	obl	WALS Ch. 81	WALS Ch. 84
eng	-0.42	0.07	0.42	SVO	VOX
jpn	-0.60	-0.14	-0.52	SOV	XOV
ara	0.18	0.59	0.55	VSO	VOX
zho	-0.77	0.39	-0.51	SVO	XVO

Table 1: The *position* values for `nsubj`, `obj` and `obl` in four languages. For example, in Japanese the `obl` relation has a lower value than `obj`, meaning that it will be placed before it; and both have a negative value, so they will both be placed to before their head. Assuming that the head is a verb, this follows the canonical XOV word order in Japanese.

OptimalOrder

Our algorithm for finding the optimal linear order that minimises dependency length is based on that of Gildea and Temperley. For each recursive subtree, we sort dependants by their *weight*: the number of words in their recursive subtree. Dependants are then placed inside-out on alternating sides of their head. Whether the alternation starts from left or right depends on the direction of the head: left-branching heads will start left-to-right; right-branching heads, right-to-left. This order will be reversed if the number of dependants is even, such that the heaviest dependant will branch in the same direction as its head. Fig. 3 shows an example of the output of this algorithm.

The optimal ordering gives an idea of the upper bound of DLM that we could expect under complete word order freedom with DLM as the only objective. In the case of languages with a high

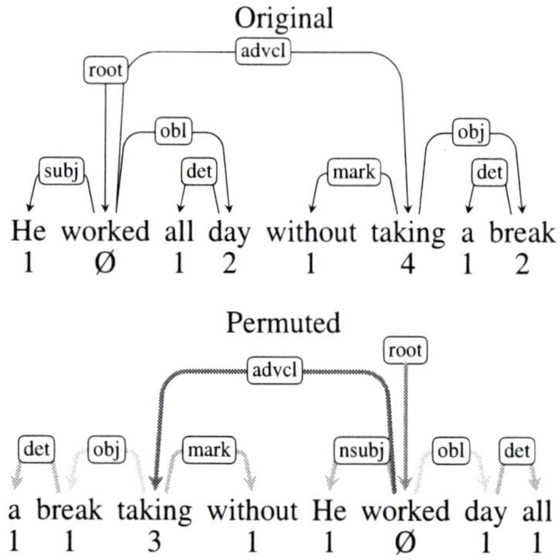

Figure 3: An example of how the OptimalOrder algorithm permutes a sentence. The colour of the edges indicates the order in which they are attached to their head: orange first; green second; blue third. Dependency lengths are shown on the bottom row of text. The permuted sentence has lower dependency lengths than the original due to the flattening effect of the algoithm.

dependency length rate, the comparison with the optimal baseline tells us to what extent this can be explained by the inherent complexity of the sentence structure.

3.2 Data

We use the CIEP+ corpus for our analysis (Talamo and Verkerk, 2022).[5] CIEP+ is a parallel corpus of translated works of modern prose in several languages, comprised of a set of some of the world's most widely translated works. The source languages of the texts varies between English, French, Portuguese, Spanish, German, and Dutch. The corpus is parsed predictively using the Stanza NLP pipeline (Qi et al., 2020), which has pretrained models in UD format with Labeled Attachment Score of at least 70% for all languages under consideration. The languages that we use, their families, and their canonical word order are shown in Table 2. These languages are not subset to those used by Futrell et al. (2015) and thus cannot be directly compared, but are the languages for which we have data in CIEP+.

We remove all punctuation tokens from the corpus, as these carry no semantic information and cause artificially long dependency lengths. In or-

[5] `https://www.uni-saarland.de/fileadmin/upload/lehrstuhl/verkerk/CIEP_outline.pdf`

Family	Language (code)	Basic order
IE Germanic	Danish (dan)	SVO
	Dutch (nld)	SVO*
	English (eng)	SVO
	German (deu)	SVO*
	Norwegian (nor)	SVO
	Swedish (swe)	SVO
IE Celtic	Irish (gle)	VSO
	Welsh (cym)	VSO
IE Romance	French (fra)	SVO
	Italian (ita)	SVO
	Latin (lat)	SVO
	Portuguese (por)	SVO
	Romanian (ron)	SVO
	Spanish (spa)	SVO
IE Baltic	Latvian (lav)	SVO
	Lithuanian (lit)	SVO
IE Slavic	Bulgarian (bul)	SVO
	Croatian (hrv)	SVO
	Czech (ces)	SVO
	Polish (pol)	SVO
	Russian (rus)	SVO
	Slovak (slk)	SVO
	Slovenian (slv)	SVO
	Ukrainian (ukr)	SVO
IE Indo-Iranian	Hindi (hin)	SOV
	Persian (fas)	SOV
	Urdu (urd)	SOV
IE Other	Armenian (hye)	SOV*
	Greek (ell)	SVO*
non-IE Finno-Ugric	Finnish (fin)	SVO
	Hungarian (hun)	SVO
non-IE Other	Arabic (ara)	VSO
	Chinese (zho)	SVO
	Indonesian (ind)	SVO
	Japanese (jpn)	SOV
	Turkish (tur)	SOV*

Table 2: Languages in CIEP+ tbat we use for our experiments. All languages have at least 20k sentences and are parsed using models with >70% LAS. Basic word order is according to WALS (Dryer, 2013). Asterisks * indicate that the language has more than one dominant word order.

der to reduce the number of parameters needed for the FittedGrammar and RandomFixed baselines, we simplify subtyped relations to their main type (e.g. `aux:pass` → `aux`). For ease of processing, we exclude non-standard tokens that are not part of the tree structure in the `conllu` format, such as enhanced dependencies and multiword tokens.[6] Finally, we exclude all sentences that, after these cleaning steps, have more than 50 tokens.

[6]The reason for this is simply that such tokens are incompatible with our permutation algorithms. We leave examination of the impact of enhanced dependencies and multiword tokens on dependency lengths for future research.

4 Results

4.1 Dependency length minimisation

We show the coefficients for the mixed-effects regression for each baseline in each language in Fig. 5. These coefficients represent the rate at which dependency length can be expected to increase as a function of sentence length for each baseline and language in the corpus. We also show an example of the regression fit in English in Fig. 4.

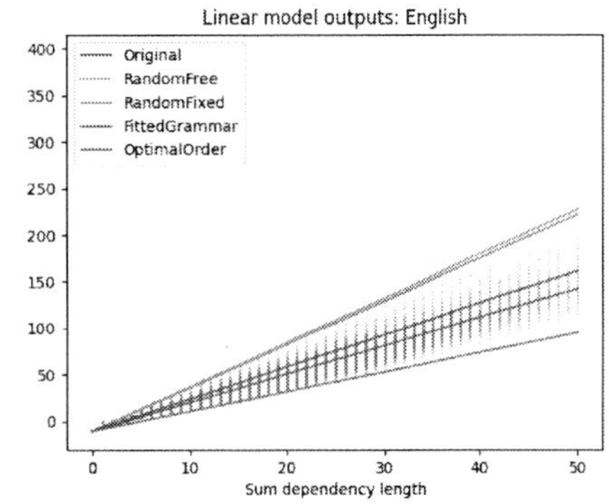

Figure 4: Dependency lengths as a function of sentence length in English. The coloured lines show the fit from the linear mixed-effects model for each baseline. Grey dots show the true (observed) dependency lengths.

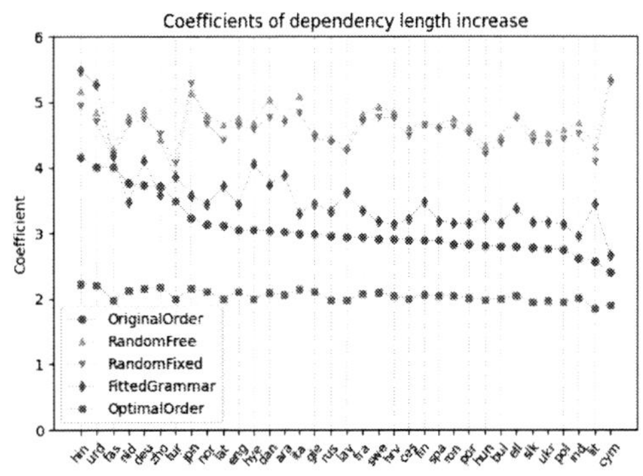

Figure 5: The coefficients of dependency length increase for all baselines in all languages. Languages are sorted in descending order by the coefficient of the OriginalOrder sentence.

Overall, we see clear evidence of DLM in all languages compared to both random baselines. We also find the same asymmetry as Futrell and Gibson (2015) and others whereby verb-final languages such as Hindi, Turkish and Japanese - and languages with frequent verb-final constructions such as German, Dutch and Chinese - show faster rates of dependency length increase. We can see this as the rising tail on the left of the OriginalOrder coefficients in Fig. 5. The same tendency is not apparent in predominantly SVO languages with free word order and rich inflectional morphology, such as Baltic and Slavic languages.

Interestingly, we find the lowest rate of increase in Welsh, a VSO-preferring language (Williams, 1980), which we might expect to generate longer dependencies because of the increased distance from the predicate to its arguments. Irish, another Celtic language that prefers VSO word order, has a coefficient more in line with the SVO languages in the corpus. We should note that Welsh has one of the lower number of sentences in CIEP+, and the LAS of the Welsh parsing model in Stanza is low compared to other languages in our corpus, so we do not make any conclusions regarding this.

OptimalOrder is consistent across languages, showing that a consistent rate of increase is possible across all the languages sampled. This optimum would not be realistic in any of the languages as it would require no word order constraints, but it does show that where some languages show a faster rate of dependency length increase, this is not likely to be the result of the underlying tree structure of sentences being inherently more complex than other languages.

Regarding the **RandomFixed** baseline, we do not find that this operates differently from **RandomFree**, and intuitively this would be explained by the outputs of all random grammars being pooled together; with the resulting data being not much different to what we would see if we simply randomized all sentences. This can and should be fixed in future research.

The **FittedGrammar** baseline is more chaotic than we anticipated. In most languages towards the right of the graph, we see a small gap between the original sentences and the FittedGrammar output, though in some languages this gap is greater than in others. Many of these seem to be languages with flexible word order, such as as the Baltic languages and Greek, but also, for some reason, Danish. This could be cautious evidence of languages using their available word order flexibility to reduce dependency lengths.

However, as we reach the SOV and mixed languages on the left side of the graph, the picture is more incoherent. In Hindi and Urdu, the fitted grammar results in a higher dependency length increase even than both random baselines. We are unsure how to interpret this, and further linguistic analysis of the permutations produced by the fitted grammar is in order.

4.2 Intevener Complexity Measure

Fig. 6 shows the coefficients of the linear mixed-effects model, this time using Intervener Complexity Measure of each sentence as the response variable.

As with dependency length, we find a clear pattern whereby SOV languages, or languages with frequent verb-final constructions, show a faster rate of increase in ICM compared with SVO languages. For other languages, however, a very similar pattern of minimisation is observed, though in this case the gap between coefficients is much smaller.

Welsh once again shows the slowest rate of increase, though in this case the effect is less pronounced. Again, Irish is not among the languages with the lowest coefficients, which indicates that this is probably not due to typological properties of VSO or Celtic languages.

The observed ICM is almost colinear with OptimalOrder for several of the languages (mainly those with SVO word order), and in some cases is lower. The OptimalOrder algorithm was developed to minimise dependency lengths, not ICM, so this is unlikely to represent the true optimum. However, this finding is compelling because it suggests that observed sentences are close to an optimal ICM, while also being clearly separated from the random baselines.

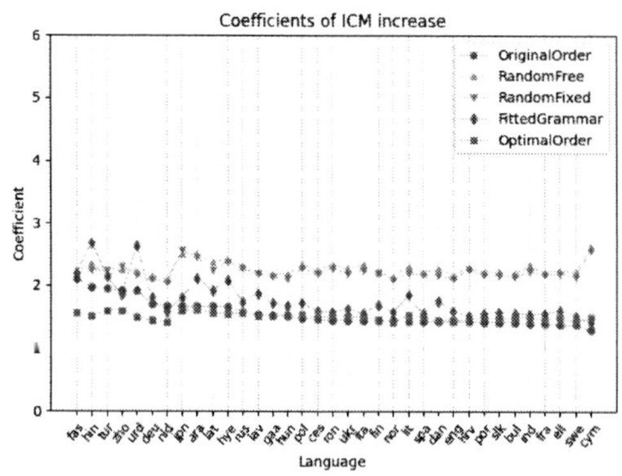

Figure 6: The coefficients of intervener complexity measure increase for all baselines in all languages. Languages are sorted in descending order by OriginalOrder coefficient.

5 Discussion

Overall, our results seem to uphold DLM as a universal, though with the ame asymmetry between verb-final and verb-initial or -medial languages. We also find this same asymmetry in intervener complexity, with the same languages showing a faster rate of increase in ICM, showing that the antilocality effect extends to this measure as well.

The next step is to turn our attention to explanations of this tendency for reduced DLM in SOV/verb-final languages. There is already work underway to explain these tendencies (Yadav et al., 2020; Jing et al., 2022).

The use of a parallel corpus has supported the results of previous research in this area. In other words, we do not see a very different picture when using a parallel corpus. An interpretation of this that dependency length and intervener complexity minimisation effects are strong enough that they show through the noise of domain and sentence variation.

However, we still maintain that parallel corpora should be used wherever possible in such studies. Our study has applied to languages as a whole, using the full range of sentences each language in the corpus. On the other hand, we hypothesise that the more focused the linguistic structures under investigation - for example, verb phrases with single object and oblique arguments (Liu, 2020), or verb phrases with two oblique arguments (Liu, 2022) - the more the noise of differing domains and sentence content will affect the results. It is particularly these kinds of studies that we believe will benefit from large parallel corpora.

A meta-study of dependency length and related experiments using both Universal Dependencies and parallel corpora would be useful to measure the extent to which such noise affects different kinds of experiments. We leave this for future research.

There are also some improvements that could be made to this study in particular.

We would like to find an algorithm for finding the linear ordering that truly optimises intervener complexity measure, so that we can properly assess how close observed orderings are to this baseline. We are unaware of such an algorithm as of yet, and Gildea and Temperley's algorithm is an imperfect stand-in. This would be particularly valuable because of the tentative evidence we find for observed word order reflecting optimised ICM.

Some previous studies have used Surface Universal Dependencies (SUD) annotated corpora (Gerdes et al., 2018) instead of Universal Dependencies. While we do not expect vastly different results, there is some contention that SUD is more appropriate for modelling syntactic difficulty and cognitive demand (Yan and Liu, 2019), and it would be beneficial to compare experiments on corpora using each of the two formalisms.

Finally, as more languages are added to CIEP+, we hope to be able to expand our analyses to more languages, particularly non-Indo-European languages.

6 Conclusion

Our replication of a keystone study on dependency length minimisation as a language universal on a much larger, parallel parsed corpus has corroborated previous findings that show evidence of systematic dependency length minimisation in a variety of the world's languages, controlling for the effect of sentence and domain variation. We find a similar effect for intervener complexity measure.

We make available our code for permuting parsed corpora according to different permutation baselines, and for analysing them in terms of dependency length, intervener complexity and other properties.[7]

We plan to use this corpus in further replications and original studies on syntactic complexity and word order constraints. Among our topics of interest are research into why dependency length minimisation is less of a pressure in verb-final languages; and the extent to which other constraints such as information locality (Futrell, 2019; Liu, 2022) and memory-surprisal tradeoff (Hahn et al., 2020, 2021) subsume dependency length as an explanatory factor for word order.

Limitations

While the design of the CIEP+ corpus is parallel in the sense that the same collection of books is to be added for each language, not all languages have the full collection. This also means that languages will have different data sizes and different book coverage. While in data exploration we did not find that the book that sentences came from was a strong random effect, it is possible that these differences may nevertheless confound the results. Book translations are continually added to the corpus, so

[7] `https://github.com/andidyer/DependencyLengthSurvey`

this problem will hopefully become lesser in future studies.

In contrast to the gold Universal Dependencies data used in many other studies, CIEP+ is predictively parsed, and parser error may propagate to give erroneous results. Interesting findings for any particular language should therefore be looked at with the performance of that language's Stanza model in mind.[8] CIEP+ does not currently have gold evaluation sets, so it is unfortunately not possible to get LAS scores for the models on CIEP+; we rely on the models' evaluation scores on the test sets of the UD corpora on which they are trained.

The use of a linear mixed effects model for plotting the increase in dependency length is not ideal due to the heteroscedacity of sentence dependency length relative to sentence length; variance of dependency length increases with sentence length, and means do not increase linearly. This is contrary to the assumptions of linear models, and may affect the reliability of the results. (van den Berg, 2021) We experimented with generalised mixed effects models with a Poisson link function, but found that this caused unacceptably long training times with the size of our data. We might overcome this with bootstrap sampling, or an alternative regression algorithm or software.

Ethics

We are not aware of any adverse impacts on any individual or group of individuals as a result of our study.

This paper and all associated code and statistical analysis was produced by human effort of the authors. At no point was any generative artificial intelligence used.

Our data is not available to share in its original form due to copyright concerns. However, upon request, we can provide the data in delexicalised form.

Acknowledgements

Thanks to Michael Hahn and Annemarie Verkerk for their supervision and feedback, and to Luigi Talamo and Luca Brigada Villa for comments and suggestions.

CIEP+ exists thanks to the work of Luigi Talamo and Annemarie Verkerk, and the many individuals who collected the required books. And, of course, the writers and translators of those books.

Finally, many thanks to the anonymous reviewers for their kind comments, critiques and suggestions.

[8] https://stanfordnlp.github.io/stanza/performance.html

References

Jennifer Arnold, Anthony Losongco, Thomas Wasow, and Ryan Ginstrom. 2000. Heaviness vs. newness: The effects of structural complexity and discourse status on constituent ordering. *Language*, 76:28–55.

Östen Dahl. 2007. From questionnaires to parallel corpora in typology. *Language Typology and Universals*, 60(2):172–181.

Matthew S. Dryer. 2013. Order of subject, object and verb (v2020.3). In Matthew S. Dryer and Martin Haspelmath, editors, *The World Atlas of Language Structures Online*. Zenodo.

Matthew S. Dryer and Orin D. Gensler. 2013. Order of object, oblique, and verb (v2020.3). In Matthew S. Dryer and Martin Haspelmath, editors, *The World Atlas of Language Structures Online*. Zenodo.

Ramon Ferrer-i Cancho. 2017. The placement of the head that maximizes predictability. an information theoretic approach. *Glottometrics*, 39.

Richard Futrell. 2019. Information-theoretic locality properties of natural language. In *Proceedings of the First Workshop on Quantitative Syntax (Quasy, SyntaxFest 2019)*, pages 2–15, Paris, France. Association for Computational Linguistics.

Richard Futrell and Edward Gibson. 2015. Experiments with generative models for dependency tree linearization. In *Proceedings of the 2015 Conference on Empirical Methods in Natural Language Processing*, pages 1978–1983, Lisbon, Portugal. Association for Computational Linguistics.

Richard Futrell, Kyle Mahowald, and Edward Gibson. 2015. Large-scale evidence of dependency length minimization in 37 languages. *Proceedings of the National Academy of Sciences*, 112(33):10336–10341.

Martin Gellerstam. 1986. Translationese in swedish novels translated from english. In *Translation Studies in Scandinavia*, pages 88 – 95.

Kim Gerdes, Bruno Guillaume, Sylvain Kahane, and Guy Perrier. 2018. SUD or Surface-Syntactic Universal Dependencies: An annotation scheme near-isomorphic to UD. In *Universal Dependencies Workshop 2018*, Brussels, Belgium.

Edward Gibson. The dependency locality theory: A distance-based theory of linguistic complexity. In *Image, language, brain: Papers from the first mind articulation project symposium*, pages 94 – 126.

Edward Gibson. 1998. Linguistic complexity: locality of syntactic dependencies. *Cognition*, 68:1–76.

Daniel Gildea and David Temperley. In *Proceedings of the 45th Annual Meeting of the Association of Computational Linguistics*, pages 184–191.

Daniel Gildea and David Temperley. 2010. Do grammars minimize dependency length? *Cognitive Science*, 34(2):286–310.

Michael Hahn, Judith Degen, and Richard Futrell. 2021. Modeling word and morpheme order in natural language as an efficient tradeoff of memory and surprisal. *Psychological Review*, 128:726–756.

Michael Hahn, Dan Jurafsky, and Richard Futrell. 2020. Universals of word order reflect optimization of grammars for efficient communication. *Proceedings of the National Academy of Sciences of the United States of America*, 117:2347–2353.

Jingyang Jiang and Haitao Liu. 2015. The effects of sentence length on dependency distance, dependency direction and the implications–based on a parallel english–chinese dependency treebank. *Language Sciences*, 50:93–104.

Yingqi Jing, Damián Blasi, and Balthasar Bickel. 2022. Dependency length minimization and its limits: A possible role for a probabilistic version of the final-over-final condition. *Language*, 98.

Moshe Koppel and Noam Ordan. 2011. Translationese and its dialects. In *Proceedings of the 49th Annual Meeting of the Association for Computational Linguistics: Human Language Technologies*, pages 1318–1326, Portland, Oregon, USA. Association for Computational Linguistics.

Natalia Levshina and Steven Moran. 2021. Efficiency in human languages: Corpus evidence for universal principles. *Linguistics Vanguard*, 7(s3):20200081.

Haitao Liu. 2008. Dependency distance as a metric of language comprehension difficulty. *Journal of Cognitive Science*, 9:159–191.

Zoey Liu. 2020. Mixed evidence for crosslinguistic dependency length minimization. *STUF - Language Typology and Universals*, 73(4):605–633.

Zoey Liu. 2021. The crosslinguistic relationship between ordering flexibility and dependency length minimization: A data-driven approach. In *Proceedings of the Society for Computation in Linguistics 2021*, pages 264–274, Online. Association for Computational Linguistics.

Zoey Liu. 2022. A multifactorial approach to crosslinguistic constituent orderings. *Linguistics Vanguard*.

Joakim Nivre, Marie-Catherine de Marneffe, Filip Ginter, Yoav Goldberg, Jan Hajič, Christopher D. Manning, Ryan McDonald, Slav Petrov, Sampo Pyysalo, Natalia Silveira, Reut Tsarfaty, and Daniel Zeman. 2016. Universal Dependencies v1: A multilingual treebank collection. In *Proceedings of the Tenth International Conference on Language Resources and Evaluation (LREC'16)*, pages 1659–1666, Portorož, Slovenia. European Language Resources Association (ELRA).

Marius Popescu. 2011. Studying translationese at the character level. *International Conference Recent Advances in Natural Language Processing, RANLP*, pages 634–639.

Tiina Puurtinen. 2003. Genre-specific Features of Translationese? Linguistic Differences between Translated and Non-translated Finnish Children's Literature. *Literary and Linguistic Computing*, 18(4):389–406.

Peng Qi, Yuhao Zhang, Yuhui Zhang, Jason Bolton, and Christopher D. Manning. 2020. Stanza: A Python natural language processing toolkit for many human languages. In *Proceedings of the 58th Annual Meeting of the Association for Computational Linguistics: System Demonstrations*.

Luigi Talamo and Annemarie Verkerk. 2022. A new methodology for an old problem: A corpus-based typology of adnominal word order in european languages. *Italian Journal of Linguistics*, 34:171–226.

Stéphanie M. van den Berg. 2021. *Analysing Data using Linear Models*, 5 edition, chapter 7. University of Twente, Netherlands.

Stephen J. Williams. 1980. *A Welsh Grammar*. University of Wales Press, Cardiff.

Himanshu Yadav, Shubham Mittal, and Samar Husain. 2022. A reappraisal of dependency length minimization as a linguistic universal. *Open Mind*, 6:147–168.

Himanshu Yadav, Ashwini Vaidya, Vishakha Shukla, and Samar Husain. 2020. Word order typology interacts with linguistic complexity: A cross-linguistic corpus study. *Cognitive Science*, 44(4):e12822.

Jianwei Yan and Haitao Liu. 2019. Which annotation scheme is more expedient to measure syntactic difficulty and cognitive demand? In *Proceedings of the First Workshop on Quantitative Syntax (Quasy, SyntaxFest 2019)*, pages 16–24, Paris, France. Association for Computational Linguistics.

Xiang Yu, Agnieszka Falenska, and Jonas Kuhn. 2019. Dependency length minimization vs. word order constraints: An empirical study on 55 treebanks. In *Proceedings of the First Workshop on Quantitative Syntax (Quasy, SyntaxFest 2019)*, pages 89–97, Paris, France. Association for Computational Linguistics.

Does Topological Ordering of Morphological Segments Reduce Morphological Modeling Complexity? A Preliminary Study on 13 Languages

Andreas Shcherbakov
The University of Melbourne
scherbakov.andreas@unimelb.edu.au

Kat Vylomova
The University of Melbourne
vylomovae@unimelb.edu.au

Abstract

Generalization to novel forms and feature combinations is the key to efficient learning. Recently, Goldman et al. (2022) demonstrated that contemporary neural approaches to morphological inflection still struggle to generalize to unseen words and feature combinations, even in agglutinative languages. In this paper, we argue that the use of morphological segmentation in inflection modeling allows decomposing the problem into sub-problems of substantially smaller search space. We suggest that morphological segments may be globally topologically sorted according to their grammatical categories within a given language. Our experiments demonstrate that such segmentation provides all the necessary information for better generalization, especially in agglutinative languages.

1 Introduction

Generalization is a form of abstraction where common patterns, or properties, that are observed across specific instances are then extended to a wider class of instances. This form of deductive inference allows humans to learn language more efficiently, form sophisticated concepts, and introduce semantic relations such as hypernymy. Still, computer systems are considered to be less successful in making generalizations from data (Lake and Baroni, 2018). Morphological inflection task is a popular playground to compare and evaluate systems' ability to generalize. The morphological inflection task is a type of language modelling that focuses on producing inflected forms from a given dictionary form (a *lemma*) and a set of morphosyntactic features (a *tagset*) that describes the word form to be produced, as in "$spider, (N; PL) \rightarrow spiders$". Table 1 provides a sample paradigm table for Czech and Turkish nouns for "cat". Annual contests on morphological inflection prediction were held since 2016, covering a variety of typologically diverse languages (Cotterell et al., 2016, 2017, 2018; McCarthy et al., 2019; Vylomova et al., 2020; Pimentel et al., 2021). With the introduction of neural systems and the availability of large datasets, the task deemed to be solved with top performing systems achieving over 90% accuracy on most languages, even morphologically complex ones such as Uralic or Turkic. Most challenging cases were associated with under-resourced languages such as Chukchi or Evenki where majority of morphological paradigms were incomplete and sparse (Vylomova et al., 2020). However, a more fine-grained analysis from Pimentel et al. (2021) and Goldman et al. (2022) revealed that accuracy dropped substantially on unseen lemmas (i.e. in the condition where train, development, and test sets did not overlap lexically).

	Czech		Turkish	
Case	Singular	Plural	Singular	Plural
Nom	**kočka**	kočky	**kedi**	kediler
Gen	kočky	koček	kedinin	kedilerin
Dat	kočce	kočkám	kediye	kedilere
Acc	kočku	kočky	kediyi	kedileri
Ins	kočkou	kočkami	–	–
Ess	kočce	kočkách	kedide	kedilerde
Voc	kočko	kočky	–	–
Abl	kočko	kočky	kediden	kedilerden

Table 1: Sample paradigm tables for Czech and Turkish "cat" (its lemma form is in **bold**). The tags follow the UniMorph annotation schema (Sylak-Glassman, 2016). Turkish paradigm omits possessive and predicative forms.

This observation led to a significant reconsideration of the shared task design in 2022. The 2022 shared task (Kodner et al., 2022) focused on controlling the training, development, and test sets with respect to observed lemmas and tagsets. More specifically, the task organizers provided four conditions in which: 1) both the test lemma and tagset were observed in the training set (but separately!); 2) the test lemma was presented in the training set

Proceedings of the 5th Workshop on Research in Computational Linguistic Typology and Multilingual NLP (SIGTYP 2023), pages 120–125
May 6, 2023 ©2023 Association for Computational Linguistics

but the test tagset was not included in the training set; 3) the test tagset was observed in the training set while the lemma was not; 4) (the most challenging where) both the lemma and the tagset appeared exclusively in the test set. The performance assessment and analysis were carried out separately for each of the four categories and revealed a notable lack of generalization ability in all submitted systems, the vast majority of which were neural sequence-to-sequence models. It is particularly striking that systems failed at modelling agglutinativity, the ability to compose novel combinations of morphemes that were previously observed in other combinations. Or, the opposite, deducing morphemes for a subset of a previously observed tagset. Many agglutination rules that seem to be simple to human learners, appear to be challenging when it comes to machines. This fact tells us that sequence-to-sequence models do not generalise well, and current approaches to morphology modelling should be reconsidered.

In this paper, we suggest that annotated morphological segmentation can significantly improve the generalization ability. We propose augmenting the inflection model with segmentation as an intermediate step. We aim to evaluate the claim that such task is easier to solve than the reinflection task in its classical setting, especially in agglutinative languages. We suggest that the reinflection task can be formalized as a classification task rather than a string-to-string transduction task. This approach dramatically reduces the search space during the inference phase as well as enhances the model's robustness to data sparsity.

2 The Dataset

In our experiments we used datasets for inflectional paradigms and segmentation for Catalan (`cat`), Czech (`ces`), German (`deu`), English (`eng`), Finnish (`fin`), French (`fra`), Hungarian (`hun`), Italian (`ita`), Mongolian (`mon`), Portuguese (`por`), Russian (`rus`), Spanish (`spa`), and Swedish (`swe`) provided in MorphyNet resource (Batsuren et al., 2021).

3 Learning the Order of Segments

We hypothesise that the order of morphological segments[1] *within a language* is defined by the order of their corresponding grammatical categories (such as grammatical number, person, case). For instance, Turkish nouns would first specify the number and then the case (as shown on Table 1).

In the dataset described above, each word form w^j stands for a sequence of $[(s_i, t_i)]^j$, where s_i is i-segment in word form j, t_i is a tagset describing the segment (*segmental tagset*; such as "$GEN; PL$" for fusional or "GEN" for agglunitative languages). Let us illustrate this notation by the following example from Catalan, taken from MorphyNet dataset.

```
        ossificar            ossificaven
V|IND;PST;IPFV|3;PL   ossificar|ava|en
```

Here, an inflected form is expressed as a sequence of three segments: s_0 = "ossificar", s_1 = "ava" and s_2 = "en". Each segment bears its respective tagset. In such a way, a *whole* word's Unimorph tagset "$V; IND; PST; IPFV; 3; PL$" associated with the word form is represented as a sequence of three segmental tagsets $t_0 \dots t_2$, where $t_0 = \text{V}, t_1 = \text{IND;PST;IPFV}$ and $t_2 = \text{3;PL}$.

As we mentioned, we suggest that segment tagsets are strictly ordered globally withing a given language. More formally, we claim that it is possible to sort all unique tag combinations $t = (t_i)_{i=0 \dots i_{max}(j)}$ topologically, i.e. to associate each *unique* t with a number $ord(t^j)$ in such a way that for each w^j we have:

$$k > i \Rightarrow ord(t_k^j) > ord(t_i^j) \qquad (1)$$

To test the hypothesis, we propose the following learning algorithm. First, we initialize $ord(t_i^j) := 0$ for all segment-wise tag combinations t_i^j. Then, in each epoch, for each w^j observed in the dataset we check whether the equation 1 has already been satisfied for all i, k. If not, we add $(i - \bar{i})$ to $ord(t_i^j)$ for each i, where $\bar{i}$ is mean i value (half the number of segments in w^j). This way, we attempt to either learn the global segmental tagset order or disprove existence of it. We repeat the procedure until the number of forms in which segmentation was compliant to equation (1), stops to increase. A simplified pseudocode which implements such a process is given below.

```
RATE = 0.01                    ▷ A tunable hyperparameter
function FITTAGORDER(tagsets, update)
    mixed := false
    last := LEFTPAD            ▷ A dummy tagset
    S = |tagsets|
    for i ∈ 0...S − 1 do
        if update then
```

[1] We will use morphological segments and morphemes interchangeably.

```
            increment L[tagsets[i]] by RATE ×(2i − S + 1), default = 0
            if L[tagsets[i]] ≤ L[last] then
                mixed = true
            last := max_{set→L[set]} (last, tagset)
        return mixed
    procedure EPOCH(samples)
        for sample ∈ samples do
            ts = segment tagsets in sample
            if FITTAGORDER(ts, false) then
                FITTAGORDER(ts, true)
                report sample as outlier
```

Indeed, we find that the global order of segmental tagsets *does* exist in all languages represented in MorphyNet. Swedish is the only language where a few (only two) exceptions were found; however, even those exceptions may be attributed to fuzziness of segment tagging rules. This result suggests that for a morphological inflection system it should be sufficient to produce a set of segments and use their global topological order to properly sort them rather than deal with segmentation order for every sample individually. Therefore, a "full scale" character-level sequence-to-sequence model can be replaced by a simpler classifier model to carry out the segmentation process. This important finding allows to reduce the model decision space without any loss in accuracy while enabling better generalization, especially in agglutinative languages (and higher robustness to training data sparsity).

4 Decomposing Tagsets

As grammatical feature combinations are often complex, one might expect that there should be numerous ways to decompose those corresponding to morphological segments, thus, making decomposition a separate complex subtask. In this section, we refute it by demonstrating the statistics on decomposition variety per distinct segmental tagset.

As both segments and their corresponding tagsets are listed for each word form in MorphyNet, it may appear that a "natural" way of segmentation modelling would look as follows. First, decompose the initial tagset into segment-wise sub-combinations and, second, map each sub-combination into a distinct morphological segment. However, as we discovered, this technique does not work well because the assignment of tag combinations to segments appears to be highly ambiguous in MorphyNet. In many cases, it is due to the tags that represent an inherent property of a lemma. These tags, therefore, are not realized as a segment (e.g., animacy in nouns). The lack of consistent rules governing tag-to-segment annotation is another source of ambiguity as it frequently leads to different tagging across similar samples. Fortunately, there is an *alternative technique* that works better. Namely, we should consider *unique combinations* of resulting moprhological segments rather than focus on the variants of tagset decomposition. Our experiments demonstrate that the number of distinct morphological segments per tagset is less than 4 for the majority of tag combinations, and only in 5% cases reaches 15 (in total, approximately 2,400 tag combinations were considered, as counted separately for each language). The stem segment of any word was replaced by a wildcard symbol matching with other word stem segments.[2] Figure 1 shows the distribution of the number of segment variants per a distinct tag combination. It is worth mentioning that more than a half of tag combinations that are realized by "15 or more segment sequences" each were Russian verb forms. The first letter of suffixes in those verbs may depend on the adjacent ending of the verb's stem. This dependency results in either copying of a stem trailing consonant or a consonant mutation. Thus, it is necessary to take adjacent letter into account in order to predict the segment correctly.

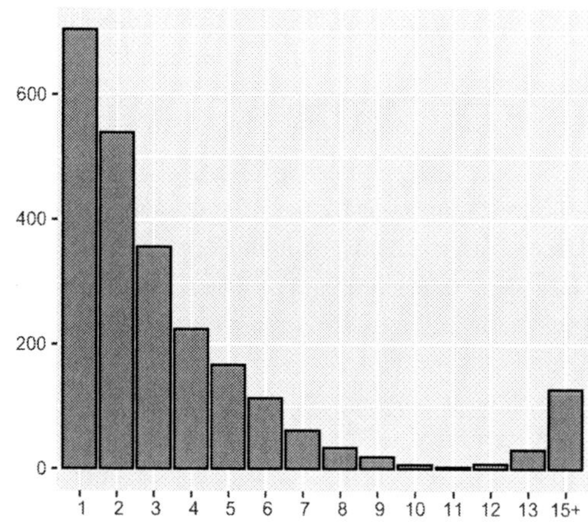

Figure 1: A frequency distribution for the number of different morphological segments per tagset. Here we consider distinct (language, tagset) pairs.

[2]To keep the setting simple, we excluded inflected forms of German compounds, in which the order of two stems was swapping.

5 Segment Composability

In Section 3 we have demonstrated that the order of segments is deterministic. Still, in the condition when the data is sparse an inflection system should be able to retrieve relevant segments from training samples, especially in agglutinative languages. Typically, the observed tagsets are different from the one that needs to be predicted. We define a *"segment composability"* measure over a segmentation dataset as a percentage of tagsets T with the following property: *The segment has ever been seen in at least two data samples, one with tagset t and one, with tagset* $t' \neq t$. While evaluating this percentage, we prune all tagsets that contain tags that only occur once, i.e. in that particular tagset (which means the tagset cannot be reconstructed from the rest of the data). A "segment composability" is a probability for a segmentation corresponding to the tagset to be reconstructed from segments observed in other tagsets, given that the predictor uses a "perfect" oracle over segments observed in a training set. The composability values measured over MorphyNet are provided in Table 2. They appear to be close to 100% for languages with high agglutinativity,[3] demonstrating a notable usability of MorphyNet segmentation datasets for the inference of unseen word forms. Here is a pseudocode explaining our approach to computation of composability.

function COMPOSABILITYRATE
  for $sample \in samples$ **do**
    $(segments, tagsets) = sample$
    $T = \{\forall tag \in \forall set \in tagsets\}$
    for $(seg, set) \in sample^{\mathsf{T}}$ **do**
      for $\tau \in set$ **do** ▷ single tags
        $uses_t[\tau] := uses_t[\tau] \cup \{T\}$
      $uses_s[seg] := uses_s[seg] \cup \{T\}$

$$combined = \left\{ \begin{array}{c} T: \\ \exists\tau : \{T\} \subset uses_t[\tau] \\ \neg\exists\tau : \{T\} = uses_t[\tau] \end{array} \right\}$$
▷ Word tag sets without exclusive tags

$$compos = \left\{ \begin{array}{c} T \in combined: \\ \neg\text{ISSTEM}(seg)\wedge \\ \neg\exists s : \{T\} = uses_s[seg] \end{array} \right\}$$
▷ "Composable" word tag sets that share all representing segments to some other tag sets

return $|compos|/|combined|$

$\mathscr{L}$	Interc., %	$\mathscr{L}$	Interc., %
cat	85	hun	88
ces	100	ita	55
deu	96	por	55
eng	50	rus	98
fin	100	spa	96
fra	52	swe	97

Table 2: "Segment composability" as measured over MorphyNet datasets.

6 From Segments to Surface Forms

Even when all morphological segments are predicted, a conversion into a surface form is yet to be done. Luckily, in most cases, such a conversion only requires to remove segment separators and concatenate the substrings. However, to account for phonotactics, additional string edit operations may be necessary. Our analysis discovered the following major cases when they are needed: (1) removal or modification of *affixes* that are relevant only to the lemma form and are not separated from the stem into a different segment. This mostly concerns verbs. For example, deletion of `-ar` and insertion of `-u-` in Spanish (`catalogar` → `cataloguem V|IND;PRS;1;PL catalogar|em`); (2) removal of adjacent duplicate letters in some languages; (3) replacement of certain adjacent letter combinations at segment boundaries as in the following Czech example: `čtverec` → `čtvercem N;SG|INST;MASC;INAN čtverec|em`.

Predicting such transformations is generally a sequence-to-sequence task. Still, it is rather specific sub-task in which source and target sequences are aligned, and only local character modifications are to be learnt. In our experiments, a hard attention model (Aharoni and Goldberg, 2017) yields nearly perfect prediction of segments "gluing" into a word.[4] German was the only exception due to compounding.

[3] High composability figures, besides a language's agglutinativity, may result from a large size of the corresponding dataset or high variety of word forms presented there. As shown in Table 2, values for closely related language may differ significantly. A high composability is particularly important for agglutinative morphology modelling. However, it shouldn't be preceived as a *measure* of a language's agglutinativity.

[4] Grammatical tags were ignored (set to some constant value).

$\mathscr{L}$	Accuracy	$\mathscr{L}$	Accuracy
cat	0.99	hun	0.98
ces	0.98	ita	0.99
deu	0.89	mon	1.00
eng	0.99	por	1.00
fra	0.99	swe	0.98

Table 3: Segments-to-form conversion accuracy achieved with a hard attention model

7 Discussion

The experiment results suggest that the usage of morphological segmentation dataset enables principal reduction of the complexity of the morphological inflection task. This allows breaking the inflection task into two consecutive stages, (1) producing segments for a given (lemma, tagset) pair, and (2) concatenating segments into a surface word form. As our experiments suggest, prediction of segments in stage (1) is a classification task with a relatively limited feature set, while stage (2) translates into a (minor) string edit task. Here, we have just outlined this perspective direction; a detailed performance exploration is yet to be done. Still, the statistics we collected in our experiments allows us to be optimistic about filling two major gaps in the state-of-the-art systems' performance on these tasks: (1) the ability to generalize to unseen grammatical tag combinations (Kodner et al., 2022), and (2) to better account for phonotactics, as described in Section 6. Also, the proposed reduction of search space should be beneficial for smaller training sets and is crucial for under-resourced languages.

Although morphological segmentation allows a decent amount of fuzziness, it facilitates the discovery of important latent variables that participate in inflection processes. We hypothesize that it would be sufficient to allow an inflection system consider the latent variables within its architecture and fit them during the training process. While the above is the only option for the languages not yet represented in MorphyNet and similar resources, the usage of annotated segmentation datasets should significantly increase generalization ability in the inflection task.

8 Conclusion

We conducted a series of experiments with morphological segmentation and demonstrated that annotated segment sequences may significantly simplify the prediction of inflected forms. We outlined that inflection task can be transformed from sequence-to-sequence into a classification task, with better capacities to address language agglutinativity challenges.

References

Roee Aharoni and Yoav Goldberg. 2017. Morphological inflection generation with hard monotonic attention. In *Proceedings of the 55th Annual Meeting of the Association for Computational Linguistics (Volume 1: Long Papers)*, pages 2004–2015.

Khuyagbaatar Batsuren, Gábor Bella, and Fausto Giunchiglia. 2021. Morphynet: a large multilingual database of derivational and inflectional morphology. In *Proceedings of the 18th sigmorphon workshop on computational research in phonetics, phonology, and morphology*, pages 39–48.

Ryan Cotterell, Christo Kirov, John Sylak-Glassman, Géraldine Walther, Ekaterina Vylomova, Arya D. McCarthy, Katharina Kann, Sabrina J. Mielke, Garrett Nicolai, Miikka Silfverberg, David Yarowsky, Jason Eisner, and Mans Hulden. 2018. The CoNLL–SIGMORPHON 2018 shared task: Universal morphological reinflection. In *Proceedings of the CoNLL–SIGMORPHON 2018 Shared Task: Universal Morphological Reinflection*, pages 1–27, Brussels. Association for Computational Linguistics.

Ryan Cotterell, Christo Kirov, John Sylak-Glassman, Géraldine Walther, Ekaterina Vylomova, Patrick Xia, Manaal Faruqui, Sandra Kübler, David Yarowsky, Jason Eisner, and Mans Hulden. 2017. CoNLL-SIGMORPHON 2017 shared task: Universal morphological reinflection in 52 languages. In *Proceedings of the CoNLL SIGMORPHON 2017 Shared Task: Universal Morphological Reinflection*, pages 1–30, Vancouver. Association for Computational Linguistics.

Ryan Cotterell, Christo Kirov, John Sylak-Glassman, David Yarowsky, Jason Eisner, and Mans Hulden. 2016. The SIGMORPHON 2016 shared Task—Morphological reinflection. In *Proceedings of the 14th SIGMORPHON Workshop on Computational Research in Phonetics, Phonology, and Morphology*, pages 10–22, Berlin, Germany. Association for Computational Linguistics.

Omer Goldman, David Guriel, and Reut Tsarfaty. 2022. (un)solving morphological inflection: Lemma overlap artificially inflates models' performance. In *Proceedings of the 60th Annual Meeting of the Association for Computational Linguistics (Volume 2: Short Papers)*, pages 864–870, Dublin, Ireland. Association for Computational Linguistics.

Jordan Kodner, Salam Khalifa, Khuyagbaatar Batsuren, Hossep Dolatian, Ryan Cotterell, Faruk Akkuş, Antonios Anastasopoulos, Taras Andrushko, Aryaman Arora, Nona Atanelov, Gábor Bella, Elena

Budianskaya, Yustinus Ghanggo Ato, Omer Goldman, David Guriel, Simon Guriel, Silvia Guriel-Agiashvili, Witold Kieraś, Andrew Krizhanovsky, Natalia Krizhanovsky, Igor Marchenko, Magdalena Markowska, Polina Mashkovtseva, Maria Nepomniashchaya, Daria Rodionova, Karina Sheifer, Alexandra Serova, Anastasia Yemelina, Jeremiah Young, and Ekaterina Vylomova. 2022. Sigmorphon–unimorph 2022 shared task 0: Generalization and typologically diverse morphological inflection. In *Proceedings of the 19th SIGMORPHON workshop on computational research in phonetics, phonology, and morphology*.

Brenden Lake and Marco Baroni. 2018. Generalization without systematicity: On the compositional skills of sequence-to-sequence recurrent networks. In *International conference on machine learning*, pages 2873–2882. PMLR.

Arya D. McCarthy, Ekaterina Vylomova, Shijie Wu, Chaitanya Malaviya, Lawrence Wolf-Sonkin, Garrett Nicolai, Christo Kirov, Miikka Silfverberg, Sabrina J. Mielke, Jeffrey Heinz, Ryan Cotterell, and Mans Hulden. 2019. The SIGMORPHON 2019 shared task: Morphological analysis in context and cross-lingual transfer for inflection. In *Proceedings of the 16th Workshop on Computational Research in Phonetics, Phonology, and Morphology*, pages 229–244, Florence, Italy. Association for Computational Linguistics.

Tiago Pimentel, Maria Ryskina, Sabrina J. Mielke, Shijie Wu, Eleanor Chodroff, Brian Leonard, Garrett Nicolai, Yustinus Ghanggo Ate, Salam Khalifa, Nizar Habash, Charbel El-Khaissi, Omer Goldman, Michael Gasser, William Lane, Matt Coler, Arturo Oncevay, Jaime Rafael Montoya Samame, Gema Celeste Silva Villegas, Adam Ek, Jean-Philippe Bernardy, Andrey Shcherbakov, Aziyana Bayyr-ool, Karina Sheifer, Sofya Ganieva, Matvey Plugaryov, Elena Klyachko, Ali Salehi, Andrew Krizhanovsky, Natalia Krizhanovsky, Clara Vania, Sardana Ivanova, Aelita Salchak, Christopher Straughn, Zoey Liu, Jonathan North Washington, Duygu Ataman, Witold Kieraś, Marcin Woliński, Totok Suhardijanto, Niklas Stoehr, Zahroh Nuriah, Shyam Ratan, Francis M. Tyers, Edoardo M. Ponti, Grant Aiton, Richard J. Hatcher, Emily Prud'hommeaux, Ritesh Kumar, Mans Hulden, Botond Barta, Dorina Lakatos, Gábor Szolnok, Judit Ács, Mohit Raj, David Yarowsky, Ryan Cotterell, Ben Ambridge, and Ekaterina Vylomova. 2021. SIGMORPHON 2021 shared task on morphological reinflection: Generalization across languages. In *Proceedings of the 18th SIGMORPHON Workshop on Computational Research in Phonetics, Phonology, and Morphology*, pages 229–259, Online. Association for Computational Linguistics.

John Sylak-Glassman. 2016. The composition and use of the universal morphological feature schema (unimorph schema). *Johns Hopkins University*.

Ekaterina Vylomova, Jennifer White, Elizabeth Salesky, Sabrina J. Mielke, Shijie Wu, Edoardo Maria Ponti, Rowan Hall Maudslay, Ran Zmigrod, Josef Valvoda, Svetlana Toldova, Francis Tyers, Elena Klyachko, Ilya Yegorov, Natalia Krizhanovsky, Paula Czarnowska, Irene Nikkarinen, Andrew Krizhanovsky, Tiago Pimentel, Lucas Torroba Hennigen, Christo Kirov, Garrett Nicolai, Adina Williams, Antonios Anastasopoulos, Hilaria Cruz, Eleanor Chodroff, Ryan Cotterell, Miikka Silfverberg, and Mans Hulden. 2020. SIGMORPHON 2020 shared task 0: Typologically diverse morphological inflection. In *Proceedings of the 17th SIGMORPHON Workshop on Computational Research in Phonetics, Phonology, and Morphology*, pages 1–39, Online. Association for Computational Linguistics.

Findings of the SIGTYP 2023 Shared task on Cognate and Derivative Detection For Low-Resourced Languages

Priya Rani[1], **Koustava Goswami**[1,2], **Adrian Doyle**[1],
Theodorus Fransen[1], **Bernardo Stearns**[1], **John P. McCrae**[1]
[1] Data Science Institute, University of Galway, Ireland
[2] Adobe Research Bangalore, India
koustavag@adobe.com,
{priya.rani, adrian.doyle, theodorus.fransen, bernardo.stearns, john.mccrae}@insight-centre.org

Abstract

This paper describes the structure and findings of the SIGTYP 2023 shared task on cognate and derivative detection for low-resourced languages, broken down into a supervised and unsupervised sub-task. The participants were asked to submit the test data's final prediction. A total of nine teams registered for the shared task where seven teams registered for both sub-tasks. Only two participants ended up submitting system descriptions, with only one submitting systems for both sub-tasks. While all systems show a rather promising performance, all could be within the baseline score for the supervised sub-task. However, the system submitted for the unsupervised sub-task outperforms the baseline score.

1 Introduction

Cognates and derivatives have been studied in various fields of linguistics with different purposes (Labat and Lefever, 2019). In historical linguistics, cognates are useful in the reconstruction of proto-languages and can aid in establishing the relationship between languages; in lexicography, cognates are helpful in the development of multilingual dictionaries. Moreover, in recent years, NLP researchers have shown interest in using cognates to enhance the performance of multilingual tasks such as machine translation, lexical induction, word embeddings and many more (Kondrak, 2005; Kondrak et al., 2003).

As there has been little work on automatic cognate identification, it is still a challenging task, especially for less-resourced languages (Jäger et al., 2017; Rama, 2016). Supervised identification of cognates and derivatives is requires a substantial amount of annotated linguistic data, which may need to be manually annotated (Kanojia et al., 2021). At the same time, finding linguists and annotators for less-resourced languages is impractical. Thus we propose a shared task which aims to provide a new benchmark for differentiating between cognates and derivatives and introduce new unsupervised approaches for cognate and derivative detection in less-resourced languages.

Cognates are etymologically related word pairs across languages which may or may not have similar spelling, pronunciation and meaning (Crystal, 2011). Cognates can be traced back to a single ancestral word form in a common earlier language stage. On the other hand, derivatives are words which have been adopted into a language either from an earlier stage of the same language, or as a borrowing from a different language. To give an example, the Spanish *libro* and French *livre*, are each derived from Latin *liber* "book", and are cognates with each other because they share this common ancestor. By contrast, the Irish word *leabhar* is derived from Latin *liber* because it was borrowed into Irish from Latin, but *leabhar* is a cognate with Spanish *libro* because *libro* has been derived from an earlier developmental language stage, i.e. *leabhar* was not borrowed from Spanish, but from Latin, a precursor to Spanish. Where multiple stages of direct derivation occur, each successive stage is considered a derivation from the last, but also from any earlier stages. For example, *leabhar* in Modern Irish is derived from Old Irish *lebor*, but also from Latin *liber*.

As will be discussed in section 3, data used in this shared task has been drawn from Wiktionary. Apart from cognates (`cog`), Wiktionary distinguishes between derived (`der`), inherited (`inh`), and borrowed (`bor`). This distinction is not maintained in this shared task, and all three are treated broadly as derivation. Languages are distinguished from one another in the shared task based on ISO-639 codes. Anything which has a discrete ISO-639 code is considered a separate language. Therefore, Irish with the code `ga` is a completely separate language from Old Irish as this has a separate code, `sga`. This prevents any confusion as to the point

Proceedings of the 5th Workshop on Research in Computational Linguistic Typology and Multilingual NLP (SIGTYP 2023), pages 126–131
May 6, 2023 ©2023 Association for Computational Linguistics

at which something ceases to be a derivative and becomes a cognate. Such confusion may occur in speech, for example, where one may say that a term was borrowed into English from French. Such a statement could lead to the supposition that a Modern English (`en`) word is derived from the Modern French (`fr`) term, however, if the borrowing took place between earlier language stages, say into Middle English (`enm`) from Old French (`fro`), the Modern English term is only derived from Old French and precursors to it, like Latin (`la`), not from Modern French. This is the case with the English word *liberal*. It was borrowed into Middle English from Old French, and is ultimately derived from Latin *liber* "free". Hence, the Modern English, *liberal*, would be considered a derivative from both Old French and Latin in our data, however, it would be a cognate with Modern French *libéral* because *liberal* is not derived directly from Modern French.

The rest of this paper is organised as follows. Section 2 describes the setup and schedule of the shared task. Section 3 presents the dataset used for the competition. Section 4 describes the evaluation methods and the baselines. Section 5 describes the systems submitted by the teams in the competition, and Section 6 presents and analyses the results obtained by the competitors. Lastly, in Section 7, we conclude the whole findings of the shared task.

2 Shared task setup and schedule

The section describes how the shared task was organized. The shared tasks involve two sub-tasks to perform multiclass classification tasks, which require that the relationship between pairs of words be identified as either a cognate relationship, a derivative relationship, or no relationship. The subtasks are:

- Supervised: Cognate and Derivative Detection
- Unsupervised: Cognate and Derivative Detection

The shared task started with the registration process through Google Forms. The participants were asked to register their team along with their affiliation, team member and the sub-tasks they wanted to participatc in. Rcgistered participants were sent a link to access the training and development data. The participants were allowed to use additional data to train their system with the condition that any additional data used should be made publicly available and to provide a proper citation of the data used to develop their model. The schedule for the release of training data and release of test data, along with notification and submission, are given in Table 1.

Date	Event
9 January 2023	Release of training data
27 Feburary 2023	Release of test data
15 March 2023	Submission of the systems
27 March 2023	Submission of system description paper
31 March 2023	Camera-ready

Table 1: SIGTYP 2023 Shared Task schedule

3 Cognate Datasets

In this section, we present the characteristics and the statistics of the dataset used for the task of cognate and derivative prediction.

3.1 Training Data

We provide annotated word pairs for cognate and derivative prediction in a format given in Table 2 in which the first column represents the first word of the word pair and the second column represents the language of the given word through the ISO code. The third and the fourth column represent the second word and its language code, respectively. Lastly, the fifth column represents the relation between the two words in each pair; cognate, derivative or none. The detailed statistics of the words pairs according to the labels are given in Table 3.

Word_1	ISO	Word_2	ISO	Label
Yannick	en	Yannig	br	der
creta	ca	creta	la	der
roh	de	raw	en	cog
gnit	en	gnit	is	cog
erudit	oc	ergueito	gl	none

Table 2: Format of the dataset

The data consists of word pairs from 34 languages including both high-resourced and less-resourced languages. Table 4 gives an overview of the languages involved and statistics of each language. This data was collected and annotated using Wiktionary.

Labels	Train	Test
Cognate	11869	98
Derivatives	39205	340
None	181408	438
Total	232482	876

Table 3: Statistics of the dataset in each category.

In the later stages of the shared task we came across a number of false negatives in the training data. Specifically, some word pairs were labelled none, indicating that they shared no relationship, however, upon investigation they were found to be either cognates or derivatives. As we were close to releasing the test data, we decided not to make any changes in the training data, but instead to simply inform the participants. This was expected to cause the least disruption to participants for a couple of reasons. Firstly, participants had already been given the freedom to manipulate the data as they saw fit, in order for them to optimise their systems. Secondly, as discussed in section 2, the participants were allowed to use datasets other than those provided. If participants had already attempted to overcome the problem by editing or removing erroneous entries from the provided training data, it was perceived that providing all participants with cleaned training data at such a late stage would have unfairly benefited those who had not adapted the training data.

Languages	Count in word_1	Count in word_2
en	22883	13414
es	14921	11996
it	12528	9804
nb	12473	9390
nn	12139	9415
pt	12118	9759
ca	11946	9434
fr	10944	12573
nl	10895	9670
gl	10437	9026
da	10280	9048
oc	8119	7904
sv	7823	7588
la	7757	37217
de	7340	9105
ro	7063	6664
pl	6346	5744
af	5465	5205
ga	4384	3872
cs	4342	4058
is	4136	4237
lb	3230	2754
no	2833	2904
gd	2833	2710
cy	2684	2742
sk	2680	2487
lv	2576	2549
sl	2481	2448
gv	1764	1651
fy	1759	1797
wa	1584	1562
br	1259	1255
kw	1244	1220
lt	1216	1280

Table 4: Statistics of the languages in the training data

3.2 Test Dataset

Similar to training data, test data for the given task consists of word pairs from 34 languages, including high-resourced and less-resourced. Table 5 provides an overview of the languages involved and statistics of each language. Though the test data was collected using Wiktionary, it was annotated manually by the experts using the Wiktionary template.

4 Methods

4.1 Evaluations

The standard evaluation metrics for evaluating and ranking the teams was F1-Score for supervised classification. For unsupervised methods, we followed the standard cluster performance evaluation process. The number of clusters will be same as the number of original classes and evaluated with the cluster accuracy using the equation shown in Equation 1,

$$ACC = max_m \frac{\sum_{i=1}^{n} 1(l_i = m(c_i))}{n} \quad (1)$$

where l_i is the ground truth label, c_i is the cluster assignment produced by the algorithm and m ranges over all possible one-to-one mappings between clusters and labels.

4.2 Baselines

This section gives a short description of the baselines used to compare the submitted systems.

Supervised: The system was a multi-layer LSTM-based network. The framework has two major stages, they are:

- Data preparation: In this stage pre-processing was carried out to remove punctuation, undesirable Unicode, conversion of cases and building one-hot vectors of both word and language information.

Languages	Count in word_1	Count in word_2
en	120	44
pt	55	17
nn	50	14
es	49	28
it	46	35
ca	44	16
nb	40	20
fr	29	38
da	27	23
ro	25	14
gl	25	21
nl	25	29
oc	25	22
de	23	42
fy	19	13
sv	18	24
pl	17	17
lb	17	06
af	17	07
is	17	18
lt	16	09
cy	16	12
no	16	17
cs	15	07
wa	15	15
sk	14	07
gv	14	08
kw	13	13
sl	13	18
lv	13	12
gd	12	10
la	12	276
br	11	09
ga	8	15

Table 5: Statistics of the languages in the test data

- Model training: After converting the data to one-hot vector various RNN model were trained. However, the best model was chose to be the baseline of the shared task. This model consisted of two hidden layers of 100 LSTM cells with only a single dense layer and softmax activation function. It uses Adam optimisation and categorical cross-entropy to calculate loss. The model was set to train for 250 epochs on a randomised selection of 90% of the training data. The other 10% was set aside for validation during training. Early stopping was applied to ensure overfitting did not occur, with the result that the actual number of epochs during training was less than 100. The input format for the model was a 34x50 matrix where 34 represents the number of languages (this was higher than the total number of unique characters), and 50 represents the buffered word-size (24) doubled as words were fed in in pairs, plus 2 as the language of each word also took up a vector each.

Unsupervised: A simple Levenshtein edit distance (Levenshtein, 1965) model was trained to perform the clustering task with the cluster set of 3.

5 Systems

A total of 9 teams registered for the shared task: 7 teams registered to participate in both the supervised and unsupervised tasks while 2 teams registered for only the supervised task. Out of these, only two teams submitted systems. Both teams submitted for the supervised task and one team submitted for both the supervised and unsupervised task. The teams who submitted their systems were invited to submit system description papers describing their experiments in the proceedings of the workshop (Beinborn et al., 2023). Since these systems are described in individual papers, we will only briefly present the main features here.

ÚFAL_supervised: The system submitted by team ÚFAL, represented by Tomasz Limisiewicz from Charles University, provided gradient boosted tree classifier trained on linguistic and statistical features. The features used by the team to train the classifiers were language model embeddings, typological information which included language identity and language group identity and orthographical information (Limisiewicz, 2023).

CoToHiLi_supervised: Team CoToHiLi, represented by Liviu Dinu from University of Bucharest, experimented with a few different multi-class classification algorithms such as Support Vector Machine, Naive Bayes, and SGD with the combination of three features graphic features, phonetic features and language features. At the end they selected the best performing classifiers to train a stackable ensemble classifier (Liviu P. Dinu, 2023).

CoToHiLi_unsupervised: The unsupervised system submitted by team CotoHiLi employed a set of features including graphic, phonetic and language encoding to KMeans algorithms (Liviu P. Dinu, 2023).

6 Results

The participants were asked to submit the final test results in the format of the training data files, with comma-separated fields for word pairs, language codes, and relationship labels. Files had to be named **team name_unsupervised/supervised** to indicate both the team's name and the sub-task in question.

Teams	F1-Score	Precision	Recall
Baseline	0.91	0.99	0.84
ÚFAL	0.87	0.89	0.86
CoToHiLi	0.83	0.87	0.81

Table 6: Results of submitted supervised systems for the SIGTYP 2023 Shared Task.

Teams	Accuracy
Baseline	0.38
CoToHiLi	0.49

Table 7: Results of submitted unsupervised systems for the SIGTYP 2023 Shared Task.

7 Conclusion

We have reported the findings of the SIGTYP 2023 Shared Task on cognate and derivative detection for less-resourced languages as part of the fifth edition of SIGTYP workshop. With the two teams that participated, we have seen different and interesting non-neural and neural systems that deal with cognate and derivative prediction task. While the baseline for supervised sub-task were based on neural networks, team ÚFAL used a gradient boosted tree classifier and team CoToHiLi came up with an ensemble classifier. However, neither team could beat the baseline set for the supervised task: the difference in the F1-Score was -0.04 for team ÚFAL and -0.08 for team CoToHiLi. Although, team ÚFAL's entry ranked first among the two supervised systems submitted, with an F1-Score of 0.87, the unsupervised system submitted by team CoToHiLi based on a KMeans algorithm beat the baseline for the unsupervised task with with an improvememt of 0.11 in accuracy.

Acknowledgements

This Shared Task was supported by the Irish Research Council as part of grant IRCLA/2017/129 (CARDAMOM-Comparative Deep Models of Language for Minority and Historical Languages) and co-funded by Science Foundation Ireland (SFI) as part of grant SFI/18/CRT/6223 (CRT-Centre for Research Training in Artificial Intelligence) and grant SFI/12/RC/2289_P2 (Insight_2).

References

Lisa Beinborn, Koustava Goswami, Saliha Muradoğlu, Alexey Sorokin, Ritesh Kumar, Andrey Shcherbakov, Edoardo Ponti, Ryan Cotterell, and Ekaterina Vylomova, editors. 2023. *Proceedings of the 5th Workshop on Research in Computational Linguistic Typology and Multilingual NLP*. Association for Computational Linguistics, Dubrovnik, Croatia.

David Crystal. 2011. *A dictionary of linguistics and phonetics*. John Wiley & Sons.

Gerhard Jäger, Johann-Mattis List, and Pavel Sofroniev. 2017. Using support vector machines and state-of-the-art algorithms for phonetic alignment to identify cognates in multi-lingual wordlists. In *Proceedings of the 15th Conference of the European Chapter of the Association for Computational Linguistics: Volume 1, Long Papers*, pages 1205–1216, Valencia, Spain. Association for Computational Linguistics.

Diptesh Kanojia, Prashant Sharma, Sayali Ghodekar, Pushpak Bhattacharyya, Gholamreza Haffari, and Malhar Kulkarni. 2021. Cognition-aware cognate detection. In *Proceedings of the 16th Conference of the European Chapter of the Association for Computational Linguistics: Main Volume*, pages 3281–3292, Online. Association for Computational Linguistics.

Grzegorz Kondrak. 2005. Cognates and word alignment in bitexts. In *Proceedings of Machine Translation Summit X: Papers*, pages 305–312.

Grzegorz Kondrak, Daniel Marcu, and Kevin Knight. 2003. Cognates can improve statistical translation models. In *Human Language Technology Conference of the North American Chapter of the Association for Computational Linguistics, HLT-NAACL 2003, Edmonton, Canada, May 27 - June 1, 2003*. The Association for Computational Linguistics.

Sofie Labat and Els Lefever. 2019. A classification-based approach to cognate detection combining orthographic and semantic similarity information. In *Proceedings of the International Conference on Recent Advances in Natural Language Processing (RANLP 2019)*, pages 602–610, Varna, Bulgaria. INCOMA Ltd.

Vladimir Levenshtein. 1965. Binary codes capable of correcting spurious insertions and deletions of ones. *Russian Problemy Peredachi Informatsii*, 1:12–25.

Tomasz Limisiewicz. 2023. Ufal submission for sigtyp supervised cognate detection task. In *Proceedings of the 4th Workshop on Research in Computational Linguistic Typology and Multilingual NLP*, Dubrovnik, Croatia. Association for Computational Linguistics.

Ana Sabina Uban Liviu P. Dinu, Ioan-Bogdan Iordache. 2023. Cotohili at sigtyp 2023: Ensemble models for cognate and derivative words detection. In *Proceedings of the 4th Workshop on Research in Computational Linguistic Typology and Multilingual NLP*, Dubrovnik, Croatia. Association for Computational Linguistics.

Taraka Rama. 2016. Siamese convolutional networks for cognate identification. In *COLING 2016, 26th International Conference on Computational Linguistics, Proceedings of the Conference: Technical Papers, December 11-16, 2016, Osaka, Japan*, pages 1018–1027. ACL.

ÚFAL Submission for SIGTYP Supervised Cognate Detection Task

Tomasz Limisiewicz
Faculty of Mathematics and Physics, Charles University in Prague
limisiewcz@ufal.mff.uni.cz

Abstract

In this work, I present ÚFAL submission for the supervised task of detecting cognates and derivatives. Cognates are word pairs in different languages sharing the origin in earlier attested forms in ancestral language, while derivatives come directly from another language. For the task, I developed gradient boosted tree classifier trained on linguistic and statistical features. The solution came first from two delivered systems with an 87% F1 score on the test split. This write-up gives an insight into the system and shows the importance of using linguistic features and character-level statistics for the task.

1 Introduction

The described system is a supervised model trained for three-way classifications aimed to distinguish cognate and cross-lingual derivatives or no relationship for pairs of words in different languages. Cognates are pairs with similar meanings and come from the same root in an ancestral language. For instance, the German "vater" is cognate with the English "father" coming from the same Proto-Indo-European root. In contrast, multilingual derivatives are words borrowed from another language potentially with some modification, e.g., the word "restaurant" in English comes from a French word with the same spelling (Crystal, 2008).

The solution used only the data provided by the organizers, i.e., 232,482 bilingual pairs in 34 European languages. The data came with the relationship labels (cognate, derivative, or no relation) scraped from Wiktionary.[1] In the examples containing derivative pairs, the order of words did not indicate the source and recipient language.

The proposed system was evaluated on the test data with 876 bilingual word pairs with hidden target labels. The evaluation metric was a macro-averaged F1 score. For development purposes, I sampled 10% of the provided training data to create a validation set not used in the model fitting.

My solution is based on gradient boosted tree classifier trained on the set of language features comprising multilingual language model embeddings, language and language group id, character-level Levenshtein distance, and a binary variable marking capitalized words.

The system obtained the F1 score of **87%** on the test set and came first out of two submitted to the shared task. The source code for the submission is publicly available at GitHub: https://github.com/tomlimi/cognate_detection.

The system description is organized in the following way: in Section 2, I describe the classification model and the hyperparameter search method; in Section 3, I introduce the features selected as input for the classifier; lastly, in Section 4, I present the results of the method together with the accumulation study and the analysis of feature importance.

2 Classification

For classification tasks, I used a gradient-boosted tree implemented in the XGBoost library (Chen and Guestrin, 2016).[2] The boosting tree is the method that enables the predictions of a large set of decision trees obtained with a gradient search. This section describes the hyperparameters used for the classifier and the method used to select them.

I chose XGBoost because it performs well for data containing real and discrete variables, and the set of input variables can be easily extended. Moreover, XGBoost can be interpreted through feature importance analysis.

2.1 Class Weighting

The cognate data were significantly skewed toward no relation class (78.0%), followed by derived pairs (16.9%) and cognates (5.1%). The task organizers

[1] https://www.wiktionary.org/

[2] https://xgboost.readthedocs.io/

Proceedings of the 5th Workshop on Research in Computational Linguistic Typology and Multilingual NLP (SIGTYP 2023), pages 132–136
May 6, 2023 ©2023 Association for Computational Linguistics

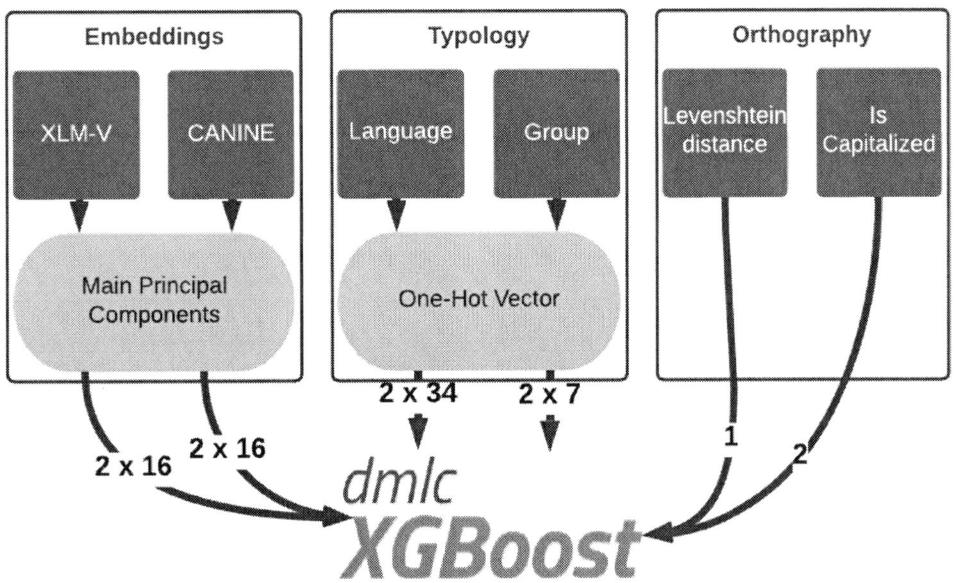

Figure 1: The visualization of features selected as an input to XGBoost classifier. For each word from the test cases, I obtained embeddings from two models, XLM-V and CANINE-C. The embeddings were compressed to 16 dimensions for each model by selecting the first principal components. The language and language group labels were fed to the classifier as one-hot vectors. Levenshtein distance between words in each pair was inputted as a real-valued variable. The last component of the classifier input were binary variables denoting if each word of the pair is capitalized.

notified contestants that the training data contains a significant share of false positives, i.e., unmarked cognates pairs. For those reasons, I weighted test examples in order to counter the imbalance, assigning higher weights to examples containing cognate and derived forms.

2.2 XGBoost Hyperparameters

The boosting algorithm was trained to maximize the area under the classification curve with gradient descent performed for 100 steps. In the parameter search, I considered the following ones:

- **eta** shrinks the weights of features.
- **gamma** minimum loss reduction needed to make a partition of the node
- **maximum depth** maximum depth of the tree.
- **minimum child weight** minimum sum of the instance weights in a leaf.
- **maximum delta step** the cap of the output in the leaf helps to counter data imbalance
- **subsample** sampling training instances for each boosting iteration.
- **column sample** family of arguments: sampling columns (features) before adding a new tree, level, or node.
- **lambda** L2 regularization on the model's weights.
- **alpha** L1 regularization on the model's weights.

2.3 Bayesian Paremeter Search

The hyperparameters are searched by Bayesian optimization (Bergstra et al., 2013) based on the Hyperopt library.[3] In this algorithm, the hyperparameter space is searched by sampling the configuration with a high probability of increasing the objective function. The search is performed iteratively, updating hyperparameter distributions after each epoch. I ran a Bayesian search for 50 epochs (in each epoch, the XGBoost was run for 100 steps).

[3] https://hyperopt.github.io/hyperopt

Parameter	Search Range	Selected
eta	0.01 - 0.3	0.275
gamma	0 - 5.0	0.642
maximum depth	3 - 20	12
minimum child weight	1 - 6	4
subsample	0.6 - 1.0	0.723
column sample (tree)	0.6 - 1.0	0.919
column sample (node)	0.6 - 1.0	0.749
column sample (level)	0.6 - 1.0	0.998
lambda	0 - 5.0	1.507
alpha	0 - 5.0	1.138

Table 1: Hyperparameter search spaces: uniform distributions in the given ranges. The value was selected with Bayesian optimization. Distributions of maximum depth and minimum child weight are discrete.

Table 1 shows the search spaces and selected parameters.

3 Feature Selection

I used an ensemble of word embeddings, typological and orthographical information as input to the XGBoost classifier. This Section describes how those features were selected and pre-processed. The visualization of all the picked features is presented in Figure 1.

3.1 Language Model Embeddings

I computed the embedding representation of the words in each test pair. I took the final layer representation of two recent multilingual Transformer-based models available through the HuggigFace interface (Wolf et al., 2020):[4] **XLM-V** (Liang et al., 2023) and **CANINE** (Clark et al., 2022). The former model tokenizes the input with a large (1 million entries) subword vocabulary. The latter splits the input into character sequences and applies a convolution layer before the proper Transformer. I used these two models aiming to merge character and subword signals.

The resulting word embeddings have high dimensionality, i.e., 1024 for each model. I decided to decrease the dimensionality of the embeddings in order to balance out the composition of the classifier input vector. For that purpose, I applied SVD decomposition on the embeddings obtained for the training set and sorted the principal components in the order of the variance explained. Subsequently, I picked the first 16 principal components for each model and used the projection matrix to obtain the representation for the development and test sets.

[4]https://huggingface.co/

	Features	Train Acc	Train F1	Validation Acc	Validation F1
1	Language ID	75.9	64.2	76.1	64.2
2	(1) + Group ID	76.6	64.7	76.7	64.6
3	(2) + Capitalized	78.4	66.3	78.6	66.4
4	(3) + Levenshtein	83.1	70.6	83.0	69.8
5	(3) + Embeddings	97.2	94.2	92.6	80.3
6	(4) + Embeddings No weighting	**98.4**	95.8	**93.8**	79.6
7	**(4) + Embeddings**	97.8	**95.3**	93.7	**82.7**

Table 2: The feature accumulation analysis results from the XGBoost classifier. Each row presents the results for the model trained on a different set of features.

3.2 Typology

I encoded language information as two class variables: the first is **language identity** (34 classes), and the second is **language group identity** (7 classes: Romance, Slavic, Germanic, Celtic, Hellenic, Baltic).

Both variables were encoded in a one-hot vector, with 34 dimensions for language and 7 dimensions for language family.

3.3 Orthography

I used **Levensthein distance** (Levenshtein, 1966) on character level as the measure of similarity between words. The second feature based on orthographical forms was the binary variable denoting for each word whether it **is capitalized**. I added this feature because I have observed that proper names are often borrowed in other languages. Therefore, the capitalized word's appearance increased the derivative class's probability.

Admittedly, the adequate way to utilize Levenshtein distance would be to compute it on the phoneme level. However, the text to phonemes models were not publicly available for many low-resource languages included in the shared task.

4 Results

I trained the classifier on top of input vectors constructed from the features described in Section 3 and using the hyperparameters picked by Bayesian search described in Section 2.3. I split the training

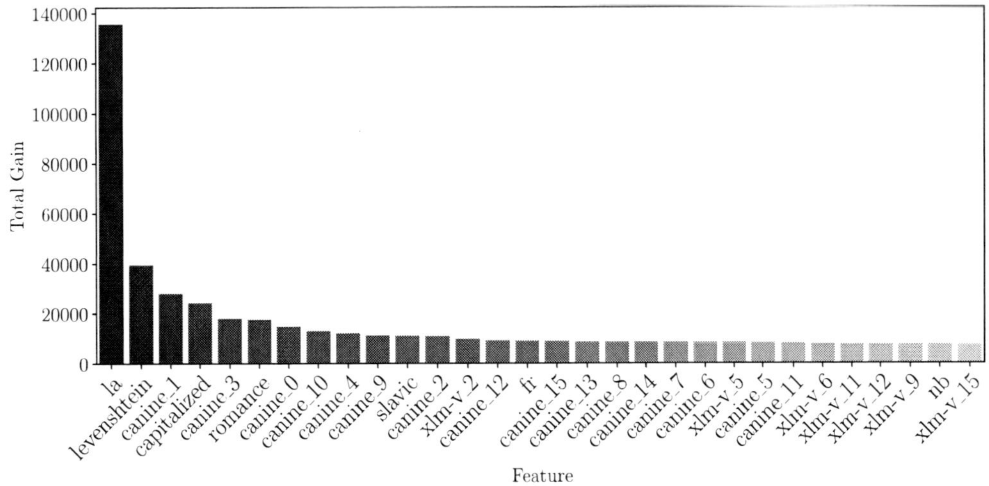

Figure 2: The sum of objective gains for when a given feature was used for a tree split. Features *la, fr, nb* are ones of 34 language ID features indicating if one of the languages in the pair is Latin, French, or Bokmål (Norwegian). *canine_x* and *xlm-v_x* denote the main principal component of language models CANINE and XLM-V, where *x* indicates the rank of the component according to the proportion of explained variance. The figure presents only 20 features with the highest total gain.

set provided by the organizers into train and validation splits containing 90% and 10% randomly selected data examples.

The submitted solution obtained **95.3%** macro F1 score on the train set and **82.7%** on the validation set. On the held-out test split, the system achieved **87%** F1 score, as reported by the organizers. This section presents the results of the accumulation study and feature importance analysis.

4.1 Accumulation Analysis

Table 2 shows the accuracies obtained by the classifier trained on subsets of features. Interestingly, the classifier trained just on language labels achieves a relatively high F1 (64.2% on the validation set). The highest gain is observed after adding word embeddings (+12.9% validation F1 increase in (8)); Levenshtein distance also visibly improves results (+3.87% in (5)). The model without class weighting (7) achieves better class accuracies and a lower F1 score due to class imbalance.

In summary: there is a visible impact of including language model embeddings and Levenshtein distance as classification features.

4.2 Feature Importance

Figure 2 presents the feature importance computed as the total gain each feature brought in the splits.

The most important feature is a binary variable indicating if one of the languages in a pair is Latin. The importance of this feature can be explained by the fact that Latin is the source language of many borrowings throughout European languages. The second feature is Levesnshtein distance, followed by one of the CANINE principal components (*canine_1*) and binary variable marking capitalized words. These three feature depends on the character composition of the analyzed words, highlighting the importance of orthographical information for cognate detection. Furthermore, character-based CANINE embeddings tend to be more influential to the predictions than subword-based ones (XLM-V).

5 Conclusions

The developed supervised system achieves competitive results in cognate detection (87% on the test set). The model was trained on a diverse set of linguistic and statistical signals. The accumulation and importance analysis showed the importance of nuance aspects of the dataset, such as Latin or capitalization, as an indication of derivative relation. The analysis also showed the high importance of using character-based representation for the task in the form of CANINE embedding and character-level Levenshtein distance.

Limitations

I acknowledge that the solution is limited in its scope. For instance, I did not use phonetical representation, which is more suitable for comparing the potential cognates across languages. Also, the solution could benefit from more complex historical linguistic analysis, e.g., obtained with Pyling package (List and Forkel, 2021).[5] However, the proposed classification method can be easily extended to incorporate additional features.

The flawed annotation of the training set causes another limitation of the method. According to information from the organizers, the dataset contained a significant number of false negatives, i.e., missing cognate relations.

Acknowledgments

I thank Abishek Stephen for his theoretical insight and valuable suggestions for using linguistic features in the classification model. I also thank Martin Popel, Ondřej Plátek, and Ondřej Dušek for their helpful comments on the previous draft of this system description. My work has been supported by grant 338521 of the Charles University Grant Agency.

References

James Bergstra, Daniel Yamins, and David Cox. 2013. Making a science of model search: Hyperparameter optimization in hundreds of dimensions for vision architectures. In *Proceedings of the 30th International Conference on Machine Learning*, volume 28 of *Proceedings of Machine Learning Research*, pages 115–123, Atlanta, Georgia, USA. PMLR.

Tianqi Chen and Carlos Guestrin. 2016. XGBoost. In *Proceedings of the 22nd ACM SIGKDD International Conference on Knowledge Discovery and Data Mining*. ACM.

Jonathan H. Clark, Dan Garrette, Iulia Turc, and John Wieting. 2022. Canine: Pre-training an Efficient Tokenization-Free Encoder for Language Representation. *Trans. Assoc. Comput. Linguistics*, 10:73–91.

David Crystal. 2008. *A Dictionary of Linguistics and Phonetics*, 6th ed. edition. Blackwell Pub Malden, MA ; Oxford.

V. I. Levenshtein. 1966. Binary codes capable of correcting deletions, insertions, and reversals. *Cybern Control Theory*, 10:707–710.

Davis Liang, Hila Gonen, Yuning Mao, Rui Hou, Naman Goyal, Marjan Ghazvininejad, Luke Zettlemoyer, and Madian Khabsa. 2023. XLM-V: Overcoming the Vocabulary Bottleneck in Multilingual Masked Language Models. *CoRR*, abs/2301.10472.

Johann-Mattis List and Robert Forkel. 2021. LingPy. A Python Library for Historical Linguistics.

Thomas Wolf, Lysandre Debut, Victor Sanh, Julien Chaumond, Clement Delangue, Anthony Moi, Pierric Cistac, Tim Rault, Rémi Louf, Morgan Funtowicz, Joe Davison, Sam Shleifer, Patrick von Platen, Clara Ma, Yacine Jernite, Julien Plu, Canwen Xu, Teven Le Scao, Sylvain Gugger, Mariama Drame, Quentin Lhoest, and Alexander M. Rush. 2020. Transformers: State-of-the-Art Natural Language Processing. In *Proceedings of the 2020 Conference on Empirical Methods in Natural Language Processing: System Demonstrations, EMNLP 2020 - Demos, Online, November 16-20, 2020*, pages 38–45. Association for Computational Linguistics.

[5] https://lingpy.readthedocs.io

CoToHiLi at SIGTYP 2023: Ensemble Models for Cognate and Derivative Words Detection

Liviu P. Dinu[1,2], **Ioan-Bogdan Iordache**[1], **Ana Sabina Uban**[1,2]
[1]Human Language Technology Research Center, University of Bucharest, Bucharest, Romania,
[2]Faculty of Mathematics and Computer Science, University of Bucharest, Bucharest, Romania
ldinu@fmi.unibuc.ro, iordache.bogdan1998@gmail.com, auban@fmi.unibuc.ro

Abstract

The identification of cognates and derivatives is a fundamental process in historical linguistics, on which any further research is based. In this paper we present our contribution to the SIGTYP 2023 Shared Task on cognate and derivative detection. We propose a multi-lingual solution based on features extracted from the alignment of the orthographic and phonetic representations of the words.

1 Introduction and Related Work

In this paper we describe our participation in the SIGTYP 2023 Shared Task on cognate and derivative detection.

As both the cornerstone of historical linguistics and a starting point of historical enquiry, automatic detection of cognates and derivatives provides access to a wide range of areas in social sciences (Campbell, 1998; Mallory and Adams, 2006; Mailhammer, 2015). Concrete examples of the usefulness of accurate prediction of cognates and cognate chains were previously mentioned in the works of Atkinson et al. (2005), Alekseyenko et al. (2012), and Dunn (2015) through linguistic phylogeny, which in turn can be applied to back tracing linguistic relatedness (Ng et al., 2010). Linguistic contact can also be inferred from such predictions (Epps, 2014), and this in turn can provide a better understanding and insight into the interaction of ancient communities (Mallory and Adams, 2006; Heggarty, 2015). While looking for similar patterns that regulate the cognitive mechanisms involved in semantic change, an extended view on cognate chains can be used as a basis for the identification of meaning divergence (Dworkin, 2006). The study of language acquisition (Huckin and Coady, 1999) as well as the challenging problem of removing false friends in machine translation (Uban and Dinu, 2020) would both benefit from an accurate understanding on the cognate pairings between any two related languages.

Today there is a vast volume of linguistic data that is yet to be analysed from a historical perspective (List et al., 2017). This illustrates the paramount importance of looking into automatic methods and algorithms that can accurately detect cognates and derivatives for both highly resourced and lowly resourced languages.

Recent years have seen a proliferation of techniques for automated detection of cognate pairs (Frunza and Inkpen, 2008; Ciobanu and Dinu, 2014; Jäger et al., 2017; Rama et al., 2018; Fourrier and Sagot, 2022). A lot of these techniques employ feature extraction from various orthographic and phonetic alignments used for training shallow machine learning algorithms in the supervised setting, or used along with clustering methods for the unsupervised approaches (Simard et al., 1992; Koehn and Knight, 2000; Inkpen et al., 2005; Mulloni and Pekar, 2006; Bergsma and Kondrak, 2007; Navlea and Todirascu, 2011; List, 2012; Ciobanu and Dinu, 2014; Jäger et al., 2017; St Arnaud et al., 2017; Cristea et al., 2021). Ciobanu and Dinu (2014) reported results on cognate detection for several Romance language pairs, in which cognate and non-cognate pairs are distinguished via features extracted from orthographic alignments that are used for training Support Vector Machines, with accuracies reaching as high as 87%.

Deep learning models for cognate detection and other similar tasks were mentioned in fewer studies. Siamese convolutional neural networks trained on character sequences for either the orthographic, or the phonetic representations of the words, and augmented with handcrafted features were shown to perform well when tested on cognate prediction for three language families, out of which the most proeminent one being the Austronesian family (Rama, 2016). Also, for borrowing detection Miller et al. (2020) employed deep learning architectures based on recurrent neural networks.

Proceedings of the 5th Workshop on Research in Computational Linguistic Typology and Multilingual NLP (SIGTYP 2023), pages 137–142
May 6, 2023 ©2023 Association for Computational Linguistics

1.1 SIGTYP 2023 Task and Data

The SIGTYP 2023 competition includes two subtasks: supervised and unsupervised classification of word pairs into three different classes: cognates, derivatives, and neither. The dataset included 232,482 annotated word pairs in 34 languages, where each word pair was annotated with a language for each word, and with one of the three categories based on the relationship between the pair. The data was annotated based on Wiktionary.

2 Automatic Cognate Detection Experiments

2.1 Methodology

The models we experimented with were all multilingual, in the sense that we trained them on the whole dataset without any split with respect to the languages of the classified word pairs. We trained classical machine learning algorithms using various sets of handcrafted features. In order to improve overall performance, we also looked into training ensemble models using the best scoring algorithms.

2.2 Features

The models were trained using combinations of three types of features:

- graphic features, extracted from aligning the graphic form of the words in a pair
- phonetic features, extracted from a similar alignment, but for the phonetic transcriptions
- language features, represented as one-hot encodings for which pair of languages the words in an input pair come from.

For the graphic features, we started by preprocessing the input words and removing the accents. The Needleman-Wunch algorithm for sequence alignment (Needleman and Wunsch, 1970) was successfully employed in previous studies (Ciobanu and Dinu, 2019) for aligning and extracting features from the graphic representation of word pairs, in order to classify such pairs as cognates or non-cognates. Using a similar approach we were able to extract n-grams around alignment mismatches (i.e. deletions, insertions, and substitutions). Another aspect we borrowed from previous studies is that for a given value of n, we extract all such i-grams that have the length $i \leq n$.

As for an example of graphic features extraction, we can look at the pair constituted of the German word "hoch" and the Swedish word "hög", annotated as cognates in the training dataset, and both meaning "tall". For the preprocessed pair `(hoch, hog)` we obtain the following alignment: `($hoch$, $hog-$)`, where `$` marks the start and the end of the alignments and `-` represents an insertion, or deletion (depending on the direction we are considering). For a chosen value of $n = 2$, the extracted features are: `c>g`, `h>-`, `oc>og`, `ch>g-`, and `h$>-$`.

For phonetic features, we employ the same method, but this time on the phonetic representation of the input words, where one could have been identified (if we did not identify the phonetic representation of at least one word in the input pair, we consider no phonetic features for this pair). To obtain the phonetic representations we used the eSpeak library[1], version 0.1.8.

All these features along with the encoding of the input languages are vectorized using the binary bag of words paradigm, and correspond to the input representation for the various Machine Learning models we trained.

2.3 Supervised classification: Ensemble Model

Using various combinations of the features described above, we experimented with training a few different multi-class classification algorithms: Support Vector Machine, Naive Bayes, and SGD Classifier. In order to compare the performance of the trained models (with various hyper-parameters) and their corresponding feature combinations, we computed F1 scores obtained from three-fold cross validation using the whole training dataset.

Out of these models we select the top performing ones and we then train a stacking ensemble classifier. We also experimented with the number of models selected and assessed the enseble performance using three-fold cross validation as well.

2.4 Unsupervised classification: Clustering model

For the clustering approach, we employed the whole set of features (graphic features, phonetic features, and language encodings) and fitted a KMeans algorithm with the number of clusters set to 3.

[1] https://github.com/espeak-ng/espeak-ng

Model and Hyper-Parameters	n	graphic	phonetic	language	F1	Acc
SGD Classifier, loss: "hinge"	3	yes	yes	yes	**0.793**	0.921
SGD Classifier, loss: "modified_huber"	3	yes	yes	yes	0.791	0.921
SGD Classifier, loss: "modified_huber"	2	yes	yes	yes	0.783	0.916
Linear SVM, $C = 0.1$	3	yes	yes	yes	0.782	**0.923**
SGD Classifier, loss: "modified_huber"	3	yes	no	yes	0.781	0.916
SGD Classifier, loss: "hinge"	2	yes	yes	yes	0.781	0.914
SGD Classifier, loss: "log_loss"	3	yes	yes	yes	0.780	0.913
SGD Classifier, loss: "perceptron"	3	yes	yes	yes	0.775	0.910
SGD Classifier, loss: "hinge"	3	yes	no	yes	0.775	0.911
Linear SVM, $C = 1$	3	yes	yes	yes	0.782	0.917

Table 1: Top ten best performing models with respect to macro F1 score for the supervised task. Best hyper-parameters and feature combinations are also reported in this table. n represents the size of the considered alignment n-grams for graphic and phonetic features. Evaluation was done using three-fold cross validation on the training data

2.5 Hyperparameters and experimental details

For selecting the best base models to be combined into the stacking ensemble for the supervised approach, and also for selecting the model for the unsupervised task, we trained various machine learning models using the *scikit-learn* Python library. The list of models and their parameters is the following (note that if not said otherwise, all other hyper-parameters are set to the defaults specified in the 1.2.0 version of the library):

- Linear Support Vector Machine (`LinearSVC`): $C \in \{0.1, 1, 10\}$
- Multinomial Naive Bayes
- SGD Classifier: loss $\in$ {hinge, log_loss, perceptron, squared_hinge, modified_huber}.

We evaluate each such model using all combinations of graphic, phonetic, and language encoding features, and using various values for the size of considered alignment n-grams ($n \in \{1, 2, 3\}$).

Lastly we select the top performing N models based on cross validation scores and train a `StackingClassifier` on the whole training set. Furthermore, we cross validate these ensembles as well in order to determine the best N.

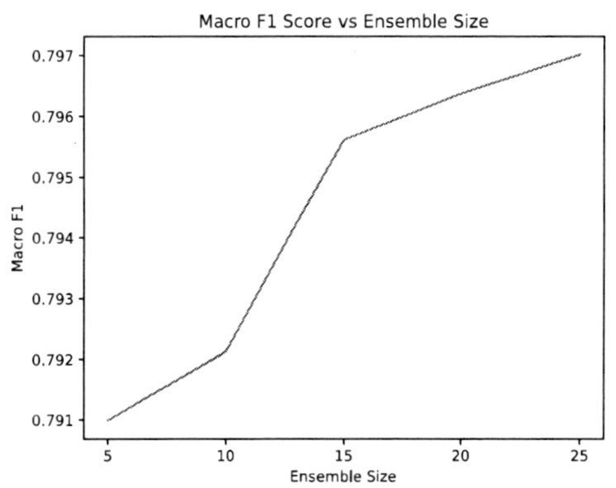

Figure 1: Computed macro F1 scores through three-fold cross validation for the supervised ensemble architectures trained using various numbers of base models.

3 Results

3.1 Supervised Task

We report metrics computed via three-fold cross validation performed using the provided training dataset. We report the macro F1 score (the metric used in the task description for evaluation purposes) and the classification accuracy. Table 1 contains the metrics computed for the top 10 performing classification models, along with their choice of hyper-parameters and features.

We also tracked the performance of the ensemble architecture for various numbers of base models. As can be seen in figure 1, slight improvements are achieved when picking more models, although at some point this process shows diminishing returns and a longer time for training.

For the supervised submission, we chose the 25 models ensemble that displayed a 0.797 macro F1 score on the cross validation experiment, while for the unsupervised one, our KMeans model displayed a clustering score of 0.816.

4 Conclusions

In this paper we described our approaches for both the supervised and the unsupervised subtasks from the SIGTYP 2023 Shared Task on cognate and derivative detection. Our methods mostly rely on feature engineering powered by sequence alignments for both orthographic and phonetic transcriptions.

As we have seen from the results reported on the train labels, the combination of graphic and phonetic features seem to provide better performance than the models relying on one but not the other. One disadvantage is the lack of phonetic transcriptions for some of the low resource languages, which should be an important item in the long list of studies still needed for these type of languages.

Our submissions for the shared task yielded a macro F1 score of 0.83 for the supervised subtask, which was only 0.04 below the best reported result, and a 0.49 clustering accuracy for the unsupervised subtask, which was the best reported result and achieved a 30% improvement over the baseline.

For future work we are considering a qualitative analysis of the errors, in order to better understand on which language pairs our models were registering better results and where they struggled to provide accurate predictions.

Acknowledgments Research supported by the Ministry of Research, Innovation and Digitization, CNCS/CCCDI UEFISCDI, CoToHiLi project, number 108/2021, Romania.

References

Alexander V. Alekseyenko, Quentin D. Atkinson, Remco Bouckaert, Alexei J. Drummond, Michael Dunn, Russell D. Gray, Simon J. Greenhill, Philippe Lemey, and Marc A. Suchard. 2012. Mapping the Origins and Expansion of the Indo-European Language Family. *Science*, 337:957–960.

Quentin D. Atkinson, Russell D. Gray, Geoff K. Nicholls, and David J. Welch. 2005. From Words to Dates: Water into Wine, Mathemagic or Phylogenetic Inference? *Transactions of the Philological Society*, 103:193–219.

Shane Bergsma and Grzegorz Kondrak. 2007. Alignment-based discriminative string similarity. In *Proceedings of the 45th annual meeting of the association of computational linguistics*, pages 656–663.

Lyle Campbell. 1998. *Historical Linguistics. An Introduction.* MIT Press.

Alina Maria Ciobanu and Liviu P. Dinu. 2014. Automatic Detection of Cognates Using Orthographic Alignment. In *Proceedings of ACL 2014, Volume 2: Short Papers*, pages 99–105.

Alina Maria Ciobanu and Liviu P. Dinu. 2019. Automatic identification and production of related words for historical linguistics. *Computational Linguistics*, 45(4):667–704.

Alina Maria Cristea, Liviu P. Dinu, Simona Georgescu, Mihnea-Lucian Mihai, and Ana Sabina Uban. 2021. Automatic discrimination between inherited and borrowed Latin words in Romance languages. In *Findings of the Association for Computational Linguistics: EMNLP 2021*, pages 2845–2855, Punta Cana, Dominican Republic. Association for Computational Linguistics.

Michael Dunn. 2015. Language phylogenies. *The Routledge handbook of historical linguistics*, pages 190–211.

Steven N Dworkin. 2006. Recent developments in spanish (and romance) historical semantics. In *Selected Proceedings of the 8th Hispanic Linguistics Symposium*, pages 50–57.

Patience Epps. 2014. Historical linguistics and sociocultural reconstruction. In *The Routledge Handbook of Historical Linguistics*, pages 579–597. London: Routledge.

Clémentine Fourrier and Benoît Sagot. 2022. Probing multilingual cognate prediction models. In *Findings of the Association for Computational Linguistics: ACL 2022, Dublin, Ireland, May 22-27, 2022*, pages 3786–3801. Association for Computational Linguistics.

Oana Frunza and Diana Inkpen. 2008. Disambiguation of partial cognates. *Lang. Resour. Evaluation*, 42(3):325–333.

Paul Heggarty. 2015. Prehistory through language and archaeology. In *The Routledge Handbook of Historical Linguistics*, pages 598–626. Routledge.

Thomas Huckin and James Coady. 1999. Incidental vocabulary acquisition in a second language: A review. *Studies in second language acquisition*, 21(2):181–193.

Diana Inkpen, Oana Frunza, and Grzegorz Kondrak. 2005. Automatic Identification of Cognates and False Friends in French and English. In *RANLP-2005, Bulgaria*, pages 251–257.

Gerhard Jäger, Johann-Mattis List, and Pavel Sofroniev. 2017. Using support vector machines and state-of-the-art algorithms for phonetic alignment to identify cognates in multi-lingual wordlists. In *Proceedings of the 15th Conference of the European Chapter of the Association for Computational Linguistics: Volume 1, Long Papers*, pages 1205–1216, Valencia, Spain. Association for Computational Linguistics.

Philipp Koehn and Kevin Knight. 2000. Estimating Word Translation Probabilities from Unrelated Monolingual Corpora Using the EM Algorithm. In *Proceedings of the 17th National Conference on Artificial Intelligence and 12th Conference on Innovative Applications of Artificial Intelligence*, pages 711–715.

Johann-Mattis List. 2012. LexStat: Automatic Detection of Cognates in Multilingual Wordlists. In *Proceedings of the 13th Conference of the European Chapter of the Association for Computational Linguistics Joint Workshop of LINGVIS and UNCLH*, pages 117–125.

Johann-Mattis List, Simon J. Greenhill, and Russell D. Gray. 2017. The Potential of Automatic Word Comparison for Historical Linguistics. *PLOS ONE*, 12(1):1–18.

Robert Mailhammer. 2015. Etymology. In *The Routledge handbook of historical linguistics*, pages 441–459. Routledge.

James P Mallory and Douglas Q Adams. 2006. *The Oxford introduction to proto-Indo-European and the proto-Indo-European world.* Oxford University Press on Demand.

John E Miller, Tiago Tresoldi, Roberto Zariquiey, César A Beltrán Castañón, Natalia Morozova, and Johann-Mattis List. 2020. Using lexical language models to detect borrowings in monolingual wordlists. *Plos one*, 15(12):e0242709.

Andrea Mulloni and Viktor Pekar. 2006. Automatic detection of orthographic cues for cognate recognition. In *In Proceedings of the 5th International Conference on Language Resources and Evaluation, LREC 2006*, pages 2387–2390.

Mirabela Navlea and Amalia Todirascu. 2011. Using Cognates in a French-Romanian Lexical Alignment System: A Comparative Study. In *Proceedings of the International Conference on Recent Advances in Natural Language Processing*, pages 247–253.

Saul B Needleman and Christian D Wunsch. 1970. A general method applicable to the search for similarities in the amino acid sequence of two proteins. *Journal of molecular biology*, 48(3):443–453.

Ee-Lee Ng, Beatrice Chin, Alvin W. Yeo, and Bali Ranaivo-Malançon. 2010. Identification of Closely-Related Indigenous Languages: An Orthographic Approach. *Int. J. of Asian Lang. Proc.*, 20(2):43–62.

Taraka Rama. 2016. Siamese convolutional networks for cognate identification. In *Proceedings of COLING 2016, the 26th International Conference on Computational Linguistics: Technical Papers*, pages 1018–1027.

Taraka Rama, Johann-Mattis List, Johannes Wahle, and Gerhard Jäger. 2018. Are automatic methods for cognate detection good enough for phylogenetic reconstruction in historical linguistics? In *Proceedings of the 2018 Conference of the North American Chapter of the Association for Computational Linguistics: Human Language Technologies, Volume 2 (Short Papers)*, pages 393–400, New Orleans, Louisiana. Association for Computational Linguistics.

Michel Simard, George F. Foster, and Pierre Isabelle. 1992. Using Cognates to Align Sentences in Bilingual Corpora. In *Proceedings of the Fourth International Conference on Theoretical and Methodological Issues in Machine Translation*.

Adam St Arnaud, David Beck, and Grzegorz Kondrak. 2017. Identifying Cognate Sets Across Dictionaries of Related Languages. In *Proceedings of the 2017 Conference on Empirical Methods in Natural Language Processing*, pages 2519–2528.

Ana Sabina Uban and Liviu P. Dinu. 2020. Automatically building a multilingual lexicon of false friends with no supervision. In *Proceedings of The 12th Language Resources and Evaluation Conference, LREC 2020, Marseille, France, May 11-16, 2020*, pages 3001–3007. European Language Resources Association.

Multilingual BERT has an accent: Evaluating English influences on fluency in multilingual models

Isabel Papadimitriou*, Kezia Lopez* and **Dan Jurafsky**
Computer Science Department
Stanford University
{isabelvp,keziakl,jurafsky}@stanford.edu

1 Introduction

Multilingual language models share a single set of parameters between many languages, opening new pathways for multilingual and low-resource NLP. However, not all training languages have an equal amount, or a comparable quality (Kreutzer et al., 2022), of training data in these models. In this paper, we investigate if the hegemonic status of English influences other languages in multilingual language models. We propose a novel method for evaluation, whereby we ask if model predictions for lower-resource languages exhibit structural features of English. This is similar to asking if the model has learned some languages with an "English accent", or an English *grammatical structure bias*.

We demonstrate this bias effect in Spanish and Greek, comparing the monolingual models BETO (Cañete et al., 2020) and GreekBERT (Koutsikakis et al., 2020) to multilingual BERT (mBERT), where English is the most frequent language in the training data. We show that *mBERT prefers English-like sentence structure in Spanish and Greek* compared to the monolingual models. Our case studies focus on Spanish pronoun drop (pro-drop) and Greek subject-verb order, two structural grammatical features. We show that multilingual BERT is structurally biased towards explicit pronouns rather than pro-drop in Spanish, and subject-before-verb order in Greek: the structural forms parallel to English.

The effect we showcase here demonstrates the type of fluency that can be lost with multilingual training — something that current evaluation methods miss. Our proposed method can be expanded, without the need for manual data collection, to any language with a syntactic treebank and a monolingual model. Since our method focuses on fine-grained linguistic features, some expert knowledge of the target language is necessary for evaluation.

Our work builds off of a long literature on multilingual evaluation which has until now mostly focused on downstream classification tasks (Conneau et al., 2018; Ebrahimi et al., 2022; Clark et al., 2020; Liang et al., 2020; Hu et al., 2020; Raganato et al., 2020; Li et al., 2021). With the help of these evaluation methods, research has pointed out the problems for both high- and low-resource languages that come with adding many languages to a single model (Wang et al., 2020; Turc et al., 2021; Lauscher et al., 2020, inter alia), and proposed methods for more equitable models (Ansell et al., 2022; Pfeiffer et al., 2022; Ogueji et al., 2021; Ògúnrẹ̀mí and Manning, 2023; Virtanen et al., 2019; Liang et al., 2023, inter alia). We hope that our work can add to these analyses and methodologies by pointing out issues beyond downstream classification performance that can arise with multilingual training, and aid towards building and evaluating more equitable multilingual models.

2 Method

Our method relies on finding a variable construction in the target language which can take two structural surface forms: one which is parallel to English (S_{parallel}) and one which is not ($S_{\text{different}}$). Surface forms parallel to English are those which mirror English structure.

Once we have identified such a construction in our target language, we can ask: are multilingual models biased towards S_{parallel}? We can use syntactic treebank annotations to pick out sentences that exhibit the structures S_{parallel} or $S_{\text{different}}$, and put these extracted sentences into two corpora, C_{parallel} and $C_{\text{different}}$. We then calculate a ratio $r_{\texttt{model}}$ for each model: the average probability of a sentence in C_{parallel} divided by the average probability of a sentence in $C_{\text{different}}$ according to the model. Our experimental question then boils down to asking if $r_{\texttt{multi}}$ is significantly larger than $r_{\texttt{mono}}$. To get an estimation of $P_{\texttt{model}}(x)$, we can extract the prob-

Proceedings of the 5th Workshop on Research in Computational Linguistic Typology and Multilingual NLP (SIGTYP 2023), pages 143–146
May 6, 2023 ©2023 Association for Computational Linguistics

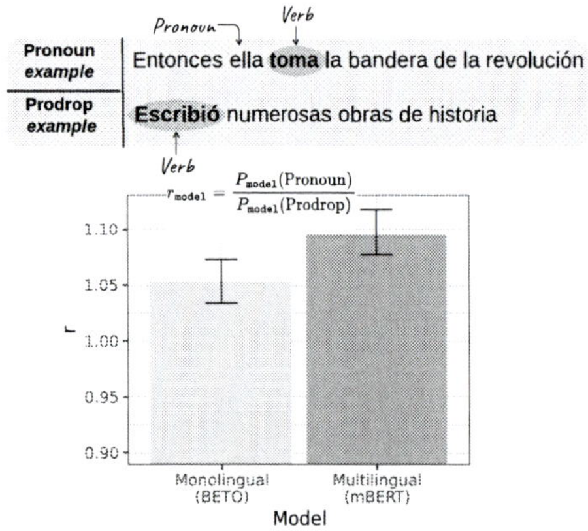

Figure 1: Results from our experiment on the Spanish GSD treebank, along with two examples from the treebank to illustrate S_{parallel} (with pronoun) and $S_{\text{different}}$ (pro-drop). Error bars represent 95% bootstrap confidence intervals.

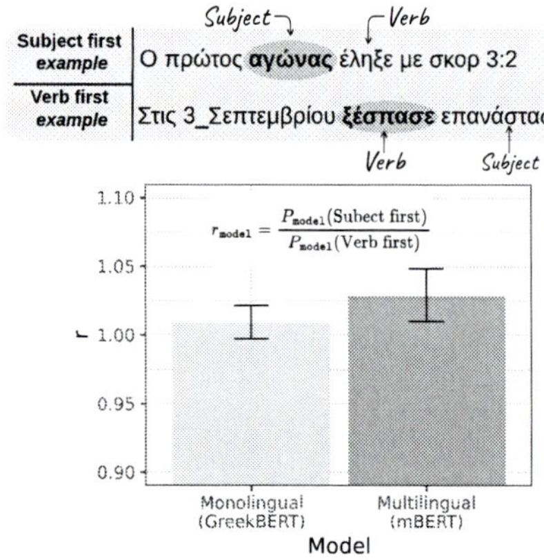

Figure 2: Results from our experiment on the Greek Dependency Treebank, along with two examples from the treebank to illustrate S_{parallel} (Subject-Verb) and $S_{\text{different}}$ (Verb-Subject). Error bars represent 95% bootstrap confidence intervals.

ability of *one word* w in each sentence that best represents the construction, and approximate the probability of x with $P(w_x|x)$. Using a carefully chosen word as a proxy for the probability of a construction is a methodological choice also made in reading time psycholinguistics experiments (Levy and Keller, 2013).

2.1 Case Study: Spanish Pro-drop

For our Spanish case study, we examine the feature of whether the subject pronoun is realized. In Spanish, the subject pronoun is often dropped: person and number are mostly reflected in verb conjugation, so the pronoun is realized or dropped depending on semantic and discourse factors. English, on the other hand, does not allow null subjects except in rare cases, even adding expletive syntactic subjects as in "**it** is raining". We extract C_{parallel} (with subject pronoun) and $C_{\text{different}}$ (dropepd subject pronoun) from the Spanish GSD treebank (De Marneffe et al., 2021). We take all sentences with a pronoun dependent of the root verb and add them to C_{parallel} (283 sentences) and all sentences where there is no `nsubj` relation to root verb and add them to $C_{\text{different}}$ (2,656 sentences), ignoring some confounder constructions. We always pick the main root verb of the sentence as our logit word w.

2.2 Case Study: Greek Subject-Verb order

For our Greek case study, we examine the feature of Subject-Verb order. English is a fixed word order language: with few exceptions, the order of a verb and its arguments is Subject-Verb-Object. Greek, on the other hand, has mostly free word order (Mackridge, 1985), meaning that the verb and arguments can appear in any order that is most appropriate given discourse context. For our experiment, we define S_{parallel} to be cases in Greek when the subject precedes the verb, as is the rule in English. $S_{\text{different}}$ is then the cases when the verb precedes the subject, which almost never happens in English. We extract C_{parallel} (Subject-Verb order, 1,446 sentences) and $C_{\text{different}}$ (Verb-Subject order, 425 sentences) from the Greek Dependency Treebank (Prokopidis and Papageorgiou, 2017). We define w to be the first element of the subject and verb: This first element is closer to the surrounding context, and so gives us a word-order-sensitive measurement of how the subject-verb construction is processed within the context.

3 Results

Results are shown in Figures 1 and 2, showing for both of our case studies that multilingual BERT has a greater propensity for preferring English-like sentences which exhibit S_{parallel}. Multilingual BERT significantly prefers pronoun sentences over pro-drop compared with monolingual BETO (bootstrap sampling, $p < 0.05$), and significantly prefers subject-verb sentences over verb-subject sentences over GreekBERT (bootstrap sampling, $p < 0.05$).

References

Alan Ansell, Edoardo Ponti, Anna Korhonen, and Ivan Vulić. 2022. Composable sparse fine-tuning for cross-lingual transfer. In *Proceedings of the 60th Annual Meeting of the Association for Computational Linguistics (Volume 1: Long Papers)*, pages 1778–1796.

José Cañete, Gabriel Chaperon, Rodrigo Fuentes, Jou-Hui Ho, Hojin Kang, and Jorge Pérez. 2020. Spanish Pre-trained BERT Model and Evaluation Data. In *PML4DC at ICLR 2020*.

Jonathan H Clark, Eunsol Choi, Michael Collins, Dan Garrette, Tom Kwiatkowski, Vitaly Nikolaev, and Jennimaria Palomaki. 2020. TyDi QA: A benchmark for information-seeking question answering in typologically diverse languages. *Transactions of the Association for Computational Linguistics*, 8:454–470.

Alexis Conneau, Ruty Rinott, Guillaume Lample, Adina Williams, Samuel Bowman, Holger Schwenk, and Veselin Stoyanov. 2018. XNLI: Evaluating Cross-lingual Sentence Representations. In *Proceedings of the 2018 Conference on Empirical Methods in Natural Language Processing*, pages 2475–2485.

Marie-Catherine De Marneffe, Christopher D Manning, Joakim Nivre, and Daniel Zeman. 2021. Universal Dependencies. *Computational linguistics*, 47(2):255–308.

Abteen Ebrahimi, Manuel Mager, Arturo Oncevay, Vishrav Chaudhary, Luis Chiruzzo, Angela Fan, John Ortega, Ricardo Ramos, Annette Rios Gonzales, Ivan Meza-Ruiz, et al. 2022. AmericasNLI: Evaluating Zero-shot Natural Language Understanding of Pre-trained Multilingual Models in Truly Low-resource Languages. In *Proceedings of the 60th Annual Meeting of the Association for Computational Linguistics (Volume 1: Long Papers)*, pages 6279–6299.

Junjie Hu, Sebastian Ruder, Aditya Siddhant, Graham Neubig, Orhan Firat, and Melvin Johnson. 2020. XTREME: A massively multilingual multi-task benchmark for evaluating cross-lingual generalisation. In *International Conference on Machine Learning*, pages 4411–4421. PMLR.

John Koutsikakis, Ilias Chalkidis, Prodromos Malakasiotis, and Ion Androutsopoulos. 2020. Greek-BERT: The Greeks visiting sesame street. In *11th Hellenic Conference on Artificial Intelligence*, pages 110–117.

Julia Kreutzer, Isaac Caswell, Lisa Wang, Ahsan Wahab, Daan van Esch, Nasanbayar Ulzii-Orshikh, Allahsera Tapo, Nishant Subramani, Artem Sokolov, Claytone Sikasote, Monang Setyawan, Supheakmungkol Sarin, Sokhar Samb, Benoît Sagot, Clara Rivera, Annette Rios, Isabel Papadimitriou, Salomey Osei, Pedro Ortiz Suarez, Iroro Orife, Kelechi Ogueji, Andre Niyongabo Rubungo, Toan Q. Nguyen, Mathias Müller, André Müller, Shamsuddeen Hassan Muhammad, Nanda Muhammad, Ayanda Mnyakeni, Jamshidbek Mirzakhalov, Tapiwanashe Matangira, Colin Leong, Nze Lawson, Sneha Kudugunta, Yacine Jernite, Mathias Jenny, Orhan Firat, Bonaventure F. P. Dossou, Sakhile Dlamini, Nisansa de Silva, Sakine Çabuk Ballı, Stella Biderman, Alessia Battisti, Ahmed Baruwa, Ankur Bapna, Pallavi Baljekar, Israel Abebe Azime, Ayodele Awokoya, Duygu Ataman, Orevaoghene Ahia, Oghenefego Ahia, Sweta Agrawal, and Mofetoluwa Adeyemi. 2022. Quality at a glance: An audit of web-crawled multilingual datasets. *Transactions of the Association for Computational Linguistics*, 10:50–72.

Anne Lauscher, Vinit Ravishankar, Ivan Vulić, and Goran Glavaš. 2020. From Zero to Hero: On the limitations of zero-shot language transfer with multilingual transformers. In *Proceedings of the 2020 Conference on Empirical Methods in Natural Language Processing (EMNLP)*, pages 4483–4499.

Roger P. Levy and Frank Keller. 2013. Expectation and locality effects in German verb-final structures. *Journal of Memory and Language*, 68(2):199–222.

Haoran Li, Abhinav Arora, Shuohui Chen, Anchit Gupta, Sonal Gupta, and Yashar Mehdad. 2021. Mtop: A comprehensive multilingual task-oriented semantic parsing benchmark. In *Proceedings of the 16th Conference of the European Chapter of the Association for Computational Linguistics: Main Volume*, pages 2950–2962.

Davis Liang, Hila Gonen, Yuning Mao, Rui Hou, Naman Goyal, Marjan Ghazvininejad, Luke Zettlemoyer, and Madian Khabsa. 2023. Xlm-v: Overcoming the vocabulary bottleneck in multilingual masked language models. *arXiv preprint arXiv:2301.10472*.

Yaobo Liang, Nan Duan, Yeyun Gong, Ning Wu, Fenfei Guo, Weizhen Qi, Ming Gong, Linjun Shou, Daxin Jiang, Guihong Cao, Xiaodong Fan, Ruofei Zhang, Rahul Agrawal, Edward Cui, Sining Wei, Taroon Bharti, Ying Qiao, Jiun-Hung Chen, Winnie Wu, Shuguang Liu, Fan Yang, Daniel Campos, Rangan Majumder, and Ming Zhou. 2020. XGLUE: A new benchmark datasetfor cross-lingual pre-training, understanding and generation. In *Proceedings of the 2020 Conference on Empirical Methods in Natural Language Processing (EMNLP)*, pages 6008–6018, Online. Association for Computational Linguistics.

P. Mackridge. 1985. *The Modern Greek Language: A Descriptive Analysis of Standard Modern Greek*. Oxford University Press.

Kelechi Ogueji, Yuxin Zhu, and Jimmy Lin. 2021. Small Data? No Problem! Exploring the viability of pretrained multilingual language models for low-resourced languages. In *Proceedings of the 1st Workshop on Multilingual Representation Learning*, pages 116–126, Punta Cana, Dominican Republic. Association for Computational Linguistics.

Tolúlọpẹ́ Ògúnrẹ̀mí and Christopher D. Manning. 2023. Mini but Mighty: Efficient multilingual pretraining with linguistically-informed data selection.

Jonas Pfeiffer, Naman Goyal, Xi Lin, Xian Li, James Cross, Sebastian Riedel, and Mikel Artetxe. 2022. Lifting the curse of multilinguality by pre-training modular transformers. In *Proceedings of the 2022 Conference of the North American Chapter of the Association for Computational Linguistics: Human Language Technologies*, pages 3479–3495, Seattle, United States. Association for Computational Linguistics.

Prokopis Prokopidis and Haris Papageorgiou. 2017. Universal Dependencies for Greek. In *Proceedings of the NoDaLiDa 2017 Workshop on Universal Dependencies (UDW 2017)*, pages 102–106, Gothenburg, Sweden. Association for Computational Linguistics.

Alessandro Raganato, Tommaso Pasini, Jose Camacho-Collados, and Mohammad Taher Pilehvar. 2020. XL-WiC: A multilingual benchmark for evaluating semantic contextualization. In *Proceedings of the 2020 Conference on Empirical Methods in Natural Language Processing (EMNLP)*. The Association for Computational Linguistics.

Iulia Turc, Kenton Lee, Jacob Eisenstein, Ming-Wei Chang, and Kristina Toutanova. 2021. Revisiting the Primacy of English in Zero-shot Cross-lingual Transfer. *CoRR*, abs/2106.16171.

Antti Virtanen, Jenna Kanerva, Rami Ilo, Jouni Luoma, Juhani Luotolahti, Tapio Salakoski, Filip Ginter, and Sampo Pyysalo. 2019. Multilingual is not enough: BERT for Finnish. *arXiv preprint arXiv:1912.07076*.

Zirui Wang, Zachary C Lipton, and Yulia Tsvetkov. 2020. On negative interference in multilingual models: Findings and a meta-learning treatment. In *Proceedings of the 2020 Conference on Empirical Methods in Natural Language Processing (EMNLP)*, pages 4438–4450.

Grambank's typological advances support computational research on diverse languages

Hannah J. Haynie
University of Colorado Boulder
Boulder, Colorado, USA
hannah.haynie@colorado.edu

Damián Blasi
Harvard University
Cambridge, Massachusetts, USA
damianblasi@gmail.com

Hedvig Skirgård
Max Planck Institute for Evolutionary Anthropology
Leipzig, Germany
hedvig_skirgard@eva.mpg.de

Simon J. Greenhill
University of Auckland
Auckland, New Zealand
simon.greenhill@auckland.ac.nz

Quentin D. Atkinson
University of Auckland
Auckland, New Zealand
q.atkinson@auckland.ac.nz

Russell D. Gray
Max Planck Institute for Evolutionary Anthropology
Leipzig, Germany
russell_gray@eva.mpg.de

Abstract

In spite of increasing attention on less-resourced languages in Natural Language Processing (NLP), equitable access to language technologies and inclusion of diverse languages in the development of these technologies remains a problem (Joshi et al., 2020). This disparity in resources and research attention is pronounced – only a handful of the world's approximately 7,000 languages receive the majority of scholarly attention (Blasi et al., 2022). Extending the reach of language technologies to diverse, less-resourced languages is important for tackling the challenges of digital equity and inclusion, and incorporating typological information into language transfer and multilingual learning is an important strategy for doing this. Here we introduce the Grambank typological database as a resource to support efforts that leverage typological features to enhance multilingual NLP.

To date, the cross-linguistic information about morphology and syntax that has been recruited for NLP comes primarily from datasets designed for theoretical linguistics research, with very little consideration of how this data may be used in computational tasks (Dryer and Haspelmath, 2013; Michaelis et al., 2013; Bickel and Nichols, 2002). As a result these existing typological datasets suffer from several limitations, including small numbers of adequately annotated languages, excessive missing data per feature, and lack of transparency in the content and coding of features (O'Horan et al., 2016). Grambank is a resource designed and curated by linguistic typologists to serve both theoretical linguistic purposes and computational uses. Its 195 morphosyntactic features cover a similar range of grammatical phenomena as prior typological databases (e.g. word order, grammatical relation marking, constructions like interrogatives and negation), but Grambank differs in its design in ways that facilitate its use in computational research.

Each of Grambank's features encodes some characteristic of the morphology and/or syntax of languages. The content of the feature set balances the description of a wide range of structures that are known to vary across languages with the availability of information for a maximal set of languages. Feature names take the form of a question (e.g. 'Are there prenominal articles?'), and values for a majority of features are binary (0/'no', 1/'yes'). Six word order features have multi-state values (e.g. 'Order A', 'Order B', or 'Both Order A and Order B'), which can easily be binarised for analytical purposes. Binary feature values avoid the ambiguity of binned or inadequately described categories, and the representation of Grambank datapoints in terms of the presence or absence of linguistic traits allows the dataset to report all strategies identified in empirical sources for expressing a particular meaning or function. This contrasts with prior typological resources that encode a single 'dominant' category per meaning or function (Dryer and Haspelmath, 2013).

The typological content of Grambank is structured as a simple list of features, with no hi-

Proceedings of the 5th Workshop on Research in Computational Linguistic Typology and Multilingual NLP (SIGTYP 2023), pages 147–149
May 6, 2023 ©2023 Association for Computational Linguistics

erarchical relationships between features (e.g. specific characteristics that are only coded if a certain value is registered for a more general feature). Care was also taken to avoid strict logical dependencies between features (i.e. situations where a certain value for Feature A entails a particular value for Feature B). Functional dependencies may still exist between features for a variety of reasons, such as communicative pressures or common processes of language change. However, the structure of the dataset eliminates a great deal of the redundancy in typological data that is problematic for tasks such as measuring language distances (Hammarström and O'Connor, 2013).

To promote transparency (Slingerland et al., 2020), the Grambank web interface includes extensive documentation for each feature, including step-by-step procedures that outline the analytical decisions made by annotators in determining feature values, illustrative examples from languages with different feature values, and references to relevant theoretical literature.

Grambank is annotated by linguists based on descriptions (e.g. published grammars) of languages. It currently includes data for 2,467 languages – around a third of the world's total linguistic diversity – from 316 different language families around the globe. This sample covers all continents (Antarctica excepted), and all 24 linguistically relevant geographic areas identified in prior research (Nichols et al., 2013). Whereas NLP research to date features languages of continental Eurasia almost exclusively, only about 20% of the Grambank sample is drawn from this region, with the remainder representing diverse languages from Africa, the Americas, Australia, Papua New Guinea, and Oceania. While Grambank is not intended to be a perfect stratified sample of language families or macroareas, it provides representation of areas and languages that are often under-sampled, including minority languages, endangered languages, languages from small language families, and isolates.

The size of the language sample in Grambank is similar to WALS (Dryer and Haspelmath, 2013), but Grambank represents a tremendous leap forward in terms of the overall number of datapoints available for characterizing individual languages, investigating language universals and tendencies, and examining the full range of grammatical diversity. Grambank advances the field by making complete or nearly complete sets of high quality, easily interpreted grammatical information available for a large and diverse set of languages. Missing data has been repeatedly presented as the most important limitation of typological data for use in multilingual NLP (O'Horan et al., 2016; Ponti et al., 2019; Bjerva et al., 2020), and this is where Grambank most clearly exceeds the prior benchmark. On average a WALS feature is coded for approximately 400 languages (Dryer and Haspelmath, 2013). In contrast, Grambank features are coded for approximately 1,500 languages on average. This means that a typical language in WALS is coded for only approximately 30 features, while it is likely to be coded in Grambank for approximately 145 features. In sum, approximately 17% of the potential datapoints in WALS have values (Dryer and Haspelmath, 2013; O'Horan et al., 2016), while Grambank pushes the total completion rate above 70%.

Typological data has been shown to be a useful tool for improving the performance of multilingual methods (Zhang et al., 2012; Ammar et al., 2016), transfer of technologies from high resource languages (Naseem et al., 2012), and a variety of other tasks that enable multilingual NLP and ultimately the development of inclusive language technologies (Rama and Kolachina, 2012; Östling, 2015; Takamura et al., 2016). Grambank represents a significant advance in the typological information that can be used to support these activities.

Limitations

The resource described herein includes information for only approximately one third of the languages of the world; its use for computational tasks involves some risk of bias related to sampling based on availability of grammatical descriptions and risk of excluding understudied languages.

The evaluation of the Grambank resource presented here relies on qualitative differences between this resource and the existing state of the art in cross-linguistic morphosyntactic data. Further analyses are warranted to examine the impacts of this resource on specific tasks.

Ethics Statement

This research complies with the principles of the ACL Ethics Policy. Cross-linguistic morphosyntactic resources have the potential to aid in the expansion of computational resources to less-resourced languages, but we note that the needs and interests of language communities vary and that digital equity and inclusivity require the involvement of those communities in research and development of technologies.

References

Waleed Ammar, George Mulcaire, Miguel Ballesteros, Chris Dyer, and Noah A. Smith. 2016. Many languages, one parser. *Transactions of the Association for Computational Linguistics*, 4:431–444.

Balthasar Bickel and Johanna Nichols. 2002. Autotypologizing databases and their use in fieldwork. In *Proceedings of the International LREC Workshop on Resources and Tools in Field Linguistics*, pages 33–40.

Johannes Bjerva, Elizabeth Salesky, Sabrina J. Mielke, Aditi Chaudhary, Giuseppe G. A. Celano, Edoardo Maria Ponti, Ekaterina Vylomova, Ryan Cotterell, and Isabelle Augenstein. 2020. SIGTYP 2020 shared task: Prediction of typological features. In *Proceedings of the Second Workshop on Computational Research in Linguistic Typology*, pages 1–11, Online. Association for Computational Linguistics.

Damian Blasi, Antonios Anastasopoulos, and Graham Neubig. 2022. Systematic inequalities in language technology performance across the world's languages. In *Proceedings of the 60th Annual Meeting of the Association for Computational Linguistics (Volume 1: Long Papers)*, pages 5486–5505, Dublin, Ireland. Association for Computational Linguistics.

Matthew S. Dryer and Martin Haspelmath, editors. 2013. *WALS Online*. Max Planck Institute for Evolutionary Anthropology, Leipzig.

Harald Hammarström and Loretta O'Connor. 2013. Dependency-sensitive typological distance. In Anju Saxena and Lars Borin, editors, *Approaches to Measuring Linguistic Differences*, pages 329–352. De Gruyter, Berlin.

Pratik Joshi, Sebastin Santy, Amar Budhiraja, Kalika Bali, and Monojit Choudhury. 2020. The state and fate of linguistic diversity and inclusion in the NLP world. In *Proceedings of the 58th Annual Meeting of the Association for Computational Linguistics*, pages 6282–6293, Online. Association for Computational Linguistics.

Susanne Maria Michaelis, Philippe Maurer, Martin Haspelmath, and Magnus Huber, editors. 2013. *APiCS Online*. Max Planck Institute for Evolutionary Anthropology, Leipzig.

Tahira Naseem, Regina Barzilay, and Amir Globerson. 2012. Selective sharing for multilingual dependency parsing. In *Proceedings of the 50th Annual Meeting of the Association for Computational Linguistics (Volume 1: Long Papers)*, pages 629–637, Jeju Island, Korea. Association for Computational Linguistics.

Johanna Nichols, Alena Witzlack-Makarevich, and Balthasar Bickel, editors. 2013. *The AUTOTYP genealogy and geography database: 2013 release*. University of Zürich.

Helen O'Horan, Yevgeni Berzak, Ivan Vulić, Roi Reichart, and Anna Korhonen. 2016. Survey on the use of typological information in natural language processing. In *Proceedings of COLING 2016, the 26th International Conference on Computational Linguistics: Technical Papers*, pages 1297–1308, Osaka, Japan. The COLING 2016 Organizing Committee.

Robert Östling. 2015. Word order typology through multilingual word alignment. In *Proceedings of the 53rd Annual Meeting of the Association for Computational Linguistics and the 7th International Joint Conference on Natural Language Processing (Volume 2: Short Papers)*, pages 205–211, Beijing, China. Association for Computational Linguistics.

Edoardo Maria Ponti, Helen O'Horan, Yevgeni Berzak, Ivan Vulić, Roi Reichart, Thierry Poibeau, Ekaterina Shutova, and Anna Korhonen. 2019. Modeling language variation and universals: A survey on typological linguistics for natural language processing. *Computational Linguistics*, 45(3):559–601.

Taraka Rama and Prasanth Kolachina. 2012. How good are typological distances for determining genealogical relationships among languages? In *Proceedings of COLING 2012: Posters*, pages 975–984, Mumbai, India. The COLING 2012 Organizing Committee.

Edward Slingerland, Quentin D. Atkinson, Carol R. Ember, Oliver Sheehan, Michael Muthukrishna, Joseph Bulbulia, and Russell D. Gray. 2020. Coding culture: Challenges and recommendations for comparative cultural databases. *Evolutionary Human Sciences*, 2:E29.

Hiroya Takamura, Ryo Nagata, and Yoshifumi Kawasaki. 2016. Discriminative analysis of linguistic features for typological study. In *Proceedings of the Tenth International Conference on Language Resources and Evaluation (LREC'16)*, pages 69–76, Portorož, Slovenia. European Language Resources Association (ELRA).

Yuan Zhang, Roi Reichart, Regina Barzilay, and Amir Globerson. 2012. Learning to map into a universal POS tagset. In *Proceedings of the 2012 Joint Conference on Empirical Methods in Natural Language Processing and Computational Natural Language Learning*, pages 1368–1378, Jeju Island, Korea. Association for Computational Linguistics.

Language-agnostic measures discriminate inflection and derivation

Coleman Haley **Edoardo M. Ponti** **Sharon Goldwater**
Institute for Language, Cognition and Computaton, University of Edinburgh, United Kingdom
{coleman.haley,eponti,sgwater}@ed.ac.uk

In the field of morphology, a distinction is commonly drawn between *derivations*, processes that form "new" words, and *inflections*, processes that merely create new "forms" of words (Dressler, 1989). While the theoretical nature of this distinction is a subject of ongoing debate, it is widely employed throughout linguistic theory, computational and corpus linguistics, and even psycholinguistics.

Dictionaries and grammars roughly agree on which morphological relationships are inflectional and which are derivational within a language. There is even a degree of cross-linguistic consistency in the constructions which are typically/traditionally considered inflections—e.g., tense marking on verbs is widely considered to be inflectional. This cross-linguistic consistency is highlighted by the development of UniMorph (Batsuren et al., 2022), a resource which annotates inflections across 182 languages using a unified feature scheme. This is despite the fact that UniMorph data is extracted from the Wiktionary open online dictionary[1], which organises constructions into inflections and derivations based on typical traditions for a given language. This is in line with Haspelmath's (in press) view of these terms as *traditional comparative concepts*, being based on the ways in which Western dictionaries and grammar books are traditionally structured.

While linguists have proposed many tests or prototypical properties of these categories, such as derivations producing larger semantic changes or occurring closer to the root of the word, difficulties in producing a cross-linguistically consistent definition have led many researchers to conclude that the inflection–derivation distinction is gradient rather than categorical (e.g., Dressler, 1989) or even to take position that the distinction carries no theoretical weight (Haspelmath, in press). In particular, Haspelmath (in press) argues that many such properties of inflection and derivation are not proven to apply in a consistent way across languages.

One major issue in evaluating these theoretical claims is the lack of large-scale, cross-linguistic evidence based on quantitative measures (rather than subjective tests). While several studies have also computationally operationalised linguistic intuitions about the inflection–derivation distinction, they have been limited in terms of the languages studied, focusing on French (Bonami and Paperno, 2018; Copot et al., in press) and Czech (Rosa and Žabokrtský, 2019). We here expand the set of measures and languages studied to evaluate whether traditional concepts of inflection and derivation relate to their claimed properties cross-linguistically.

We develop a set of four quantitative measures of morphological constructions, including measures of *both* the magnitude and the variability of the changes introduced by each construction. Crucially, our measures can be computed directly from a linguistic corpus, allowing us to consistently operationalise them across many languages and morphological constructions. That is, given a particular morphological construction (such as "the nominative plural in German") and examples of word pairs that illustrate that construction (e.g., '*Frau, Frauen*', '*Kind, Kinder*'), we compute four corpus-based measures which quantify the idea that derivations produce *larger* and *more variable* changes to words compared to inflections. We then ask whether, for a given construction, knowing just these measures is sufficient to predict its inflectional versus derivational status in UniMorph.

In particular we consider for each construction:

- $\|\Delta_{form}\|$, the average edit distance between the base and constructed forms,
- $\|\Delta_{distribution}\|$, the Euclidean distance between the distributional embeddings of the base and constructed forms,
- var(Δ_{form}), the average edit distance between the edit sequences between base and

[1] https://en.wiktionary.org

Proceedings of the 5th Workshop on Research in Computational Linguistic Typology and Multilingual NLP (SIGTYP 2023), pages 150–152
May 6, 2023 ©2023 Association for Computational Linguistics

Features	Logistic	MLP
Majority class (Inflection)	0.57	–
$\|\|\Delta_{distribution}\|\|$	0.67	0.68
$\|\|\Delta_{form}\|\|$	0.59	0.60
var($\Delta_{distribution}$)	0.76	0.76
var(Δ_{form})	0.71	0.71
Form/distribution magnitude*	0.66	0.67
Form/distribution variability*	0.84	0.84
Form magnitude/variability*	0.70	0.75
Distribution magnitude/variability*	0.77	0.77
All measures*	**0.86**	**0.90**

Table 1: Accuracy in reconstructing Unimorph's inflection–derivation distinction by various supervised classifiers.

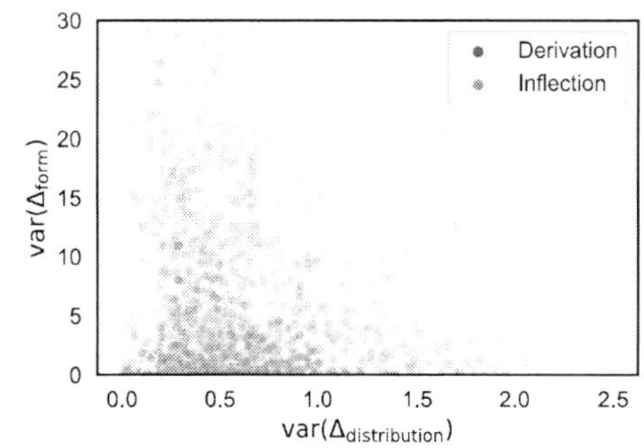

Figure 1: Our two most predictive measures for inflectional and derivational constructions in UniMorph. While these measures can be used to correctly classify 84% of UniMorph constructions, they display a clearly gradient mapping onto the categories.

constructed forms within a construction,

- var($\Delta_{distribution}$), the total variance of the difference vectors between base and constructed form in the distributional embedding space.

If, across languages belonging to different language families and morphological typologies, the UniMorph annotations can be predicted with high accuracy based on our measures, this would indicate that traditional concepts of inflection and derivation *do* correspond to intuitions about the different *types* of changes inflection and derivation induce.

To explore this, we train a logistic regression classifier and a multilayer perceptron (MLP). Since we are interested in the cross-linguistic consistency of our four predictors, the models are not given access to the input language or any of its typological features. In experiments on 26 languages[2] (including five from non-Indo-European families) and 2,772 constructions, we find that both models are able to predict with high accuracy whether a held-out construction is listed as inflection or derivation in UniMorph (86% and 90%, respectively, for the two models, compared to a majority-class baseline of 57%). We additionally find that our distributional measures alone are more predictive than our formal ones, and our variability measures alone are more predictive than our magnitude ones; still, combining all four features yields the best results.

We also identify *how prototypical* various categories of inflections are in terms of our measures. We determine that inherent inflectional meanings are particularly likely to be classified as derivation by our model, in line with Booij's (1996) characterisation of inherent inflection as non-canonical.

We provide initial evidence about non-Indo-European languages, obtaining 82% accuracy compared to 91% for Indo-European languages. While still indicating generalisation, this suggests that the application of the inflection–derivation distinction to non-Indo-European languages may be less consistent as suggested by Haspelmath (in press). For example, Turkish is a highly agglutinative language with, in traditional descriptions, an exceptionally rich inflectional system—reflected by an extremely large number of inflectional constructions and relatively small number of derivations in our dataset. Our classifier over-uses the label derivation for this language, suggesting a degree of mis-alignment with the way linguists typically operationalise inflection and derivation in this language.

Nevertheless, together these results provide large-scale cross-linguistic evidence that, despite the apparent difficulty in designing diagnostic tests for inflection and derivation, these concepts are nevertheless associated with distinct and measurable formal and distributional signatures that behave consistently across a variety of languages. Further analysis of our results does not, however, support the view of these concepts as clearly discrete categories. While our measures largely discriminate inflection and derivation, we still find many constructions near the model's decision boundary between the two categories, indicating a gradient, rather than categorical, distinction (Figure 1).

[2] cat, ces, dan, deu, eng, ell, fin, fra, gle, hun, hye, ita, kaz, lat, lav, mon, nob, nld, pol, por, ron, rus, spa, swe, tur, ukr

References

Khuyagbaatar Batsuren, Omer Goldman, Salam Khalifa, Nizar Habash, Witold Kieraś, Gábor Bella, Brian Leonard, Garrett Nicolai, Kyle Gorman, Yustinus Ghanggo Ate, Maria Ryskina, Sabrina Mielke, Elena Budianskaya, Charbel El-Khaissi, Tiago Pimentel, Michael Gasser, William Abbott Lane, Mohit Raj, Matt Coler, Jaime Rafael Montoya Samame, Delio Siticonatzi Camaiteri, Esaú Zumaeta Rojas, Didier López Francis, Arturo Oncevay, Juan López Bautista, Gema Celeste Silva Villegas, Lucas Torroba Hennigen, Adam Ek, David Guriel, Peter Dirix, Jean-Philippe Bernardy, Andrey Scherbakov, Aziyana Bayyr-ool, Antonios Anastasopoulos, Roberto Zariquiey, Karina Sheifer, Sofya Ganieva, Hilaria Cruz, Ritván Karahóğa, Stella Markantonatou, George Pavlidis, Matvey Plugaryov, Elena Klyachko, Ali Salehi, Candy Angulo, Jatayu Baxi, Andrew Krizhanovsky, Natalia Krizhanovskaya, Elizabeth Salesky, Clara Vania, Sardana Ivanova, Jennifer White, Rowan Hall Maudslay, Josef Valvoda, Ran Zmigrod, Paula Czarnowska, Irene Nikkarinen, Aelita Salchak, Brijesh Bhatt, Christopher Straughn, Zoey Liu, Jonathan North Washington, Yuval Pinter, Duygu Ataman, Marcin Wolinski, Totok Suhardijanto, Anna Yablonskaya, Niklas Stoehr, Hossep Dolatian, Zahroh Nuriah, Shyam Ratan, Francis M. Tyers, Edoardo M. Ponti, Grant Aiton, Aryaman Arora, Richard J. Hatcher, Ritesh Kumar, Jeremiah Young, Daria Rodionova, Anastasia Yemelina, Taras Andrushko, Igor Marchenko, Polina Mashkovtseva, Alexandra Serova, Emily Prud'hommeaux, Maria Nepomniashchaya, Fausto Giunchiglia, Eleanor Chodroff, Mans Hulden, Miikka Silfverberg, Arya D. McCarthy, David Yarowsky, Ryan Cotterell, Reut Tsarfaty, and Ekaterina Vylomova. 2022. UniMorph 4.0: Universal Morphology. In *Proceedings of the Thirteenth Language Resources and Evaluation Conference*, pages 840–855, Marseille, France. European Language Resources Association.

Olivier Bonami and Denis Paperno. 2018. Inflection vs. derivation in a distributional vector space. *Lingue e linguaggio*, 17(2):173–196.

Geert Booij. 1996. Inherent versus contextual inflection and the split morphology hypothesis. In *Yearbook of Morphology 1995*, pages 1–16. Springer.

Maria Copot, Timothee Mickus, and Olivier Bonami. in press. Idiosyncratic frequency as a measure of derivation vs. inflection. *Journal of Language Modelling*.

Wolfgang U Dressler. 1989. Prototypical differences between inflection and derivation. *STUF-Language Typology and Universals*, 42(1):3–10.

Martin Haspelmath. in press. Inflection and derivation as traditional comparative concepts. *Linguistics*.

Rudolf Rosa and Zdeněk Žabokrtský. 2019. Attempting to separate inflection and derivation using vector space representations. In *Proceedings of the Second International Workshop on Resources and Tools for Derivational Morphology*, pages 61–70, Prague, Czechia. Charles University, Faculty of Mathematics and Physics, Institute of Formal and Applied Linguistics.

Gradual Language Model Adaptation Using Fine-Grained Typology

Marcell Richard Fekete
Aalborg University
Copenhagen, Denmark
mrfe@cs.aau.dk

Johannes Bjerva
Aalborg University
Copenhagen, Denmark
jbjerva@cs.aau.dk

Transformer-based language models (LMs) offer superior performance in a wide range of NLP tasks compared to previous paradigms. However, the vast majority of the world's languages do not have adequate training data available for monolingual LMs (Joshi et al., 2020). Multilingual LMs like mBERT (Devlin et al., 2019) and XLM-RoBERTa (Conneau et al., 2020) offer a solution to this state of affairs, and their joint pretraining on data taken from a large set of languages results in surprisingly robust cross-lingual representations (Pires et al., 2019; Wu and Dredze, 2019, 2020). This lends them the ability to also carry out zero-shot transfer, solving tasks in a target language without language-specific supervision (Wu and Dredze, 2019; Üstün et al., 2020, 2022).

However, multilingual LMs may struggle when it comes to adapting to additional languages (Conneau et al., 2020; Pfeiffer et al., 2020; de Vries et al., 2021). This is especially true if these languages are resource-poor (Wu and Dredze, 2020; Rust et al., 2021; Pfeiffer et al., 2020, 2021), or have typological characteristics unseen by the LM during its pretraining (Üstün et al., 2020, 2022). The performance of multilingual LMs might suffer even on resource-rich languages due to the lack of model capacity to adequately incorporate language-specific parameters and vocabulary (Conneau et al., 2020; Pfeiffer et al., 2020; Üstün et al., 2020, 2022), although some success has been achieved with model adaptation techniques that add extra language-specific parameters to multilingual LMs (Houlsby et al., 2019; Pfeiffer et al., 2020; Üstün et al., 2020, 2022).

Beyond standard training methods for multilingual LMs, monolingual model adaptation techniques may help to overcome the relatively low adaptability for resource-pour languages (de Vries et al., 2021), by adapting monolingual LMs to closely related target languages. Ács et al. (2021) do not find that language-relatedness is a significant indicator in determining whether transfer would work best for various Uralic languages using various monolingual and multilingual LMs. In contrast, de Vries et al. (2021) observe a positive correlation between the typological similarity of the LM and target languages and the success of transfer when looking at Gronings and West Frisian. While these studies reach conflicting conclusions, it is possible that differences in specific model adaptation techniques may explain the discrepancies in their findings; the former study fine-tunes LM weights using training data from target languages, while the latter retrains the lexical layer while freezing all LM weights.

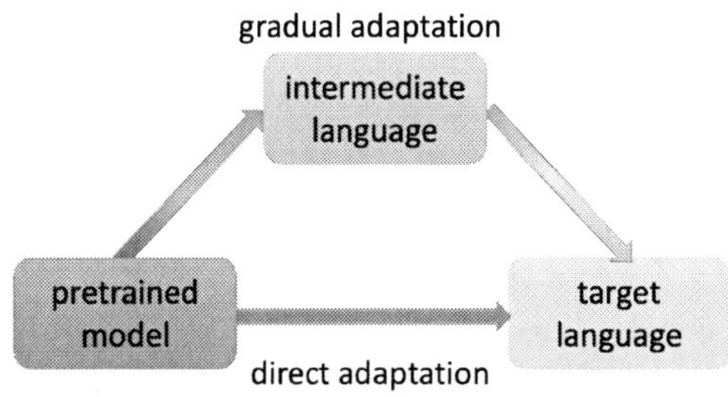

Figure 1: Gradual adaptation proceeds from the source language to the target language through an intermediate language in order to maximise cross-lingual transfer to the benefit of the target language.

In this paper, we build upon previous work on monolingual model adaptation, extending it in a new, flexible, typologically-informed framework of *gradual* model adaptation. Instead of directly adapting a monolingual LM to a target language, we propose that adaptation should take place in multiple stages (see Figure 1), based on the insight that cross-lingual transfer is enhanced by typological similarity (Pires et al., 2019; Üstün et al., 2020, 2022; de Vries et al., 2021). We hypothesise that by ensuring high typological similarity between the languages involved throughout the gradual adapta-

Proceedings of the 5th Workshop on Research in Computational Linguistic Typology and Multilingual NLP (SIGTYP 2023), pages 153–158
May 6, 2023 ©2023 Association for Computational Linguistics

tion process, we can facilitate this transfer. Gradual model adaptation is also informed by principles of curriculum learning, which aims to find an ideal ordering of training instances in order to enhance LM learning (Bengio et al., 2009). In this case, the instances are in fact languages, while the ordering is based on typological similarity.

The explicit consideration of typology sets our work apart from a majority of model adaptation approaches that either do not consider the individual properties of languages (Pfeiffer et al., 2020, 2021; Artetxe et al., 2020; Rust et al., 2021; Bapna and Firat, 2019), or consider solely their genealogical relations (Wu and Dredze, 2020; Ács et al., 2021; Faisal and Anastasopoulos, 2022). When it comes to typologically informed approaches such as Üstün et al. (2020, 2022), they typically use features extracted from hand-crafted typological resources such as WALS WALS (Dryer and Haspelmath, 2013) and URIEL (Littell et al., 2017).

However, such hand-crafted typological resources are typically quite coarse-grained, and fail to represent the in-language variation in terms of features such as word order (Ponti et al., 2019). German, for instance, has verb-second word order except for in subordinate clauses, while Hungarian subjects may precede or follow their verbs depending on topicalization. While de Vries et al. (2021) quantifies language similarity using a lexical-phonetic measure, we opt for using structural vectors derived from counts of dependency links (Bjerva et al., 2019). These provide a fine-grained and data-driven measure of typology, and we derive them from Universal Dependencies 2.11 (UD; Zeman et al., 2022).

We select our candidate languages from the Germanic subset of UD, and measure pairwise cosine similarity values between the structural vectors of these languages (see Figure 2). We evaluate the performance of BERT models such as English BERT (Devlin et al., 2019), German BERT (Chan et al., 2020), Norwegian BERT (Kummervold et al., 2021), Danish BERT (Hvingelby et al., 2020) and Dutch BERTje (de Vries et al., 2019) on language modelling and POS-tagging. We use data from UD to fine-tune LM weights on the target task, using two languages distinct from the model language m: besides target language t, we also use data for an intermediate language i. Language i is selected such that, in terms of cosine similarity of its structural vector with the structural vectors of m

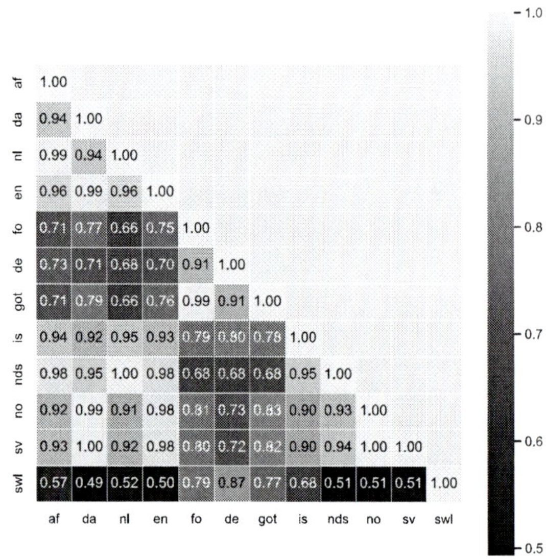

Figure 2: Pairwise cosine similarities between the structural vectors of Germanic languages in UD. The structural vectors compared derive from counts of dependency links following Bjerva et al. (2019).

and t, it is as close to equidistant as possible from both. For example, if m is German (*de*) and t is Norwegian (*no*; cosine similarity of .73), i might be Icelandic (*is*; cosine similarity from German .80 and from Norwegian 0.90) (see Figure 2). We found the POS-tagging is close to a performance ceiling even when fine-tuning our models on small amounts of training data in language t. Typically only 500 sentences are enough to reach F1-scores of 0.85-0.95 depending on the languages involved. This is why we aim to also evaluate our approach on dependency parsing. Moreover, we are expanding to the technique of retraining the lexical layer as an alternative of fine-tuning LM weights.

Our main contribution is the introduction of gradual model adaptation, a monolingual mdodel adaptation framework that is capable of incorporating various measurements of typological similarity in designing intermediate model adaptation steps. By encouraging cross-lingual transfer, this approach may lead to improved performance of LMs on resource-poor languages. Additionally, the framework of gradual model adaptation might also allow us to assess the correlation between various – typological and non-typological – language similarity measures, as well as the efficacy of cross-lingual transfer.

References

Judit Ács, Dániel Lévai, and Andras Kornai. 2021. Evaluating transferability of BERT models on Uralic languages. In *Proceedings of the Seventh International Workshop on Computational Linguistics of Uralic Languages*, pages 8–17, Syktyvkar, Russia (Online). Association for Computational Linguistics.

Mikel Artetxe, Sebastian Ruder, and Dani Yogatama. 2020. On the cross-lingual transferability of monolingual representations. In *Proceedings of the 58th Annual Meeting of the Association for Computational Linguistics*, pages 4623–4637, Online. Association for Computational Linguistics.

Ankur Bapna and Orhan Firat. 2019. Simple, scalable adaptation for neural machine translation. In *Proceedings of the 2019 Conference on Empirical Methods in Natural Language Processing and the 9th International Joint Conference on Natural Language Processing (EMNLP-IJCNLP)*, pages 1538–1548, Hong Kong, China. Association for Computational Linguistics.

Yoshua Bengio, Jérôme Louradour, Ronan Collobert, and Jason Weston. 2009. Curriculum learning. In *Proceedings of the 26th Annual International Conference on Machine Learning - ICML '09*, pages 1–8, Montreal, Quebec, Canada. ACM Press.

Johannes Bjerva, Robert Östling, Maria Han Veiga, Jörg Tiedemann, and Isabelle Augenstein. 2019. What do language representations really represent? *Computational Linguistics*, 45(2):381–389.

Branden Chan, Stefan Schweter, and Timo Möller. 2020. German's next language model. In *Proceedings of the 28th International Conference on Computational Linguistics*, pages 6788–6796, Barcelona, Spain (Online). International Committee on Computational Linguistics.

Alexis Conneau, Kartikay Khandelwal, Naman Goyal, Vishrav Chaudhary, Guillaume Wenzek, Francisco Guzmán, Edouard Grave, Myle Ott, Luke Zettlemoyer, and Veselin Stoyanov. 2020. Unsupervised cross-lingual representation learning at scale. In *Proceedings of the 58th Annual Meeting of the Association for Computational Linguistics*, pages 8440–8451, Online. Association for Computational Linguistics.

Wietse de Vries, Martijn Bartelds, Malvina Nissim, and Martijn Wieling. 2021. Adapting monolingual models: Data can be scarce when language similarity is high. In *Findings of the Association for Computational Linguistics: ACL-IJCNLP 2021*, pages 4901–4907, Online. Association for Computational Linguistics.

Wietse de Vries, Andreas van Cranenburgh, Arianna Bisazza, Tommaso Caselli, Gertjan van Noord, and Malvina Nissim. 2019. BERTje: A Dutch BERT Model. ArXiv:1912.09582 [cs].

Jacob Devlin, Ming-Wei Chang, Kenton Lee, and Kristina Toutanova. 2019. BERT: Pre-training of deep bidirectional transformers for language understanding. In *Proceedings of the 2019 Conference of the North American Chapter of the Association for Computational Linguistics: Human Language Technologies, Volume 1 (Long and Short Papers)*, pages 4171–4186, Minneapolis, Minnesota. Association for Computational Linguistics.

M. S. Dryer and Martin Haspelmath. 2013. *The World Atlas of Linguistic Structures*. Max Planck Digital Library, München.

Fahim Faisal and Antonios Anastasopoulos. 2022. Phylogeny-inspired adaptation of multilingual models to new languages. In *Proceedings of the 2nd Conference of the Asia-Pacific Chapter of the Association for Computational Linguistics and the 12th International Joint Conference on Natural Language Processing (Volume 1: Long Papers)*, pages 434–452, Online only. Association for Computational Linguistics.

Neil Houlsby, Andrei Giurgiu, Stanisław Jastrzebski, and Bruna Morrone. 2019. Parameter-Efficient Transfer Learning for NLP. In *Proceedings of the 36th International Conference on Machine Learning*, page 10, Long Beach, California.

Rasmus Hvingelby, Amalie Brogaard Pauli, Maria Barrett, Christina Rosted, Lasse Malm Lidegaard, and Anders Søgaard. 2020. DaNE: A named entity resource for Danish. In *Proceedings of the Twelfth Language Resources and Evaluation Conference*, pages 4597–4604, Marseille, France. European Language Resources Association.

Pratik Joshi, Sebastin Santy, Amar Budhiraja, Kalika Bali, and Monojit Choudhury. 2020. The state and fate of linguistic diversity and inclusion in the NLP world. In *Proceedings of the 58th Annual Meeting of the Association for Computational Linguistics*, pages 6282–6293, Online. Association for Computational Linguistics.

Per E Kummervold, Javier De la Rosa, Freddy Wetjen, and Svein Arne Brygfjeld. 2021. Operationalizing a national digital library: The case for a Norwegian transformer model. In *Proceedings of the 23rd Nordic Conference on Computational Linguistics (NoDaLiDa)*, pages 20–29, Reykjavik, Iceland (Online). Linköping University Electronic Press, Sweden.

Patrick Littell, David R. Mortensen, Ke Lin, Katherine Kairis, Carlisle Turner, and Lori Levin. 2017. URIEL and lang2vec: Representing languages as typological, geographical, and phylogenetic vectors. In *Proceedings of the 15th Conference of the European Chapter of the Association for Computational Linguistics: Volume 2, Short Papers*, pages 8–14, Valencia, Spain. Association for Computational Linguistics.

Jonas Pfeiffer, Ivan Vulić, Iryna Gurevych, and Sebastian Ruder. 2020. MAD-X: An Adapter-Based

Framework for Multi-Task Cross-Lingual Transfer. In *Proceedings of the 2020 Conference on Empirical Methods in Natural Language Processing (EMNLP)*, pages 7654–7673, Online. Association for Computational Linguistics.

Jonas Pfeiffer, Ivan Vulić, Iryna Gurevych, and Sebastian Ruder. 2021. UNKs everywhere: Adapting multilingual language models to new scripts. In *Proceedings of the 2021 Conference on Empirical Methods in Natural Language Processing*, pages 10186–10203, Online and Punta Cana, Dominican Republic. Association for Computational Linguistics.

Telmo Pires, Eva Schlinger, and Dan Garrette. 2019. How multilingual is multilingual BERT? In *Proceedings of the 57th Annual Meeting of the Association for Computational Linguistics*, pages 4996–5001, Florence, Italy. Association for Computational Linguistics.

Edoardo Maria Ponti, Helen O'Horan, Yevgeni Berzak, Ivan Vulić, Roi Reichart, Thierry Poibeau, Ekaterina Shutova, and Anna Korhonen. 2019. Modeling language variation and universals: A survey on typological linguistics for natural language processing. *Computational Linguistics*, 45(3):559–601.

Phillip Rust, Jonas Pfeiffer, Ivan Vulić, Sebastian Ruder, and Iryna Gurevych. 2021. How good is your tokenizer? on the monolingual performance of multilingual language models. In *Proceedings of the 59th Annual Meeting of the Association for Computational Linguistics and the 11th International Joint Conference on Natural Language Processing (Volume 1: Long Papers)*, pages 3118–3135, Online. Association for Computational Linguistics.

Ahmet Üstün, Arianna Bisazza, Gosse Bouma, and Gertjan van Noord. 2020. UDapter: Language adaptation for truly Universal Dependency parsing. In *Proceedings of the 2020 Conference on Empirical Methods in Natural Language Processing (EMNLP)*, pages 2302–2315, Online. Association for Computational Linguistics.

Ahmet Üstün, Arianna Bisazza, Gosse Bouma, and Gertjan van Noord. 2022. UDapter: Typology-based language adapters for multilingual dependency parsing and sequence labeling. *Computational Linguistics*, 48(3):555–592.

Shijie Wu and Mark Dredze. 2019. Beto, bentz, becas: The surprising cross-lingual effectiveness of BERT. In *Proceedings of the 2019 Conference on Empirical Methods in Natural Language Processing and the 9th International Joint Conference on Natural Language Processing (EMNLP-IJCNLP)*, pages 833–844, Hong Kong, China. Association for Computational Linguistics.

Shijie Wu and Mark Dredze. 2020. Are all languages created equal in multilingual BERT? In *Proceedings of the 5th Workshop on Representation Learning for NLP*, pages 120–130, Online. Association for Computational Linguistics.

Daniel Zeman, Joakim Nivre, Mitchell Abrams, Elia Ackermann, Noëmi Aepli, Hamid Aghaei, Željko Agić, Amir Ahmadi, Lars Ahrenberg, Chika Kennedy Ajede, Salih Furkan Akkurt, Gabrielė Aleksandravičiūtė, Ika Alfina, Avner Algom, Chiara Alzetta, Erik Andersen, Lene Antonsen, Katya Aplonova, Angelina Aquino, Carolina Aragon, Glyd Aranes, Maria Jesus Aranzabe, Bilge Nas Arıcan, Hórunn Arnardóttir, Gashaw Arutie, Jessica Naraiswari Arwidarasti, Masayuki Asahara, Katla Ásgeirsdóttir, Deniz Baran Aslan, Cengiz Asmazoğlu, Luma Ateyah, Furkan Atmaca, Mohammed Attia, Aitziber Atutxa, Liesbeth Augustinus, Elena Badmaeva, Keerthana Balasubramani, Miguel Ballesteros, Esha Banerjee, Sebastian Bank, Verginica Barbu Mititelu, Starkaður Barkarson, Rodolfo Basile, Victoria Basmov, Colin Batchelor, John Bauer, Seyyit Talha Bedir, Juan Belieni, Kepa Bengoetxea, Yifat Ben Moshe, Gözde Berk, Yevgeni Berzak, Irshad Ahmad Bhat, Riyaz Ahmad Bhat, Erica Biagetti, Eckhard Bick, Agnė Bielinskienė, Kristín Bjarnadóttir, Rogier Blokland, Victoria Bobicev, Loïc Boizou, Emanuel Borges Völker, Carl Börstell, Cristina Bosco, Gosse Bouma, Sam Bowman, Adriane Boyd, Anouck Braggaar, Kristina Brokaitė, Aljoscha Burchardt, Marie Candito, Bernard Caron, Gauthier Caron, Lauren Cassidy, Maria Clara Castro, Tatiana Cavalcanti, Gülşen Cebiroğlu Eryiğit, Flavio Massimiliano Cecchini, Giuseppe G. A. Celano, Slavomír Čéplö, Neslihan Cesur, Savas Cetin, Özlem Çetinoğlu, Fabricio Chalub, Liyanage Chamila, Shweta Chauhan, Ethan Chi, Taishi Chika, Yongseok Cho, Jinho Choi, Jayeol Chun, Juyeon Chung, Alessandra T. Cignarella, Silvie Cinková, Aurélie Collomb, Çağrı Çöltekin, Miriam Connor, Daniela Corbetta, Marine Courtin, Mihaela Cristescu, Philemon Daniel, Elizabeth Davidson, Leonel Figueiredo de Alencar, Mathieu Dehouck, Martina de Laurentiis, Marie-Catherine de Marneffe, Valeria de Paiva, Mehmet Oguz Derin, Elvis de Souza, Arantza Diaz de Ilarraza, Carly Dickerson, Arawinda Dinakaramani, Elisa Di Nuovo, Bamba Dione, Peter Dirix, Kaja Dobrovoljc, Timothy Dozat, Kira Droganova, Puneet Dwivedi, Christian Ebert, Hanne Eckhoff, Sandra Eiche, Marhaba Eli, Ali Elkahky, Binyam Ephrem, Olga Erina, Tomaž Erjavec, Aline Etienne, Wograine Evelyn, Sidney Facundes, Richárd Farkas, Federica Favero, Jannatul Ferdaousi, Marília Fernanda, Hector Fernandez Alcalde, Jennifer Foster, Cláudia Freitas, Kazunori Fujita, Katarína Gajdošová, Daniel Galbraith, Federica Gamba, Marcos Garcia, Moa Gärdenfors, Sebastian Garza, Fabrício Ferraz Gerardi, Kim Gerdes, Filip Ginter, Gustavo Godoy, Iakes Goenaga, Koldo Gojenola, Memduh Gökırmak, Yoav Goldberg, Xavier Gómez Guinovart, Berta González Saavedra, Bernadeta Griciūtė, Matias Grioni, Loïc Grobol, Normunds Grūzītis, Bruno Guillaume, Céline Guillot-Barbance, Tunga Güngör, Nizar Habash, Hinrik Hafsteinsson, Jan Hajič, Jan Hajič jr., Mika Hämäläinen, Linh Hà Mỹ, Na-Rae Han, Muhammad Yudistira Hanifmuti, Takahiro Harada, Sam Hardwick, Kim Harris, Dag Haug, Johannes Heinecke, Oliver Hellwig, Felix Hennig, Barbora Hladká, Jaroslava Hlaváčová, Florinel Hociung, Petter Hohle, Marivel Huerta Mendez, Jena Hwang, Takumi Ikeda, Anton Karl Ingason, Radu Ion, Elena Irimia, Ọlájídé Ishola, Artan Islamaj, Kaoru Ito, Siratun Jannat, Tomáš Jelínek, Apoorva Jha, Katharine Jiang, Anders Johannsen, Hildur Jónsdóttir, Fredrik Jørgensen, Markus Juutinen, Hüner Kaşıkara, Andre Kaasen, Nadezhda Kabaeva, Sylvain Kahane, Hiroshi Kanayama, Jenna Kanerva, Neslihan Kara, Ritván Karahóǧa, Boris Katz, Tolga Kayadelen, Sarveswaran Kengatharaiyer, Jessica Kenney, Václava Kettnerová, Jesse Kirchner, Elena Klementieva, Elena Klyachko, Arne Köhn, Abdullatif Köksal, Kamil Kopacewicz, Timo Korkiakangas, Mehmet Köse, Alexey Koshevoy, Natalia Kotsyba, Jolanta Kovalevskaitė, Simon Krek, Parameswari Krishnamurthy, Sandra Kübler, Adrian Kuqi, Oğuzhan Kuyrukçu, Aslı Kuzgun, Sookyoung Kwak, Veronika Laippala, Lucia Lam, Lorenzo Lambertino, Tatiana Lando, Septina Dian Larasati, Alexei Lavrentiev, John Lee, Phng Lê Hồng, Alessandro Lenci, Saran Lertpradit, Herman Leung, Maria Levina, Cheuk Ying Li, Josie Li, Keying Li, Yixuan Li, Yuan Li, KyungTae Lim, Bruna Lima Padovani, Krister Lindén, Nikola Ljubešić, Olga Loginova, Stefano Lusito, Andry Luthfi, Mikko Luukko, Olga Lyashevskaya, Teresa Lynn, Vivien Macketanz, Menel Mahamdi, Jean Maillard, Ilya Makarchuk, Aibek Makazhanov, Michael Mandl, Christopher Manning, Ruli Manurung, Büşra Marşan, Cătălina Mărănduc, David Mareček, Katrin Marheinecke, Stella Markantonatou, Héctor Martínez Alonso, Lorena Martín Rodríguez, André Martins, Jan Mašek, Hiroshi Matsuda, Yuji Matsumoto, Alessandro Mazzei, Ryan McDonald, Sarah McGuinness, Gustavo Mendonça, Tatiana Merzhevich, Niko Miekka, Karina Mischenkova, Margarita Misirpashayeva, Anna Missilä, Cătălin Mititelu, Maria Mitrofan, Yusuke Miyao, AmirHossein Mojiri Foroushani, Judit Molnár, Amirsaeid Moloodi, Simonetta Montemagni, Amir More, Laura Moreno Romero, Giovanni Moretti, Keiko Sophie Mori, Shinsuke Mori, Tomohiko Morioka, Shigeki Moro, Bjartur Mortensen, Bohdan Moskalevskyi, Kadri Muischnek, Robert Munro, Yugo Murawaki, Kaili Müürisep, Pinkey Nainwani, Mariam Nakhlé, Juan Ignacio Navarro Horñiacek, Anna Nedoluzhko, Gunta Nešpore-Bērzkalne, Manuela Nevaci, Lng Nguyễn Thị, Huyền Nguyễn Thị Minh, Yoshihiro Nikaido, Vitaly Nikolaev, Rattima Nitisaroj, Alireza Nourian, Hanna Nurmi, Stina Ojala, Atul Kr. Ojha, Hulda Óladóttir, Adédayọ Olúòkun, Mai Omura, Emeka Onwuegbuzia, Noam Ordan, Petya Osenova, Robert Östling, Lilja Øvrelid, Şaziye Betül Özateş, Merve Özçelik, Arzucan Özgür, Balkız Öztürk Başaran, Teresa Paccosi, Alessio Palmero Aprosio, Anastasia Panova, Hyunji Hayley Park, Niko Partanen, Elena Pascual, Marco Passarotti, Agnieszka Patejuk, Guilherme Paulino-Passos, Giulia Pedonese, Angelika Peljak-Łapińska, Siyao Peng, Cenel-Augusto Perez, Natalia Perkova, Guy Perrier, Slav Petrov, Daria Petrova, Andrea Peverelli, Jason Phelan, Jussi Piitulainen, Rodrigo Pintucci, Tommi A Pirinen, Emily Pitler, Magdalena Plamada, Barbara Plank, Thierry Poibeau, Larisa Ponomareva, Martin Popel, Lauma Pretkalnina, Sophie Prévost, Prokopis Prokopidis, Adam Przepiórkowski, Robert Pugh, Tiina Puolakainen, Sampo Pyysalo, Peng Qi, Andriela Rääbis, Alexandre Rademaker, Mizanur Rahoman, Taraka Rama, Loganathan Ramasamy, Carlos Ramisch, Fam Rashel, Mohammad Sadegh Rasooli, Vinit Ravishankar, Livy Real, Petru Rebeja, Siva Reddy, Mathilde Regnault, Georg Rehm, Ivan Riabov, Michael Rießler, Erika Rimkutė, Larissa Rinaldi, Laura Rituma, Putri Rizqiyah, Luisa Rocha, Eiríkur Rögnvaldsson, Ivan Roksandic, Mykhailo Romanenko, Rudolf Rosa, Valentin Roșca, Davide Rovati, Ben Rozonoyer, Olga Rudina, Jack Rueter, Kristján Rúnarsson, Shoval Sadde, Pegah Safari, Benoît Sagot, Aleksi Sahala, Shadi Saleh, Alessio Salomoni, Tanja Samardžić, Stephanie Samson, Manuela Sanguinetti, Ezgi Sanıyar, Dage Särg, Marta Sartor, Mitsuya Sasaki, Baiba Saulīte, Yanin Sawanakunanon, Shefali Saxena, Kevin Scannell, Salvatore Scarlata, Nathan Schneider, Sebastian Schuster, Lane Schwartz, Djamé Seddah, Wolfgang Seeker, Mojgan Seraji, Syeda Shahzadi, Mo Shen, Atsuko Shimada, Hiroyuki Shirasu, Yana Shishkina, Muh Shohibussirri, Maria Shvedova, Janine Siewert, Einar Freyr Sigurðsson, João Ricardo Silva, Aline Silveira, Natalia Silveira, Maria Simi, Radu Simionescu, Katalin Simkó, Mária Šimková, Haukur Barri Símonarson, Kiril Simov, Dmitri Sitchinava, Maria Skachedubova, Aaron Smith, Isabela Soares-Bastos, Barbara Sonnenhauser, Shafi Sourov, Carolyn Spadine, Rachele Sprugnoli, Vivian Stamou, Steinhór Steingrímsson, Antonio Stella, Abishek Stephen, Milan Straka, Emmett Strickland, Jana Strnadová, Alane Suhr, Yogi Lesmana Sulestio, Umut Sulubacak, Shingo Suzuki, Daniel Swanson, Zsolt Szántó, Chihiro Taguchi, Dima Taji, Yuta Takahashi, Fabio Tamburini, Mary Ann C. Tan, Takaaki Tanaka, Dipta Tanaya, Mirko Tavoni, Samson Tella, Isabelle Tellier, Marinella Testori, Guillaume Thomas, Sara Tonelli, Liisi Torga, Marsida Toska, Trond Trosterud, Anna Trukhina, Reut Tsarfaty, Utku Türk, Francis Tyers, Sveinbjörn Hórðarson, Vilhjálmur Horsteinsson, Sumire Uematsu, Roman Untilov, Zdeňka Urešová, Larraitz Uria, Hans Uszkoreit, Andrius Utka, Elena Vagnoni, Sowmya Vajjala, Rob van der Goot, Martine Vanhove, Daniel van Niekerk, Gertjan van Noord, Viktor Varga, Uliana Vedenina, Giulia Venturi, Eric Villemonte de la Clergerie, Veronika Vincze, Natalia Vlasova, Aya Wakasa, Joel C. Wallenberg, Lars Wallin, Abigail Walsh, Jing Xian Wang, Jonathan North Washington, Maximilan Wendt, Paul Widmer, Shira Wigderson, Sri Hartati Wijono, Vanessa Berwanger Wille, Seyi Williams, Mats Wirén, Christian Wittern, Tsegay Woldemariam, Tak-sum Wong, Alina Wróblewska, Mary Yako, Kayo Yamashita, Naoki Yamazaki, Chunxiao Yan, Koichi Yasuoka, Marat M. Yavrumyan, Arife Betül Yenice, Olcay Taner Yıldız, Zhuoran Yu, Arlisa Yuliawati, Zdeněk Žabokrtský, Shorouq Zahra, Amir Zeldes, He Zhou, Hanzhi Zhu, Anna Zhuravleva, and Rayan Ziane. 2022. Universal dependencies 2.11. LINDAT/CLARIAH-CZ digital library at the Institute of Formal and Applied Linguistics (ÚFAL), Faculty of Mathematics and Physics, Charles University.

On the Nature of Discrete Speech Representations in Multilingual Self-supervised Models

Badr M. Abdullah **Mohammed Maqsood Shaik** **Dietrich Klakow**
Language Science and Technology (LST), Saarland University, Germany
{ babdullah, mmshaik, dietrich }@lsv.uni-saarland.de

1 Overview and Research Question

Self-supervision has emerged as an effective paradigm for learning representations of spoken language from raw audio without explicit labels or transcriptions. Self-supervised speech models, such as wav2vec 2.0 (Baevski et al., 2020) and HuBERT (Hsu et al., 2021), have shown significant promise in improving the performance across different speech processing tasks. One of the main advantages of self-supervised speech models is that they can be pre-trained on a large sample of languages (Conneau et al., 2020; Babu et al., 2022), which facilitates cross-lingual transfer for low-resource languages (San et al., 2021).

State-of-the-art self-supervised speech models include a quantization module that transforms the continuous acoustic input into a sequence of discrete units. One of the key questions in this area is whether the discrete representations learned via self-supervision are language-specific or language-universal. In other words, we ask: *do the discrete units learned by a multilingual speech model represent the same speech sounds across languages or do they differ based on the specific language being spoken?* From the practical perspective, this question has important implications for the development of speech models that can generalize across languages, particularly for low-resource languages. Furthermore, examining the level of linguistic abstraction in speech models that lack symbolic supervision is also relevant to the field of human language acquisition (Dupoux, 2018).

2 Approach

To answer our research question, we conduct a series of experiments with spoken language identification (SLID) as a probing task. Our intuition is that if we can accurately predict the language of a short speech sample (~10 sec) from its discretized representation, this would suggest that the model has learned language-specific discrete units that are unique to each language. On the other hand, a difficulty in predicting the language would suggest that the model has learned a common set of discrete units that are shared across multiple languages.

Experimental Data. We use a balanced subset of the Common Voice speech corpus (Ardila et al., 2020) consisting of 16 languages that span diverse sub-groups within the Indo-European language family, namely: Romance (Catalan, Portuguese, French, Spanish, Italian), Germanic (German, Dutch, Swedish, Frisian), Slavic (Ukrainian, Russian, Polish), Celtic (Welsh, Breton), Hellenic (Greek), and Indo-Iranian (Persian). Our language sample exhibits a considerable degree of typological diversity with respect to various phonological features, including the Consonant-Vowel Ratio, which is high in Russian but low in German, French, and Swedish (Maddieson, 2013). In addition, stress location patterns are highly variable in Russian and Spanish, but fixed in languages such as Greek, Persian, and Welsh (Goedemans and van der Hulst, 2013). We use ~6.75, ~3.75, ~4.25 hours per each language for training, validation, and evaluation sets, respectively. A speech sample in our study is an utterance of a few seconds of read speech.

SLID Classifiers. For the set of languages in our study, we obtain discrete presentations from two pre-trained speech models: (1) monolingual English wav2vec 2.0 (W2V2), and multilingual model XLSR-53 (XLSR) (Conneau et al., 2020). We use the English W2V2 model to establish a comparison with a model that did not observe the languages in our study during pre-training.

Baseline. We use the majority class as a baseline, which corresponds to chance performance since our training and evaluation dataset are balanced.

Discrete Classifiers. Next, we train three different SLID classifiers on the discretized representations

Proceedings of the 5th Workshop on Research in Computational Linguistic Typology and Multilingual NLP (SIGTYP 2023), pages 159–161
May 6, 2023 ©2023 Association for Computational Linguistics

of utterances in our study from both W2V2 and XLSR: (1) a Naive Bayes (NB) classifier, and (2) a linear classifier based on multi-class logistic regression (LC-D), and (3) a unidirectional LSTM (LSTM-D). NB and LC-D discard the sequential nature of representations and view each speech sample as a bag of discrete units. With the LSTM-D classifier, we can examine how much we gain by incorporating sequential information when decoding the language ID from the discrete sequence.
Continuous Classifiers. To investigate the effect of the discretization step on the extractability of language ID information from the model representations, we need to compare to SLID classifiers trained on continuous representations. To this end, we train linear classifiers on the representations from all transformer layers (after applying mean pooling). In this abstract we focus on classifiers trained on the output of the local convolutional encoder (LC-C0) and the contextualized transformer layer that yielded highest accuracy in both model (LC-CX). We also train a unidirectional LSTM on the sequence of contextualized vectors (LSTM-CX), identical to those used to train LC-CX.
Skyline. Finally, we fine-tune the pre-trained models to predict language ID to establish a reasonable upper-bound of the performance on the SLID task.

3 Preliminary Results

Activated Discrete Units. First, we find that the set of activated units are nearly identical across the languages in our study, which implies that the models do not learn units that are predictable features of the identity of the spoken language.

SLID Experiments. Table 1 shows the results of our SLID experiments. We observe that the non-sequential classifiers trained on discrete units (NB and LC-D) yield only modest improvements over the majority class baseline. This indicates that the languages in our study exhibit similar distributions over the discrete units. We do not observe considerable differences between the monolingual W2V2 and multilingual XLSR models in this case. However, W2V2 surprisingly outperforms XLSR for the sequential discrete classifier (LSTM-D), which indicates either that the monolingual model is more successful at approximating the languages' phonotactics or that the multilingual model projects the audio frames onto a shared discrete space where language identity is more difficult to extract compared to the monolingual model.

	Classifier	Accuracy (%)	
		W2V2	XLSR
Baseline	Majority class	6.25	6.25
Discrete	Naive Bayes	11.84	13.28
	LC-D	13.89	12.78
	LSTM-D	**39.78**	32.10
Continuous	LC-C0	22.00	22.57
	LC-CX	47.04	59.54
	LSTM-CX	58.70	**59.80**
Skyline	Fine-tuned	*54.96*	*59.72*

Table 1: The performance of spoken language identification using different classifiers.

Discrete vs. Continuous Classifiers. If we consider the performance of the continuous classifiers, we observe a higher accuracy compared to their discrete counterparts. This demonstrates the ease of extraction for the language ID information from the continuous representations. Moreover, we find that sequential models (e.g., LSTMs) trained on the representations from a middle layers to be successful in predicting the language ID compared to lower and higher layers in the transformer, which indicates the language ID information emerges as a product of the contextualization in the transformer block. This is evident in our results since the linear classifier on middle layer representations (LSTM-CX) in XLSR performs as good as the skyline fine-tuning setting. It is worth pointing out that XLSR has observed the languages in our study during pre-training, which can explain the high accuracy in predicting the language via a linear classifier from continuous representations in the middle layers.

4 Conclusion

We summarized the findings of our experiments whereby we investigate the nature of the discrete units in multilingual, self-supervised speech models. We employed language identification as a probing task and demonstrated the difficulty of predicting the language of an utterance from its discretized representation. Our findings support the hypothesis that latent, discretized speech representations in self-supervised models correspond to sub-phonetic events that are shared across the world's languages, rather than language-specific, abstract phonemic categories.

Acknowledgement

This research is funded by the Deutsche Forschungsgemeinschaft (DFG, German Research Foundation), Project ID 232722074 – SFB 1102.

References

Rosana Ardila, Megan Branson, Kelly Davis, Michael Kohler, Josh Meyer, Michael Henretty, Reuben Morais, Lindsay Saunders, Francis Tyers, and Gregor Weber. 2020. Common voice: A massively-multilingual speech corpus. In *Proceedings of the 12th Language Resources and Evaluation Conference*, pages 4218–4222.

Arun Babu, Changhan Wang, Andros Tjandra, Kushal Lakhotia, Qiantong Xu, Naman Goyal, Kritika Singh, Patrick von Platen, Yatharth Saraf, Juan Pino, Alexei Baevski, Alexis Conneau, and Michael Auli. 2022. XLS-R: self-supervised cross-lingual speech representation learning at scale. In *Interspeech 2022, 23rd Annual Conference of the International Speech Communication Association, Incheon, Korea, 18-22 September 2022*, pages 2278–2282. ISCA.

Alexei Baevski, Yuhao Zhou, Abdelrahman Mohamed, and Michael Auli. 2020. wav2vec 2.0: A framework for self-supervised learning of speech representations. *Advances in neural information processing systems*, 33:12449–12460.

Alexis Conneau, Alexei Baevski, Ronan Collobert, Abdelrahman Mohamed, and Michael Auli. 2020. Unsupervised cross-lingual representation learning for speech recognition. *arXiv preprint arXiv:2006.13979*.

Emmanuel Dupoux. 2018. Cognitive science in the era of artificial intelligence: A roadmap for reverse-engineering the infant language-learner. *Cognition*, 173:43–59.

Rob Goedemans and Harry van der Hulst. 2013. Fixed stress locations (v2020.3). In Matthew S. Dryer and Martin Haspelmath, editors, *The World Atlas of Language Structures Online*. Zenodo.

Wei-Ning Hsu, Benjamin Bolte, Yao-Hung Hubert Tsai, Kushal Lakhotia, Ruslan Salakhutdinov, and Abdelrahman Mohamed. 2021. Hubert: Self-supervised speech representation learning by masked prediction of hidden units. *IEEE/ACM Transactions on Audio, Speech, and Language Processing*, 29:3451–3460.

Ian Maddieson. 2013. Consonant-vowel ratio (v2020.3). In Matthew S. Dryer and Martin Haspelmath, editors, *The World Atlas of Language Structures Online*. Zenodo.

Nay San, Martijn Bartelds, Mitchell Browne, Lily Clifford, Fiona Gibson, John Mansfield, David Nash, Jane Simpson, Myfany Turpin, Maria Vollmer, Sasha Wilmoth, and Dan Jurafsky. 2021. Leveraging pre-trained representations to improve access to untranscribed speech from endangered languages. In *IEEE Automatic Speech Recognition and Understanding Workshop, ASRU 2021, Cartagena, Colombia, December 13-17, 2021*, pages 1094–1101. IEEE.

Author Index

Association for Computational Linguistics
209 N. Eighth Street
Stroudsburg, Pennsylvania 18360

ISBN 978-1-7138-7387-7

9 781713 873877

CURRAN ASSOCIATES INC.
proceedings.com